consider it done

consider
it done

Accomplish 228

of Life's Trickiest Tasks

Julie Subotky

Crown Archetype
New York

Copyright © 2011 by Julie Subotky

All rights reserved.

Published in the United States by Crown Archetype,

an imprint of the Crown Publishing Group,

a division of Random House, Inc., New York.

www.crownpublishing.com

CROWN ARCHETYPE and colophon are trademarks of Random House, Inc.

Library of Congress Cataloging-in-Publication Data

Subotky, Julie.

Consider it done : accomplish 228 of life's trickiest tasks / Julie Subotky.—1st ed.

p.   cm.

1. Conduct of life—Miscellanea. 2. Life skills—Miscellanea.

3. Interpersonal relations—Miscellanea. 4. Home economics—Miscellanea. I. Title.

BF637.C5S83 2010

646.7—dc22

2010017640

ISBN 978-0-307-59157-9

eISBN 978-0-307-59158-6

Printed in the United States of America

Cover design by Jessie Sayward Bright

Book design by Maria Elias

10 9 8 7 6 5 4 3 2 1

First Edition

For the palikari and his baba with
an abundance of love and gratitude

contents

3. in the name of love

4. sneaky but (mostly) harmless

5.   mind your business

6.   crowd-pleasers

7. seemingly impossible

8. life and death

9. home sweet home

10. lions and tigers and pets, oh my!

11. food and drink

12. show me the money

13. unusual yet useful

14. annoying (but necessary)

introduction

It's all in a day's work. At least in my day.

Do you ever wish you had a person to call when you hit a stumbling block as you slog through your never-ending to-do list? I'm that person.

Through the years I have worked my way through countless to-do lists for hundreds of busy people. Sometimes I help with an everyday task, like purchasing a unique birthday gift, and sometimes it is a quirky request, like when a client called from Belgrade needing a Moulin Rouge costume for a party he was on his way to—in New Zealand.

How did I get to be the most resourceful woman in New York City? After graduating from college, I wanted a job that allowed me to have fun while helping others. But not exactly clear what that would be, I left California and headed to Aspen, to ski for the winter season. That's where I noticed that there were a lot of people out there who needed a resource for getting things done, so I started taking on tasks and figuring things out.

Before long, I was doing everything from gift wrapping and party planning, to arranging jet charters and hot air balloon rides, and accomplishing any random or bizarre task that came up. That was the start of my company, Consider It Done. Once Consider It Done took off in Aspen, it seemed only natural to bring it to New York City—home to some of the busiest and most time-starved people on the planet.

In New York City, Consider It Done grew faster than even I'd imagined. I originally thought I would be mostly doing things like picking up dry cleaning and organizing closets, but I soon found that people needed assistance with *everything*. For most people, there are just not enough hours in the day! Busy professionals needed help moving and throwing theme parties. Corporations needed help getting organized. Foreign diplomats needed help booking their travel and planning their schedules.

Business was booming and I was doing things I never would have suspected—tracking down culinary oddities, booking snake dancers for parties, overseeing the construction of an ice-skating rink in a client's basement. You'd be surprised at the kinds of requests you get when you run a company called Consider It Done, and I've come to the conclusion that each of us has an odd item or two on our list every now and again.

After spending many years accomplishing life's trickiest tasks, I have been able to come up with all kinds of creative solutions and methods for carrying out even the most outrageous requests, because as I've learned, one way or another, there's always a way to get it done.

People are fascinated by the things that my company does. By relaying stories about how I've gotten things done, I hope that you will discover some helpful tools that you can use to get your own daily tasks, and out-there ideas, accomplished. Getting things done may come naturally to me, but really, it *can* be taught. Just because your Google search brings you to a dead end, don't give up. Think again, and take another road. With persistence, you'll eventually get there, too.

The tasks I've included in this book are numerous and varied, but they are by no means exhaustive. I believe that if someone can think of it, then it's possible to make it a reality. I love figuring things out and making them happen. Every day, by thinking big and being flexible, I find unexpected solutions to seemingly unsolvable problems. The answer may not look exactly as I first imagined it would when I first started, but as long as I keep the goal in mind, it *always* gets done.

So the next time you have something slightly tricky to do, be unstoppable. If you look to work out solutions, rather than waiting for answers to magically appear, you'll soon find yourself checking even the craziest projects off your list. Maybe you'll never need to accomplish most of the tasks in this book. Maybe you will. My intention is to teach you how to approach any task that challenges you. And have fun while you do it.

disclaimer

This book contains all sorts of advice and suggestions, none of which are intended to be legal advice (especially since I'm not a lawyer). Nor are the solutions guaranteed to work for everyone, but they worked for me and for countless others.

When following any of the suggestions in this book, keep in mind that laws change, and you should always be aware of current rules and regulations and stay on the right side of them as you get your tasks done.

Each reader should exercise his or her own judgment and discretion when implementing any of the ideas, suggestions, or advice in this book. I'll provide good ideas and creative solutions, but you're on your own as to how you use them.

Here's to getting things done!

1. relatively speaking

How to Turn Your Great-Aunt's Hideous Jewelry into Something You'll Actually Wear

Great-Aunt Betty's polyester suits may not be your idea of recyclable cool, but the baubles she gave you are a different story. Those rings and necklaces (especially the expensive ones) don't have to sit forlornly in your drawer taking up space. It's time to give the family jewels a new lease on life.

One option is restoration. Unless it was really cheap to begin with, jewelry is almost never permanently ruined. Have your local jeweler fix that broken hinge, reset that loose diamond, or repolish that lackluster ring. If you want to give your jewels a quick clean at home, most jewels can be cleaned with a simple and inexpensive mix. Combine three parts water and one part ammonia, then clean with a toothbrush. Don't do this with your pearls—they will scratch—but for most other jewels it should get them sparkling in no time. If you're not sure, check with any jeweler, and he or she will be able to let you know if the solution is good for your gems. Alternatively, pick up some at-home jewelry cleaner from a site like www.hagertyusa.com.

A slightly more radical option is reinvention: taking the item apart and reconfiguring its components—the stone, the band, and so on—into something you actually want to wear outside the safety of your bedroom. You don't even have to restrict yourself to the same type of piece—a necklace chain can be melted down into a band for a ring, the stone from a brooch can become a pendant, and so on. Personalized jewels aren't just for the Beyoncés and Jay-Zs of the world. Hundreds of designers are available who will work with you to incorporate or recast your existing jewels into a new masterpiece that's more to your taste without charging you an arm and a leg. Not sure exactly what you want? Most designers have computerized software that allows them to create a preview of what the finished product will look like before the work even begins.

If you're more interested in hawking than you are in refashioning, check out gold prices—jewelers and a growing number of Internet-based companies will swap your ugly treasures for cold hard cash. Or, easier yet, sell the jewelry online via sites like Craigslist or eBay and put the proceeds toward a new sparkler that somehow reflects the spirit, if not the style, of your well-meaning benefactor. Great-Aunt Betty would want it that way.

This is also a great way to put the jewelry from your ex to good use!

How to Get Out of Going to a Family Reunion

Family reunions are a huge ordeal. They involve spending a ton of money on a flight to a place you don't want to go and a weekend (or God forbid, longer) with dozens of people you either don't know or don't like (or both).

Most people feel this way, yet when the reunion rolls around, everyone expects everyone else to show up. Unless you're some nut who enjoys seeing slide shows of your third cousin Billy's trip to Bermuda or pretending you care about how many times your aunt Amanda's grandkids have made the honor roll, you may, understandably, look for a way out.

But finding a way out is close to impossible. These aren't spur-of-the-moment events. They are big affairs, planned months in advance, and rain or shine you are expected to be there. If you get sick, people expect you to come medicated. If you have to work, they expect your boss to understand. And if it's your birthday or anniversary, even better: come celebrate with your second cousin thrice removed.

To get out of a family reunion, you need an ironclad preexisting engagement, one that was already planned well before you heard about the reunion, and one that trumps a reunion in both size and importance. There is only one such engagement.

You need a wedding.

Not *your* wedding, of course. You have to have been invited to someone else's, someone who is very important in your life and yet whom no one in your family knows and will never have the opportunity to ever meet. It shouldn't be too difficult to come up with someone, since you're going to make this person up.

It's got to be an old friend, perhaps from college, who has since moved to a city far away from both where you live (which also allows you to use the old "I haven't seen her in seven years" line) and where your family reunion will be held. If someone in your immediate family can't recall ever having heard of this person with whom you were "quite close" for a meaningful portion of your life, you might ask indignantly, "What do you *mean* you don't remember Jenny?" You'd *really* love to attend the family reunion, you'll tell them, but you just couldn't live with yourself if you missed your friend's special day. You just can't believe, out of all the weeks in the year, the two events happen to be scheduled at the same time! What are the odds?

When the day finally arrives, you'll have to create some decent alibis. Don't just let the reunion go by without a word—your family will be suspicious, and you'll never hear the end of it (if you ever even see any of them again). Here's a quick game plan, but all families are different so feel free to adjust this to suit your own needs:

- Send a group e-mail the day before the reunion to all attendees telling them how much you'd rather be with them than in Alberta for dear Jenny's wedding. If your fake wedding is in a different time zone (as it should be), change your computer's clock before you send the e-mail. It's a small detail that most of them won't notice, but in case one does, you're covered. After all, if you're going to do this thing, you might as well do it right.
- Stage some wedding photos. Tell your best friends what you've done, and ask if they'll help. Go to a friend's apartment, or a classy bar, dress in tuxedos and gowns, and snap a few group shots. Post them to your Facebook page with a subtitle that references the wedding (people post wedding photos all the time, so it won't be out of place, plus no one will be offended at having been snubbed by Jenny, since there is no Jenny), or just e-mail the photo to a few relatives with some sort of wistful caption ("I bet the reunion is ten times wilder than this wedding—wish I were there!"). Sounds elaborate, but your mock wedding with your friends could turn out to be a blast.
- At least once over the course of the weekend, go into a basement or somewhere with bad cell-phone reception and call your closest family member (parent, sibling, etc.). When the service cuts out, tell them that whatever Podunk town you're in has bad reception, but please say hi to the family for you. They will. And everyone will be reminded of how thoughtful you are to call even though you couldn't make it.
- Update your Twitter feed, Facebook status, and any location-based cell-phone apps to indicate that you're at the wedding. Most of your relatives won't check, but one or two will (most likely the ones who also wish they were somewhere other than the reunion and have nothing better to do than to keep checking their e-mail), and if your digital whereabouts don't match up with your ability, you'll be busted.
- Bask in the joys of modern technology.

It might sound like a lot of bases to cover, but it's worth it. Just remember, this is a stunt you can only get away with once, so if the reunion is in Hawaii, think twice about dodging it and save the wedding excuse for next time. Instead, pack your bags and plan to spend the time learning to surf or doing some other activity you can guarantee won't include your long-lost cousin from Milwaukee.

How to Hire a Fake Fiancé to Escort You to a Family Reunion

If you have to explain to your great-aunt Mildred—and everyone else at the family reunion for that matter—why such a smart, pretty young lady like yourself (cue the cheek pinching) hasn't managed to snag a husband, you'll literally go insane. So if this is your situation, you have two options: (1) blow off the reunion (see "How to Get Out of Going to a Family Reunion," page 2) or (2) take a page from a number of successful Hollywood chick flicks and hire a fake fiancé (or just the standard fake boyfriend or girlfriend) to escort you to the event. Of course, as most moviegoers know, such a strategy will likely involve mistaken identities, madcap chases, and unexpected emotional complications that change the protagonist's (I mean, your) life forever. So if you're willing to put up with all this and go ahead with your farcical adventure, be careful. There may be consequences, even if they are a long way down the road.

Before choosing your ideal suitor, consider your motives. Just what are you trying to accomplish? I'm assuming (hoping) that since this is a family event, you're not trying to make someone jealous, so dashingly handsome shouldn't really be your top requirement. (Although, let's face it, if you're going to spend the weekend with someone, it's always a welcome perk.) More likely your goal is simply to get those meddlesome old biddies off your case and prove that, yes, *somebody* will agree to marry you (and you also avoid being set up with your great-aunt Mildred's chiropractor's nephew Barry—again). Or perhaps you're just fulfilling a dying relative's only wish—to see you happy (aka, married). If either of these are the case, you'll want to choose someone who seems sweet, doting, and charming. And of course the most important thing is that your union seems realistic.

For this reason, it's often preferable to choose a friend over the more expensive, time-consuming (albeit more cinematic) option of hiring a stranger to pose as your fake fiancé. It should be a good friend (after all, this is not something you can inflict on a casual acquaintance), but also someone whom no one else in your family knows too well. This is an important precautionary measure; if you choose someone the family is attached to, like an old family friend, there will be a lot of broken hearts, not to mention a lot of explaining to do, when the marriage doesn't pan out. But by choosing a friend over a hired stranger, you might even be able to convince your family that the two of you have chemistry. Plus, the actual reunion will be a lot easier to get through. Hey, it might even be fun. At least you won't have to hang out with your family as much— even your aunt Mildred will be careful to give you two lovebirds some alone time.

Warning: Even if it's just a friend, you might have to kiss a few times, in public, to seal the deal and convince everyone else it's legit. Discuss this with your friend beforehand, and practice a few times. But try to keep it as platonic as a PDA can be, while still being convincing (little-to-no tongue, please, otherwise he might get the wrong idea). A few other ways to keep it looking real . . . hold hands (A LOT; you are, after all, newly engaged), and do all those irritating new couple things, like eating off each other's plate and finishing each other's sentences and telling your engagement/how-we-met story over and over.

Quick tip: Be sure your story is a good one, and that both of you have all the details straight!

If you don't have a friend who can (or is willing to) pull this off, you'll have to go with a stranger, which means you'll have to pay for the service. Yes, for all practical purposes it's like you're hiring a prostitute. But morally, it's far superior. Find a local escort service on the Internet. These exist for males as well as females, and they are entirely legal if you play by the rules. (Unfortunately, not everyone does, so if you want to avoid a potentially awkward situation after the reunion, make sure you're completely up front with your escort about your intentions *before* the event.) The other way to find a person to hire is by going through friends. Hopefully your friends don't have many prostitutes on speed dial, but one of them is bound to know an out-of-work actor or two, who would probably relish the extra cash, and the challenge—they can think of it as good practice for a future role. If your friends don't hang with the actor set, just stop by a local theater and when the curtain goes down after the show, find out where the actors' after-parties are, and get acquainted with the thespians yourself. To be honest, this may cost you just as much, and be equally as awkward as calling an escort service . . . but at least the performance at the reunion should be a showstopper.

Beware: If your life is like a romantic comedy, this story is likely to end with you falling in love (for real) with the fake fiancé. Maybe that's something you want, maybe it isn't. Just keep it in mind.

How to Teach Your Elderly Relative to Be Internet Savvy

Ah, the cycle of life. Once upon a time, she guided you through life's uncertain waters and shared her hard-won wisdom of the world, and now it's time to do the same for her. While navigating the Web may seem as obvious to you as switching on a light, the same may not be true for your pre-Internet-era relative who still thinks cookies only come in jars, and a firewall is part of an Evel Knievel stunt. While this technological cave dwelling might be charming, you're sick of not being able to reach her by e-mail. It's time to get her a learner's permit and send her down the electronic superhighway.

Start small. Get her going on a simple computer—maybe one that's a cheerful, unintimidating color. Unless she's planning to make a late entry into filmmaking, digital publishing, or music production, skip the fancy applications; she probably doesn't need more than an Internet browser. Introduce her to the basic lingo, and give her a quick lesson on the anatomy of a webpage: home pages and hyperlinks, browser windows and back buttons, search boxes and search engines, and so on. If necessary, make sure she knows how to adjust font size so that staring at the screen doesn't strain her eyes. Then set her up with an e-mail account (Gmail is probably the most user-friendly) and show her how to use it. Maybe send a few practice e-mails or do a few practice web searches together. It may seem infantilizing to you, but remember, she's probably as lost as you were when she first taught you how to drive a stick shift.

The Internet can be overwhelming even for experienced users, so after showing her how to use Google, Yahoo!, and other major search engines, zero in on her specific interests. Does she like cooking? Introduce her to some good recipe sites, and help her to bookmark them for easy access. Then show her some sites pretty much every older relative on the planet would use, if he or she knew of their existence. This includes photo-sharing sites, and free calling and video services like Skype (so now she won't have to miss her grandchild's first steps even if she lives miles away). You might even consider making a cheat sheet and taping it to her monitor or, if you really want to wow her, come up with some handy tips and have them printed on a custom-made mouse pad (try www.zazzle. com). Set her up with a way to troubleshoot, especially if you live far away and—though you love her and everything—you don't particularly relish the idea of frantic phone calls at all hours of the night. Sign her up for a GoToMyPC.com account, which provides 24/7 customer support, including training videos and user guides, and recruit a computer-savvy neighbor or friend to come by if disaster strikes. If you want to be able to keep a handle on her online activity from afar (all in the name of helpfulness, of course), give yourself access to her e-mail account. This allows you to clean up her mess without her knowing—and hey, remember when she snuck in your room and read your diary? Now's your opportunity for payback.

One computer skill you probably *don't* want to teach her: online shopping. That is, unless you're okay with her spending your inheritance on the collection of antique frog figurines she found on eBay.

How to Speak with Your Unborn Baby

From a scientific point of view, a mother and baby are connected because they share the same blood supply. The baby gets the nutrients that allow it to grow and develop directly from the mother. Some also believe that a mother and her baby share an instinctive spiritual bond—that a "mother's intuition" develops long before the baby is actually born. And others even believe this connection is so intense that mothers and babies can communicate through the womb. There is no way to be certain if this is true or not, but let's just say for now that it is.

When a fetus is only about sixteen weeks old, it begins to hear. Research shows it picks up the sounds of the mother's stomach rumbling and her heart beating, and that even a sudden noise may startle it, waking it from a nap and causing its limbs to jump. At nineteen weeks, the hearing is even better, and through the ocean of amniotic fluid and a paste that covers and protects its ears, an unborn baby may be able to detect the sounds, however muffled, of not only the person carrying it around all day, but others nearby. And studies also show that, although of course the baby can't understand what you're saying, talking to your child in utero will strengthen the bond a mother feels toward the baby she has yet to hold in her arms.

So if you're expecting a new little angel, try a bit of reading to your belly. It doesn't matter if the words come from Shakespeare, the *Onion*, or even some type of gibberish. The mere act of speaking should make you feel closer to the baby you are soon to meet, so talk away.

So why not talk *to* that little being as well? If it feels weird speaking to your stomach, start slowly. Maybe after a kick say, "You liked that smoothie, did you?" or let your baby know what's going to happen next ("We're going for a long walk now"). Pretty soon you'll be having all kinds of conversations with your new unborn companion. Don't be embarrassed; it's actually good practice to get used to the embarrassing things you will do in public after the baby is born, like picking up a pacifier that falls on the sidewalk and licking it clean before giving it back to your tot.

Although a little more scientifically suspect, some say that the baby can communicate back. If you buy this, go to a quiet place, ask your baby a question and then see what pops into your head. What if that is not your wheels turning, but the baby actually answering you? Ask it what names it likes or what colors it wants in the nursery and see what comes up. At the end of the day, it's either you or the baby talking, so why not have a little fun with it? Don't worry, if anyone you know thinks it's crazy. Just blame it on the fact that you're pregnant. Pregnant people are allowed to do whatever they want, including act crazy.

All of this will help a mom and a dad feel like actual parents months before the first labor pains begin, so that by the time the little one pops out into the world, everyone feels like they know each other already. Added bonus: Your baby can't talk back yet—so enjoy!

There are some at-home prenatal monitors that let a mother-to-be hook up fetal speakers on a maternity belt, attach a microphone, and speak in soothing tones directly into her belly (just in case the baby can't hear her normally) throughout pregnancy. It also lets her record the sounds her baby makes and e-mail them to family and friends.

How to Welcome a New Mom Home from the Hospital

The baby's here, everyone's healthy, the families are overjoyed, and your friend's life is about to return to (sort of) normal. But what kind of friend would you be if you weren't there to welcome that bundle of love, and his exhausted mother, when they arrive home from the hospital?

Here's the thing about coming home for the first time as a new mom: it's a mixture of old and new. She is returning to her old life, but with a whole new twist on things. So when welcoming her home, it's important to keep this in mind.

Just like many situations, it's the little things that count. Stocking the fridge with her favorite foods (which might be different now that she's no longer pregnant, so don't go wild restocking the chocolate-covered pickles), making sure there are fresh sheets and towels available, and even DVRing her favorite shows will go a long way in helping her readjust to her old life.

Sometimes it's as simple as hanging a WELCOME HOME sign (include info on the baby and maybe a little drawing of a stork) on the front door. It's guaranteed to put a smile on her face, plus it alerts the neighbors that the new family member has arrived, and that they may now begin offering gifts, baked goods, and free babysitting services. (And though there may already be a nursery set up for the baby, you can always add a few last-minute toys, supplies, and accents to the room to surprise the new mom when she gets home from the hospital.)

Remember, nothing will help a new mother feel as cared for as the relief of not having to do anything, so offer her a day or two of babysitting so she can do whatever she wants—whether it's reading, catching up on those recorded shows, getting a massage or a haircut, or just taking a nap. She won't even know how much she really needed it until it happens, so unless she's not comfortable letting the baby out of her sight (or you're not comfortable being responsible for the little one), don't take no for an answer.

For the first couple of days, *everyone* will want to come by and see the baby, and a new mom may need help managing the traffic, so ask her if you can step in and take charge (or just insist). Pick up food for guests, and head over just to clean (or send someone over to do the scrubbing— no reason to ruin your own manicure!).

The name of the game here is letting the mom rest and not have to worry about anything. After all, she'll have the rest of her life to worry, so if you can put her mind at ease for just a few days, you'll have done your part. Now about those sleepless nights . . . well, that just may be the one place where new parents are on their own.

If you are the father of the baby, take a week off work (tip: if you have to check the sports scores, use your BlackBerry, and do it where she can't see you!), rub your wife's feet often (she has been standing on them carrying a lot of extra weight for the last nine months), and don't freak out if she feels like crying (a lot). And take this opportunity to hone your diaper-changing skills—if you really want to help, you're going to need them.

∞ How to Stay Sane as a New Mom

Just about the time in your pregnancy you were starting to enjoy the attention and getting used to letting other people do things for you (like give you their seat on the train or let you off the hook for not helping with the dishes), your nine months are up, and suddenly it's no longer all about *you*. Face it, as soon as that baby arrives, all eyes are off you and on your new little bundle of joy (and if you're like most new moms, that part is a relief). But if you thought pregnancy was tough, it can be more than a little challenging to get down with the notion that for the next eighteen *years* (or more!) you're going to be responsible for the well-being of this new person. And you wouldn't have it any other way . . . but how is it possible to stay sane at this critical point in your life?

Relax. It was a long and (literally) sober journey guiding your little one into this world, but she's here now and if you want to be a good mom, you're gonna have to be a *sane* mom, and that's why you need some *you* time, beginning immediately.

Keep in mind that for the first twenty-four hours after your baby is born, your hormones are going to pretty much sucker punch you, making even the smallest task seem like an insurmountable obstacle. Let it go. If you need to bitch, bitch. If you need to cry, cry. You just pushed out a *baby*, and now is the time that *everyone* will let you off the hook—so enjoy it, maybe even milk it a little.

Remember this: The first step in becoming a good mom is coming to terms with your new life. And although books are good resources and your childless friends might be wonderful and supportive, when you're really in the throes of adjusting to motherhood, it's often very helpful to talk to other people going through the same thing. So go make some new mom friends. Invite them over for playdates. It's perfectly OK to pretend that you are doing it for the baby; after all, every eight-week-old needs some new pals, doesn't she?

Things will get considerably easier once you acknowledge the fact that sleep isn't going to happen for a very long while. Yes, you can dream about staying in bed until noon on a lazy Sunday morning, but know that your best dreams in the near future will be daydreams. And readjust your expectations about what you can get done with a new baby. Even if you are supermom, don't attempt more than one outing per day at the most. Trust me, just getting out the door will feel like a heroic feat in and of itself.

That said, leaving the house is key to staying sane as a new mom. Get yourself a fantastic babysitter and rest assured your baby will be just fine without you for a few hours. Don't kid yourself—there are a few things motherhood doesn't change and getting a mani/pedi is a necessity, just like before. You'd hire a babysitter to go to a business meeting, so don't feel guilty getting one just to go get your hair done.

And it's OK to leave the house at night, too. The sooner you come to terms with the fact alcohol does not affect your breast milk (as long as you drink it a couple of hours before nursing), the better. (If you'd like to err on the side of caution, you can always learn to pump and dump.) Institute a Mommy Margarita night. Even if you just have one, you will start to feel like an adult. If you don't want to risk hard alcohol, stick with beer. Rumor has it that (in moderation) beer helps with milk production, so really, you're doing your bambino a favor.

Finally, give yourself a break about the baby weight and be sure to invest in some "in-between" clothing to wear while you get rid of the few extra baby pounds. This is not the time to be starving yourself to make it back into your skinny jeans. The brand Lululemon is just *made* for new mothers and a few new items in your wardrobe will make you feel like a new woman.

Quick tip: Black is always a tempting color, especially when you're not as tiny as you were last year, but I'd advise going with some prints about now—they'll do a better job of hiding that spit-up you'll have on your shoulder for at least the next six months.

Know that this will all be *so* much easier the second time around!

How to Make Baby Food from Scratch

You cook for yourself and your spouse. You even cook occasionally for the dog. But when it comes to your eight-month-old, it's awfully tempting to buy jar after jar of premade baby food from a supermarket shelf. Even if you're buying organic, and the list of ingredients certainly seems harmless enough—sweet potatoes, water—if feels funny to be giving the kid processed foods when you only eat foods that you cook yourself.

Let me clue you in on one thing: The thought of making baby food is more difficult than actually *making* the food. You can make your own baby food in a couple of really simple ways. The most important distinction between baby food and grown-up food is the texture. So first, you'll need something with which to grind up the solid food. You can use a regular blender, an immersion blender, a hand-cranked food mill, or sometimes even the back of a fork will do the trick. The food just needs to be prepared so that the baby can mush it around and swallow it without anyone having to worry about choking. There are also plenty of baby food-making kits on the market—and a surprising number of baby food cookbooks. A few of the kits come with their own grinders, as well as instructions, a cookbook, nutritional guidelines, and the trays you'll be freezing the food in (which are simply glorified ice cube trays). Do yourself a favor, though, and save this money for his or her college fund; instead of buying a fancy kit, use the tools you have on hand and look up instructions on the Internet. It's not beef bourguignon, it's baby food. Either way, you don't need new gadgets to get this done.

The process is surprisingly simple. Soften the foods by cooking them however you like—steaming, baking, boiling—then mash them up with enough of the cooking water to get the right consistency. Simply blend for a few seconds and voilà, you have ready-to-eat baby food. I'd recommend making large batches at once and freezing them in ice cube trays so you have some on hand for the days you don't feel like Julia Child.

Hint: Once frozen, pop the food out of the trays and store the cubes in Ziploc bags so you can grab a serving when you need it.

Steam some extra of whatever the baby is going to eat (minus the mashing and blending, of course) and add it to your own dinner plate. If you're like most people, you're feeding your baby healthy vegetables, so this may help put you on the track to healthier eating.

There are different theories on how to thaw the food. Some people are horrified that you would go to the trouble of making your own baby food and then defrost it in the evil microwave, but the dangers of this method have yet to be confirmed. No judgment here, so if you do decide to use the microwave, just place the cubes in a glass bowl—not plastic—and zap. Otherwise, you can thaw the cubes in the refrigerator overnight (not at room temperature, because of bacteria concerns), or to get it done in a hurry, place the cubes in a double boiler (or in a bowl that sits in another bowl of hot water) on the stove.

Whether your baby food is homemade or store-bought, be sure to check with your pediatrician about when the baby should be introduced to certain foods, because there are concerns about allergies and digestive development. And when it comes to certain vegetables, such as carrots and spinach, you'll have to educate yourself on nitrates (though some say that concern is way overblown). Still, you can use the above method for any number of fruits and vegetables, and eventually poultry, fish (be careful of the bones and no shellfish), and even meat.

If you are so busy that it's hard enough to get a meal on the table for you and your partner these days, and you catch yourself taking more and more shortcuts—like takeout—don't feel guilty about taking some shortcuts with your baby, too. Feed her from a jar if it makes you less stressed out. Or cook some food (you can even use some of your own leftovers, if they're healthy enough), and buy others premade.

Finally, one of the best ways to get your baby interested in good food is to have him sit with you at mealtime and give him things from your plate—as long as it doesn't require chewing. You can smash up bits of rice with the back of a spoon and give it to him or offer him some of your mashed potatoes or a taste of a banana. This will introduce your baby to new flavors, as well as the ritual of meals, and makes dinnertime more relaxed for everyone.

And don't feel pressured to do what all the other moms are doing. What's good for you is good for your baby.

Think potluck. You make the carrots and have your new mom friends each make another dish, then bring your ice chest to the next playgroup and swap veggies. Don't think too much about the fact that just last year you were going out to dinner every Saturday night, and now swapping brussels sprouts for squash puree has suddenly become the high point of your week. My, how quickly things change!

How to Get Your Kids to Sleep in Their Own Beds

Letting your kids sleep with you in your bed when they're upset, lonely, or scared of the monster in the closet is fine to do once in a while, but it can be a dangerous habit to fall into. Trust me, the first few times you let junior snuggle in with you, you'll feel like the best parent in the world, but if it becomes a regular thing, it could do more harm than good in the long run for both your child's development and for your sanity (not to mention your sex life).

The key is not letting it get that far. But of course as anyone who has been in this situation knows, that's easier said than done. And if it does start to become a habit, you should take action immediately to break it. One good tip is to set a time limit—anywhere from ten minutes to an hour—for how long your child can stay in your bed (you might want to start with an hour and then gradually subtract ten minutes every night). Be clear that after the time is up, you'll be moving your little one back to her own bed whether she is asleep or not (it's better if the child is awake, so she is aware of what's happening). If you spring this on her without warning, she may become confused and even more distressed, but if you set the limit ahead of time, she can prepare herself. Kids crave structure, so make sure you are very clear and that you stick to what you say, even when they beg for more time.

Another strategy is to climb into bed with your kid for a little while—his or her bed, that is. What your child really wants is attention and comfort, not necessarily the feel of your specific bed and blankets. By getting into your kid's bed as he or she falls asleep can provide the same comfort, but you remain in control. You can leave as soon as your kid falls asleep, and *you* decide which nights you come in and which nights you don't (you do run the risk of falling asleep yourself, though, so either set a watch or tell your spouse to come wake you after a set amount of time).

Of course, this too can be emotionally damaging if it becomes a habit, so reserve it for necessary occasions, like if your kid has, say, just watched a scary movie (bad call on your part) or had to deal with the death of a pet. If your kid feels like it's a routine, you won't be in control of his reaction when the routine ends. If you do sense this is happening, work your way out of the room gradually. In other words, for a few nights you can lie in the child's bed. Then for a few nights sit next to the bed holding his hand. After that sit across the room in a chair and finally, go back to your own room. If you take this one step at a time, it will be easier for your child to accept. Slow and steady wins the race here.

Another option is bribery. This works for some families and you know who you are. No judgment here.

Perhaps the best solution, though, is to simply take steps to make your kid more comfortable in his or her own bed. You know your own child best, so figure out the specific problem. Fear of the dark? Purchase a night-light (and maybe do a nightly sweep for monsters). Fidgety and unable to sleep? Put a glass of warm milk by the child's bedside, and/or buy a clock radio or iPod dock that has a "sleep" function, as some kids can fall asleep quicker and easier with soft music in the background. Scared of creaky noises? Try drowning them out with a white noise machine (sleep experts swear by them). Whatever the specific issue, also invest in a special pillow or special mattress pad so that your kid will be so comfortable in his bed he'll never want to leave, even on stressful nights (though this might create other problems—like getting him to school on time).

Remember: At the end of the day (or night as the case may be), they are only little and vulnerable for a very short while. At some point, they will outgrow it. I don't know of any teenagers who sleep with their parents.

How to Convince Your Kids That Doing Dishes, Cleaning Their Room, and Doing Chores Is Fun

Remember that famous story from the novel *The Adventures of Tom Sawyer*, where Tom got out of the painful chore of whitewashing the fence by tricking a friend into thinking it was such a fantastic activity that the friend actually offered to *pay Tom* for the pleasure of doing it for him? This isn't just a funny story; it's a really valuable lesson in parenting.

Most parents use one of two fairly easy techniques to get kids to do chores: carrots and sticks (OK, maybe more like ice cream, and revocation of video-game privileges). What I mean is if the kids do what they are told, they're rewarded, and if they don't do it, they're punished.

But while rewards (otherwise known as bribes) and consequences can convince your kids to do chores some of the time, bear in mind, they'll also have an unintended effect: they will imply that there's something inherently *bad* about doing chores. After all, a child will be quick to figure out, if there's a reward at the end, the journey must be boring. If it were fun, the activity would be the reward in itself, right?

And that's what chores have to be.

To get kids to do (and enjoy) their chores in the long run, you have to stop offering bribes and/or doling out punishments. And since there's nothing that kids like more than games (except maybe ice cream), turn the chores into games.

This might be challenging at first (and if so, you might want to turn this chore into a game for yourself!), especially if your kids are used to getting rewarded for chores (that's why this method works much better on the younger set, and why starting early is key). So the first step is to turn the chore into a fun thing that you can do *together*. If you're doing the dishes, turn on some music and dance while you wipe. If you're cleaning up a room, don't just drop stuff in the trash or place dirty clothes in a hamper: make it a game of basketball. If you're sweeping or mopping, turn it into a race to see who can finish his or her side of the room fastest. Depending on the age and personality of your kids, you can even assign point values to various chores (i.e., for every toy you clean up, you get one point), and see who gets the most points in ten minutes. But don't let them trade in points for prizes (the activity itself is the prize, remember?)—that's just a disguised bribe. And NEVER refer to the chore by its plain old "work" name (e.g, "washing the kitchen floor" or "cleaning your room") in front of your child. Give it some kind of fun-sounding name, like mop racing, or hamperball.

The most important thing is that you do the chores *with* your kids and show that you're having fun doing them (or at least pretend you are). This is really why they'll want in on the game. After a while, you'll be able to phase out your participation, and soon enough, your kids will be doing the chores themselves. It's easy to modify the games so they can be played solo; instead of racing, give them a timer, and see if they can beat their personal best at cleaning their room. Before you know it, your kids will be cleaning the house without your having to ask, just for the fun of reporting back how many points they got or baskets they scored or records they beat. Hey, who knows, they may even offer to pay you for the privilege.

How to Start a Family Game Night Tradition

Spending quality time with your kids (and spouse) often gets left off the daily to-do list, but instituting a weekly family game night is a fun way to get everyone together, for more than just a few minutes, on a regular basis. After a while, it won't just be a distraction from your daily routine—it will become an integral part of it.

If your kids, or even your spouse, roll their eyes at the mention of family game night (party poopers), you may have to do some work to get them excited. First, get some *new* games. Even if you have some classics that you love in the back of your closet, kids (and husbands) love new things, so try starting out with something novel, like Taboo, Apples to Apples, or Buzzword. Plus, playing some of the newer games can help you feel younger and in the know. If you don't want to invest in any new games, do a game swap with the neighbors. If you have older children, make sure you buy age-specific games that will be a bit of a challenge; if the game is too easy for them, they'll lose interest. If, however, it's too difficult, they may get frustrated, so start with something you think will be a little challenging and have an easier game ready as a backup. Also, if you have younger kids, try one of the many new games that have "junior" versions, which are easier for younger children (and will make them feel more grown-up) but are still fun for adults. Have kids of different ages? Though the instructions won't tell you this, the adult and junior versions of many newer games can be *combined* and played at the same time. For example, if you are playing Taboo, use both versions and simply have adults and teens draw cards from the regular game and kids draw cards from the junior version.

Once you have your games ready, do *not*, whatever you do, announce "It's time for family game night!" Everyone's seen those Hasbro commercials, and while they may look like heaven to parents, they're cheesy to kids. If game night is regulated and "official," it's already uncool. Better to institute a tradition of having pizza on game night and calling it "pizza night" instead. Even if you end up playing every Thursday night, don't let your kids realize it's becoming a pattern; act like it came up organically, and your kids will be more likely to get into it. Make it even more special by baking cookies or making popcorn, and your kids will be excited for game night (I mean "having popcorn and staying up late night") all week long.

Another way to make it more fun is to come up with your own family "rules." For example, the winner gets to choose what's for dinner the next night or the loser has to make the beds for everyone in the house for the next week. It's always exciting to put a little extra spin on things.

If it doesn't catch on, it's most likely the game, not your family. If board games aren't doing it, consider multimedia-based games like Scene It? If you have a video-game console, like Wii or Playstation, look into family or party-style games like Buzz or Rock Band. Sure, they don't have the same feel as a good old-fashioned game of Scrabble, but, hey, times have changed, and even if you're facing a TV screen, you're still getting in some quality time with the family.

Remember: It's about your bigger vision—keeping your kids happy and bringing the family together. So who cares what you're actually doing. Your job is simply to set the stage, and then let the games begin!

Make sure the games are interactive and social. Much to your husband's dismay, getting your family to sign up for Fantasy Baseball is *not* a good choice for game night.

How to Create a Family Crest

"What gift should I send the family that invited us to stay in their vacation home for a week? They have everything?" This is a question I get a lot. Then, one day I came up with a terrific idea. Make them a family crest. It's unique and fun *and* then you can use the emblem to personalize their gifts forever.

Crests were invented in the Middle Ages to identify warriors who were dressed in armor. Each knight chose symbols and colors to distinguish himself, and then the crest was passed down for generations. Certain guidelines existed back then, but really, since we are no longer walking around in suits of armor, there is no official way to make a family crest; just design something that somehow reflects the background or interests of your family (or the family you are making it for) and you've got your crest.

First, choose the basic design. A typical crest is a shield shape, but yours can be any shape you want. There are no strict rules here, but my advice would be to keep the outline relatively simple and feel free to decorate the edges or create a border.

Next, choose a color. For a more traditional-looking crest, you might go with a muted color like silver or gold, but don't limit yourself. There's nothing wrong with a hot pink family crest if that's what best expresses your family.

Quick tip: The type of crest and the colors you choose can have different symbolic meanings (although if you just happen to like how it looks, that's OK too). For example, gold symbolizes generosity, silver or white symbolizes peace, and blue symbolizes truth and loyalty. For a more comprehensive list, check out www.fleurdelis.com/meanings.htm.

Most crests are divided into four parts, with symbols placed in each section. If your family, even if generations ago, came from another country, it's common to have an emblem representing that country (perhaps a flag) in one section, and an emblem representing the country you (or they) reside in now (if it's the United States, you could use a symbol like a bald eagle) in the opposite one. But again, you can use any symbols you like that have special meaning to and represent your family (although try to use things that are timeless, rather than just things you think are cool right now, so that the crest can last for many years and be passed down from generation to generation). Have a little fun with it. For example, the family I once helped a client make the crest for had a ski house, so we used skis in it (instead of medieval swords).

Many crests also contain monograms or phrases, "mottos" if you will. Some families choose to put each family member's first initial on the crest, which is fine if it's only for now, but it won't hold up over time as your family grows. I recommend choosing a group of words that resonates with you and is meaningful and special to your family. Don't have a family motto? What a great family activity—create one! And to up the customized gift appeal, consider translating it into another language—perhaps the language of the country where your family came from. Everything seems just a bit more symbolic when it's in another language, doesn't it?

Last, don't just design your crest: *do* something with it! Upload your design to a website like www.CustomInk.com where you can put it on T-shirts, mugs, or a wide range of other items. Have a copy framed in your home. Send an electronic image to your extended family. Include it in your next holiday greeting card. It's a great conversation piece, and besides, if you don't show it off, what was the point of making it in the first place?

Quick tip: If you're not artistically inclined, visit www.MakeYourCoat OfArms.com, where you'll get assistance with every step of the process, from designing your crest to printing it on a variety of products. Using the website is completely free—ordering items is the only thing that'll cost you.

How to Tell Your Mother You Got a Tattoo

If your mother has a tattoo, well then, you probably don't need this section. But for those whose mothers aren't adorned with permanent body art (and I assume this is most of us, but who knows), figuring out how to break the news to your mother (or grandmother) that you got a tattoo can be tough. So, lesson number one: Think things through *before* you get your tattoo. If you can't stomach the thought of telling your mother, just be smart and have it placed somewhere that she will not see it, ever.

I had a friend who got a tattoo just above her bikini line. The perfect spot—or so she thought, until she found herself going to Florida on vacation with her entire family. She *knew* her grandmother would freak out. When she told me it was a flower, I assumed she was safe, that no one would even notice it. What I didn't realize was this was no little rose petal—the tattoo she got was a monster flower, larger than the palm of her hand! She sure didn't plan that well.

Look, we've all done things we regret (usually when we were younger, and maybe not quite so wise, aka: more daring). And if the shame of the act itself weren't enough, having to confess to our parents only made things worse. But while the pain of owning up to your mom is bad (what is it about mothers that can instantly make a grown man or woman become like a fourteen-year-old who's late for curfew?), having her find out about it on her own will be infinitely worse. So if there's even a small chance this could happen, I'd advise biting the bullet.

If you lived in a sitcom, you might think the best thing to do would be to introduce the idea slowly. Ask your mom what she thinks of tattoos. Then cleverly steer her into saying she sees nothing wrong with them. A few days later, ask if she'd ever consider getting one. Trick her into saying yes. A few days after that, ask what she'd think if you got one. Now she can't possibly object, right?

Wrong. Because if there is one thing you should know about sitcoms, it's that these things never go off as planned—that's why they are fun to watch! Besides, unless your mother has a not-so-secret love of tattoos, she'll likely shut down your questions right from the get-go. Rather than warming to the idea, the more you press the issue, the more suspicious she'll become. Sure, it might be good TV material, but it's not a good life strategy.

Best to just get it over with, and better if you can get your mother when she's feeling relaxed . . . so, consider plying her with a few drinks. There's something about drinking and getting a tattoo; somehow, they seem to go hand in hand. Invite your parents to a nice dinner and have a bottle of wine that you insist on opening right away. And if your mother decides not to drink? Well, then you should consider consuming her share. It's amazing what a few glasses will do for your courage. And by all means, avoid the other sitcom cliché, chickening out at the last minute and making up some other bogus story instead (surprise! I'm pregnant). It will only make things worse, and you'll undoubtedly be exposed by the end of the episode, er, evening, anyway.

The bottom line is that a mother loves her kids, and even if at first she seems mad (or worse, "disappointed"), she'll get over it. No matter what, it's better for her to find out from you than to notice it poolside at the family reunion.

How to Get Rid of Your Kids' Things Once They Move out of the House

Have you let time freeze and kept your kid's room looking exactly like it did in 1983 (when she was twelve)? It's a little strange at Christmastime, isn't it, when your daughter and her husband have to squeeze into her old twin bed surrounded by stuffed animals and old horse show ribbons strung across the walls? Eighteen-plus years under your roof has probably added up to a lot of stuff, from preschool potato stamp prints to a B+ high school term paper on Martin Luther King Jr. Some parents try to hang on to old memories by keeping their kids' room as a shrine, but really, it's OK to move on, especially once the kids are done with college and have their own homes where they could store all this stuff. So how do you go about getting rid of your grown kids' things and maybe finally get some use out of that extra bedroom?

The most important thing is that you involve them in the process.

Honestly, even if your kids are in their thirties, live across the country, and haven't cracked open their middle-school yearbook in two decades, they'll probably be hurt and upset if they come home for their next visit and find that their childhood bedroom has been converted into a home gym. It would likely be a mistake to plow through their old rooms—filling garbage bags as you go—without warning. Tell them (gently) that you've decided to clean out their room, and give them until an agreed-upon date to have everything that they would like to keep cleared out (or you'll be getting rid of it). Be sure that they agree to do this in a timely manner; set a firm deadline and stick with it. If your kids don't live nearby and you have the extra time on your hands, offer to help (how very thoughtful of you) by going through their stuff and making lists so they can tell you what they want you to hold on to for them and what you can toss.

Chances are, you'll be more sentimental about the stuff than your kids are. I have been hired plenty of times to assist parents in parting with their kids' things, and for the record, it's usually the parents who don't want to say good-bye.

If you want the room cleared out right away (maybe you have a guest coming into town who might not be comfortable sleeping in a room wall-papered with My Little Ponies), it may be as simple as just getting a big box and packaging everything all up for them. If you have the space, say, in a garage or an attic, store it until the next time they are home for a visit. If not, just ship it right off to them and let them decide what they want to do with their old high school soccer trophies and cheerleading outfits. Whatever strategy you choose, be careful not to work too hastily so you don't end up throwing away something you, or your kids, will later regret.

If you're the sentimental sort, it can feel heartbreaking to part with all those old finger paintings and math tests. One way to ease the pain is to make albums for them (or for yourself), including just a few originals from each stage of their childhood, and trashing the rest. You can even take pictures of the stuff if you can't bear to let it go.

How much you decide to keep is up to you. Some people are hoarders, some are clean-slaters. It's healthy to fall somewhere in between. Instead of thinking of it as "getting rid" of old stuff, tell yourself you're "organizing." And remember, organizing isn't about simply making room to accumulate more stuff (though generally that's what happens). It's about coming up with a strategy to hang on to what means a lot to you, and thinning out the rest along the way. If you need help, check out the

National Association of Professional Organizers (www.napo.net). Yes, there is such an organization and the members really know what they're doing. And if you think you have a real problem getting rid of things, take a test to see if you might be a compulsive hoarder at http://www.pamguide.com.au/anxiety/hoard_test.php (if you find you do have a problem, the site will provide resources for where to get professional help).

Here's a way to avoid this problem in the first place. As soon as your kids leave home, redo their rooms, keeping enough of their stuff that it will still feel like home when they come to visit but clearing enough out so that you can use the space as you wish while they are away. They'll feel special that you made them a nice adult room to come home to, and you won't feel like you kicked them out too quickly.

How to Commission Someone to Paint a Family Portrait

Just because you want to commission someone to paint a family portrait doesn't mean that you hang out at country clubs and carry around a copy of *The Preppy Handbook*. A family portrait isn't a vain indulgence of blue bloods. It's a meaningful, personal memento that can be enjoyed for generations. And it's a lot easier to do than most people imagine. When I was asked to commission one for a client, the trickiest part was getting everyone in the family to commit to the same sitting date.

If you decide to get a family portrait done (and would prefer it didn't look like it was modeled after a page in the Ralph Lauren catalog), consider going a nontraditional route. Choose a local artist you really love, regardless of whether or not he or she is a portrait artist (or has ever done portraits before). A good artist will ask you these types of questions: What are you trying to capture? What kinds of things does your family like to do together? (If the answer is "nothing" or "I don't know, I can't stand them," consider it a clue that you probably don't need to get a family portrait painted.) In fact, if you choose someone who has *never* done a portrait before, you might end up with a fascinating piece of art with a unique new take on portraiture. Call it modern portraiture? If you genuinely like the artist's style, it's worth the risk. Who knows, Aunt Sally may look even better in a more "abstract" painting.

If you don't already have someone in mind, visit local art galleries and studios, which you can usually find even in small towns. Don't rush it: if you don't see something you love right away, wait until the gallery changes its inventory and showcases work from a new artist.

While you are busy finding the painter, be sure someone else in the family is rallying the troops. They will need to get everyone to agree on what to wear (or keep it simple by instructing everyone on what to wear) and make certain that the location is convenient for all. And don't stress out if one person just can't make it. I'm sure with the aid of a photo, the artist will be able to paint them right in.

If you find the person through a gallery, ask in advance about a ball-park price for a commissioned piece (based on the price of the artist's other works). Just remember, as with anything else, custom is usually a bit more expensive, but if you call the artist directly and cut out the middle-man (like the gallery), you'll probably pay less. Most local artists, especially ones who have not yet "made it big," will be willing to do the portrait for a reasonable rate simply because it's a new opportunity and a guaranteed sale.

Want to do it even more cheaply? Try seeking out an art school student. Most art school students are strapped for cash (you've heard the term *starving artist*) and will jump at the opportunity. You'll save some money, and you might discover a new and unique artistic visionary.

If you want a more traditional-looking portrait, and you start your search online, as most people do, be careful. Websites like www.Portrait Artist.com will set you up with local artists, but be sure to do your homework, and find examples of his or her other work to make sure you like the style. Commissioning a painting can be a very personal thing, so call up the artist to ensure that you click. Don't be shy and ask if you can speak with some references.

If you don't care so much about quality, various websites create portraits from digital photos that you upload. Though most of them claim to have "real" artists who paint the portrait from your photo, the final product can sometimes have a pretty generic, computer-generated look. Check out some samples on websites (e.g., www.PaintYourLife.com), to see what I mean. If the quality works for you, it'll save you a ton of cash; prices start around $100 (though that increases based on the number of people in the photo and the size of the portrait). The good news is that you only have to pay 20 percent up front so if you don't like the work, you can simply decline it and keep 80 percent of the fee. But the really great part is that since they're painting from a photo, you won't have to put your five-year-old through his worst nightmare, sitting still posing for hours on end.

How to Get Your Wife to Let You Watch the Game in Peace

It's game time, and you're ready: you've got your chips, your brews, and your buddies, and nothing's going to stop you from cheering your team to victory. Except maybe your wife. She may be the love of your life, but when you want to focus on the giant TV, it can be hard to keep that fact in mind. So how do you make sure she gives you your "you time"?

Well, first of all, having people over to watch is a great way to send the message that this is important to you. If the game feels like an *event*, she's less likely to interrupt, and with other people around, she won't want to cause a scene. It's important to take care of all the arrangements yourself, though—don't be the guy who has a bunch of friends over but expects his wife to do all the shopping and cooking.

A great idea that benefits *everyone* is to arrange something a little special for her to do while the game is on. Make an appointment for her—a spa treatment, massage, or manicure—and drop her off. You don't even have to pretend you don't have an ulterior motive—as long as you're giving her something to enjoy, she'll be all for it. If she's going to be around, though, you can also negotiate with her beforehand. In return for some guytime with ESPN, for example, offer to take the kids out all morning so she can do her thing or offer to handle dinner (be sure to say "handle" and not "cook," just so there are no misunderstandings). Again, it doesn't matter if it's obvious that you're just doing this because you want to watch the game. You're still a good guy for offering.

Touchdown.

2. around the world

How to Guarantee Your Luggage Won't Get Lost

Let's face it, short of traveling only with carry-ons, there's no surefire way to ensure your luggage gets to go on the same vacation you do: airlines are just *that good* at losing your stuff. Fortunately, there are definitely ways to increase the odds that your bag arrives safely in Honolulu with you.

First, if you can shell out the extra dough (or book far enough in advance to get a good deal), fly direct. Most lost bags go missing because they don't make connecting flights in time, or they're placed on the wrong connecting flight. Flying direct means your bag only has to make it on *one* plane, which vastly increases the odds you'll walk out of the airport with it.

Second, when you check in, remember to make sure that the tag placed on your bag has the correct destination marked on it. Sounds obvious, but often people are so distracted by other things, like worrying about whether their toothpaste is going to get confiscated at security, that they don't bother to take two seconds to double-check this simple thing.

You check your own ticket to make sure you are getting on the correct plane, don't you? So why wouldn't you extend the same courtesy to your luggage?

I realize that weapons on a plane (even fake ones) are a sensitive issue in this day and age, but I want you to know that if you are the sort of person who doesn't mind ruffling a few feathers, another way to make sure your bag arrives at your destination is by getting a FAKE weapon like a starter pistol (the things they fire at the beginning of a race) or a flare gun and packing it in your checked bag. At check-in, declare you have an unloaded weapon. (*Note:* This means letting the check-in agent know you've packed a weapon in your bag, not yelling "I have a gun!," which is a good way to guarantee you'll end up in jail.) The agent will put a tag on your bag to this effect. Trust me, the airline will make *extra* sure a suitcase containing a weapon isn't lost. This might feel wrong, but it is safe and perfectly legal to do—traveling photographers do it all the time to ensure they see their equipment again.

Another tip is to consider the choice of bag itself. Everyone knows that if you have a generic black suitcase you should tie a brightly colored ribbon on it so you can easily identify it at baggage claim, right? Exactly! Everyone knows and does this, which means it doesn't really decrease the odds of someone mistakenly taking your bag. On the other hand, if you travel with a neon purple bag with glitter stickers all over it, odds are no one else will take it home by mistake. Plus, if it gets put on the wrong plane, a bag that looks like it's a prop from an '80s music video will be much easier to locate and recover. After all, what are the airline employees going to remember better, your Jem and the Holograms bag or the 158 black duffel bags with red ribbons tied on them they saw that day?

How to Make the Best of Being Stranded in an Airport

Being stranded at an airport when your flight is delayed is most people's worst nightmare. But when you think about it, an airport may actually be one of the better places you could be stranded.

After all, airports are specifically designed to help you kill time. Everything you need is right at your fingertips. Plus, the diversity of people passing through airports is unmatched almost anywhere else, so it's the perfect place to people watch—or even meet people. You can relax, read, shop, eat, and drink—what more to life is there? In fact, if you didn't think of it as being "stuck" or "stranded," you just might go there to have some fun.

For one thing, airport bars can have some terrific happy hours. Head over to a bar and grill and have a few drinks with your meal to drown the sorrow of being delayed. If you're traveling alone, sit at the bar and order food off the bar menu—you might meet other solo travelers there and strike up a conversation to pass the time. If you're single, have some fun and flirt. You can even test out that pickup line you've been wanting to try; chances are you'll never see the person again. Though I myself have never met anyone in an airport, I've seen enough movies to know that airports are a great place to find love. If you don't believe me, ask Billy Crystal. If getting plastered and looking for romance isn't your thing, get some shopping done instead. Airports, especially the duty-free stores, are great places to buy gifts (for someone else, or yourself). The prices are usually affordable and often tax-free.

Quick tip: If possible, always travel with your laptop or PDA. Many airports now offer free wireless Internet access, so you can get some work done while you're stuck at the gate. The bonus is that no one from the office will bother you because they think you're on a plane.

If you're stuck for a good number of hours, try visiting the nearest airport hotel and poking around. It may have a better restaurant (or bar) than what you'd find in the terminal, and it may also have a pool, gym, or spa that you can sneak into, even if you're not actually staying there. In some hotels, you might need a key card to get in, but if you're willing to wait for someone else to go in (or come out), just slip in behind them. Since you're traveling, you're likely to have gym clothes (or perhaps even a bathing suit) with you, so take advantage of the opportunity and grab a good workout or go for a relaxing swim.

Note: If you don't travel frequently, learn to keep a change of clothes and/or workout clothes in your carry-on bag, just in case.

Another option is to check out some of the airlines' executive clubs (e.g., American's Admirals Club, Continental's Presidents Club, Delta's Sky Club, United's Red Carpet Club, or the US Airways Club). If you're a frequent flyer, consider buying a membership to the club of your choice, but if not, and this will be a onetime occurrence, most clubs offer a day pass for around $40 or $50. Most offer free food, drinks, newspapers and magazines, television, computer workstations, and a quiet place to relax or do some work. If you are stuck overnight and don't want to pay for a hotel, an airline club is a great alternative; it will be much safer and quieter than simply sleeping in the terminal. Be sure to first verify that the club is open twenty-four hours, and make arrangements for the staff to wake you up, if necessary, so you don't miss your flight.

Quick tip: If you have an American Express Platinum card or higher, you may be eligible for automatic free access to three clubs: American, Delta, and Continental. If you fly often, this might be a good reason to get an AmEx card or upgrade to Platinum.

Still stressed? Pamper yourself. Many airports now have small spas that offer services like massages or manicures. If there was ever a time to treat yourself to this kind of luxury, this is it. After all, you've already spent a couple hundred dollars on the flight, so splurging a little more to help keep yourself calm and sane is probably worth the extra money.

Still not excited about spending the day in the airport? Think really hard about what you would be doing on a lazy day in your own home. Reading? Sleeping? Drinking? Shopping? It's all right there. I could go on, but I think you get the point. Trick yourself into thinking that you're *choosing* to spend the afternoon at the airport and you just might have a good time.

How to Efficiently Pack for a Trip

At one point in time, I was traveling nonstop for business. Yes, I had clients all over the world and was always on a plane. When I started out, I was not the most efficient packer and would inevitably end up with a bag that was too large for the overhead (because it was crammed with too many items that would never get worn and, of course, lacked the one thing I actually needed). Luckily, it didn't take me long to mend my ways, and before long I was packing as efficiently as George Clooney in *Up in the Air*. What a relief. There is nothing like being able to lift your suitcase gracefully up into the overhead compartment and sail out of the airport thirty minutes ahead of all those suckers waiting for their luggage. Plus getting dressed in the morning was a lot easier once I only had a choice of a few versatile outfits that were already neatly ironed and ready to throw on.

The key to being a good packer is in the prep work—shopping. To pack efficiently you first need to own just a few key items that easily go from day to night, don't wrinkle, and can be mixed and matched with each other. A black skirt is key, as are a couple of solid-colored cardigans. Keep all items in the same color scheme—basic—so you can make your wardrobe decisions on the fly and wear items again (if necessary, without people thinking of you as the girl who always wears the red dress).

Once you've picked out your travel outfits, the best way to pack them is to roll everything up, from socks and underwear to pants and cotton shirts. One of the biggest fallacies about packing is that rolling clothes will make them wrinkle—in fact, exactly the opposite is true. By rolling everything instead of folding, you prevent it all from moving around and getting out of place during travel, which is what causes the wrinkles in the first place. Just make sure to roll everything tightly, and wedge it securely into the suitcase. Plus rolling clothes actually saves space (though items are the same size whether you fold them or roll them, only rolling allows you to fit items into the nooks and crannies of the bag), so you'll be able to fit in that red dress, after all—just in case of a special occasion.

Don't even think about trying to bring all of your toiletries. Buy some small travel sizes (the essentials only) just once and refill them. If you prefer, pick up clear plastic bottles from The Container Store or Bed Bath & Beyond (these are extremely cheap, usually around $1 each, and they're reusable). Plus, if you're flying and don't want to check your bag, you'll need all liquids in three-ounce containers, anyway.

Don't be afraid to get creative with your toiletries, either. Conditioner may be meant for your hair at the end of a shower, but it also works reasonably well as shaving cream, and body wash will do for shampoo in a pinch (some companies, like Axe and Old Spice, have started making two-in-one body wash *plus* shampoo). And, of course, if you're staying at a hotel, don't pack anything they're likely to provide: soap, shampoo, mouthwash, a hair dryer, and so on.

Once you pack the perfect bag, take two extra minutes and create a packing list. Slip it into one of the zippered compartments in your luggage that you never use and pull it out before every trip. Between knowing ahead of time what you want to pack and not having to bother with folding, you'll be packed and on your way to the airport in ten minutes flat. You can send me a postcard to say thanks.

Need more help? Visit www.OneBag.com, which has pages and pages dedicated to traveling light and fitting everything into one bag.

How to Hire Your Own Security Guard to Take You Around a Dangerous City

Maybe you like living on the edge, or maybe you need to go to a dangerous city for business, or maybe it's just that you like to have an entourage follow you wherever you go—whatever the reason, a time may come when you'll want to hire your own personal security guard to accompany you around a dangerous city. From Mogadishu to Ciudad Juarez and back home to Camden, New Jersey, the world is full of cities bristling with carjackings, muggings, kidnappings, hotel room break-ins, and so on, so why put yourself in unnecessary danger?

Hiring a beefy, well-trained bodyguard, especially one who can understand the customs and protocol of a particular country, can ensure your safety and help you navigate your way around a dangerous hood.

You can hire a security guard once you arrive in the city you're visiting, but if the city is really formidable, you will need to prepare ahead of time, lest you end up with someone unreliable, or connected to the wrong crowd. It makes much more sense, and is bound to be safer, to bring someone from home, or at the very least have an agency stateside. Either way, double-check the person's credentials and make sure he or she has experience in the specific place you are headed. If you do get someone local, find a legit native source who can vouch for this person, or beware: you could be hiring your own kidnappers.

If you decide to use a stateside agency, the best way to find someone, as with everything, is a referral. If you don't know anyone who has ever hired a bodyguard, been a bodyguard, or knows a bodyguard, search the phonebook or online for an "executive protection agency."

Once you find a company, you'll want to check its permits and licenses, and call and ask a lot of questions. Does your guard speak the language in the country you are going to? Does he know the culture? Does he have current passports and immunizations? What about ties to police or other agencies in the country you will be visiting? All these things are very important, and you'll also want to verify that your bodyguard knows how to handle weapons—and if he knows first aid and CPR, all the better (you will, after all, be in dangerous territory).

You should also let the agency know whether you have additional requirements. For instance, if you're a woman, would you prefer to have a woman guard than a man? How important is it that the person you hire looks like he or she fits in with your lifestyle? You might want the bodyguard to be able to hit a cocktail party with you and keep up with the small talk so as not to stand out. Or maybe you *want* people to know you have security with you. These are all things agencies anticipate you asking, so don't hold back. If you speak with someone who won't comply, try somewhere else.

Remember: always get a photocopy of the security guard's driver's license and social security card.

Don't just *ask* for references. Do yourself a favor and take the time to actually call them. You're talking life-and-death scenarios here, and there are no "do-overs."

If you are bothering to get a security guard, you'll probably want the person to be armed (otherwise, what's the point?). And although it is possible with the proper permits, it's extremely difficult for *anyone* to travel with weapons. Even if you do clear security, many countries have regulations preventing people from bringing arms into their country, so if you must have an armed guard with you, see "How to Get Armed Security Guards on a Commercial Flight," page 59.

Prices for security vary widely depending on how many protective agents you have and whether or not you need round-the-clock security. If you want 24/7 protection, that means that one guy will need to sleep, so you'll need to hire two men. We're talking from $500 to $1000 for a twelve-hour shift up to even $100,000/week or higher if you'll be in a *really* sketchy place. If an agency is charging much less than this, I'd stay away; after all, if you are hiring security, it is probably for good reason and—saving a few bucks should not be the name of the game here. You get what you pay for.

Remember: Even if you have a security guard watching out for you, don't do anything stupid. Keep a low profile and try to blend in as best you can. Just attend to your business, and get back home. And don't feel strange about hiring a security guard if you think you need one. I've traveled with high-profile people who need security guards and even armored cars. Once you get used to having someone with a wire in his ear and a firearm at his hip following you around, just knowing that person is there will help you sleep a lot more soundly.

Best not to tell your mother about the trip until after you're back—and maybe not even then.

How to Know What to Bring When Traveling with a Baby

Preparing for a vacation was certainly easier before your baby came along, but the process needn't be overwhelming. Not many people realize this, but the younger your baby is, the easier travel can be. Once you have a crawler—especially a toddler—on your hands, everything becomes trickier, and a vacation can feel less and less like the R&R you once knew. So do yourself a favor and book that trip to Hawaii before your little one starts walking and talking.

The first thing to do is to make a list of everything you'll need for the baby—*and* for yourself. If you thought lists were important before, now that you have a child (and the frazzled, sleep-deprived baby brain that goes along with having a child) lists are your new best friend (and key to your sanity). It's all too easy to get caught up in diapers and baby shampoo only to get to the beach and discover you forgot your own bathing suit—oops.

The basics for your little one are easy:

1. Diapers. I'd advise enough for the time you'll be in transit plus two extra days' worth just in case; unless you're going to a remote cabin in the middle of nowhere (an ambitious choice indeed), you'll be able to buy more when you arrive at your destination.

2. Plastic bags for messy diapers, food, and clothes. Just please make sure you don't mix the contents of these.

3. Items for the bathroom, including hand sanitizer, soaps, lotions, and diaper cream.

4. Bibs.

5. Toys and books.

6. Clothes. This includes a sun hat (even if you're not going anyplace particularly warm, a baby's skin is sensitive, and you'll still want to protect it from the rays) and two baby outfits for every day you'll be gone (unless you're going to Grandma's and will be able to do laundry).

7. And finally: pacifiers if your baby uses them. It's also not a bad idea to have some basic medicines, especially infant Tylenol or Motrin. And bring a spare shirt for yourself for the trip there, in case of the inevitable spit-up stains.

What food you bring for your baby depends, of course, on his or her age and stage. It couldn't be easier to travel with a baby who's exclusively breastfed and not eating solid food yet. If you're flying, feed during take-off and landing (check online for Hooter Hiders easy cover-ups); it helps ease the pressure in baby's ears and will help to calm her if she gets rattled. If you'd rather not breastfeed on the plane (understandable), check with the airline you are flying on, but most allow three ounces of formula or expressed breast milk. If not, bring powdered formula and ask a flight attendant for water. If your baby is eating solid foods, bring what she'll need for the trip there, but chances are you can stock up on more when you get where you're going—unless, again, you're traveling to some remote place, or a country where the food might be so unfamiliar your baby won't like it. Remember though, since every food is new to a baby, she has just as much of a shot of liking the hummus as she does the pureed broccoli; take this opportunity to broaden her tastes a little, and don't hesitate to try her on the local fare.

I once had a client whose kids would *only* drink vanilla soymilk. Which is fine, I guess (who am I to judge) except that they don't carry it in the Greek Islands (we checked). So we loaded up a suitcase full of the stuff and they checked the bag right on through. Sounds silly, but the kids were happy and then my clients had an empty suitcase to fill with goodies to bring back from their trip.

You'll need a collapsible stroller and/or a sling or front carrier (an excellent way to schlep baby around airports and new cities, leaving your hands free) and a car seat for taxis or the rental car (and for the plane if the baby gets her own seat). Be sure to have a plan for sleeping arrangements wherever you're going. You could bring a portable crib or play yard, but most hotels will rent you such an item, so check. No crib? Let your tiny baby nap in a baby carrier, and at night create a safe space (like on a mattress on the floor) or try cosleeping for a few nights. As long as your baby is not mobile, you still have some flexibility here.

New toys are the best distraction on a long trip, but don't bring them out all at once. Introduce a new toy or book every couple of hours, and save some for the trip home, too.

Try wrapping all new toys (even silly little $1 items like little wind-up toys); kids love to unwrap things (some even like to play with the ribbon), and it will keep them busy for longer.

And get creative with what counts as toys. Q-tips make great mini building tools (like tiny Lincoln Logs), they're the perfect size for those airplane tray tables, and can amuse a kid for hours. And don't forget about iPhone apps; you'd be surprised how many apps exist for entertaining tots, and this way you don't even have to pack anything extra.

When it comes to entertainment, get creative and think simple. If you forget to bring the bag of toys, make up a story or write the story about your trip (from your kids' perspective) and have them do the illustrations; it's an activity that can last you the whole trip and will leave you with a great keepsake from your vacation!

How to Find a Custom Tailor in a Foreign City

Just after 9/11, I was in London with a group of politician clients who were scheduled to have tea at the House of Lords (yes, they actually do that kind of stuff over there) before speaking at a rally. The day before the rally, the politicians were informed that due to the dangerous political climate, they would be required to wear bulletproof vests as a precautionary measure.

Well, if there's one thing bulletproof vests do (besides protect you from bullets), it's mess up an outfit. The mens' shirts wouldn't fit over the bulky vests. Buying new shirts was an option, but although a larger size might slip over the vest, it would be too big in the neck and sleeves. Of course they also wanted to look good in all the footage that would inevitably be taken at the rally—not to mention for teatime with the British aristocracy—so there was only one solution. They'd need custom-tailored shirts. Issue was, I didn't have a single custom tailor in London in my Rolodex.

As with anything you find yourself needing in another country, the first and easiest way to start is to contact a hotel concierge. Concierges are basically professional problem solvers, and they tend to be locals, so they know where to find anything and everything you might need. The more expensive the hotel, the better the concierge tends to be. If that doesn't work, and you're traveling on business, call some of the colleagues you're friendly with in that foreign office. They may have to ask around, but if there's a risk of you showing up to give a presentation to all their shareholders in pants that are ripped down the inseam, I think they'll be willing to spend a few minutes to help you out.

In this case, our concierge was able to act quickly and refer me to the best tailor in the city . . . who then laughed at my request for four custom shirts in less than twenty-four hours. But it turned out he knew of *another* tailor who was good at quick turnarounds, and he proceeded to make the referral. The second tailor was certain he could accommodate us and asked what time the men could come in to be measured.

Unfortunately, I then ran into another slight snag in the plan: the politicians were already overbooked, and there was no way an in-person measuring session was going to happen. So, thinking fast, I got a crash course on how to take shirt measurements (in the metric system, no less!) After a few awkward moments of getting a little more up close and personal with my clients than I would have liked, I had the measurements the tailor needed, and he was able to get us the shirts in the nick of time.

Of course, this was a unique situation, but if you travel a lot, particularly for business, there's going to come a time you're in desperate need of a tailor, and being in a strange city, even one where you don't speak the language, shouldn't prevent you from getting something altered or repaired. Are you really going to let the last-minute discovery of a tear in your bridesmaid dress ruin your best friend's Paris wedding?

How to Get a Passport Issued— Overnight

Your bags are packed, your dress is perfectly pressed, and the ceremony is in two days. You have one foot out the door to your bachelorette party when you remember that you need your passport to go to Bora Bora for your honeymoon—and it's expired.

You're packing the whole family up for your two weeks out of town when you realize, you've had an addition to the family since your last jaunt abroad. Could you really have forgotten that your baby needs a passport?

You're single and generally unattached, you just got laid off, your lease is up next week, and you have just enough saved for a month's stay, with no strings attached, in Mexico. But wait, your passport expired ten years ago.

Yes, all three of these situations have happened to my clients.

Whatever the circumstances, you, too, may at some point find yourself in need of a passport right away. But as it turns out, there's no reason to despair. A standard passport application will take about six weeks; however, to obtain your document within twenty-four to forty-eight hours, you can simply make an appointment with your regional passport office (call 877-487-2778 to find a location nearby and to make an appointment). Be prepared to wait in line and pay an additional expediting fee (in addition to the regular application fees), but hey, you snooze, you lose. If you'd have taken the time to look at the expiration date on your passport when you planned your trip instead of waiting until the day before you were leaving town, you wouldn't be in this pickle.

If you can't make it to the regional office, search online for an authorized passport outfit near you and head there with the required materials and an additional chunk of cash (usually a few hundred dollars, and they won't take personal checks).

Here's what you'll have to bring with you: a form DS-82 (which you can get at www.travel.state.gov), two regulation passport photos (the best place to get these taken is at a store that sells photography equipment, although some drugstores and most Mail Boxes Etc., and other such stores, will do it for you), proof of U.S. citizenship (your old passport, if you have one, or a birth certificate will do the job), and proof of your identity (driver's license, naturalization certificate, government or military ID card).

With all that in hand, the application filled out, and your pockets full of dough, you'll be able to get the new passport in less time than it takes to get through international security at El Al Airlines. Still, do yourself a favor and take a time-out to check your passport right now. Find the expiration date and add a reminder into your calendar two months before. Then come back, turn to "How to Get the Best Seat on an Airplane, page 45, and go ahead and book that trip to Thailand you keep talking about!

How to Get to Everest Base Camp

If you've read *Into Thin Air* by John Krakauer, it was probably enough to deter you from attempting a Mount Everest ascent. Still, if you want to taste the romance of that infamous peak without risking life and limb, you can always hike to the Everest base camp, one of the most popular trekking routes in the Himalayas. If you're reasonably fit and like a good adventure, this could be the trip of a lifetime.

First thing you should know when considering whether this vacation is right for you is that you won't have to carry your own bag—ever. Porters are plentiful and you shouldn't feel guilty hiring one, because these guys need work and who better than you to contribute to the local economy? Hiring the locals for this approximately eighteen-day round-trip trek will not only save your back but will let you leave the nitty-gritty details—like making sure you're going in the right direction—to someone else so you can focus on the spectacular views. Trust me, by the end of your trip you will want to take these guys home with you to help navigate everyday life in your town or city.

There are a few ways to go about finding a good guide. A popular method is to book a group tour with a trekking company. All-inclusive trips usually provide experienced and certified English-speaking guides and porters. This is the slightly pricier option but the simplest solution. The disadvantage to group trekking, though, is that you'll have to stick to a tight schedule, so if you feel like lingering at a particular village along the way, you're out of luck. And you might get left behind if you need an extra day to recover from altitude sickness (which you'll recognize if you feel hungover when all you've consumed the night before is a boiled egg and some tea).

If you decide, like I did a few years back, to do this the adventurous way, you can simply choose a route and then find your own guide and porters when you get there. Get yourself to Kathmandu; then just ask some locals for recommendations. Start with your hotel; its staff should know where you can find someone to get you to the peak. Not staying at a fancy hotel? Don't worry. In a city like Kathmandu, everyone's got a friend he wants to refer you to. Someone who works at your two-star hotel, or your taxi driver, or your waiter will know a guy who knows a guy who will take good care of you. Who are you kidding? You're a Westerner with dollar bills.

Even if you can't locate someone in Kathmandu, you can still hop the plane to Lukla, which is one of the highest airports in the world (this flight alone is part of the adventure and highly recommended). Don't be alarmed by the airplane you'll have to take to get there—the inside may look like that of a rickety old school bus, but the flight is so breathtaking it'll distract you from the fact that the airplane's seat belts wouldn't help you in a fender bender, never mind thousands of feet up in the air.

After you land, you'll see a plethora of porters and guides milling about the airstrip waiting for the opportunity to escort you through the mountains to base camp. Once you have your guide and your porter, you are ready to hit the trail. Enjoy the fact that you are unreachable by cell phone, and keep in mind that although your trekking trip will sound awesome when you get home, there are few luxuries on this journey.

Here are some insider tips to help prepare you for what lies ahead:

1. The "showers" are generously named. You will have a stall with a hose coming through the top. Your guide or porter will then warm water by the fire for a few minutes and pour it through the spout. The on/off switch is your voice—scream when it's too freezing to take and he'll stop pouring.

2. Consider yourself lucky if you come across a "bathroom." And by that I mean four pieces of wood for privacy and a platform over a very deep hole, to squat.

3. High bridges (the kind you see James Bond swinging from in the movies) actually do exist—and they are everywhere. They are wobbly, especially when many people (and yaks) are crossing at the same time. So if you are scared of heights . . . well, come to think of it, if you're scared of heights you probably should just consider another adventure altogether.

4. Don't eat the chicken. You will know why when you see these dirty scrawny birds picking up scraps from under your lunch table. If you need a little protein and run out of Luna bars, have your guide ask at the teahouse for some peanut butter (they all seem to have it hidden in the back).

5. Bring duct tape. It helps with blisters and lots of other things that you can never plan for. It's a must-have in your backpack for any adventure.

Just because you won't have to carry your own bag doesn't give you a free pass to overpack. You need one change of clothing, extra socks, a rain jacket, some snacks, a good sleeping bag, and a camera. ALWAYS remember: Eat *before* you're hungry and drink *before* you're thirsty. There are no 7-Elevens on the way to base camp.

How to Get the Best Seat on an Airplane

You've booked an exorbitant ticket, stood in security lines, removed your shoes, had your shampoo confiscated, and endured endless delays. So now that you've finally made it onto the plane, the last thing you want is to find you'll be spending the next six hours sitting inches from the restrooms, or in the same vicinity as a screaming infant. To make matters worse, the guy who checked in *after* you is stretching his legs in the exit row, while you're scrunched in the middle seat between two snoring strangers with your knees at your neck.

How can you avoid such a fate?

Contrary to popular belief, scoring the best spot on the plane is not so much a matter of luck as of strategy. Step one: Identify the plum positions. To some extent, those depend on your own preferences and habits. Exit rows are key if you are tall and leggy (but aren't an option for children under fifteen); window seats are best if you are prone to falling asleep while airborne (but are less ideal if you have a small bladder); aisle seats are good for the impatient since they allow for faster disembarking at the end of the flight. If you're a nervous flier, seats over the wings tend to feel less turbulence, but the jury's out as to whether you're more likely to survive a crash if you're sitting at the front or back of the aircraft (though hopefully it won't come to that!). To help choose your ideal spot, check out websites like www.seatguru.com that compare seat width, legroom, and laptop and video facilities for a range of airlines and aircraft (unfortunately these sites can't predict the seat assignments of restless babies).

Once you've decided where you want to sit, there are a number of ways to get there. Since prime-real-estate-like exit rows go fast, it's crucial to choose your seat as early as possible, preferably when you book your ticket. If you book online and seat assignments are not an option, you can try calling the airline directly to see if they will reserve you a place. (But always double-check later: airlines can change aircrafts and reassign seats at the last minute, so keep an eye on your flight to make sure that you're still in the seat that you want.)

Still not happy? Don't be a wallflower—ask directly for an upgrade when you check in at the gate. You'd be surprised how many people don't, and you may just score a row to yourself, or, if you're in luck, even an empty business or first-class perch. Similarly, let the airline know if you're sick, or have any other compelling reason to be allocated a better seat (consider speaking in a hushed voice about the terrible problem that sends you to the bathroom every thirty minutes—can you say aisle, please!). If you're not above being a little (OK, more than a little) sneaky, call and tell an agent you'll be traveling with a small child, then at the last minute decide to leave the (imaginary) little tyke at home (if you show up solo, it's unlikely the person at the check-in counter will reassign your seat). Or you might mention you'll be flying with crutches—so what if you don't really need them. It's your call, but hauling a pair of crutches through the airport could be worth the extra few minutes it takes to trudge through the terminal if it gains you an upgraded seat for the next five hours.

Volunteering to relinquish your seat on an overbooked flight can also set you up for seating bliss when you eventually get on the next one. It may mean that you have to alter your travel plans by a few hours or spend a night in an airport or airport hotel (see "How to Make the Best of Being Stranded in an Airport," page 30), but you often get a pretty hefty coupon, cash, or upgrade in return. If you travel frequently, also be sure to leverage your elite status. It can mean that you get early dibs when it comes to choosing seats.

Then there are the more creative (but less scrupulous) options: listen to loud music or pretend to be sick so that your neighbors will move, leaving you next to the empty seat. If you do decide to go that route though, be warned: karma's a bitch thirty thousand feet up.

How to Make People Think You're a Local Even If You're a Tourist

There's nothing a local hates more than being mistaken for a tourist, especially in his own neighborhood. And no question about it, being a local has a lot of benefits—people are less likely to take advantage of you, sell you things you don't need, or roll their eyes when you walk by. When you're a local, you are cool and in the know. You know the best places to go, get the best prices on everything, and back doors open everywhere you turn. But if you think the only place you can pass for a local is in your hometown, think again. With enough planning and a few tricks, you can make even the most grizzled local wonder how he's never met you before.

For starters, don't rely on guidebooks; they are a dead giveaway and will direct you to touristy places where no local would be caught dead. Like in New York City: you'd be surprised at how rarely most New Yorkers actually go to midtown (other than to meet out of towners), yet the focus of most New York City guidebooks seems to imply that midtown is one of the hottest areas to spend time (it isn't). So, instead of using a guidebook, I recommend getting in touch with people who live in the place you are going, then have them give you the real scoop. Where do *they* go to dinner? If you can't find *anyone who knows anyone* who lives where you're going, you must not be utilizing Facebook properly.

Speaking of networking sites, even if you're not single, consider browsing match.com or other dating sites—they're a great tool to find hot spots. Search the profiles to find out people's favorite restaurants, clubs, and activities; trust me, there will be plenty to choose from.

And although I've never tried it and hesitate to recommend it, if you don't have the time to do this legwork, or just can't seem to track anyone down, some guidebooks, like the Lonely Planet guides or the *Not for Tourists* series (only available for some cities), will steer you to places off the beaten path and give you insider tips. Online review sites like yelp. com can also help you find hotels, attractions, restaurants, and bars in any area; just make sure to read the tips and reviews from real locals, who know the area and know all the places you might otherwise miss. Be aware, though, that you run the risk of relying on information from only the select group of locals who fill out their opinions online.

You may be better off picking up the newspaper when you first arrive in town. In a small town it's easy to find the local paper, but in a bigger city like New York where there are several to choose from; that means those that don't have national circulation, like the *Post* or the *Village Voice*, instead of the *New York Times*. Many cities distribute free papers on the subway, so give those a quick read as well. Or at least hold them up and pretend to read them while on the subway; it's generally only locals who read the free papers, so it's instant street cred.

Which brings me to the next point: real locals *ride public transportation*. If you're going to a big city, study the subway and bus maps beforehand, and if you know you need to get someplace specific, check www.hopstop.com to map out your path ahead of time (nothing will brand you as a tourist faster than having to look at a map or, God forbid, ask for directions). If you decide to hoof it instead, the GPS feature on most smartphones can go a long way. If you don't have such a device, write down directions before you leave the hotel (obviously, the people at hotels know you don't live there, so you don't have to pretend to know where you are going in front of anyone there).

If you must take a taxi, know that bossily directing the taxi drivers is another thing only locals do. Look up the recommended route on Google maps, and let the driver know how you want to get to your destination. Phrases like "take the bridge" or "don't go down Broadway, it's a mess this time of day" will make you seem like you know what you're talking about and keep the driver from jerking you around.

From the moment you arrive, keep your eyes and ears open. Listen in on conversations at Starbucks or the local coffee shop. Figure out who the locals are and subtly tail them. Not sure where to go for happy hour? At a ski resort, watch for the guy walking around town in his ski boots and follow him. And when you get there, get to know the bartender. All locals know the bartenders. Plus, bartenders can get you into restaurants even when there is a wait and will give you the dirt on everything in town.

Another big rule is to steer clear of any and all clothing with the city's name on it—no real Aspenite wears an Aspen sweatshirt (unless he got it for free in some event goody bag), and you'll never see a D.C. resident wearing an FBI hat (even people in the FBI don't wear them, as that would probably be a poor idea when going undercover). If you must get souvenirs for people back home, find something unique in a small store that doesn't necessarily declare the name of the place you went to, something you can only get in New York, but doesn't scream "I heart New York." It's much more personal, the story of how you found the place will be far more interesting, and your sister won't wonder if it's from the last shop you saw in the airport on your way back home.

If all else fails, break out a wad of cash. All locals love tourists who like to spend money in their town, so if you can't join 'em, at least get 'em to like you for the week.

How to Find a Dentist in Another Country

No one expects a dental emergency while on vacation in another country, but a few years ago, while a client of mine was enjoying an expensive Italian meal in Venice, she bit down on something hard, heard a crack, and ended up with a loose tooth. She knew she'd have to deal with it eventually, but hoped she could wait until she got back to the United States.

Unfortunately, an hour later, her tooth was still throbbing, and she knew she'd need immediate medical attention. Though she could have searched for a dentist online, finding an Internet café seemed just as challenging as finding a dentist or hospital. Plus, it's a bit scary to just go blindly to any old dentist you find on the Internet (especially in a foreign country). Though she was traveling with an International Emergency Card, the service directed her to a deserted building that apparently *used* to be a hospital. Dead end. Literally. She put in a call to us, but with the time change, we didn't get the message in time.

Luckily, on her way back to the hotel, she spotted two police officers and approached them. Though she didn't speak any Italian, she repeated the words *dentist* and *hospital* while pointing to her tooth, and they got the picture. They tried to explain how to get to the nearest dentist, but the language barrier proved difficult, so my client very resourcefully pulled out her map of Venice and the officers drew an X to mark the spot. Thankfully, it turned out to be a functioning dentists' office that was open for business—and they even had an employee who spoke English and was able to translate.

If you find yourself in the same situation but don't happen upon any helpful police officers (or you have even more trouble explaining what you need), don't despair. Just use a travel dictionary or Internet translator to look up the word for *dentist,* and then use Google Maps—which works internationally—to locate the nearest one. In advance of your trip, you should also buy a membership with International SOS (www.internationalsos.com) or a similar international emergency service. (With any luck, they'll send you to a real, practicing dentist, unlike what they did with my client.) If you can't find a dentist, or if it's already late at night when most dentists' offices are closed, do a Google Maps search to find a nearby hospital. At the hospital they can at least give you something for the pain and then refer you to a local dentist if necessary (most international hospitals have at least one doctor or nurse who speaks English).

If your dental problem is *not* an emergency but you still need to get it taken care of (maybe you're abroad for an extended period) before you make it back stateside, the best thing to do is to start asking people you know for references. If you have any friends from the country you're visiting, or know anyone who has ever lived there for any amount of time, call them up, even if they're not currently in the country, and even if they didn't live in the same city you're visiting. Their connections could lead to someone who can help you out—for example, a dentist in Rome may have a colleague he can recommend in Venice. Also, check your Facebook friend list (or other social networking site) for anyone whose name sounds like it may be from the country you're in. Even if you haven't spoken to the person in years, most people will be glad to help in an emergency.

As you may have guessed by now, some of my favorite resources are the concierges at big fancy hotels. If you can't find a personal referral for a local dentist, just call the concierge where you are staying and ask for a reference. Alternatively, you could stop by a local pharmacy (outside the United States, almost *all* pharmacies are adorned with the same symbol, a green neon plus sign). Pharmacies abroad aren't like Walgreens or CVS in the United States—they usually carry only the prescription stuff, so the shopkeeper (akin to a U.S. pharmacologist) should be well connected to the medical world and, with any luck, will have a recommendation for the best local dentist. If they don't speak too much English, try the international language of pain: pointing to your teeth and moaning. Most people will get the picture.

How to Hike the Appalachian Trail

Hiking the entire Appalachian Trail can be one of the most rewarding experiences of a lifetime—and at the same time, one of the most challenging. Whether you're an avid hiker or a relative novice who wants to try something new, completing the trail is within your reach, but it helps to know what you're getting yourself into. Current statistics say that almost two thousand people begin hiking the trail each year, yet only somewhere between five hundred and six hundred finish the entire thing. Most of those people don't finish simply because they are not fully prepared. The Appalachian Trail is more than just a weekend stroll on a dirt path with your friends; it's a serious, several-month-long commitment that requires some serious planning. Still, if you're determined and you follow a few easy steps, you can be part of the elite 25 percent who come home saying that hiking the trail was one of the best experiences of their life. (*Hint:* Now's a good time to consider adding it to your bucket list, see "How to Create a Bucket List," page 197).

The first important thing to know is that the trail stretches over two thousand miles! Whew! It starts in Georgia and ends in Maine (or vice versa, depending on where you begin). An extremely speedy, professional hiker can complete the trail in about four months; a very slow hiker who stops for days at a time in small towns can take up to seven. Most people, on average, take about five to six months. To accomplish this undertaking in less than six months, you will need to hike almost every day (though a break here and there, either for rest, scenic visits, or to avoid bad weather, is fine), for about six to ten hours a day (about ten to fifteen miles).

So even if you hike at a reasonable clip, this undertaking means putting other aspects of your life on hold. If you can't take, say, more than a few weeks off from work, or be away from your family more than a few weeks at a time, you are "allowed" (according to unofficial Appalachian Trail hiking code) to split the trip up and it still technically "counts." About 20 percent of people who complete the entire trail do it in segments, usually over multiple years. This can be a great way to accomplish your goal while keeping your life intact, and it can make the actual journey seem easier. It'll take six years instead of six months, but think of it as spreading out the fun.

If you plan to hike the whole trail in one stretch, be sure to consider weather conditions. For example, if you're thinking about starting the hike in the winter or spring, begin in Georgia so that it's turning into summer by the time you enter chilly New England. If you start in the summer, begin in Maine for the opposite effect. Also, consider the difficulty levels: the southern sections of the trail are much flatter and easier, while some of the trail's most difficult mountains are in Vermont, New Hampshire, and Maine. So think about whether you'd prefer to start out easier and work your way up, or get the hard part over with early on. Also, think about whether you would like to hike with a huge group of people, or to take a more personal journey. About 90 percent of thru-hikers begin in Georgia, so if you like crowds and want to meet people, go with the flow, but if you really want a solitary experience, start in Maine and do the reverse commute.

Quick tip: If you're considering hiking with a friend or two, make sure they're *really* good friends. You are going to spend every waking hour with these people for the next six months, so it would be better if you really like them. Or, consider making this the time to fly solo. You're likely to make some new friends along the way (and new people tend not to get on your nerves quite as much).

Other logistics include food and lodging. You will not have to rely on hunting and fishing for your own food, but you will have to plan your meals in advance. The Appalachian Trail goes through many small towns, but when it doesn't (like in the White Mountains of New Hampshire), there are Appalachian Mountain Club (AMC) huts at periodic intervals that provide food, water, and shelter. If you want to feel like you are really roughing it, you could organize mail or food drops, but understand that neither is necessary, since you'll pass by either a town or an AMC hut almost every day if you're walking at a fifteen-mile-a-day pace. Same goes for a tent. Sure, you can bring one, but it is possible to sleep in an AMC hut or other shelter every night (it will cost a bit more money, though, so many thru-hikers only stay in huts when the weather is lousy).

Once you've made all these arrangements, you're well on your way! Make sure you have all the proper gear, but travel light. Consider what you will do in an emergency—your cell phone may not get reliable service, so have a backup plan. And check out some websites, like www.appalachiantrail.org. This site can help you prepare your entire trip from start to finish.

The trail was established in 1921, and to date only about ten thousand people have ever completed the entire route. So if you like a challenge and your boots were made for walking, lace 'em up.
Lewis and Clark would be proud.

How to Book a Ferry to a Greek Island

So you want to go to take a vacation in Greece? Trust me, what you *really* mean is that you want to visit the Greek Islands. Athens is a must see, but my advice is to visit the major sites and move on as quickly as possible. There are *thousands* of the most gorgeous islands in the world (although only a couple *hundred* are inhabited) off the coast of Greece, so take advantage of the opportunity and head out to sea.

With there being so many islands, the most convenient (and cost-effective) way to check them out is by ferry. Ferries in Greece are the equivalent of Greyhound buses in the United States, and an extremely popular way to island-hop on your vacation. Just make sure to book the ferries you want in advance; sometimes people think that they can just get over there and jump on a boat, and while you certainly *can* do this, you may end up letting the ferry availability dictate the islands you visit, rather than you deciding on your destinations.

But before you book, prepare yourself. Making the arrangements for vacationing in the Greek Islands is never as simple as you might think. With a married last name of Papadopoulos, I understandably get calls about this every spring. "Help! I can't understand these websites. The ferry schedules are conflicting and the cabin situations make no sense. Not to mention, the descriptions of the seats and cabins seem to be written backwards. And how can I coordinate the different stops? It's just not clear and there are different boats and different ports and I have no idea what I'm doing!"

Well, here's the inside scoop. Even if you're Greek and read and speak the language, it's still close to impossible to understand what's going on, so I'd recommend using a travel agent, and letting him or her take care of the ferry reservations. If you aren't using a travel agent, at least find someone who speaks the language to do the booking for you. Don't know anyone who speaks Greek? I guess you could try calling yourself, but just know that you are not guaranteed anything, ever, and allow some time for the ensuing lengthy and confusing conversation—I dare you to complete the whole transaction in under an hour. In addition, know that the schedules change all the time, so be sure when you book your ticket that you are working off a schedule that will apply during the dates of your trip. If you're already *in* Greece, *Athens News* publishes the ferry schedule for the coming week every Friday, and your hotel should be able to provide you with a copy. The website www.ferries.gr is a great source for the most recent schedules and booking information. Or better yet, ask the hotel concierge to handle the ticket and then cross your fingers when you arrive at the port.

There are a few other things to know when you plan your Greek getaway. The last weekend in July and the first three weeks in August are when Greeks (and almost all Europeans) travel to the islands for their own vacations, so advance reservations are a must. The days before Greek Easter are also crowded, as large numbers of Orthodox Greeks travel to Greece to be with their families for the holiday. If you like festive holidays, this is a good time to go, but check your calendar first, because Greek Easter is not the same as other Easters.

More things to know about ferries: There are slow ferries and fast ferries, and you get what you pay for. The fast ferries (similar to the Acela Express trains from New York to Washington, D.C.) are the better option if you want to cover a lot of ground (or water, in this case), although slower ferries have multiple stops on their itineraries and can seem like minicruise ships, without the all-you-can-eat buffet (thank goodness, as that could get pretty ugly on those choppy waters).

Some ferries travel through the night and will have various room/sleeping accommodations. You can never be sure exactly what you are getting until you step foot on the boat, so best not to expect five-star-hotel-like quarters even if you pay for the priciest room aboard.

Sometimes I think that the Greeks like to make things a little difficult on purpose in the hopes of keeping out the riffraff. But if you can get past the tiny cabins, the language barrier, and the confusing schedules, you've got it made. And even if it doesn't go exactly as planned, take my advice and just go with it. All the Greek Islands are amazing, so break out the sunscreen, turn your cell phone off, and enjoy the view.

How to Get Valerian Root to Kuwait (or Another Weird Substance into a Foreign Country)

Oh sure, you think this is ridiculous now. But when you're stuck in Kuwait (or another country where it's impossible to get *anything*) on business and can't sleep, you'll come crawling back to find out how to get this natural sleep aid delivered to your doorstep.

This is one of those crazy requests I just couldn't make up if I tried. One of our clients once called asking for our help—her boyfriend was in Kuwait on business, complaining that he just couldn't sleep. Sure, he missed her, but what he needed most was something called "valerian root." In case you're not up on the uses of valerian, it is helpful for treating many ailments, but it's most commonly (as far back as the ancient Greeks) used to treat insomnia. (Incidentally, the flowers on this plant have a sweet smell and are also often used to make perfume.) It is natural and legal, but not readily available in some countries (like Kuwait).

My first step was to call the Kuwaiti Consulate. The person I spoke to there confirmed that valerian was, in fact, legal in Kuwait, but I called the Kuwaiti Embassy as well just to be sure. Whenever you're sending something into another country, it never hurts to double-check—the person who told you it's legal may just be trying to get you off the phone and not actually know for certain so be sure to do your due diligence.

With two sources confirming its legality, I set to work. I called the embassy again and asked a lot of questions to find out what I needed to do to make sure the package didn't get confiscated at customs. Turned out the recipient would need a certificate of approval to pick up the item from customs once it arrived in Kuwait. And the certificate needed to be issued and picked up in person from the Ministry of Public Health in Kuwait. I asked if there was any possible way to get the certificate here in the States and include it in the package (making it easier for my client's sleep-deprived boyfriend), but the answer was a resounding no. It *must* be done on the other side.

Of course, it doesn't have to be Kuwait or valerian root—if you need anything shipped to another country, most of the preceding steps still apply (though things like foods, medications, and valuable items are more likely to come with restrictions). Confirm with the country's embassy and/or consulate whether or not the product is allowed in, then find out what the steps are for claiming the item on the other side. The last thing you want is for it to get stuck in customs; not only will you probably never see it again, but you and/or the recipient could end up in legal trouble.

The last step I took with the valerian was verifying the fastest and most reliable shipper (with tracking of course); once I locked that in, the herb was on its way. Although my client could have easily hopped on a plane to hand deliver the goods (wouldn't her boyfriend have been surprised), truth be told, it was just a few phone calls and one certificate of approval later and he was sleeping like a baby.

If you're going to go to all the trouble, just be sure you send enough to last him until he gets home to the comforts of his own bed!

How to Book a Hot Air Balloon Ride

Very few things are as adventurous, romantic, unique, or just plain exciting as a hot air balloon ride, and hot air balloon rides are safer than you might think, so if it's not on your bucket list (see "How to Create a Bucket List," page 197), consider adding it now. Though hiring a hot air balloon may seem, well, out of reach, there are plenty of companies that can help you realize your dream of floating above scenic vistas in a giant, lighter-than-air vessel. I once had a client who wanted to propose in a hot air balloon, and it was surprisingly easy to pull off.

We started where anyone would, online. We quickly found that due to air traffic laws, if you live in a city, you'll almost definitely have to travel at least an hour away, but there's no way around that. Check out www. HotAirBallooning.com, which has a list of balloon ride companies across the country (only sixty-two total, and not in every state, but it's a decent list) as well as other important information you'll need to know for your trip.

If you're booking a balloon ride, make sure to have a backup date, because you might not be able to fly on the day you plan to. Hot air balloons only fly in good weather conditions, so if it's rainy, cloudy, or even windy, you'll be staying on the ground. (On the plus side, this makes ballooning one of the safest forms of aviation that exists.)

We found a hot air balloon company in Snowmass, Colorado, which was perfect because the couple loved to ski there. The trickiest part of the whole maneuver was that the balloons go up at dawn (yes, even more romantic, but a bit challenging to get your bride-to-be out the door for a 5:00 A.M. surprise!). He ended up telling her that he had to get up early to pick their friends up from the airport and she had to go with him to navigate. Worked like a charm, and the proposal (and the balloon) went off without a hitch. He later told me that the scariest part of the whole thing wasn't being thousands of feet off the ground, but the thought of dropping the ring!

Because there are relatively few commercial ballooning companies, you might not find one near you. If that's the case, try to find a hot air balloon festival (amazingly beautiful!). They usually happen in the summer or fall, and local ones are likely to crop up within driving distance of wherever you live, even if a commercial ballooning company is nowhere to be found.

If you're looking for a free ride, go to a festival and don't be shy—mingle with the pilots and crew members before the balloons take off. Ask them questions, and express your interest in learning more and possibly taking a ride. If you meet the right person and hit it off, you may be able to score a free ride (or at least one for a reduced fee). Who knows, they may want to take you up just for fun.

If you don't find anyone who is willing to have his or her balloon chartered, ask if you can join the crew. Many pilots will be receptive to new crew members, and if you're willing to devote some time to it, they might take you on. You may not get off the ground right away—the crew's primary responsibility is to drive the "chase vehicle" that follows the balloon—but eventually, you may earn the chance to go up in the balloon.

If you really get hooked on ballooning, consider joining a local "Balloon Club." Yes, these exist, and they often organize flights, contests, festivals, informational and safety sessions, and so on. They tend to be a friendly bunch, not, you know, the type to be full of hot air (sorry, I couldn't resist).

How to Get the Brand of Chewing Gum You Got Hooked on in Japan

Let's face it, visiting exotic places has its downsides. For one thing, no matter how hard you try, you're probably not gonna find Toll House cookies in Japan, and possibly not even your favorite flavor of Doritos. And the reverse is also true—the brands and flavors that are big in Japan are only a distant memory once you come back stateside. So how can you replenish your stash once your carry-on full of the Japanese gum you got hooked on runs out? We once had a client who, after a trip to Tokyo, was left with fond memories of a delicious sugarless plum gum, and nothing more than a wrapper to show for it, so we were enlisted to help him get his fix.

So where to begin? Well, for starters, most major cities have Japanese specialty stores, or at the very least, Asian grocery stores. Such stores always have a candy section, and if your gum was popular enough in Japan, chances are one of these stores will stock it. Worst-case scenario, if you don't see it on the shelf, speak to a manager there and try to find out if he knows of a place where you can get some, or if he can special order it for you. It helps if you can show people an actual pack or wrapper, since you might very well mispronounce the name, or not even know what it's called. That's why it's important to, at the very least, keep your last wrapper even after your gum has all been chewed!

Also, a growing number of websites have been designed for Americans who want to purchase Japanese products; for example, there's a good chance that www.jbox.com or www.asianfoodgrocer.com will have what you're looking for. If you're not sure what the exact name of the gum is, try describing it to someone at a Japanese market or even a customer service rep for one of the sites to get an idea of what you're looking for. (Luckily, ours happened to be *Ume*, meaning plum).

If you strike out with these sites, or can't figure out the name of the brand, try eBay or Craigslist (they often include photos, so if you don't know the name, you can probably identify it by sight). In fact, eBay is where we ended up getting our client his gum. A German eBay auction was selling some gum that looked like our client's, and just to be sure we brought someone in to translate and make sure it was a match. It was, and we were able to get him enough cases of the stuff to last until his next trip to Japan.

Even if there isn't an auction for your particular type of gum on eBay, you might find a user who's selling other kinds of candy or gum from Japan to people in the United States, so contact the seller directly to inquire about your brand.

Still no luck? Head out to the airport, find someone on his or her way to Tokyo, and pay the person to pick some up on the way back. Granted, this is a bit of a pain, and you might (understandably) feel a little weird approaching a stranger and asking him or her to buy you gum, so alternatively, try posting a Craigslist ad for anyone who's headed to Japan in the near future (same idea, but you won't have to drive to the airport, or speak to the person face-to-face—sometimes ya gotta love the anonymity of the Internet!). Just be careful not to get suckered by someone who will take your money, with no intention of getting your gum. It's best to offer to reimburse the person upon delivery.

One last tip: If your travels to Japan were business related, try contacting a business associate (or an assistant at the associate's office) to see if he or she can pop some in the mail. And maybe, just maybe if you are still searching . . . you could call the concierge at a high-end Japanese hotel, supply him with your FedEx number and see if he'd do you a favor. But seriously, if you are the kind of person who is going to go to these lengths to get your hands on an obscure brand of Japanese chewing gum, next time you travel *anywhere*, remember to take an extra suitcase so you can stock up on whatever else you get hooked on!

How to Get Armed Security Guards on a Commercial Flight

Usually, I'm so busy thinking about how to get something done, I don't even think about how bizarre the thing I'm trying to get done *is* until afterward (and then it only occasionally occurs to me). So when I was hired to work with a former politician and terrorism expert, and we needed to get his armed guards to accompany us on a flight from New York to D.C. for an interview, it honestly didn't seem all that weird to me.

Once I'd diligently compiled all the lengthy and necessary paperwork, screenings, and approvals (the process was actually easy to facilitate; the airline let me know what they needed and the security guards had all the forms ready, since they did this all the time), and the guards—and their weapons—were safely on the plane, I figured I was home free. But as the plane idled on the runway for over an hour, my client and I began to get anxious. I asked the flight attendant if we were going to sit for a while, and if so, could we please deplane as we had to make it to an interview and would need to catch a train if we were going to get there on time. Well, to my surprise, the flight attendant replied, "If *you* deplane, we'll be able to take off immediately." Turns out, *we* were the reason the plane hadn't taken off!

Apparently, even with all the required approvals in order, the ultimate decision about whether or not to take off rests with the pilot, and ours wasn't comfortable with the armed guards being on board. Although I could have argued that we were going to be safer than any other flight up there, I kept my mouth shut. He finally agreed to fly, but only after *all* passengers and *all* baggage were unloaded from the plane and bomb-sniffing dogs were taken past the luggage and through the entire cabin. It took two hours, but we finally took off and ended up making the interview in the nick of time. Needless to say, we did not make any new friends on the flight!

However, this all happened pre-9/11. Nine years later, it's a different story. Now, it's challenging to get a bottle of *shampoo* through security, so you can imagine how difficult it now is to get guys with guns on board an airplane.

Law enforcement officers traveling on official business can gain the necessary approvals fairly easily, but for private security firms there are many more forms and approvals, and the required permits can be very costly. And even then, there's no guarantee. So if you are hiring your own security to travel with, you will most likely need to transport their firearms in your checked baggage. Special specific rules also exist regarding the types of containers and packing you must use (call the airlines to ask for the guidelines), and the firearms *must* be unloaded as well as declared at the ticket counter during the check-in process. True, your guard will be unarmed during the flight, but so will everyone else.

If, for whatever reason, you really must take the weapons on board, charter a private plane. Just remember that your security specialist will still need to be certified to carry a weapon in whatever states you are traveling to *and* from. And if you need armed protection in another country, the rules for transporting the weapons will probably be even stricter, so you'll want to consider arranging for the guards to get weapons after they arrive.

How to Travel on a Major Holiday Without Losing Your Mind

When you're a kid, there is nothing better than the long-awaited Christmas break. Whether it is a trip to Grandma's or a ski vacation, the idea that the holidays mean getting out of town is something that has been instilled in us since grade school. And although vacations during the holidays can be fun, sometimes they are more trouble than they're worth: wrapping up loose ends at work, finding a pet sitter, and so on. There's the stress of getting it all together to leave town in the first place. Then there are the crowded airports and delayed flights to deal with, not to mention the fact that the hotels jack up their prices. Every restaurant is jam-packed, and a masseuse with a free schedule is a rare find unless you're smart enough to book the Christmas before (which incidentally is not such a bad idea—because if you are like most people, you end up in the same place year in and year out anyway, so why not consider booking that spa day early?).

However, I've traveled enough, and booked travel arrangements for clients enough, at the holidays that I've come up with some handy tricks and tips for getting to your destination with your sanity intact.

The first one is (and you'll like this one), stretch your vacation and fly a little earlier and stay a little longer than everyone else. Avoiding the heaviest travel days are key for your sanity, and hey, a little extra vacationing never hurt anyone.

Next, when at all possible, fly private. If you're on a budget, spend it on the travel and stay in a less expensive hotel if you need to. Trust me, it's the easiest way to keep your sanity. If you can't quite manage to scrape the funds together, see if you can round up a few friends and all chip in. Or consider hitching a ride on a private jet. Seriously. People don't like empty seats on their planes, so go hang out at the private airport and make some new friends. You'll be glad you did. Avoiding public transportation will make your travel itself a holiday.

If you can't swing the chartered plane, there are ways to make the airport experience less painful. First of all, few things in this world are more stressful than racing for a plane (you've seen *Home Alone*, haven't you?), so with security getting tighter and tighter and lines at airports and train stations getting longer and longer (especially at the holidays), you should leave at least an hour earlier than you think you need to.

Dressing for comfort is also key. (*Note:* comfortable does not mean slob.) Be comfortable, but that doesn't mean you have permission to wear your pajamas. Planes and airports can swing wildly in temperature, so layer. To make things easier at the security checkpoint, don't forget to designate a pair of slip-ons for your travel shoes. Just make sure they are as comfortable as your laced sneakers—you might be wearing them awhile.

Resign yourself to the fact that you'll be waiting around a lot. One way to make all that waiting time less painful is to allow yourself a few special treats. For example, stock up on that one special snack food you love but never let yourself eat, and pack it in your carry-on. Use this opportunity to indulge in the trashiest of trashy books and magazines you can find—without any guilt. And maybe pack some Sudokus to fill up your time. Turn off your cell phone while you're at it; it will help keep the stress at bay. Since everyone thinks you're on a plane, you've got a free pass to tune out. Another activity that can keep you endlessly entertained while you're waiting for your flight (and doesn't even require planning ahead) is people watching. Seeing people who are in much more annoyed states than you are can be quite calming, even amusing. Play a game with your kids to see who can spot more agitated travelers and make up funny stories of their plights.

Be prepared to meditate. No, you don't have to sit cross-legged on a mat facing Mecca and chant (although if you're game, go for it; everyone else is so in their own head at this time of the year, more than likely no one will notice). If you prefer, do some less obvious forms of meditation that won't draw a crowd. Ever heard of vision boards? These can work wonders. Just cut out photos of your favorite people, places, and things to do, paste them on some cardboard, and stick it in your carry-on. When travel stress goes up, look at your photos, and remind yourself of all the great memories you'll create on this vacation. Take deep, yet quiet breaths while waiting in long lines. Aim to keep your body in a tranquil state, thinking peaceful thoughts. Not into the mind-body stuff? Another way to chill out in public is to put on your headphones and listen to some serene and mellow music on your iPod.

Don't underestimate the stress-reducing benefits of having a car service pick you up on both ends. And when you get into the car, make sure to smile at the driver. Remember, he probably wishes he were on vacation, but instead he's stuck working. So give him a little gift of your warm smile and see how much nicer he treats you.

Remember: 'Tis the season to be jolly! There's always plenty of booze at the airport bars if you need it.

3. in the name of love

How to Blow a First Date

I've blown a few dates. I've blown a few dates that I didn't even realize
were dates (which, now that I think about it, may have contributed to my
blowing the date). And after a few accidental blown dates, I started to
realize what I was doing, and I was able to correct my mistakes on future
dates. But every once in a while, I could tell a date was going poorly right
away, and those date-blowing strategies I had long ago employed came
out again—this time, on purpose.

Whether you're reading this to try to *avoid* blowing a date, or you're
thinking of blowing it on purpose, the techniques for killing the mood
are the same. But if you do it on purpose, just make sure you're at least a
halfway-decent actor, or your date will think you're being quirky or aloof
and become even more attracted to you.

The top two strategies are interconnected: talking only about yourself and not listening to what the other person has to say. These seem
somewhat obvious, but they're the most surefire ways to get him signal-
ing for the check. The most effective conversation topics to this end:
your cats, the anatomy of ex-boyfriends, your addiction to prescription

painkillers, the plot of your favorite Sandra Bullock movie (nobody likes spoilers).

Another good strategy: Get really drunk. Sloppy, slurry drunk. If you can get him picturing a future of having to hold your hair back over the toilet every time you go out for a night on the town, he won't be calling you the next day (which is good because you'll probably be hungover). Just make sure you don't get so drunk that you forget you didn't like the guy in the first place (or do something you'll regret in the morning).

Quick tip: If you're a guy, the quickest way to kill the date is to talk about sex. Ladies, if you employ the same strategy, it will probably have opposite results and will most likely lead to—gasp!—sex.

There are also ways to ruin the date before it even begins, which can be especially efficient. First, choose places for the date where you can't talk, like loud clubs, concerts, or other similar venues. Not being able to hear each other is a perfect excuse for an early exit. A similar tactic is to choose a really bad movie—or better yet, one you want to see but that he's sure to hate. Also, remember that physical appearance matters. Obviously you can't change the way you look, but you can always "forget" to brush your hair, or dress like it's the early '90s.

Want to *really* kill the relationship before it even begins? Invite another friend (or two, or more) along on the date (bonus points if the friends are of the opposite sex), and act like it's no big deal ("I asked Bob and Phil to join us, I hope that's OK"). It will totally mess with your date's head. He might get the message that you're not that into the whole thing, or he could think you didn't even realize your date was a date. Either way, it won't be a romantic evening, and it should be enough to kill any confidence he might have managed to muster up to ask you out again.

Quick Guide: Top 10 Easy Ways to Blow First Date

10. Answer your cell phone . . . a lot. The more times the better. If it stops ringing, start sending text messages and e-mails.
9. Talk with food in your mouth.
8. Tell your date he has food in his teeth (even if it's not true—he'll never know the difference).
7. Pretend to add up the calories of everything on your plate—and his.

6. Suggest skipping out of the restaurant without paying and when he looks horrified, say, "What's the big deal? I do it all the time."

5. Invite him to go with you to your parents' house for the weekend and meet your family.

4. Say "I love you" at the end of the night.

3. Say "I love you" *before* the end of the night (bonus if you say it in a baby voice).

2. Casually reference a random fact about him that he definitely hasn't told you and when he looks surprised, tell him you read it on Google.

1. Tell him you always judge a person's character by the last three text messages he's sent, then ask to read his. *Note:* Be sure you have rigged yours to be extra-creepy and say—"I'll show you mine!"

How to Impress Your Date with Your Drink Order

"I'll have a Gin Rickey, please."

Having a unique signature drink not only breaks the ice on a date, it's also a good conversation starter at a cocktail party. You can launch into what's in this unique cocktail, how you were introduced to it, and why you like it so much. Instant conversation.

Plus, ordering a unique drink like this makes you look interesting; it shows that you're a little offbeat and a bit adventurous, someone worth getting to know. The more obscure the drink, the more impressive it is. For example, Harvey Wallbangers or Moscow Mules are drinks that most bartenders know how to make, but the average person has no clue as to what they are, other than they sound interesting.

For an added wow factor, do some research and know where your favorite fallback beverage comes from, and what the story is behind it.

Of course, certain classic drinks can also make you look impressive, as long as you order them with an air of sophistication. A "Bombay Sapphire martini, up, slightly dirty," for example, shows distinction and lets your date know that you're not to be underestimated. If you order a classic drink like this, the key is to order it in a very specific "signature" way. For example, with martinis, give a specific brand of gin (if you want to look sophisticated, it must be gin—see "How to Make the Perfect Martini," page 296) and indicate whether you like your martini "dry" (almost no vermouth) or "wet" (a lot of vermouth), "up" or "on the rocks," and indicate how "dirty" you'd like it (how many olives/how much olive juice).

No matter what you request, the cardinal rule of impressive drink ordering is to do it with authority. Indecisiveness or uncertainty says you don't know very much about whatever it is you end up asking for, and, frankly, makes you seem a little boring. But the more conviction you give your order, the more impressive the drink will sound.

Another trick, if the place has an original cocktail menu, is to ask the waiter a question before selecting a drink from it. Questions like "Is it triple distilled?" "Do you make your own simple syrup?" or "Is it on fire?" will show that even though you're ordering off the menu, you know what you're talking about, so stand back.

Wines are tricky because you might not know right away what you're going to be having for dinner, and nothing is more impressive than pairing a wine perfectly with a meal. In this case, it's perfectly acceptable to ask your waiter for a wine recommendation when you order; just be sure you ask questions like "Is it full bodied?" or "Yes, but what *region* of the Loire Valley?" Even if you know very little about wine, it's easy to fake authority—just choose a wine on the more expensive side that you haven't heard of (but not the *most* expensive, that's an obvious ploy) and announce how excited you are that they actually carry it, as you've been looking for it for a while. If it's awful, you can always say the previous year's vintage was better.

Finally, beer. Whatever your lifestyle is, if you're looking to impress someone with your beer order, the word *light* should never be uttered. Neither should the words *Coors* or *Budweiser*. Pick a microbrew from the menu—if you don't know that much about beer, remember these basic concepts: hefeweizens, ales, IPAs (India Pale Ales), and lagers are lighter (in coloring and flavor), while porters, stouts, and barley wines are heavier.

And don't forget to order an after-dinner drink. Port, hands down, is very impressive.

Basically, as long as you stay away from ordering a Bud Light, a gin and tonic, a Long Island iced tea, or a glass of merlot, you should be okay—just order anything else with authority, demonstrate a discriminating taste, and you'll make an impression. And if your date orders one of the above no-no's, excuse yourself and climb out the bathroom window. (It's what's done in polite society.)

How to Signal to Your Dinner Date That You Need the Heimlich (and Still Get Asked on a Second Date)

You're on a date. It's going pretty well, and you're fairly sure your companion's into you. While your date regales you with tales of his exotic travels, you take a bite and start to chew. But as you swallow, something's wrong: the filet mignon is stuck in your throat.

Suddenly everything is happening in slow motion. It is definitely the time to remain calm. Don't panic—chances are someone knows the Heimlich and can get to you quickly. The problem, though, is your date. Will the image of your bulging eyes and spastic gestures as you spew a piece of partially masticated meat across the room be what lingers in his mind after the evening is over? Will this indelible image nix any and all possibility for future romance? In other words, is there a chance in hell he'll ever call you again? Stick with me, and you may just be able to emerge from this unfortunate incident unscathed.

First things first—you need to alert your date to the immediate problem; after all, the prospect of a second date won't really matter if you're dead. If you're really choking, you won't be able to speak, so pat your chest and try to cough. If that doesn't work, try grabbing your throat with one hand and gesturing wildly with the other. This should be enough for him to stop talking and ask if you're okay. If it's not, you might not *want* another date with him.

When he asks what's wrong, point to your throat and shake your head, then make a fist with your hand and gesture toward your chest. This should signal to him that you are choking, and he should either commence the Heimlich or get someone else who can. If he thinks you are jumping into a game of charades, let's just say that's another clue that you've got the wrong guy.

Assuming he's found someone to administer the Heimlich (any respectable restaurant should have someone on hand who is versed in such things, so if yours doesn't, another red flag), now it's time to face the fact that there's no graceful way to get through a Heimlich. You're going to convulse and you're going to spit food out, so accept it. It's what you do *after* the maneuver that counts.

Graciously thank whoever saved your life, whether it's your date, your waiter, or an innocent bystander. If it's your date, tell him how lucky you were that he knew what to do, and ask him where he learned it. Try to move past it and get back to normal chitchat. Like any mishap on a first date, you want to address what happened, but not dwell on it. In this instance, it's definitely okay to crack a few jokes at your own expense, just make sure it's nothing disgusting like "Did you see how far I shot that piece of lobster?"

Now, this is a shrewd move and not everyone will be able to pull it off, but you can even turn it into an opportunity to flirt a little, by playfully blaming him for making you laugh so hard you choked (don't worry if you weren't actually laughing at the time, he'll want to believe he's that witty, so he will).

Now, you might be tempted to immediately go to the restroom after the Heimlich to make sure you don't have bits of steak all over your face, but whatever you do, resist this impulse. Why? Consider the scenario carefully. You'll be leaving your date alone to ponder what just happened, and to replay the whole ugly incident in his mind. Not to mention that he may start twittering or posting on Facebook that his date—you—almost choked to death. Weigh this with the possibility that you might have food on your face or look slightly disheveled, and well, I'll leave it to you to decide which is the lesser of two evils.

Call me a romantic, but I truly believe that nothing—not even a near-death experience—can screw up a love connection if it's meant to be. This could be the incident that brings the two of you together! I'm not saying that you should attempt it on purpose, but if it happens on its own, you just never know. Stranger things have happened.

At the end of the evening, you can bring it up one more time (and one more time only) with a comment like "Thanks again for saving my life" or "I'm glad I'll live to go out with you again, I had such a great time" to let him know you're both grateful and interested in seeing him again. If you play your cards right, you won't be remembered as "the one who almost bit the dust," but as "the girl who choked on her food but was really cool about it," which is always enough to warrant a second date.

How to Convince Your Single Friend to Join a Dating Website

In the early days of the Internet, people were skeptical of dating websites, and for good reason. Meeting a complete stranger on the computer? Scary. But as time passed, the Internet got less frightening and oddly enough, as more and more people signed up, everyone became *more* trusting of online matchmaking services. After all, if everyone's doing it, it can't be too dangerous, right?

Whether or not you buy this logic, given the sheer number of people on these sites, *some* successful matches are bound to be made in cyberspace. Still, if you have a single friend who's having no luck in the real world of dating, convincing him or her to join the virtual dating world isn't always easy to do. For many, joining an online dating pool is admitting defeat; others fear they'll be relegated to the world of weirdos—those are the only people who actually join these sites, right?

That's where your friend's wrong. Plenty of perfectly sane people meet on dating sites, and if done right, it can actually be much easier and more efficient to screen out the kooks online than it is in everyday life. But if your friend is still reluctant, it may just be your job to convince him or her. Why bother? Because it's nice to care about your friends. And because I'm guessing this is the friend who is constantly complaining about how *awful* the dating scene is and whining about how hard it is to meet anyone *normal*. And let's face it, listening to all the complaining can be exhausting for you, loyal friend that you are.

So to convince your wary friend to jump on the online dating bandwagon, first try explaining to her that online daters are not necessarily losers, they just haven't found the right person yet (here's where you gently point out that your friend hasn't either, and *she's* not a loser). This is just another avenue. Go online *with* your friend and browse some of the profiles on the sites like match.com, nerve.com, JDate.com, or eHarmony.com—let her make the choice. You'll be able to show her that most people seem pretty normal. Sometimes all it takes is the extra step of actually searching the site with her to be able to point it out. The irony is that when you're not actually attached to meeting someone, shopping for a mate online can be a lot of fun, so see if she's open to just trying it out for the sheer fun of it all.

Luckily, most dating websites offer a free trial, so once you are sitting down with your friend you can help her take the plunge right then and there. Dive right in and contact someone, maybe even actually set up the first date. This is key because once your friend sets up a meeting, she'll be committed to some degree, and she may even see how much fun and easy it can be to go date-surfing.

Quick tip: Can't even convince your friend to log on? Tell her you will write her profile and post it for her. Sometimes this is the biggest hurdle—a psychological hurdle more than anything else.

Still having trouble? Convince your friend that online dating isn't the sole future of her dating experience: it's just a *supplement*. She should continue to go out, make new friends, and meet people anywhere and everywhere. But adding a date here and there that was initiated online can't hurt. As long as your friend is convinced that online dating is *enhancing* her existing social life rather than detracting from it, she may be willing to give it a shot.

If all else fails, try creating an online dating support group. Yes, it's true, the number one motivating factor for joining a dating website is having friends who are doing it as well. If your friend doesn't already have a support group like this, create one for her. It's simple; just simultaneously convince at least one other pal to join a dating website and then put the two in touch with each other. It will help them both to commiserate with others who are going through the same thing, not to mention they will see that meeting people online is all right . . . because other normal people are doing the same thing.

How to Set Up Two of Your Friends— and Not Get Blamed If It Doesn't Work Out

Sure, we all occasionally like to play matchmaker, but how often does it actually work out? Unless you're Yente from *Fiddler on the Roof,* probably not very often. And when your matches turn sour, who do your friends blame? Hint: not themselves.

But there are ways to bring people together and, more important, not take the rap when they come apart, as long as you follow a few simple guidelines.

The number one rule of friend matchmaking is to never set up friends in the same social circle. Here's why: *They already know each other!* If they hang out a lot and they're both single, chances are there's a very good reason they haven't gotten together. Maybe they're just not attracted to each other, or maybe they like someone else. Whatever the reason, it's not right, and forcing it leads to trouble for everyone. Plus, if they break up, everyone in the group will be forced to take sides, completely ruining the dynamic. And it will be all your fault.

The best combinations are people from different areas of your life. Maybe one of your friends from college would be great with a buddy from yoga class; maybe your coworker would match perfectly with someone from your book club. Since they don't know the same people, if things go wrong, you can still continue to see both of them in different environments.

The key to setting people up is to be selective. Remember, it's the quality of the setup, not quantity. You may not set people up often, but when you do . . . they better be ready, because you know a good match when you see one (Trust me, I have credibility here, I have multiple marriage success stories). Being choosy also works to your advantage because once word gets around that your setups work, people looking to meet someone will flock to you, increasing your pool of people to choose from.

Once you've identified a match it's time to decide how you'll orchestrate the setup. You have two choices here: either subtle or straightforward. If you are not the straightforward type, invite the potential couple out in a group setting (like a party) and casually introduce them to each other. Of course you will still spend the evening dropping subtle-as-a-train-wreck hints, like "Jake here also likes *Annie Hall*" or "You both had such similar music tastes I *knew* you would hit it off," but really direct hinting can't be helped.

If you are a seasoned matchmaker, you may prefer the more direct path. I personally prefer this option, but you have to be prepared to put your own butt on the line, because if they don't hit it off, they're coming back to you, and it may not be pretty. The key here is that you *must* be extremely up front and honest with both parties. Keep in mind that the more promises you make, the more of the blame you'll get if it doesn't work out. Do not say, "I promise you'll love him," and "She's the best person ever." Instead try something clear and to the point (without your opinion), like, "Would you like me to make an introduction?" People do this in the business world all the time, so why not with life partners? This way if it doesn't work, you'll still emerge with a solid reputation.

The secret to keeping your friendships intact is that if it *doesn't* work out, give each person your condolences and let them know you're there if they need you, but do *not* take sides or listen to them bash the other person. Just like that, you've become the good friend who's there to support them, and not the person who made the whole fiasco happen in the first place.

Bottom line: It never hurts to make an honest and well-thought-out introduction. It's true, most setups don't work—but it only takes one, and when that one magical match occurs, it's really worth it.

How to Reject an Unwanted Suitor

When I was single, a well-meaning relative once asked me, "Did a weird guy call you recently?" My response was, "No, but if he's weird, why would he be calling me?" The answer was, obviously, because my well-meaning relative gave his well-meaning relative my phone number. No, he never called, but plenty of other slightly strange or otherwise unwanted suitors did. So if a borderline-crazy person in whom you have less than zero interest is chasing you around town, and you don't want any part of it, you have a few options. You can either avoid him for as long as it takes for his passion to subside, or get *him* to avoid *you*.

The first option could take from days to months. In my experience, the more unwanted the suitor, the longer it takes him to get the message. So remember you need to have the stamina here. Unwanted suitors tend to be very persistent, calling and e-mailing you incessantly, sending you flowers for no special occasion. You know, doing everything you want, only you want it from the bad boy next door, not the sweet dork in your IT department. If you've already explained to this person that you aren't interested, it's key that you not return any of these calls or e-mails. You can send one simple note thanking him for the flowers, no more. You might feel a little guilty, but trust me—if you really aren't interested, you're not doing anyone any favors by leading him on.

If you see this person in certain places on a regular basis, you may have to avoid these venues, at least at the usual times. Change your lunch schedule, your gym schedule, your coffee break schedule—whatever the case may be, just mix it up a little (besides, if you mix up your own routine, you may open yourself up to the possibility of meeting the *right* suitor). For me, out of sight tends to be out of mind, and once he stops pestering you, you can always resume your regular routine. Another wimpy avoidance technique is to schedule things with him far out on the calendar and then have something come up or reschedule once it gets close. But beware—unless you're up front, he could be back at any moment, trying to win your heart yet again.

Your other option is to *get him to avoid you*. The quickest and best way is to just be honest with him and tell him you're not interested. Most sane human beings will back off upon hearing this. Problem is, he may not be sane—if he were, you might be willing to date him. You could go the old

"I'm in a relationship" (or getting over one) route, but be warned that he might return in the future. In my experience the best way to get him to avoid you is to talk about/flirt with other guys (a lot) around him. If there's one thing men can't stand, it is to be made to feel inferior to other men. On one occasion, I had a friend who was trying to shake a particularly persistent suitor at a bar. She tried everything: ignoring him, hiding in the bathroom, even introducing him to another random female patron, but he wouldn't give up. Finally she made out with the bartender. In front of him. That did the trick. Or, if you're feeling really gutsy, tell him you're gay. That'll either keep him away forever, or make him even more attracted to you.

And then there's my favorite approach—let him think it's all his idea. Get him to think that *he* is the one rejecting you. Go watch *My Big Fat Greek Wedding* and you'll see what I mean. Men love to think it's all their idea.

Yes, unfortunately, getting rid of unwanted suitors can be like tearing off a Band-Aid. If you rip it off really quickly, it only hurts for a second (for you, that is; he may be heartbroken for weeks). So just bite the bullet and end it quickly and decisively.

It's the only way to go.

How to Be a Cute Valentine

Valentine's Day is traditionally about romance. But somehow, over the years it's become less and less about love and more about outdoing your significant other with a stunning display of cuteness. So yes, with that kind of pressure, people often need assistance (and ideas) for wooing (and wowing) their mates.

First off, know that you don't have to spend a lot of money to be original. Here's one supercreative (and in my opinion quite romantic) idea: How about naming a star after the person you love most in the universe? The two most popular star-naming companies are the International Star Registry (www.starregistry.com) and Name-A-Star (www. nameastar.com). For as little as $30, you'll get a certificate, a picture, and information about the star that you can wrap up and give to your loved one (technically, stars are *officially* named by the International Astronomical Union, but the certificate you receive looks real and unless your Valentine is *in* the International Astronomical Union, he or she won't know the difference!) It's also easy to write a sweet (yes, on any other day it might be considered cheesy) poem to go along with your gift. Perhaps start with "Star light, star bright, the most beautiful star I see tonight" . . . then make up the rest. Aww.

Another option is to put a twist on the typical romantic dinner. How about arranging to go to a favorite restaurant and hire serenaders for the finishing touch? If you think this might have the opposite effect and the embarrassment could send your sweetie heading for the door, you could hire a chef to prepare a private dinner at your house and surprise your Valentine with serenaders in the privacy of your own home. You'll have the same experience of an amazing and romantic dinner, but in a more intimate setting (lots of things that seem obnoxious in public can be romantic in private—this is one of them).

Don't want to spring for the Philharmonic? You can always find someone with a violin looking to make a few extra bucks. Try the local high school, which always has an orchestra. Trust me; your date will be so blown away by the gesture, he or she won't notice if the music's a little off-key. This is one of the few instances where it really is the thought that counts.

Remember: The key to being a cute Valentine is to make your gift as personal as possible. If you hire a violinist, have him play your date's favorite song; if you name a star after her, choose one in her zodiac sign's constellation. Whatever you do, make it meaningful. The more thought you put into it, the more romantic it will be.

Still looking to be original? What about a singing telegram? You could send one to the office or surprise your loved one somewhere he'd least expect it, like the gym (see "How to Arrange a Singing Telegram," page 136).

How to Get a Custom Engagement Ring Designed

OK, here's the deal. An engagement ring is meant to be worn *every* day *forever*. It should be nice. Not only should it be nice, it should be perfect. So if you find yourself about to pop the question to your soon-to-be-betrothed (assuming, that is, you get the ring right), a custom design is an extra-special personal touch. A one-of-a-kind ring for your one-of-a-kind love.

Before you go to a designer, it helps to have some idea of what she wants, especially since custom can't be returned. This is easier if she knows what you're up to. Have her provide some photos of styles she likes. (Don't rely on your memory. If she starts pointing out stones and settings at cocktail parties, by the time you sit down with the jeweler, it's sure to all be one big blur.) If your plan involves keeping it a secret, speak to her friends (obviously not the big-mouth friends who will blab because they just can't keep anything from each other) and get an idea of what she likes. You can also go through her rings or other jewelry and take some snapshots, but this is a little riskier because you may come across pieces that you think she never wears because she is saving them for a special occasion, when in reality they're sitting in her jewelry box unworn because she thinks they're tacky.

You'll also need to know what size ring you're looking for. This is pretty easy if she knows you're buying a ring—just ask. Most women know their ring size. If it's a surprise, just snag one of her rings. This is the least of your worries, since it's pretty easy to resize a ring.

The next step is choosing the designer. Ask your female friends if they know a good custom designer, or put in a call to some local jewelry stores and see if they would be willing to create a custom piece. Check jewelry design schools; this will be less expensive and who knows, you may find an unknown creative genius. In a big city, head to the diamond district; just be sure you take someone knowledgeable with you so you don't end up getting fleeced. Obviously, before you make a decision, you'll want to see as many examples of this person's work as possible.

Once you have chosen a designer, give him or her all the stuff you have—the ring size, photos, and so on. The designer will then create a few drawings or design samples for you to choose from. Then, you'll get to select the cut and quality of the diamond. Once you have that, you'll get to work on the setting. Your designer should be able to walk you through the process and before long, you'll have a custom bauble.

Best of all, once you've found a custom ring designer who knows your soon-to-be-wife's style, you'll never have to come up with an original birthday gift again. Just leave that to the designer. My custom ring designer, Simon Cardwell (www.designsbycardwell.com), was able to not only create a gorgeous engagement ring, but another great piece to celebrate the birth of our first child!

And, ladies, there's nothing wrong with doing some of the legwork yourself—if you give your guy all the info and ideas for what you'd like, it'll make the whole process a lot easier for him (and it's pretty damn fun for you, too).

How to Put an Engagement Ring in a Fortune Cookie

America's love affair with hiding life-changing jewelry in pastries knows no bounds. We're all suckers for the moment when that special someone finds a diamond in her éclair and exclaims "Yes!" Unfortunately, often-times engagement rings (especially the cost conscious—i.e., smaller—ones) can pose a choking hazard (among other tiny disasters), which is why, if you must hide your love away in an edible item, it might be a good idea to pop the question with something that won't be accidentally scarfed down.

Seriously, if you're planning to hide an engagement ring in a dessert, consider choosing the one dessert that's rarely ever consumed: a fortune cookie. These are the only cookies I know of that are never, ever bitten into without being opened first (and whether or not they've ever been bitten into *after* being opened is also up for debate). But how to get the ring in there?

Well, there are a few ways. The simplest, but also the most expensive, is to have a professional baker whip the cookies up for you. Or, if you're a whiz in the kitchen, and want to try to handle it all on your own, look for a recipe at www.chinesefood.about.com.

But you also should know that it's actually possible to place a ring (or any other little surprise!) inside an already baked fortune cookie. It is, however, a bit of a trial-and-error process; so it's probably a good idea to buy a whole box of cookies, just to make sure you have plenty of backups.

Grab a cookie and steam it until it becomes flexible enough to open (yes, the process is not unlike tampering with the mail). You can do this either by holding it over a pot of boiling water for a few minutes or by wrapping the cookie in a damp (not soaking) paper towel and microwaving it for about forty seconds. Once the cookie is removed from the steam/microwave, you'll have twenty seconds or so to open up the cookie's flap, pop in the ring (and maybe pop in a fortune slip of your own), and close it up before it hardens again.

The last step? Make sure your intended gets the right cookie!

Other small tokens also fit inside fortune cookies. Once you master this trick, it will take less than one minute to sneak your own custom-made fortunes into a cookie on take-out night.

How to Propose at the Philharmonic (or Any Other Classy Public Venue)

Everyone wants his (or her) wedding proposal to be memorable. But sometimes making memories is more than a one-man job, and that's where I come in. I once had a client who really wanted to make it one for the books, but to pull it off, he needed some help.

His girlfriend had been going to the New York Philharmonic her whole life, and he knew it held a special place in her heart. So we put a plan in motion for a one-of-a-kind proposal that was sure to be music to her ears. Really, it was pretty simple, and easy to replicate in pretty much any other venue.

Once he had his grandmother's ring and the tickets to a performance he knew she'd love carefully tucked in his pocket, we called Lincoln

Center. Since it's hard to say no to someone who wants to use your venue for a memorable moment like a marriage proposal, the person who answered the phone was all too happy to be in on the plan. We arranged for a small section of the lobby, right next to the doors from which the audience would exit during intermission, to be cordoned off with a velvet rope.

Behind that velvet rope we set up a table and chairs with champagne, glasses, and roses—the perfect romantic nook. Best of all, we had a photographer standing by.

We put all of this together after the music started, and when our client exited the concert hall with his girlfriend during intermission, he suggested they sit down at the table. His girlfriend was a little hesitant at first, as she thought the whole thing was set up for someone else (a VIP of course)! But once they ventured behind the velvet rope, and he got down on one knee, she quickly realized it was meant for her. Naturally, everyone applauded when she said yes.

But that wasn't all! Not only did the photographer capture the moment, when the performance started again, the conductor congratulated the happy couple in front of the rest of the audience. The whole thing went off without a hitch, and the couple is happily married today.

The best thing about this kind of proposal is, unless you count the tickets and the Champagne (Okay, and the ring), it doesn't cost a penny. Just contact your venue of choice and see what they can do for you. People love a love story, so don't be shy when asking!

How to Return Your Ex's Stuff

Breakups are ten times worse when you live together. The whole moving-out process can be awkward, painful, and just plain miserable; worst of all, you always seem to be missing *something*. Sure, you can put your best face forward and say "it's just stuff," and hey, soon you will be in a new relationship and have new stuff (*better* stuff that won't remind you of your ex!). But the bottom line is that sometimes you want your U2 *Greatest Hits* CD back, and who really knows if you'll ever see anything that you left behind again.

Well, many of us know how this feels, so if you want to be the bigger man (or woman), you owe it to the person you formerly loved to return his or her belongings. It's the least you can do (unless of course the person cheated on you, in which case it's okay to donate everything to charity or burn it all on the cheater's front lawn). And it doesn't even have to be painful; the trick is knowing how to return said things without ever having to be in communication with the person. (It's just easier to cut it off altogether, don't you think?) How? Just have someone else do the returning! You get the credit for being nice *and* you won't have to see or even speak to the person. Plus, you're going through a painful breakup—what better time to hit your friends up for favors? I once informed a client of this as I assisted him in reorganizing his closets (and his life) after his breakup.

His (former) fiancée had gotten cold feet and broken off the engagement, and he was both angry and hurt. As I helped him clean out his now spacious apartment, we discovered dresses and other decidedly feminine items that had been accidentally left behind. He *wanted* to just trash it all, but of course once I filled him in on the fact that he was a nicer guy than that, he realized that returning the items was the right thing to do. But not to worry, I told him, I would take care of the whole thing. So I simply took the items back to the office and mailed everything out to her the very next day.

About a week later, I got a call from the client—she had called him, absolutely livid that he had returned her stuff without so much as a note, in a box marked with our company name as the return address. Turns out that although she was thrilled to have her items back, she thought it was a bit harsh to receive a box in the mail from an ex with a huge sticker that said "Consider It Done!"

Fair enough. But once he explained that he simply wanted to return her belongings, she found the gesture to be so sweet that they ended up back together.

The moral of the story: All's well that ends well. So be a nice guy (or gal) and enlist someone (though perhaps not me) to return your ex's items.

How to Bake an Engagement Ring into a Soufflé

"How did he do it?" Propose, that is. Every bride-to-be has a wedding proposal story, and everyone who sees that ring on her finger will want to hear it, believe me. So if you're the one doing the proposing, you'd be well advised to give her a story she'll want to repeat a thousand times. But no pressure. Pulling off a brag-worthy proposal is surprisingly easy—it just takes a little bit of planning.

Now, there are a few things in life guaranteed to please a woman, and, yes, one of them is chocolate. Another one is a diamond ring. So you're guaranteed success when you combine the two—baking a ring right into hot melting chocolate.

How to make this magic happen? First, find a chocolate soufflé recipe that has you baking in individual ramekins, rather than in one soufflé dish, so that you can make sure she gets the portion that contains the ring. (*Note:* Be sure to mark the dish that will be *hers*.) Follow the recipe. The batter will be the consistency of wet pudding. Drop the ring in the designated dish, and it should sink, becoming completely invisible from the top.

You're almost there, but before you bake, think about this: after she sees the ring and you pop the question, the first thing she is going to want to do is put on the ring. And it will be covered in chocolate, possibly detracting from the breathless oohs and ahhs that only a gleaming, sparkling jewel can garner. So consider wrapping the ring in foil before dropping it into the unbaked soufflé.

Last step: Bake for ten or fifteen minutes. As it cools, it will give you time to cool off yourself—you'll need it on the night you are proposing.

Doing this at home has a lot of potential pitfalls, so unless you are a pastry chef, I wouldn't recommend it. Head to a proposal-worthy restaurant instead, and arrange it with the chef (don't worry, you'll still get all the credit). I've said it before, because it's true, everyone loves a love story, so the chef may not even charge you for it. Just make sure you trust him or her not to lose the ring in the chaos of the back kitchen, or your wedding proposal may go down the drain—literally.

Now the obvious question: What if she eats the ring? If you've just spent two months' salary on this little beauty, it would be a crime for it to be swallowed, sight unseen. Solution: Serve it with (or ask the chef to serve it with) a tiny spoon to eliminate the chance of her taking an extra big bite.

Another possibility is to give your chosen one a faux soufflé. Put the ring in its box and the box inside an empty ramekin. Cut out a round piece of cardboard so that it fits inside the ramekin, over the ring box. Bake the actual soufflés, slice off the top of a finished one, and set it on top of the cardboard. She'll try to dig in with her spoon, hit something hard, and find her ring. Surprise!

If you are also cooking dinner, I'd advise making something light so she's guaranteed to eat most of her dessert. What if she just has one small spoonful of your rich chocolaty masterpiece and never gets to the actual ring? Disaster.

How to Get a Wedding Dress Shipped Halfway Around the World

Recently, on a typical Tuesday afternoon, a client called and asked that I send her wedding dress (only used once!) to Zambia. Apparently her nanny's sister was about to be married, and she'd volunteered her dress. You may think that shipping something like a dress overseas is relatively straightforward—but not necessarily. Shipping to Africa, where airports and roads aren't always in the best shape, is trickier. Plus, a wedding dress is more than just large, it's delicate; extra care needs to be taken at every step, because one tear in the box could ruin the entire dress. But we didn't have much time to harp on the details: the wedding was just *two and half weeks away*. The dress needed to arrive quickly, or it would be useless.

If you ever find yourself in a similar situation, remember that the most important thing is packaging. You'll want a box that can get tossed around a bit. If you still have the box that the dress came in, use that, since it's probably the perfect size. If not, visit a store that sells wedding dresses and ask if they'll give you a box; they usually have them lying around.

Sending a dress is not like sending a box of toys—you'll need a box that is exactly the right size and shape, so those specifically made for storing wedding dresses are best.

We used the Vera Wang box the dress came in, but we made sure to cross out and tape over the "Vera Wang" labels and logos—we were afraid that anyone who got a glimpse of them might realize how valuable the contents of the box were and try to make off with it. If you think any labels on your box might attract unwanted attention, you should do the same (yet another reason to break out the duct tape).

After concealing all the designer evidence, we took the box to a Mail Boxes Etc., where we knew we would have our choice of shippers. Good thing, too, since it turned out that neither FedEx nor DHL nor the U.S. Postal Service shipped to this specific town in Zambia at all. Luckily, UPS was able to deliver to her. We were very pleased to hear this, until we learned the cost of sending the dress: $700. We were ready to look elsewhere (e.g., buying a spot in a container and sending the dress by boat), but when we checked in with the client, she asked us to pay the hefty price to ensure on-time delivery.

After paying the steep fee to ship the dress, we breathed a sigh of relief and then forgot about the whole thing—until the day before the wedding, when we got a call from the client saying that the dress hadn't arrived (I should have known; it was all going too smoothly). We called UPS to track the package (all major shippers give you a tracking number for just this purpose) and found out that the dress had "arrived," which was curious since our client's nanny's sister definitely had not received it. If you're shipping to a country like Zambia, with a smaller-scale postal system, you may run into the same problem; mistakes can be made, and they'll often go unnoticed for days. After many phone calls to postal offices all over the country, we tracked down the dress, which, of course, had been delivered to the wrong place. We contacted the recipient, and she sent someone over in person to retrieve it. Sure enough, after a few hours of travel, he was able to get his hands on the dress.

In this case, the operation was a success, so if you're in a similar situation, now you know how to make it happen. However, before you go through all these steps, consider sending someone to Zambia (or flying there yourself) and delivering the dress in person. Depending on the country, commercial airline tickets could end up being much less expensive than shipping costs; and that way, someone gets to take an exotic vacation!

How to Convince Your Single Friend to Quit a Dating Website

Dating websites can be a good way to meet people, if used properly. But that's a big "if." I've seen it happen time and time again. The more people use these services, the more they lose touch with why they ever went on there in the first place. Instead of focusing on meeting Mr. or Ms. Right, they get sucked into the spiral of serial online dating and end up hooking up with Mr. or Ms. Wrong instead.

Although there are many online success stories (most of which have been featured in eHarmony or match.com commercials), there are just as many, if not more, horrifying ones. If you have a friend who may be getting too hooked on online dating or is consistently meeting the wrong types of people, the least you can do is to help him or her snap out of it.

First, you can try talking to the person honestly. Some people get so obsessed with these online communities that they stop thinking rationally. A quick and simple reminder can often jolt them back into reality. If this doesn't work, you can try a more elaborate method to show someone the true dangers of online dating. How? You guessed it, create a fake scenario to prove that you never *really* know what you're getting when you meet someone online.

Here is how it goes. A friend joins a dating website. It's not going horribly, but it's not going well, either. You see the signs of obsession percolating: He is starting to spend more time on the dating websites than working. He spends hours tallying the number of "winks" he receives from potential mates. Dates have now completely taken over every free evening—and with a different person every night. Your friend needs a wake-up call and you are just the one to deliver it.

Here's how: Create a phony profile that you know your friend will be attracted to. Make sure to have all the pieces in place—fake picture, fake e-mail address, fake Facebook page. A true friend would even go as far as to get a pay-as-you-go cell phone so that your friend and the potential suitor will also be able to start exchanging texts.

Ultimately the decision will be made to meet for a date. This is when you show up. Your friend thinks she can't be fooled? Surprise.

With any good luck, your friend won't be too mad and will get the point, which is that you should always remember to use dating websites wisely. If you fear this person's wrath, you can also modify the prank and send a lot of sketchy, out-of-line messages to your friend from your fake identity. This might be enough to turn him or her off to the whole thing—and you'll never have to reveal it was you all along (though this might be a little excessive, especially if you have to keep that secret for the rest of your life).

Even if you don't really care if your friend is using or abusing a dating website, this is a funny April Fool's Day prank.

How to Plan a Wedding in Two Weeks

Sometimes doing things at the last minute is simply easier. It's a different kind of pressure, and sometimes you need that extra adrenaline to kick yourself into gear. But planning a wedding in two weeks?! Impossible, right? Well, think again.

Coordinating the details of a wedding is a ton of fun, but being on the planning side all the time, I get to see all the bazillion details and decisions that go on behind the scenes, and trust me, it isn't always pretty. First, there are all the initial decisions—the date, the venue, the invitations—and then all of the decisions leading up to the day itself—the dress, the flowers, the guest list, I could go on and on. And then the actual wedding day arrives with still more decisions—like how to put out all the inevitable fires. So you might be able to see why some people would want to spare themselves all the nonsense that goes along with all these months of planning and just cut to the chase, make the decisions and have it happen.

People have plenty of reasons for planning a last-minute wedding (in addition to the one you're probably thinking). Maybe you have an army fiancé who's gotten a sudden furlough, and you just can't wait another year. Or you could be headed to grad school in two weeks, and married-student housing would save you a bundle. Perhaps your true love is about to be deported. Whatever your reason, you really can plan a lovely and perfect wedding in only a couple of weeks. Yes, it helps if you are flexible but, in this day and age, an overwhelming abundance of choices are out there to make your day perfect. With just two weeks' notice, you can even create the vision you've had of your big day since you were eight years old. Really. If you want a quickie wedding, you don't have to go to Las Vegas anymore to get one (unless of course that is your fairy tale, in which case, just skip over the rest of this section).

The key to planning a wedding in two weeks is decisiveness and efficiency, as the big decisions have to be made quickly. The number one priority to nail down, right away, is where you will have the wedding and/ or reception. Once you find a place, book it immediately. Of course, finding a respectable venue that can fit you in at the last minute can be tricky, so here's a hint: call a favorite restaurant to see if they'll host the wedding on a day they're closed to the public (or in the early afternoon if they only serve dinner). This can be a good bet because they can easily take care of a lot of the details for you. They'll clear a space and provide chairs for the ceremony, and they may even be able to provide flowers. Plus, you know you will like the food, so assuming they have a bar, one of the only remaining decisions will be choosing the kind of champagne you will serve.

If a neighborhood restaurant isn't available (and your own backyard is too small), get online and start searching restaurants nearby. You'll find something, just keep at it and remember to be flexible. Once you make a decision, don't look back. It never fails that the minute you're sure about what you have chosen, another great option will be put in front of you, so even though it might be tempting, don't doubt yourself. There's no time for that. Plus, getting married is not the time to doubt yourself on any front.

Now, of course, you'll have to let your guests know where and when you'll be having your nuptials. Hand-painted and calligraphied invitations may not be happening, but luckily, plenty of places online can be used to create your own beautiful invites in a hurry. If you are really running behind schedule, consider an e-vite. Normally I would *not* recommend this, and Emily Post would certainly be appalled, but you're under a tight timeline, so do what you need to do. If you've got to have a head count, you might want to follow up with some quick phone calls to your guests; although beware, if you put them on the spot, the people you invited only out of politeness might feel pressured into actually coming. Enlist a relative no one knows to make the calls for you—yes, if you are planning your wedding in two weeks, you will need to do some serious delegating, so let everyone who offers help out.

Now you are two weeks out minus one day. You have a place, and your guests are making their reservations, so the next order of business is a dress. Book appointments at every bridal shop in town and start trying them on; you often can still have your dream gown. I once had a client who was getting married in New York, and when her dress from Australia hadn't arrived a week before the wedding, she started to panic. We were told it was stuck in customs halfway around the world and I was about to hop on a plane to dig it out myself when she decided to try off-the-rack dresses at J.Crew. Incredibly, she found something that she liked enough to wear on her big day. Two days before the wedding, the original dress actually showed up. But she had moved on, and the J.Crew dress was now her number one choice.

You may not be able to get a custom wedding gown made just for you in such a short amount of time, but you will still look great. Try getting a sample from a showroom. Often these items will have only been worn on the runway, and showrooms likely even have someone available to do the alterations (anyone who tells you it takes six weeks to alter a wedding dress is lying). It's an added bonus if you are a sample size and can walk right out of the store with something beautiful that fits like a glove. Check boutiques and department stores, too; they just may have something that will pass as a wedding dress and help your bridesmaids do the same. Or just choose a color and tell your bridesmaids each to get a dress of her choice. They'll still look coordinated, and you'll win points for being the chillest bride ever.

Next, the marriage license. Some states require a waiting period between when you apply and when you can actually get married. However, you don't need to actually have a marriage certificate on your wedding day; in fact, many people don't. If you decide to get married overseas, for example, you would not actually be married at the ceremony; you would have your (phony) wedding ceremony in the south of France and then go to city hall to get married. The day with the guests is the one that counts (and what most couples celebrate each year), the other is just a piece of paper. Another reason to not have a marriage certificate on your wedding day is it means you can have someone not ordained, like a friend or relative, "marry you" and then zip down to city hall and tie the official knot. And while we are on the topic of officiant, if you do want one at the last minute, city hall can provide a list of judges or justices of the peace who may be available in two weeks' time. There is always someone, so don't sweat this part.

Last touches are simple: florist, cake, photographer, music, hair and makeup, favors, and you're done. To a nonplanner this may sound like a lot, but honestly, so many options are available that unless you are getting married in the middle of nowhere, you will be able to find something beautiful and perfect in no time.

Take a look at a wedding magazines and find samples of arrangements that you like and take them to your florist. For last-minute arrangements, simple and in season is best. Choose a florist you trust to do a good job and leave the rest to him. Cake: same as the florist. Choose a bakery or chef you like, show them each a photo, and have a little flexibility. For music, listen to some bands online and then call around to see who is available. Often a DJ is a good option, and there is always one looking for a gig (even if that DJ is your cousin and his iPod). Hair and makeup: Go to your own salon and see if your regular person is available, and if not, choose someone else from your salon who is and get a trial run-through. Again, there are plenty of stylists who need work, so if you're flexible, not to worry. Not enough time for favors? Think again. See "How to Customize Anything," page 152, for how to make custom honey jars, cookies, candles, or anything that represents the two of you. Customized cocktail napkins are a supernice touch and have a quicker turnaround time than you'd think.

This may all sound like a lot to take care of in fourteen short days, but in some ways, it's much easier to do it all at the last minute. If you've ever been around a bride-to-be in the six months leading up to her wedding, you'll see why. If you plan the entire event quickly, you're cramming all the stressful decisions into just two weeks, and before you know it the planning will be over and you'll be enjoying the party. Congratulations!

Relax. Your friends and family just want to be there with you on your special day, and they aren't going to sweat the details, so why should you? Plus, you're getting *married.* **It's not really about the party, is it?**

How to Surprise Your Bride with a Fireworks Display

Surprising your bride with a display of fireworks will be an unforgettable experience—for you and everyone else in town. There's nothing more spectacular, thrilling, and even romantic, and you'll be sure to have a dramatic conclusion to your evening. Besides, natural beauty—white sandy beaches, snow-covered mountain ranges, quiet chalets in the woods—is overdone anyway. A wedding night fireworks display is as original and memorable as it gets. But whether it's a private show just for two, or the culminating event of your wedding reception, take care to do it right—and do it big.

That said, there is always the chance things just may not go according to plan. I was once called in to save the day when the tugboat carrying the fireworks to an island wedding broke down. Could I get a new tugboat to be sure that the fireworks display went off without a hitch? Well, a couple of planes, trains, and automobiles later, I did figure out a way to get the fireworks there—minutes before the show was rained out. So much for a big bang.

However, if you have your heart set on it, your best bet is to look online for a licensed pyrotechnician who has done parties and events. Better yet, visit your town's chamber of commerce and find out who the staff hires for the town's Fourth of July fireworks display. You should be able to walk in and get this information easily, as it's public record, but if they can't give you a good reference, check a few neighboring towns, especially if you remember that they put on a good Fourth of July show. Once you've got a name, call him up, and if he's not available on the date you need, ask if he can refer you to a friend.

If you're going for more of the homegrown type of extravaganza, you'll have many choices. Types of fireworks vary in degrees of danger-ousness and awesomeness (these are related). Smaller types of fire-works—like sparklers, smoke bombs, fountains, cracklers, and other novelties—are legal in many states for anyone to purchase. For the most part, these types of fireworks stay on or near to the ground, and they don't explode all at once. As they get bigger—things like sky fliers, missiles, bottle rockets, and others actually fly into the air and then explode—many states require you to have a license to purchase and operate them. These are the type you'll need if you want to make it a truly spectacular event.

Remember: If fireworks are illegal to buy in your state without a permit, they're technically illegal to set off, so don't try buying them in a neighboring state and driving them across the border. For an easy-to-use directory of state fireworks laws, visit www.AmericanPyro.com.

If your state bans *all* fireworks, don't fret! They're still allowed if you have a proper permit—so you'll just have to find a licensed pyrotechnician.

If you happen to live in a state where most fireworks are legal without a permit, you may be able to purchase everything yourself ahead of time, which can save you some money, but make sure you hire a professional to set them off. You *can* pull off your own fireworks display, but you don't want to be messing around with explosives all evening. On your wedding night, you'll want to plan in advance so that everything runs smoothly each step of the way.

Even if you have friends who think they can handle it, there is always the potential for something to go wrong, and a killer fireworks display could really turn into a "killer" fireworks display, so unless your friends are trained professionals, hire outside help. You'll pay more than you would by doing it yourself, but you'll be guaranteeing (probably) that everyone—especially your beloved—walks away in one piece.

How to Take Care of Your Man

Ever wonder the secret to keeping your man happy?

Always carry a pillow and a sandwich.

Men are easy. If he's cranky, he's either hungry or tired, so keep it simple and everybody wins.

4. sneaky but (mostly) harmless

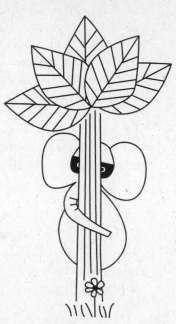

How to Politely and Lawfully Blackmail Anyone

Blackmail is one of the thorniest topics in the legal world today. Although lawyers and legal scholars generally agree that it is (and should be) illegal, figuring out what constitutes blackmail can be tricky.

Consider the recent case of David Letterman. As you've undoubtedly heard, he had an affair with a member of his staff, and a man named Robert Halderman found out about it—by perfectly legal means—and figured this was the perfect opportunity to make some cold hard cash. If he wanted, Halderman could've sold that information to the tabloids, which also would've been entirely legal. What he was taken to court for, however, was simply *threatening* to sell the information if Letterman didn't pay him $2 million—just the threat was considered criminal, not anything he actually *did*.

So if you want to blackmail someone and avoid legal proceedings, you must avoid making any explicit connection between the thing you want and the information you have the ability to expose. "If you don't do X, I will reveal Y," that sort of thing.

Instead, what you need to do is very subtly imply that there will be consequences if the person doesn't do what you're asking, but you have to do it in a way that lets you maintain *deniability* (and can't be proven in court). The best tactic is to just ask for what you want simply and politely. Then, in a separate conversation—that part is key—casually drop a few subtle hints to let on that you know what you know (e.g., if what you're after is a promotion and you happen to know that your boss has been having late-night trysts with his secretary, you might want to casually comment, a few days after asking for your promotion, that "Janine was working late again last night. You must be riding her really hard").

Unfortunately, if your boss refuses your request anyway, you may be out of luck. Making an explicit threat is a bad idea; even if it doesn't land you in jail, you're setting yourself up to be a target for revenge (don't think the person can't dig something up on you if he or she tries hard enough), and you could ruin your personal relationships, reputation, and possibly your career if your plot is ever revealed publicly.

Bottom line: I'm not a lawyer, and I'm certainly not suggesting any laws be violated. What I suggest is if you want something badly, skip the blackmail part and just ask nicely. As Zig Zigler said "You can have everything you want, if you will just help enough other people get what they want."

How to Hire a Private Investigator

The Internet has made snoops of us all. Let's face it, is there anyone among us who hasn't succumbed to the siren call of the search box and typed in the name of an ex, a secret crush, or a long-lost friend from kindergarten? Still, there are times in everyone's stalking career when Google just isn't enough.

Hiring a private investigator might seem a bit old school in our golden era of information, but bringing in the hired gumshoe can have some real advantages. For one, no matter how many Google searches you do, you just can't get certain information online, and that's exactly the information private investigators (or PIs, if you're hip) are trained to sniff out. Plus, it's fairly cool to think of a Humphrey Bogart/Sam Spade type running around town in a trench coat on your behalf.

Still, if you're planning on securing a sleuth, you'll need to do some detective work of your own. It's not a question of how to find one (Yellow Pages or an Internet search should be enough to get you started), but what to look for when choosing the person you'll pay to pry.

First, confirm that your potential Magnum P.I. actually has a license, which is a legal requirement in most states for anyone doing investigative work. This will rule out people with criminal pasts, as well as questionable companies offering sketchy services like "background checks." Not only are these services unregulated, their information often consists of little more than a simple database search of old public records, which you could do on your own. Even if you've found a legit company, pay attention to the title of the person you hire. Generally, only a detective agency's main investigator needs to be credentialed, which means that many investigative positions—like store detectives, bodyguards and bounty hunters—don't need a license at all. Your local Department of State can provide an updated list of licensing requirements.

Even if undercover agents do show you paperwork, you'll want to do a lot of homework to make sure it's legit. After all, these people make their living being shady, so how hard do you think it would be for them to forge a few documents? Ask for references of both clients and attorneys they've worked with. If they can't produce these immediately, look elsewhere. A good PI will always have references on hand. Also get their license number, and check with the licensing agency to be sure that it's both kosher and current. The International Association of Security and Investigative Regulators (www.iasir.org) can let you know which agency is in charge of licensing in your state. You can also check sites like www.pinow.com, and with the Better Business Bureau to see if your guy (or gal) is facing any consumer complaints.

If your PI passes these initial tests, the next step is to schedule a consultation by phone or in person. A good rule of thumb is to treat hiring a PI the same way you'd treat hiring a babysitter—after all, both must be trustworthy, dependable, and willing to watch your loved ones for hours at a time. A sitter will just cost you less. Ask a PI the same questions you'd ask a babysitter (except for "Can you help Timmy with his algebra?"), starting with the person's background. What did your PI do prior to this gig? Was he a police officer? In the military? In a Guns N' Roses cover band? How'd she gain the skill set she's trying to sell you? The answers to these questions will tell you a lot about his or her abilities. Don't be shy: Request details about any PI's law enforcement or military backgrounds (most PIs are ex-police or ex-army). What crime unit was the person in? What was his or her title?

Probe each PI's education, work experience, and training, because training requirements differ from state to state. A Big Apple snoop, for example, must pass a state test and needs six thousand hours of investigating experience, while Colorado requires no training at all—only a business license (although don't put too much stock in this; there's no recognized curriculum or institution for training PIs, although a lot of programs offer courses). Also inquire about their confidentiality policies, equipment that may be used (if bamboo and matches are on the list, stay away), whether they'll testify in court for you if needed, and how you'll be billed. And confirm who will actually be chasing down your quarry. You may be interviewing Dog the Bounty Hunter, but is he, or one of his sidekicks, going to be doing the work?

Also, know what *not* to expect. Private investigators can't pose as law enforcement officers, tap phones, or obtain cell-phone records without court approval. Since you're the boss, you may be liable for any damages that your PI causes. So make sure the person you hire is insured—or "bonded" in professional lingo—against property damage, car accidents, and natural disasters.

Then, yes, you *must* get it all in writing. Like with any job, you'll want to clearly define what you're paying for, what's expected, and who's responsible for any issues that might arise.

Remember: Whatever the dirt you're seeking, if you're hiring a PI in the first place, it's probably something pretty delicate and personal. So make sure you trust your PI—you don't want just *anybody* digging those skeletons out of your closet.

How to Answer a Question If You're Called on in a Class/Meeting and Weren't Paying Attention

We've all been there at some point: the teacher calls on you in class (or the workplace equivalent, the boss calls on you in a meeting) while you're spaced out, not paying attention, or otherwise engaged, and you have no clue as to what to say next. It's just a fact: no matter how much you try to concentrate, brains wander. So read on and prepare yourself now, while you're paying attention.

Though you can always admit defeat and confess that you were daydreaming, here are a few key strategies to help you talk your way out of it just as smoothly as Ferris Bueller on his day off.

First, ask the professor (or your boss) to repeat the question, but not in so many words. If you just say, "Can you please repeat that?" everyone will know what's up. Rather, respond as if you were paying attention and heard the question, but didn't quite understand what it meant. Say, "I'm not exactly sure what you mean by that," or something similar. If it turns out to be a very simple, straightforward question, you might be in hot water, but most of the time, the professor will rephrase the question, giving you enough time to formulate a response.

If you're in the middle of a group discussion, a solid strategy is to shift the question back on the last person who spoke (or, if you were so spaced out that you can't even come up with that, just take a gamble and choose someone who tends to frequently speak out in class). Say that you agree with what so-and-so said, but that you were hoping they could elaborate. With any luck, that person will jump right back in, and you can proceed to agree profusely until your brain can think of something else to say.

One of the best tactics by far, though, is to change the topic completely. This takes just a tiny bit of preparation. Always come into class (or the meeting) with something to say about the topic at hand, then, if you find yourself in this situation, say something like, "Actually, what I found more interesting was . . ." or "Before we talk about that, can I ask a question about . . ." If you actually have something coherent to say, the person in charge will probably indulge the digression without realizing you're avoiding the question at hand because you weren't paying attention.

All of these tactics require some chutzpah and some basic acting skills. If you think you have what it takes, go for it. But if you do, jump into it full force so that you come across as confident and smart. If not, you can always resort to coming clean and apologizing. If you share the reason why you were not paying attention (especially if it's a sympathetic one, like "my daughter is home with the flu and I was just worrying about her"), it usually counts for a lot. Just remember, you usually only get one shot at a good excuse, so choose wisely.

Take preventive measures. The likelihood of being called on twice in one class is low, so if you are particularly distracted or tired, voluntarily speak up early on and *then* tune out. Chances are if you've already participated, you won't get called on again that same day. And hey, if you really need extra tips, refer back to the guy who could talk his way out of anything, Ferris Bueller.

How to Cheat at Scrabble

Scrabble games can get pretty intense. I've played some that have ended in shattered dreams and tears. Obviously, the best way to avoid this is to ensure there's a clear winner (you)—even if you have to bend a couple of rules to do it.

Before you become a full-on, mustache-twirling cheater, there are a few street-legal ways to stack the odds in your favor. Before you go into the game, brush up on your obscure words. Pay careful attention to the difficult letters like Z, Q, and X. If you memorize the fair game words like *qat* or *qaid*, you have an advantage from the get-go. There are a number of websites that list the clutch Scrabble words, such as http://homepage. ntlworld.com/adam.bozon/scrabblelists.htm, or just buy and study the Scrabble dictionary. Some people think winning at Scrabble is about having a good vocabulary. It's not. It's about knowing which combination of letters will yield the most points. Who cares what a *zek* is? If it's legal, it's fair play. Remember that there are also a plethora (another good Scrabble word) of short words that are worth a bunch (yes, *za* is actually a word). Learn them.

If you've got the letters to spell *quartzy*, you are in luck—it's the highest-scoring word possible, when played on the right spaces.

If you have an iPhone or another smartphone that uses applications, you might want to download a Scrabble word checker, like Is That a Word?, which will tell you if a word can, in fact, be played. Using your phone to this end under the table will not only help you cheat (it's practically not cheating!) but also help you call BS on your friend's bogus word without risking your turn.

But wait, there's more you can do on your phone! Websites like www.scrabulizer.com and another phone app, LexeMe, can tell you what words you can make with your tiles. A word of caution: Use these sparingly and discreetly—chances are, if your friends are smart enough to be beating you in Scrabble, they'll be smart enough to know you're not checking the score of the Yankees game on your phone every time it's your turn. I once had a coworker with whom I would sometimes play online Scrabble on dull days at the office. He destroyed me every time. Then one day I happened to be passing his office between turns, and what website did I see up on his screen? www.scrabblecheat.com. Busted! I never trusted him again. Point is, if you're going to go this route, don't get caught.

If you've got the vocab, but not the tiles, there are two ways around that. One is only morally questionable, but the other is full-on devious. The first one is this: when taking your tiles, you might "accidentally" grab an extra few and just drop the ones you don't want back in the bag. The other way, which is really only for the hard-core cheaters, is to carry your own extra tiles (choice letters like *Z*s, blanks, and *S*s) on you, and swap them for your own. Just pray your friends don't keep track of how many of each letter are on the table. If they do, tell them it must be a "weird set."

Remember: All's fair in love, war, and Scrabble. So follow the above to make sure you never lose again.

People love to win at Scrabble. It makes them feel smart. So choose your battles. Sometimes it's good to let your husband (or wife) win . . . letting someone beat you isn't just nice, it's the easiest kind of cheating.

How to Avoid Eating a Host's Terrible Cooking Without Being (Too) Rude

In a perfect world, only professional chefs (or at least very talented amateurs) would give dinner parties. Unfortunately, sometimes dinner party hosts *think* that they are professional chefs—or else they simply forget that one of the most important requirements for a successful dinner party is edible food.

Nevertheless, it's their party and they'll cook if they want to. So as a gracious guest it is your duty not to burst their bubble. And whether your cooking-impaired host is a good friend, a coworker, or a boss, chances are you don't want to offend by refusing to eat the person's laborious concoction. Then again, you don't want to have to eat something disgusting, either. Here are a few ways to escape with both your taste buds *and* your host's pride (not to mention your friendship) unscathed.

1. Offer to help plan or set up for the party, then casually suggest making it a buffet. After all, it's the easiest way to serve and will free her up so she can enjoy the party as well. Bonus for you is that in this scenario, each guest chooses how much of what goes on his or her own plate, making it much less likely that the hostess will notice exactly how much (or little) you're eating.

2. Plant some seeds ahead of time. If your host is already well known for bad cooking (or the menu just *sounds* awful), mention some new diet, illness, or medication you're on that has altered your eating habits. But do it ahead of time (multiple times, if possible). If the night of the party is the first your host hears about your newly discovered gluten

allergy, she'll be suspicious, but if you've been complaining about your stomach issues for weeks, it will seem legit. Avoid giving too many particulars, as your host might make substitutions for you. Instead, just warn your host that you might not be able to eat very much (or at all), but that you couldn't resist the invitation to one of her *fabulous* dinner parties. This lets her know you're excited to be there, even if you'll need to stick with salad (a fairly safe bet).

3. If it's a sit-down meal, offer to help serve, and conveniently put small portions on your own plate (strategically of course, so it isn't completely obvious). Not only will you get credit for eating everything on your (small) plate, she will remember how helpful you were in the kitchen.

4. Drink. A lot. Wine makes everything taste better. One bite, one sip (or one bite, one glass as the case may be). Before long you'll either be happily eating your meal without even tasting it, or you'll be the sloshed guest who is so entertaining that no one will even pay the slightest bit of attention to how much you are or aren't eating. Warning: Watch yourself after having too many cocktails. Alcohol is like truth serum; don't let it slip out that the host can't cook to save her life.

5. The old standby: Think back to your childhood days and quietly move food around on your plate to create the illusion of eating. You might have to take a few bites for believability's sake, but with a little maneuvering, when the plates are cleared, it'll look like you had more than you actually did. Be very careful with this, though, as it is not really very sneaky, and the host may know what you are up to (especially if she has kids and/or did it at her mother's kitchen table—apples don't fall far from the tree). After all, she's not stupid, just a terrible cook. If she's on to you, say that you had a late lunch, but the cornflake-encrusted anchovies are just so good, could you possibly take some to go?

6. If you know one of your friends is a poor cook, you can also preempt further nightmarish dinners by suggesting you skip dinner and go out for drinks instead. Or you could help her hone her skills by giving her a fancy cookbook as a gift. Just watch out because in my experience, this can be taken as a reason to plan more dinner parties, which would, of course, include you! Consider the gift of private cooking

lessons, and set it up so that the chef comes to assist your friend with the cooking for her next gathering.

You could just be an adult, suck it up, and eat the unappetizing food. Really, how bad could it be?

How to Get Bumped Off a Flight So You Can Get a Free Ticket

Passengers hurtling through the airport in a desperate bid to catch their departing airplane is one of the stock clichés of movieland. Less depicted, however, are the savvy travelers whose goal is to miss, rather than make, their flight. While intentionally derailing one's own smooth passage may at first, seem illogical, the benefits can be considerable: above all, a free ticket. Of course, just missing any old flight won't get you a free ticket; the key to securing such heightened rewards is to end up on an overbooked flight, and to graciously volunteer to surrender your seat—in return, of course, for a free upgrade or flight coupons.

Although it's difficult to predict which trips are likely to be full, you can at least increase your odds by choosing a popular destination at a busy travel time, like Disneyland in March (when all the kids are on spring break) or a ski resort at Christmastime. Then, be sure to book your flight by phone, rather than online. When you speak to the reservations agent he or she will tell you how many seats are still available, if you ask. If it is almost full, don't hesitate—grab a seat.

Time of day also matters when you're aiming to be ousted. You are less likely to be bumped in the morning, when flights usually go off without a hitch and people are also more likely to oversleep, leaving empty seats. The prime time for overstuffed flights is after lunch, when planes are packed with the people who either missed their morning flights or were supposed to be on other connections that were canceled or postponed.

Even if you are on an overbooked flight, you may not be lucky enough to get the boot; sometimes the airline will just dump people at random without bothering to ask for volunteers. So if your goal is to be bumped off your flight, be proactive. As soon as you get to the airport, ask the attendant at the check-in counter if the flight is oversold. If it is, volunteer to give up your seat, and if they already have volunteers, ask to put your name at the top of the list. If not, ask again at the gate, and keep asking (nicely!) if you still haven't heard anything as take-off time draws near. You may even want to hover around the desk area and get to know the person making the decision. Consider bringing the attendant a cup of coffee if it looks like it's been a long day. Airline staff tend to get yelled at when flights are overbooked and travelers have to change their plans, so whomever you talk to may want to help you just for the sake of having a grateful and satisfied customer for a change.

If you're a frequent flier, try to leverage your loyalty to the airline and your familiarity with airline staff in order to get plucked from your flight. It really does work wonders. I've both traveled and booked travel for many clients and when I frequently used a particular airline, I would always call the same person when I needed assistance. After a while, once he recognized my voice on the end of the line, he was suddenly able to change tickets without charging a fee, split round-trip tickets and magically turn them into two one-ways, or put my clients to the top of the "to be bumped" list and then get them on a free flight the following day.

A final tip when finagling getting bumped from your flight: Pack a carry-on bag. It's much less work for the airline staff to bump passengers who aren't checking luggage. Make sure the gate attendant is aware that you are traveling sans suitcase, and he or she might just sneak you to the top of the list.

Fly out of smaller airports where it's easier to get to know the staff by name. Booking agents and flight attendants have a lot more "power" with regard to who does and doesn't get on the plane than most people think, and it's totally their call as to when and how they use it.

How to Join a Secret Society

According to numerous firsthand reports (as well as a little book-turned-movie you may have heard of called *The Da Vinci Code*), secret societies do exist . . . though I suppose the reports make these societies not quite as "secret" as they might hope to be. Nevertheless, even though their existence has been documented, the only way you'll truly be able to learn the inner workings of a secret society is by joining one.

Of course, secret societies are pretty selective about who they let in (that's part of the appeal, everyone wants in on a secret), so before attempting to make your case for why you should be one of the lucky few, do a little homework. Thanks to the Internet, you can find a lot of information about most societies. The Freemasons are by far the most well known, followed closely by groups like the Illuminati, the Knights Templar, and others. You won't be able to learn *everything* about the society online, but you should at least be able to find out the basics, like the types of members they have, the purpose for existence, and so on. Many secret societies recruit their members at colleges and universities (like Skull and Bones or the Order of the Bull's Blood), so if you've already graduated, it limits your options but doesn't eliminate you altogether.

Next, you'll have to make contact with the group, or at least with a single member. This is by far the hardest part of the process. A true secret society won't exactly advertise in the phone book (hence, *secret* society, duh) so up until recently it would've been almost impossible to join one unless they recruited you. Today, however, information leaks from time to time, and it usually happens online. If you do manage to find some contact information for someone who is in the society, befriend the person and try to get him or her to invite you to join (without letting the person know that's what you're doing).

If you can't find anyone who outwardly admits to being a member of the group you want to join, search for local meeting places. Masonic temples—where Freemasons meet—are perhaps the easiest to find, but every secret society has to have a meeting place, and if you look hard enough, you should be able to find it. If it's a really exclusive society, just showing up at the meeting and asking to join probably won't work (and might even be dangerous!), so try pretending to be a janitor or employee at the meeting venue (whether it's a local church basement, lodge, or back room of a restaurant). Hang around, sweep the floor, and see if you can get to know a person or two.

Still in college or grad school? This is the most opportune time to join a secret society, so take advantage. The best route: Get superinvolved in lots of nonsecret organizations and clubs. Secret societies often pick the most active and influential students on campus to join their ranks, so taking on leadership roles in various campus organizations is your best shot at getting invited.

Quick tip: Secret societies that recruit after college go by the same principle, so if you really want to be recruited, just become a powerful, influential, respected member of your community over a long period of time. Easy, right?

Still can't find a secret society to join? Create your own! First, choose a name (the spookier the better), and then choose something to protect (most secret societies have a mission to protect something, whether it's a document like the Constitution or an idea like national progress or world peace). Recruit a few members but be selective (that's the whole point, remember?). Write a charter, develop a mission statement, and invent some rites of passages, secret handshakes, passwords and code words, and other cloak-and-dagger stuff. Whether your society grows into something huge over the coming years or stays small, local, and exclusive, starting your own is the easiest way to join a secret society—plus, you'll get to be in charge.

How to Sneak into a Marathon

Not everyone knows this, but marathon spots are typically awarded by lotteries, so just because you train, it doesn't mean you'll get to run. Some like to use this as an excuse to never actually train for one, but that's weak. I've snuck into multiple marathons, so even if you don't win a spot, put away the excuses and get your running shoes back on.

After a transatlantic flight to London, my two friends and I showed up to check in for the London Marathon. When they told us they didn't have our names, we acted shocked—why would we fly all the way to London if we weren't registered to run in the marathon? No one would be that crazy, right? Logic was on our side, as it will be on yours.

But this argument alone did not get us a number. We were told to wait to speak to a supervisor, which we did . . . for most of the day. But patience and persistence won out (in my experience it usually does), and we finally were able to explain our predicament. By this point, several registrants hadn't shown up to claim their numbers, and as luck would have it, there we were needing (if not begging) for those very spots! Whether it's because they get injured during training, or just give up and decide not to run, marathons always end up having no-shows (which means unused numbers), so it pays to hang around and try to snag a spot at the last minute.

In this case, only two of us were able to pick up the unclaimed numbers, but we had three runners. This forced us to learn another sneaky maneuver. If you find yourself one number short, take that bib they give the entrants to check items, and place this number *under* a sweatshirt, just sticking out enough to look like you have an official bib on. Voilà! It looks enough like an actual registration bib to keep people from getting suspicious. This is how all three of us were able to run in the London Marathon despite none of us having won spots in the lottery!

When the New York Marathon came around, I once again found myself without a number. With my training complete and the marathon just days away, I called just about everyone I knew to see if someone had an unused registration number. Finally, a friend of a friend at the *New York Times,* one of the marathon's sponsors, let me use her name. Turns out, the name of someone who works with a major sponsor of the event can be enough to get a person in.

Another solution: Volunteer to run with the handicapped, which not only will get you into the race (though you may not be able to run at the pace you'd like), but will also allow you feel even better about your achievement, since you did such a good deed. Or consider the less virtuous route: join a running club or training group a few months before the race and meet other runners. Someone is bound to drop out and bingo—you'll score your bib just like that.

I guess you have to be a bit daring (or trusting) to put in the time and effort to train when you are not even sure that you will be allowed to run in the race. But, hey, at least you'll be in good shape.

How to Replace Your Daughter's Deceased Pet Bunny Before She Gets Home from School

For any parent, keeping your child happy (and, by extension, ensuring your own peace of mind) is the emotional center around which daily life orbits. So it's natural that as a parent, when that first bunny, goldfish, or hamster inevitably passes, you'd want to spare your kid the pain that comes with losing something she loves. And short of the lame "Fluffy went to go live on a farm upstate with a bigger yard" excuse (which she either won't buy anyway or will figure out the situation later and be traumatized that you lied about her dearly beloved), the only way to do this is replace the deceased loved one with a body double. After all, if you couldn't tell Brad Pitt from his stunt double in *Fight Club*, is Libby really going to notice if Thumper is suddenly a little heavier, or if the tip of his ear miraculously changes from brown to black overnight? Sounds a little devious, I know, but believe it or not, I have been asked to help a client do this.

If you decide that it's too soon for the Grim Reaper to pay an official visit, it's important to pick the right time to swap the old bunny for new. Wait until your kid has left for school or is fast asleep; this not only gives you plenty of time to complete the transaction, it will also create as much distance as possible between one Thumper sighting and the next.

Find your substitute by calling or visiting pet stores, with a picture in hand, to ensure a decent match. Remember, there's more to rabbit replacement than matching size and fur color. Kids will notice if their pet doesn't seem as friendly, hungry, or active, so you'll also ideally want one with a similar personality, too. Provide the store clerk with as much information as you can about bunny's habits and lifestyle to help with the search.

Desperate times may require desperate measures. If your stand-in is perfect except for that white splotch on his paw, consider a quick makeover. Steer clear, of course, of anything poisonous or irritating to the skin and eyes; but a hint of natural food coloring, or nontoxic hair dye shouldn't do any harm and could provide a short-term fix—at least until the next bath.

Still, even if all that searching, subterfuge, and primping produces a decent doppelgänger, you might want to stop and think about whether you *really* want to go through with the swap (my client couldn't actually go through with it). Experts suggest that with children honesty is the best policy when pets die because it's an important, if painful, first step in their learning to handle grief and bereavement. As for that look-alike rabbit you worked so hard to find? Donate him to a school where there are even more kids to shower him with love.

How to Get Out of a Speeding Ticket

When most of us get a speeding ticket or other type of moving violation, we just accept the ticket, pay the fine, and get on with our lives (vowing to be a bit more careful when we drive, at least in the spot where we were caught). But regardless of whether or not you actually *did* commit the violation, if you get a ticket, you should always at least try getting out of it. What have you got to lose?

The general consensus says that talking your way out of a ticket is *way* easier if you're female. Unless of course the officer pulling you over is a woman, in which case the favored method (can you say, flirt shamelessly?) probably won't work. Since there's no surefire way to guarantee that once those lights flash and you're pulled over on the side of the road that flirting will be enough to get you off the hook, here are a few tricks you can use to try and reduce, if not completely get out of paying, the fine.

Keep in mind that the person pulling you over has done this before. He's heard it all, and it's unlikely that your typical excuses will work on him. Arguing with him, or telling him your brother is a cop/trooper/state senator will just piss him off, so don't even bother. Don't offer more information than is being asked for either—if an officer wants to know *why* you were speeding, it's okay to say tell him you're late to pick up your kid or you're racing to make a doctor's appointment, but don't share this unless he asks, or it will surely sound like an excuse. I mean, most people speed because they are late for something, so you have to imagine he's not really listening to your lame story because he's heard it before.

Unless he hasn't. And that's how you can almost be guaranteed being granted a pass—by being completely out there and original. I knew someone who got pulled over and without even thinking, he whipped out his cell phone and said, "Scotty, beam me up, I'm in trouble." The officer just happened to be a Trekkie, too, and started cracking up. Needless to say, the driver was free to go with just a slight scolding.

Then there is also the old reverse psychology method; act like you actually *want* a ticket. Look him in the eye (or the aviators) and say, "I know, you have to give me a ticket now, I was speeding." You may be surprised at this one, but most people don't like to be told what to do, especially people of authority. So when he hears you tell him to give you a ticket, he will now want to *not* give you the ticket just so that he gets to make the call. It seems ridiculous, but hey, it's actually an old sales trick, and it works.

Even if you end up with a ticket, there's still hope. As Woody Allen said, 90 percent of success is just showing up. Because most people who get tickets choose to pay the fine rather than appear in court, those who actually *do* show up are frequently rewarded with the charges being dropped, especially if they've got a decent case. So if you're willing to put in the time and appear at the courthouse, the odds are in your favor. Plus you might get to miss an afternoon of work; just be sure to leave yourself plenty of time to drive carefully (and slowly) back to the office.

How to Cut Any Line

Everyone is talking about the new burger hot spot and you have *got* to try it. So you head over on your lunch break to see what all the hype is about . . . only the line is what seems like miles long. Certainly too long for you to wait in it and still make it to your next meeting within the hour. But you are there, and you really don't want to leave empty-handed, plus you're really hungry and those burgers do smell good . . . so how are you going to get your lunch and zip back to the office quickly?

You have to think fast. I run around the city every day getting things done that my clients needed done yesterday, so I usually don't have time to wait in lines. Here's the secret: The easiest way to jump to the head of the line is to offer to pay for whatever the person at the front is purchasing. Just tap him on the shoulder and ask if you can pay for his stuff along with yours—this is important, because if you pay for your stuff *and* the other person's at the same time, no one else in line will have cause to complain (they may even think you know each other), because it basically takes the same amount of time as one person making a purchase. If you turn it into two separate transactions, though, it's more like you're cutting in front of everyone.

If the person you're trying to bribe is purchasing more than you'd care to pay for (or if you're in line at Tiffany's or Neiman Marcus), you can always offer the individual cash to swap places with you. Few people would turn down the offer of a $20 or a $50 just to wait a little longer, unless they're in as big a hurry as you are.

But if you're trying to save money, it never hurts to put on your most earnest (read "pitiful") face and just ask. Don't give specifics; just say that it's very important that you get out of there quickly and would he or she mind terribly switching with you. Think about it—no one ever asks, so if someone did, I don't know about you, but I would figure it was really important.

Be sure not to abuse these strategies; you wouldn't want to have bad line karma following you around the block.

How to Start a False Rumor

Look, I don't blame you for wanting to know how to start a false rumor. Sometimes, desperate times call for desperate measures, times when you've got to get down and dirty to get what you want, be it a promotion, an exboyfriend back, or just plain old revenge. That's what false rumors are for.

But I should give you fair warning: before you sow the seeds of your rumor, you should carefully weigh the consequences. Think of the people who will get wind of the rumor and how they might react. You want to make sure that the rumor will actually accomplish your nefarious goals, and this means taking into consideration any chances of it backfiring.

When attempting to spread a false rumor, creativity is your worst enemy. Sure, it can be tempting to concoct a wild and imaginative story, like, saying that your coworker is leaving the office for hours at a time to go to orgies. The problem with that is that it's *too* creative—so creative that no one will believe it. And once your rumor has been snuffed out as a bald-faced lie, it will be dead in its tracks, and you'll probably have made an enemy (or several) for life. A better rumor might be that your coworker has started going on three-martini lunches with her male supervisor. It's not as exciting, but it is believable, and just scandalous enough that people will want to pass it on.

When creating your rumor, the most important rule is one that screenwriters follow: be consistent with your characters. Make sure the rumor is something that others could actually see that person doing. It might be tempting to tell everyone that Bob in Accounting is embezzling funds, but if Bob is someone who is known to volunteer at a soup kitchen and rescue stray animals, you might have chosen the wrong rumor to start about Bob. In addition, make sure you get your backstory straight. Someone is bound to ask "Well, how did *you* find out?" Make sure you have a plausible answer.

Another potential pitfall is including too much or too little detail. Too little and the tale could be too vague to be convincing; too much and it'll be suspicious. Think of rumors you've heard. They never have *all* the details, but they do have just enough to sound real.

So you've got your goal, your target, and your rumor. Now you just need to get it out there. Again, take a page from Hollywood screenwriters: know your audience. The first people to hear your rumor are as important as the rumor itself, since they'll be the ones to either spread it like wildfire or put out the flame. I'd go straight to the biggest mouth you can find. Every office or group of friends has that one person who just can't keep a secret, and that's your go-to gossip disseminator. The key is to not come right out with the rumor. Find a way for the rumormonger to "accidentally" find out without you actually telling him or her (like maybe leaving a piece of mail where the person can't help but see it). Anything that tips the person off to the rumor without anyone having to actually say it has the makings of authentic gossip.

Option two is to have a conversation with the blabbermouth and make a few veiled references to your made-up rumor. But you should still resist telling the person the "dirt" for a bit. This will make it seem like you are trying to keep it a secret. Once gossip girl has "dragged it out of you," make sure to give her another, mysterious source: "*Someone* told me that . . ." Never make it sound like you got it firsthand. Finally, use phrases like "You didn't hear it from me, but . . ." and "Don't tell anyone I told you this, but. . . ." Don't go so far as saying "Swear you won't tell anyone," as this might backfire if she actually keeps her mouth shut.

As the rumor spreads, you can help fan the flames by asking other coworkers, "Did [name of gossip] tell you about Mary's affair with the pool boy?" This further distances you from the actual rumor.

If you follow these tips, within days (even hours, depending on the strength of the rumor and your busybody's mouth) your false rumor will go from your brain to everyone else's lips. Machiavelli would be proud.

How to Sneak Booze into Pretty Much Anywhere

Every so often you're going somewhere, like the movies or the park, where you may just want to chill out with your after-work glass of wine, but, well, it's not allowed. Or what about the places, like concerts, where it's OK to drink, but a beer costs "how much!?" There are just too many places that *should* allow you to bring your own booze that don't, like baseball games or your great-aunt's wake. So how do you ensure some liquid fun at places like these?

Well, if you're thinking of using an old-school flask, forget it. First, flasks are often bulky and easy to spot, whether in a pocket or a purse. Second, flasks are severely limiting in terms of what you can take with you—they're really only good for straight booze.

Disposable flasks, however, are one of the great inventions of the twenty-first century. Remember those Capri Sun juice drinks you had in kindergarten? The ones in the metallic-looking bags? Disposable flasks are basically Capri Sun juice containers for grown-ups. They're metallic pouches with a plastic screw-on cap that you can stash just about anywhere, without getting busted, since they don't have that telltale outline. Best of all, they're freezer safe, meaning you can make daiquiris or margaritas and take them with you to your next picnic or dry work event (Okay, maybe the second one is not the wisest of choices). Just mix up your favorite drink recipe, funnel it into some disposable flasks, and you've got a portable party.

If you're worried that a group of grown women chugging out of juice pouches might look suspicious, there's an easy way around that. If the place you're going offers drinks, alcoholic or non, ask for some ice water. Ice water is free, and the server will give it to you in a standard cup. Now all you have to do is go to the restroom, pour the water out (keeping the ice if your portable beverage requires it), and transfer your concoction to the cup.

Of course, a more imaginative option is to invest in a product like the Beer Belly or the Wine Rack, both made by the same company and available at www.thebeerbelly.com. The Beer Belly is a large plastic pouch that can be filled with beer (or anything else) and secured by a strap to fit over your stomach. A hose travels under your shirt and then up through your collar, allowing you to drink the pouch's contents inconspicuously. Under a shirt, the Beer Belly just looks like you've got a little gut, making it a breeze to pass through security at a game.

The Wine Rack is the same concept, but designed for women. It resembles a tank top but is also a secret pouch containing the drink of your choice. Both of these are growing in popularity at sporting events and concerts, but no security guard will check for them. They are designed to be pretty inconspicuous, and the situation could get pretty awkward if it turns out you *don't* have one.

Finally, there's the college student approach—mixing your drinks in a standard soda bottle. Of course, if you have a cosmopolitan in your Coke bottle, you might draw some suspicious glances, but chances are no one will comment. Just remember to drink responsibly and, if you're found out, chug and deny. They got nothin' on you!

How to Ace a Bail Hearing

In the game Monopoly all it takes is a small fine or a few rolls of the dice to "Get out of Jail." If only life were as simple. For the most part, if you were unfortunate (or stupid) enough to get yourself arrested and would prefer to avoid getting too comfortable in the Big House while your case is being resolved, you'll need a judge to decide to grant you bail and release you from custody.

Because seeing a judge can be time-consuming and costly, some states have bail schedules that preset specific bail amounts for common crimes, so you can just pay and go without a hearing. If you do have to appear before a judge though, you'll need to use your powers of persuasion to convince her that you're *not* either (a) a danger to the community or (b) a flight risk. Things you *don't* want in this situation: an outstanding warrant, probation or parole, a history of failing to turn up in court, immigration problems, and especially not a prior conviction for weapons possession or a violent crime. Those are pretty much a one-way ticket to the cell block. Do not pass go.

If you don't face any of those problems, one way to improve your chance of getting bail is to keep your mouth shut. I don't care how cogent or impassioned you think your plea of innocence is—leave the talking to a professional. You have the right to a state-hired lawyer, but he or she may not be very experienced (remember the movie *My Cousin Vinny?*) or have much time to devote to your case, so if it is at all an option, get your own attorney. If you do speak, remember to be humble and remorseful. Even if you are innocent and wrongly accused, righteous indignation will get you nowhere except up the river. Dress well but conservatively. If your everyday uniform is pearls and furs, leave them at home. You want to come across as a nonentitled, respectful, and upstanding (albeit recently fallen) member of society who doesn't have the cash to skip town—or a nicer wardrobe than the judge. Friends, family, employers, teachers, and religious leaders who can testify to your reliability and good character can sometimes help, so consider inviting them to the hearing (it's cheaper than inviting them to dinner). Documents such as leases, school records, phone bills, evidence of community membership, and letters of reference also help. And, of course it never hurts to have your mother come down with some home-baked cookies.

Remember: A bail hearing isn't the forum to argue your innocence; it's only an opportunity to plead that you shouldn't be incarcerated before your case is heard. As tempting as it may be to reenact a scene from *A Few Good Men,* exert some self-control and wait for your day in court to get things off your chest.

Another helpful pointer: Be on time, or even show up early. You'd be surprised at what punctuality can do.

How to Beat a False Rumor

If someone you know read the earlier piece on how to *start* a false rumor, you might become the unfortunate victim of malicious gossip. And it would be all my fault. So the least I can do is give you some tips on how to shake the rumor. And if all else fails, go to "How to Start a False Rumor," page 109, so you can get your revenge.

First things first: It's not the rumor itself that's the problem. The real issue is that someone's pissed enough at you to start one. If someone started a false rumor about you, there's a reason, and figuring out that reason is an important step to clearing your name. So grow up, be an adult, apologize for what you did, and resolve any issues head-on.

If the person who is mad at you won't accept your (heartfelt, I hope) apology and continues to spread the rumor, well, now you have my permission to play a bit dirty. Send a mass e-mail to anyone you think has heard the rumor, and deny it—firmly but NOT defensively. Call out the person who started it (hey, she had her chance to make this all go away) and explain why she's out to get you (extra credit if it's embarrassing to her, as in "Jen started this rumor because she's upset with me for telling her new boyfriend about that unfortunate skin condition").

There is also the off chance that someone with a big mouth just misunderstood something. Maybe the person saw you hugging someone who's not your spouse (um, yeah, it was your *brother*), or maybe she assumed you were photocopying your résumé because you thought you were about to be fired (when really your boss asked you to do it because he was updating your profile on the company website). Whatever the case, finding out the root of the rumor will help you figure out what to do next (i.e., clear it up in an adultlike manner if at all possible).

One thing to keep in mind is that often rumors start from *some* small truth; in other words, the thing that was said about you might be off base, but at the same time actually expose something true about you. For example, that rumor about you making résumé photocopies because you got fired might not be true, but if, in order to deny it, you have to tell people you were making copies for job interviews, it could end up doing more harm than good.

Like news cycles, rumors have a shelf life that ends when something juicier comes along. So if you think trying to deny it will just make matters worse, take a vacation. When you get back, people will probably be on to the next gossip topic of the moment. Or take a page from the celebrity playbook. There's a rumor that Brangelina are about to split? They know that if they start making noises about another international adoption, *that'll* be the headline in the next issue of *US Weekly*.

In the long run, whether the rumor is 50 percent true or 100 percent false, keeping quiet about it is usually better than denying it. If you don't address it at all, the whole thing will remain a mystery and people will wonder if the whole thing was even true in the first place. After all, what people really want is something to gab about, so the more you play into it, the more people will keep talking. Remain unflappable and the rumor just may disappear as quickly as it started.

> Still don't feel vindicated? If you're okay with getting messy, starting another rumor is always an option. Two can play at this game and payback's a bitch.

❧ How to Squeeze Your Way into a Will

If you have a rich (possibly even childless) aged relative or even next-door neighbor, the thought may have guiltily, crossed your mind that you'd like to be included in his or her will. The money has to go somewhere, after all, and you know you'd put it to good use. If she's really well-to-do, chances are she's thought this through already, considered all her siblings' descendants and cousins millions of times removed, and knows exactly who she wants to leave money to. Still, even if you don't think you've made the short list, it's worth trying to sneak your way in. Who cares if you're not related, where there's a will, there's a way, right?

Obviously, the best plan is to let her get to know you and love you so that she will genuinely choose you as a recipient of her fortune. But this may take a while, and let's face it, when we're talking inheritance, time may be of the essence. So a shortcut, if you're just starting to get to know her, is to focus on shared interests (if you can't find any, fake it). If you're a burgeoning filmmaker who needs money to get started on a project, and the person is a longtime film buff, make sure you talk about your dreams and aspirations. It doesn't hurt to drop hints about your troubled finances, if you can do it without seeming sleazy. You never know, if she likes you enough (or even if she just likes that you are interested in her), she might just want to help out—perhaps even while she's still alive!

Another way to work your way into others' wills is to find out what charities they support and get involved there. Make sure they know about it, and possibly even plant the idea that you will continue to support the organization after they are gone—and wouldn't it be great if you had enough money to be sure that the organization is always taken care of?

If the person is already batty, she probably has someone taking care of her final affairs already—a sibling, niece, nephew, or grandchild, for instance. Get on good terms with this person (the conservator of her estate, in legal terms), as that individual already has her ear. If, in your search for the conservator, you discover that in fact none exists, see to it that you take on the role yourself—and quickly. If Great-Auntie Warbucks can't quite remember who you are by the time the subject of amending the will comes up, you're out of luck. Or, if you're a real jerk, maybe not . . . so be your sweetest self.

These things can be tricky, of course. Even if you manage to worm your way into the will, the closer relatives could contest it after the death, saying she was not of sound mind when she updated her will. Things often get messy (think Brooke Astor's son), and you don't want to be known as the pariah or become the talk of the town, so proceed with caution.

5. mind your business

How to Find the Perfect Job

There might not be a simple step-by-step solution for finding the ideal job; sometimes it can take a lifetime of seemingly random choices and decisions to ultimately get you to the perfect vocation. I personally believe that the best job is doing something that you love. But of course, figuring out how to turn your passion into a viable occupation that pays the bills is sometimes easier said than done. Only you know what you love, so trust yourself, even if it seems off the wall. And don't always listen to other people. Let them choose their own path; this is your journey.

To start your quest for the perfect profession, pretend there is a "job genie" who can grant you any job that you desire (just bear with me here). But the genie knows nothing about you, so you will have to provide some clues to help him become crystal clear when granting your wish. Get out a piece of paper (I know, I heard you groan, but this is your career we're talking about) and write down the three things that you most enjoy doing in life. Now spin around three times (for the genie, but also to have a little fun with it!) and ask yourself if any jobs exist that involve doing one or more of the things on that list. Let's say the things on your list were cook, read, and spend time with your kids. In an ideal world, your perfect job might then be to own a catering company that you operate from home—and maybe do book reviews for cookbooks on the side. But of course, a few practical considerations must be taken into account when deciding if the job is a good fit, so weigh your options before jumping in headfirst.

A few of the biggies are as follows.

Money: This is obvious. If you are someone who says salary is just not a factor at all, then good for you. You're one of the lucky ones. But for most people, money *is* a factor, so when the goal is to have the perfect job, the trick is to ask yourself just *how* important a factor money is to you. In other words, how much money do you wish to make (given your financial situation) while doing what you love?

Schedule: If you want to work the night shift so you can surf all day, that's your prerogative. Many people work nine to five, but if your job is a more demanding one, you may find yourself working from seven in the morning to seven at night . . . or later. If these are your hours, I hope that you really do have the perfect job *and* that you love it, since you are spending so much of your time there. If you do choose a career where you'll have to work long hours, you could also end up resenting your job, even if you love it at first. I would like to be able to tell you how you can have it all, but you'll need to figure out on your own how to make that happen. Just know that it *can* be done.

Qualifications: Maybe you have the financial cushion to live comfortably while your new catering business is getting off the ground. But what if you have no professional training or experience in your chosen career? Just because a little boy dreams of being an astronaut doesn't mean he'll land a job at NASA, right? That's true, but it's the little boys (and girls) who work hard, with their goals in mind, who do end up at NASA. Point is, be realistic about whether you're qualified to do what you want to do, and if you aren't, figure out what you need to do to get there. Maybe you need to take classes or work your way up the ladder to your ideal job, or if you're starting your own business, maybe you need to invest in some training or hire the right people to get you there. If it's really what you're meant to do, one way or another, you'll get there.

If you're already on a career path and your job is less than perfect for you, consider taking an online job assessment (check www.livecareer. com) to see if anything new and exciting piques your interest. Sometimes, people get locked in a line of work for not-so-good reasons—parents' expectations, past decisions, inertia, and so on. You may find that you're well suited for a line of work that you've never even heard of before. Remember, it's never too late to make a change. If you don't believe me, ask the genie what he thinks. The perfect job is worth wishing for.

How to Write a Résumé

At Consider It Done, I've seen hundreds of résumés. People send them to us when they want to work for us, and clients send them to us when they've hired us to search for staff. So I can tell you this: you want yours to stand out from the crowd. I know you've probably heard this all before, but really, it's competitive out there, so spend serious time updating, tweaking, and perfecting your résumé for each new opportunity. (Yes, the work starts even before you land the position!) Customize your résumé for the particular job you are applying for, and I guarantee you'll maximize your chance of landing an interview and getting hired.

Quick tip: You can often examine the specific description of and qualifications necessary for the position/job you are interested in on the company's website.

Before I even get in to the actual résumé writing tips, let me say one thing. Follow directions. Does that sound obvious? It isn't. You would be shocked to find out that 90 percent of job applicants don't follow simple directions like which forms to submit, or where to e-mail them. And guess what? This may disqualify you before your résumé even gets read. Think about it. Why would I even *consider* hiring someone who can't follow directions? After all, how you do anything is how you do everything, therefore—automatic disqualification. I'm a member of a national business group with hundreds of business owners and one of the best tips I received about screening potential candidates is to use the application process to see if the person can even follow simple instructions, so believe me when I say, businesses are looking at this.

Now that you've followed the directions for submission (I hope), here are tips for the actual document. They are what I like to call the Three Bs of résumé writing: benefits, bullets, and brag.

First, of course you'll be listing the positions you've held. What you want to do here is focus on the quantifiable benefits you have brought to companies in the past (something you've increased or decreased, percentages of growth, etc.), *and* what you will do for their company. Specifics are key. So if the new position will include cold calling, don't just say, "I did cold calling for a brokerage house"; instead say, "I initiated 200 cold calls a day with a conversion rate of 30 percent, ranking #1 of 100 reps in the company." See the difference? And always be thinking "What can I do to benefit this company?" To find out what benefits to focus on, do your homework. Read about the company's mission and values on its website, look for its press releases, and check the news or investor relations section on its webpage.

Second, use bullets to highlight your points. Be pithy (easy on the adjectives), and be sure that there is a lot of white space so that your accomplishments stand out. You want to be able to catch a reader's eye quickly. Think situation, action, result. Example: "I took over a dormant team and implemented a CRM solution; as a result, we increased sales by 20 percent."

Third, brag. A résumé is no place for modesty. What did you do that rocked? Be sure to include your greatest accomplishment with each position and if you don't know, call a colleague. Include when you got promoted, but also include details like *why* you were granted the advancement.

Keep one master résumé on your computer that includes *all* of your previous jobs and qualifications. Update this master file with each new job or experience. Whenever you apply to a new position, start with this master file and whittle it down, deleting anything that's not relevant to the current job opportunity and customizing to show exactly how you can benefit the company where you're applying. This way, you won't have to start from scratch every single time you need a new résumé. Keep cutting from the master résumé until it's a short, quick, and easy-to-read document that will stand out.

Even if a company doesn't ask for one, *always include a cover letter*. As with the résumé, you can start with a template that describes you, your experiences, and your goals. Then with each new job application, write a new paragraph that's specific to the particular company and why you are the perfect fit.

Once you've written the résumé, give it to a friend or family member for feedback. Don't argue with criticism, just take it in as information and consider implementing the suggestions. If it takes the person more than a few minutes to read it, time to simplify. And remember, you don't have to wait to see a job ad to send a résumé. Be proactive by figuring out where you want to be, and go for it.

How to Get Monogrammed Dress Shirts

The tradition of monogramming initials on men's shirts began for practical reasons: ensuring everyone got the right shirt back from the laundry. Today, the practice is more about style. Monogrammed shirts just look classy. If you've decided to upgrade your wardrobe or simply have a hankering to go old school, a monogrammed dress shirt can be a real treat. Here are a few ways to go about getting one.

The best way to monogram a dress shirt is to go see a professional tailor. Your local seamstress (a key person to have in your posse) should be able to turn an off-the-rack Gap shirt that cost $35 into one that looks like it cost $200. If you're splurging on the monogram, you might as well go all out; don't just have the tailor monogram the shirt, have him make you your own shirt and *then* monogram it. You'd be surprised that most tailors will do this for less than the cost of a new shirt at Barneys, and the fit will be a lot better. Don't have a good tailor? The best way to find one is word of mouth. Ask the snappiest dresser you know to refer you to his guy (or gal).

For a DIY monogram, simply draw the initials directly on the fabric, then, using thick thread and beginning from under the shirt, bring the thread up and across the width of the first letter, repeating the pattern and setting each stitch down as closely as possible to the previous one. Classic monogram placement on a dress shirt is on the left panel, where the pocket would be, or on the cuff. If the thought of such work makes you go cross-eyed, ask around to see if anyone you know has an embroidery machine. You choose the letters and the machine does the work for you.

Another choice is to check out a design-your-own-shirt website. These have been popping up all over the Internet and will spare you the trauma of sewing while still being more affordable than a custom shirt from a high-end shop. You simply provide your measurements, choose fabric, color, cuff and collar style, and a few weeks later a custom-made shirt will arrive on your doorstep. Even some moderately priced retailers, such as J.Crew and Lands' End, offer monogramming for an additional fee on many of their items.

Remember: It's class you're after; showiness is not the ticket. The best monograms are done subtly, not too large and in a color that's not too far off the color of the shirt itself. Stick with the simple three block letters in a row or go for a subtle variation like the classic design of a diamond shape, with the larger center initial standing for your last name. When it comes to monogramming, all that's called for are three initials, tops. Embroidering your full name on your cuffs will make it seem as if you just can't remember who you are.

Sometimes even small changes in your wardrobe can give you the confidence boost you may need to make larger changes in your life. If the shirt fits, wear it!

How to Get Your Office Mate to Use Her "Indoor Voice"

We all know the type: that one person who seems to not realize that cubicle walls aren't soundproof. Nothing is more distracting or grating than having to listen to someone else's loud conversation while you're trying to focus on work. As much as you live for your morning latte, there has been more than one occasion that you'd be willing to sacrifice it by tossing it on the offender's head for just a little peace and quiet.

You could simply tell him or her to shut the hell up, but that isn't exactly going to generate a peaceful environment. Fortunately, you've got some better options for how to achieve tranquility at your desk.

Give her the benefit of the doubt. Maybe she doesn't even realize that people can hear. Let her know that you can hear her by casually referencing something you overheard. "I happened to overhear you are having medical problems. Do you want the name of a good ob-gyn?" should get her to keep it down, if she doesn't want everyone in the office to know her business. Of course, some people speak loudly precisely because they *do* want everyone to know their business, so if the preceding strategy doesn't work, face the fact that she is one of them.

Not only doesn't she care if people know what she is up to, but she doesn't care if she is distracting other people. If this is the kind of person you have on your hands, you might try (a) having the boss sit the cute new guy next to her (if he's cute enough, he'll render even the loudest of loudmouths speechless), or (b) having the boss sit the office gossip next to her (she won't be able to get a word in edgewise).

Still no luck? Start speaking to her only in whispers. It's weird, but have you ever noticed how a conversation that's half whispered invites the other person to respond in whispers, then all of a sudden you find yourself saying, why are we whispering? So unless she's *totally* oblivious, she'll match her volume to that of the people around her. It's genius. The key is remembering to whisper around this person at all times.

There's also the "Pavlov effect." Remember Pavlov, the psychologist who found that when dogs were fed after hearing a bell, eventually, they began to salivate at the mere sound of the bell? Well, you can create the same effect with your coworker! Every time your desk phone rings (whether naturally or because you're secretly calling it from your concealed cell phone), ask her if she could "just be a little bit quieter," as it's an important call. After a while, every time the phone rings, she'll lower her voice without even realizing it. Best of all, she might just get in the habit of quieting down *without* the phone ringing. Even if you can't teach an old dog new tricks, maybe you can teach your office mate a thing or two.

Finally, you may need to resort to the completely blatant and not at all subtle way. Get to work early and put up some signs that say PLEASE KEEP CONVERSATIONS AT A REASONABLE VOLUME all around the office. Maybe even ask your coworker, in a horrified voice, "Do you think they mean us?!" She'll likely quiet down, but just to prove that it's not her.

If none of these quite do the trick, go the direct route and share with her the fact that you get extreme headaches when exposed to incessant loud noise (almost as bad as migraines) and ask her if she could please keep it down as a personal favor to you. It's not really a made-up medical condition; all the chatter really *does* give you a headache, doesn't it? Whether or not she believes you is not the point. Unless she's a total monster, she'll shut up anyway.

Failing *all* of these, good-quality sound-canceling headphones can be purchased for less than $100. But you might want to take them off every once in a while, just in case she says something interesting.

How to Pretend You Follow the TV Show All Your Friends/Coworkers Talk About

For whatever reason, *everyone* in your office is always talking about the same show. Except for you. Maybe your cable box is out and you haven't gotten around to getting a new one. Maybe your cat knocked over your TV and it shattered into a million pieces. Maybe you don't even *like* TV. But still, you don't want to feel left out at the watercooler, so here are some tips to pull off conversation like you're in the know.

To make people think you follow a show, you'll need the CliffsNotes. What I mean is that you'll not only need to know the basic plot summary, but also need to have your own theories and opinions. We're talking more than a cursory knowledge of the program; the three-line synopsis you find by doing a Google search isn't going to cut it.

Start with Wikipedia, which tends to have a lot of detailed info on current TV shows, including character sketches (or for reality shows, background info on contestants) and summaries of past seasons. TVGuide.com is another great place, as it usually has at least a page on all the major shows, and they are updated the morning after a new episode airs. (Hint: If you fall behind, your excuse is that you have it TiVoed but haven't gotten to it yet, so no spoilers!) These pages usually include a short recap of major events, as well as questions and theories about where the show is headed. This is especially useful for reality series, as the conversation will inevitably be about who was or wasn't voted off the previous evening (and who *should* have been voted off instead). *American Idol*, for example, is almost always recapped the morning after; the recap might even feature an interview with whoever went home that night, as well as a poll about who's next to get the boot. A quick glance at this info will give you enough to chime in as to whether you were excited or disappointed that the trashy girl with the good hair got nixed or how you're looking forward to the underdog (you'll know the name from your cheat sheet) winning it all.

For scripted series, you might need a little more than just the bare-bones info. A lot of shows—*Grey's Anatomy, Gossip Girl,* and *Mad Men,* for example—have frequently fluctuating character relationships and scandals that you'll need to have an opinion on, if you want to prove you're in the know.

Your best bet here is to quickly log in to Television Without Pity (www.televisionwithoutpity.com), where you will find detailed, opinion-ated weekly recaps and discussions of just about any show that people might talk about. Television Without Pity does its recaps in a humorous tone, so you might even pick up a few jokes to use when discussing a show (just don't quote them verbatim—a lot of people who watch the shows also read the recaps). The AV Club (www.avclub.com) also has recaps that include choice quotes from episodes, which are especially convinc-ing. In addition, both sites have message boards to discuss episodes, meaning you can glance at what others thought of the program and where the series is heading. Feel free to claim those opinions as your own. Con-sider subscribing to blogs and you will automatically get the updates be-fore your morning coffee.

When actually talking to your friends or coworkers, it's important to not say *too* much—if you draw too much attention to yourself, you might get drawn into a discussion that your basic knowledge won't cover. Just give a few choice opinions or observations ("I couldn't believe he kissed her!" or "I bet so-and-so will be out next.") and nod and smile for the rest of the conversation. Pretty soon you'll feel like a part of the cult—just don't spend more time studying your cheat sheet than it would take you to actually watch the show!

How to Surf the Internet at Work Without Being Busted

The time-honored tradition of pretending to be productive while actually procrastinating at work has been taken to glorious new levels by the invention of the Internet. The Web is such a vast fountain of both fascinating information and time-killing nonsense that an entire eight-hour day can easily be spent looking for exes on Facebook and laughing at funny pictures of cats doing absurd tricks.

But of course, looking at pictures of cats probably isn't in your job description (if it is, please let me know—I may want your job), so unless you have some other way of paying the bills, you're going to need to at least *appear* to be working whenever a boss or coworker stops by. So, how to be lazy while appearing productive?

Two words: *Alt Tab*. In case you're not familiar with the ins and outs of computer keystrokes, Alt Tab is pretty much the most useful one ever. Hold down the "Alt" key (the Apple Command key if you're using a Mac) and hit the "Tab" button, and you can go from shoe shopping to spreadsheet building in the blink of a prying eye. If you're using a Mac with the "Spaces" feature, this works even better, because you can have all your Internet windows in one of the spaces and all your work spaces in another—it won't even look like you have an Internet browser open at all!

Another way to stealth surf is by sticking with sites that are primarily text, like blogs or online magazines. Believe me, if someone's just walking by, he won't focus on the actual words on the screen, and it'll look like you're reading an important e-mail or document. You can also open a window with a very worklike thing (a graph, spreadsheet, company site, etc.) right next to whatever it is you're *actually* looking at; at a quick glance, people will probably recognize the work thing first, and not even notice what's open beside it.

If you *are* caught, though, don't Alt Tab out of the browser or close the window after you know your boss has seen it—at this point, it's better to own it. Trying to hide it will only draw attention (sort of like when you get toilet paper stuck on your shoe). If you are called out on it, the best excuse is that you clicked on a link in an e-mail someone sent you—it's definitely believable. Just know you can only go this route once.

> **To avoid dealing with this altogether, learn to inconspicuously use the web browser on your phone for work-time procrastination.**

How to Actually Get the To-Dos on Your List Done

Life is filled with things we need to get done. For many, this list of tasks is long—and seems to only get longer and longer. If you are someone with a long to-do list that never seems to shrink, know that you are not alone. After all, I started a business for the simple reason that so many people need help getting things on their to-do lists done.

For some, keeping a to-do list may seem like an extra task in and of itself, so they avoid it altogether. This is silly. In reality, a list is just a simple reminder of the things that you want to accomplish, and it's not nearly as overwhelming once you learn to manage it properly.

The key to a successful to-do list is *recognizing that there will always be something on the list.* Sure, we all love the feeling of checking things *off* the list. But know that for each thing you check off, you'll probably add on two new things, so when you accept the fact that yes, there will always be stuff on the list in some way, shape, or form, a certain type of freedom sets in.

My husband took a while to jump on the to-do-list bandwagon. Although he'd constantly complain about all of the things he had to do, he was a champion postponer, so his list would grow and grow and he would never get to check things off. That's when he would boycott making lists altogether. I suggested that perhaps it wasn't the *list* itself that wasn't working, but he was certain that his own head was a better place to keep track of everything. One day, I finally stopped suggesting he make a list. It may come as no surprise to you, that at exactly that time, all of a sudden, he decided that a list might be a good idea after all. Soon enough, he was writing down things he needed to do and either delegating them or doing them himself. Yes, another great benefit to actually writing down your tasks is that it gives you the ability for you to *easily delegate your to-dos*. Brilliant! The point here is not to show you that I was right about the list (which I was) but that it only worked once he came to the conclusion on his own.

Following are other key things to remember when creating a to-do list you'll actually use.

Write it down. You might feel your list is so long that it would be impossible to put everything down, even if you used an entire ream of paper. But once you start putting the items down on paper, you will find there *is* an actual end to the list. Plus, it's a proven fact that our brains can't hold more than five to nine things in short-term memory at a time; now that you have your list, you won't have to store any, and your brain will be able to focus on actually getting those things done. A written to-do list will also allow you to *check things off* when they are complete, giving you a wonderful sense of accomplishment. Great job!

Get a notebook just for your to-dos. Keep it in the same place all the time so you always know where to find it. And get a cool notebook, something you'll like looking at. It may sound silly, but a notebook that's appealing will make you want to use it. Whatever you do, don't scrawl your list on the back of a torn envelope or a page you ripped out of your daughter's secret diary. Scribbling a list on a ragged piece of paper will put you in the mind-set that the list is more of a disposable "reminder" and less of a list of things you *really* need to get done.

If you're not the notebook type, maybe a *digital to-do list* is for you. Going fully digital offers several advantages. In addition to offering mobility, digital task lists make it easy to reorder tasks, track due dates, and move tasks to different days on the calendar. You'll be able to create family to-do lists that everyone can have access to. In addition, you can easily delegate tasks (useful for business projects as well as for dishwashing assignments) and even get automated reminders by e-mail or text message. Some good digital task tools include Gmail tasks, rememberthemilk.com, or if you're an iPhone user, try Zenbe or DoBot ToDos.

And if you're on the digital plan, you'll most likely have access on your phone, which will allow you to check off boxes while you're on the go. Try Jott or Reqall when you want to be hands free. Both applications track tasks and allow you to add items by voice. Speak and you shall be heard, or at least be transcribed.

Include next steps on your list. There is always a next step. Sometimes it is making a phone call, sometimes it is filling out a form, sometimes it is running a follow-up errand. Whatever the next step is—write it down. This will help you get things done more efficiently during the day. For example, when you pull out your list and are reminded you need to make a dentist appointment, the phone number will be right there. There's no need to get on the computer where you'll be distracted by the seventeen new e-mails in your in-box; you'll be able to just sit down with the number right in front of you and immediately dial.

Give every task a deadline. This will help you prioritize and also put the pressure on—it's a great way to hold yourself accountable. But if you miss the deadline, don't let yourself off the hook. Keep the to-do task on the list and add a new (and impending!) deadline.

Set aside time each day to review your list. Use this time to update your list. Anything that didn't get done should go on the list again . . . don't just keep it on the list, write it again. Having to write the same thing over and over will get so annoying that you'll probably do it just to get the damn thing off your list.

Make it fun. One fun way to stick to your list is to assign points to each item—the more involved, complicated, or undesirable the task, the more points it's worth. Come up with a reward for yourself (chocolate, shoes, or a nap are good ones to start with) for getting a certain number of points. The idea here is to make your to-do list less like a daunting collection of tasks and more like a scavenger hunt.

Before you start bad-mouthing the to-do list, try keeping one diligently for thirty days. Go ahead, start now. And whatever you do, *don't* put "make to-do list" on it and cross it off—that's cheating.

Quick tip: Often times, things don't get accomplished because when we have a small window of time to get the tasks done, we don't know where to start. Give yourself some time to calmly think about what you want to get accomplished. It's interesting that without the pressure to quickly complete the task, solutions will just pop into your head. Make list-keeping an enjoyable part of your day—maybe sit in a special comfy place and have some tea. You'll be amazed that by taking a short break from the doing, more will actually get accomplished.

∞ How to Win Your Office Oscar Pool

Every year it's the same story if you work in an office (particularly one that has a lot of women): someone somewhere will take it upon themselves to organize an alternative "March Madness" in the form of an Oscar pool. It's a ton of fun, and there's a chance to take home a nice chunk of cash. There's just one problem: you're never the winner. Well, it's time to make plans for green, because this year, it's yours.

The issue usually is that you're thinking like an amateur—making your choices according to the films and stars that you liked best. But this isn't the way to do it. Many people don't really realize how "political" the Oscars (and many other awards) are—it's not always about what's best, but what's "supposed" to win.

For example, if you had *Brokeback Mountain* as your Best Picture winner a few years ago, you, just like the film, went home empty-handed. Remember the big uproar about how the voters chose *Crash* because it had an "easier" message than the controversial *Brokeback*? Unfortunately, no one knew that until *after* the awards had been handed out. So when making your pick, don't just think about the quality of the movie, but about its themes and message. If they're divisive, or off-putting to some segment of the population, the movie probably won't win. Think of the people on the voting panel as being politicians, not actors. Nine times out of ten they'll go with the "safe" choice.

Also, actors who have been nominated many times but have never taken home the prize are good choices, as are actors who have been in many successful movies but have never been nominated.

Unless you're a real movie freak, you probably don't know all there is to know about the nominated films, so before you fill out your "bracket," do some homework. Start by checking out some entertainment-related magazines and websites, like E!'s website or *Entertainment Weekly*'s special Oscar issue—many of these will have pages devoted to predicting the winners. Of course, these can be subjective, so find at least three sources and compare them. Where are their choices the same? Where are they different? If these three sources have the same favorites for certain categories, you can be pretty confident that your odds are good. When they differ, you want to pay close attention to the reasons—do they explain why Movie A is favored over Movie B, or does the selection seem arbitrary or based on their own personal taste? If your source talks about behind-the-scenes drama or Academy politics, it may have the inside scoop, so factor that in to your decision.

Another tip to keep in mind: It may sound stupid, but if one category has two much-buzzed about movies or actors who seem equally matched, you might want to go with the person you consider to be the third in line. Most awards shows go by number of votes, so if two nominees receive equal votes, the third choice gets the award. Nonsensical, of course (why give the award to the *third* best?), but often this is how it works.

Finally, despite all this, don't ignore your own instincts. So-called experts have been wrong before, and they could be wrong this time too. There's something to be said for going with your gut—sometimes, the dark horses win big. Just think of Seabiscuit (the actual horse, as well as the movie).

How to Get a Lazy Coworker to Shape Up

Sooner or later, most people run into a workplace situation where a colleague is not quite pulling his or her weight. And let's say that the person is smart and competent but just plain old lazy. Although your first impulse might be to scream at this person or go to your boss, keep in mind that very little good can come of either of these options. If you tell your boss, and the lazy coworker isn't immediately fired, you'll have to work with someone who knows (or suspects) you ratted her out, which may make your work situation even more unbearable than dealing with a slacker. And yelling, well it's not good for your health.

But there is a backdoor route that will make sure your coworker either shapes up or ships out, while allowing you to maintain a civil relationship. Start by constantly offering help. If you see her sitting around or she looks like she's not working, ask her if she needs a hand with something. The more you ask, the more she'll realize people have noticed that she's not really performing. If she doesn't either pick up the pace or start to actually *work* for a change, keep offering your help, only now do it loudly, and sometimes maybe even in front of your boss (or cc him on the e-mail). At the very least, knowing you are on to her will keep your coworker on her toes, as she'll want to keep up appearances in front of the higher-ups (she's smart, remember). So offer, and say it like you mean it. In most cases, sooner or later, your boss will catch on, and you'll most likely emerge looking like the capable and compassionate employee, and your coworker, the slacker that she is.

Another even better way to get your dud of a coworker to step up her game is to present the situation to your boss directly, but in a tactful way. Tell your boss you noticed the coworker is struggling, and ask if there's any way you can help her to work more effectively. Act like all you care about is helping her do a better job. This will make you sound like you want what's best not only for your coworker, but for the company (bosses love that, and, besides, if you don't want that, then it might be time for you to take a look at "How to Find the Perfect Job," page 117), while still cluing your boss in on the fact that the coworker's performance may not be up to par.

What you want to avoid is being a tattletale. Grow up. If you go running in to your boss to complain about someone, sure, he'll find out that the other person is not doing her job, but he'll also find out that you're a whiner. A complaint is just another thing he'll have to deal with and you are the one who just added it to his plate, so congratulations, you just landed yourself a spot in the annoying bucket. Plus, your boss may decide not to deal with it at all, but have the two of you clean it up, leaving you no choice but to sit face-to-face and give the person honest feedback about why you are unsatisfied with her performance. Way to go.

Remember: The goal should not be to get anyone in trouble, but to get the person to step up, pitch in, and contribute to the team. Time for you to take responsibility and have it be different. Notice what this person is good at and look to bring out that quality. Identify your coworker's strengths and passions and try to align them with other tasks and projects that are taking place in the office. People naturally get excited and work harder at things they are good at. For example, if someone is friendly and social, send her to a networking event, where she'll be more likely to add value.

If this doesn't work, you may need to put some heat on. Try making sure that the most high-profile assignments end up on her desk, so that she's forced to get it together. Eventually, her true colors will show. And if she does step up, well, that's what you really wanted anyway, right? Win-win all around.

How to Organize Your Desk

A well-organized desk is inviting. It beckons you over to come sit down and get some work done, doesn't it? It *almost* looks like it will be fun to pull your chair up and get started. A clean and organized desk means you can tackle anything. And it does wonders for your productivity.

Some people are just naturals at this. But if you're not, and you find yourself putting things off that you need or want to get done—all because you don't like to sit at your messy desk and look at all the piles of paper and disorganization—maybe it is time (or maybe it has been time for a while) for a little desk makeover.

But before you can make your desk *look* organized, you have to actually *get* it organized. There's a big difference. Organizing doesn't mean just piling everything up in one corner of your desk or stuffing everything into a drawer (although if you need to take a baby step, consider this hiding method so that at least the top of your desk is clean while you tackle the rest of the mess).

For an easy way to begin, keep this in mind: only the bare minimum stays on the top of your desk. In addition to your computer, have an in-box of some sort and something to hold a few pens and pencils (choose something unique that you like to look at, like an interesting jar you picked up on your travels somewhere). All other office supplies go in a drawer, and all other papers are either tacked to a bulletin board (if it's something you reference every day) or filed, preferably in color-coded folders. Better yet, you can scan them into a digital file and store them on your computer, then toss/recycle the hard copies. Take a field trip to The Container Store for some desk and drawer organizers. You'll be reminded of back-to-school days, with all your shiny new essentials. It's motivating.

To keep your desk clutter free, consider implementing the following process. The first time anything comes across your desk zone, either toss it, act on it, or file it. Of course, papers tend to accumulate, even if you are good at filing or throwing things away. One executive I know has a method for dealing with this. All incoming papers go onto the top of one stack. Every Friday, late in the day before she leaves the office for the weekend, she takes the bottom 25 percent of the pile and throws it away. That's right, directly in the trash bin. She believes that if she hasn't had to look at the papers for a month (which is when they'll be at the bottom of the stack), then she probably won't have to ever look at them. There is a slight risk in using this method (i.e., that you may actually *need* something from the bottom again), but it forces you to throw things away, which minimizes clutter.

There are plenty of books and websites with advice about organization, so check out a couple and choose a strategy (or mix and match from a couple) that you think will work best given your work style and habits. Whatever you choose, remember that organization isn't a onetime event—it's ongoing. At the end of the day, be sure to put everything you used that day back in place. This will take less than five minutes even if it seems that you have a lot to tidy up. And once a month or so, go through some of your files and get rid of things you don't need anymore. Pretty soon, being neat will become a very low-maintenance habit. Then don't be surprised if you hear your desk calling your name.

6. crowd-pleasers

How to Hire a Snake Dancer

Back in November 2006, Guns N' Roses were performing at Madison Square Garden, and we got the call to plan a sexy, edgy, and crazy after-party befitting of such an outrageous band. Like any wild rockers, Slash and crew had some pretty out-there requests, but that's what we were there for. Pinball machines? Check. Little people running around? No problem. Snake dancer? Uh-oh. And did I mention we had twenty-four hours to pull it all together?

A few calls to some . . . er . . . gentlemen's clubs yielded the name of one woman who is known for sexy snake-dancing. It came as no surprise that she happened to be in Vegas for the weekend. What did come as a surprise is that everyone we spoke with pointed us back to the same person. One snake dancer in all of New York? Couldn't be. I tried the circus, but they don't do snakes—I guess they scare the kids. (I located a guy who books vaudeville acts—not a huge help in the snake-dancer department, but a good find for my Rolodex. You never know when that'll come in handy.)

Then I thought—what if we just got a belly dancer to dance with a snake? Well, after calling just about every Middle Eastern restaurant in Manhattan, that idea didn't seem quite so brilliant after all . . . there were some takers, but none who could make themselves available that night. Then, I realized I'd overlooked a whole sea of people who would dance for money—no, not strippers—dance students! And students have the most flexible schedules of anyone; surely I'd be able to find *someone* who was free that evening.

So after a few calls to local dance schools, I found a dancer who was willing to manage a snake. But of course in snake dancing, the dancer is only half of the attraction. We needed a snake, and I wasn't too keen on purchasing one.

There being no 1-800-rent-a-snake, I called some pet shops. Perhaps unsurprisingly, none of the store owners were too keen on renting me one of their snakes for the evening (quite frankly, I don't think they believed me when I said I needed it for a Guns N' Roses after-party), but one of the owners I spoke to referred me to his friend who had a pet snake he would be willing to lend out—in exchange for an invite to the party.

We needed him there anyway (you know, to make sure the snake was comfortable with the dancer, behaved at the party, and had someone to entertain him on breaks), so that's how it came together. We picked up the snake, the snake owner, and dancer and got them all to the party just in the nick of time. The dancer got to make some extra cash doing what she loved, the pet owner got to hang with Guns N' Roses, and the snake— well, the snake seemed to have a good time too.

How to Arrange a Singing Telegram

Admit it: Ever since that amazing, unforgettable scene in the movie *Clue* (if you haven't seen it, go rent it immediately), you've wanted to surprise someone with a singing telegram. Well, you're in luck, because I'm about to tell you how.

When singing telegram requests come in (yes, it's a fairly common request among our clients), everyone in our office gets excited. We once arranged one to greet someone just as he pulled up to his hotel in New

York City. Right there on the street corner. We had it timed perfectly so that when the birthday boy arrived and got out of the cab at the hotel, he was greeted with a musical birthday message. Wow—was he surprised. Good thing we also arranged to have a photographer there to capture the moment!

There are plenty of places that will arrange for someone to deliver a singing telegram, particularly if you live in a large city. Some companies, like www.americansingingtelegrams.com, will set up telegrams nationwide.

The most challenging part of arranging a singing telegram isn't so much finding the people to belt one out, it's working through all the details. Many services will give you choices for the type of costume the singer will wear, as well as choices for the message itself. Is it a private message, or will there be a party going on? If there's going to be a party, you'll want to make sure the message is appropriate for the group, and not (too) embarrassing for the recipient. The keys to a successful singing telegram are anticipating the situation, and customizing the message.

If you're surprising someone randomly, you'll need to take steps to ensure the recipient will answer the door. Oftentimes, to avoid solicitors (or Girl Scouts selling cookies) people won't go to the door unless they are expecting a delivery or a friend. So come up with a reason why you'll be stopping by on Sunday at 3:00 P.M.— maybe to drop off the casserole dish you borrowed, or to borrow your friend's little black dress, and when he or she opens the door to let "you" in—surprise, it will be a singing telegram instead.

A singing telegram might be a bad idea for someone who's frequently grouchy. Remember, not everyone likes surprises, and if you think your friend might be one of these people, sending him candy might be a better idea. But then he'd miss out on a fake Marilyn Monroe singing "Happy Birthday," and that's just tragic.

How to Choose the Perfect Karaoke Song to Impress a Crowd—Even If You Can't Sing

At any karaoke night, the stakes are high: choose the right song, and everyone in the bar will love and respect you; choose badly, and prepare for the most uncomfortable four minutes of your life. The good news is that if you can't sing, fear not; impressing a crowd has very little to do with voice quality. It has almost everything to do with song choice. The bad news is that if you're singing karaoke in the first place, massive amounts of alcohol tend to be involved. So watch out, because this can seriously impair your musical judgment (i.e., "'Like a Virgin' would be a great idea!" No, it wouldn't. Especially if you're a guy.). To avoid falling into this party mood-killing trap, here are some things to consider when deciding on your song:

1. Choose something that everyone will know but that no one would have thought of. That's a tall order, I know, which is why you should think about this *before* you get to the bar and are faced with the pressure of flipping through the giant book of songs. Give it some thought and start to build your repertoire *right now.* An even better idea is to pick a song everyone will not only know but also want to sing along to. Scroll through the top-rated songs on your iTunes playlists, and make a list of whatever jumps out at you. Don't be afraid to ask around. If a quick poll of your friends generates enthusiastic nods (and preferably a bit of spontaneous singing), you're good to go. If your friends don't know what song you're talking about, forget it. To make sure no one else would've thought of your song choice, don't pick a pop song from the past few years—go back a bit further.

2. Get the audience involved, not just when you're performing, but in your choice of song. Shout out some options, and go with whatever gets the best response. Then, during the performance, encourage the audience to get involved by holding up your mic to specific people in the crowd. After all, if it sounds terrible but others are singing too, you'll still be considered a success.

3. Know your range. There are a ton of great songs that we all wish we could sing. But despite what the alcohol-soaked voice in our brain might try to tell us, most of us can't carry a tune to save our life. If you have to go falsetto or bring it down an octave, the song is definitely out of your range, so don't attempt it. Plenty of other songs are available for you.

4. If you have no idea what your range is, or have no idea what I was talking about in tip 3, your situation is a bit more dire. But there is a solution: pick a song with almost no range at all, which usually means rap. If you pick the right rap song (and learn the words ahead of time), you can wow the audience with your mad skills, and they'll never even know you can't sing. Or try some easy classics like "Love Shack" or "We Didn't Start the Fire." These are crowd-pleasers and don't necessarily require hitting the right notes. For the chorus (which *should* usually be more forgiving and easier to sing in tune), let the crowd help out.

5. Don't take yourself seriously. Remember when cheesy boy bands like Backstreet Boys and N*SYNC were popular? Well, they still are. At karaoke bars, that is. Same with the Spice Girls, Britney Spears, Hanson, ABBA, and many more. You don't have to choose a serious song to get a seriously positive reaction. In fact, choosing a serious song is discouraged. Guys singing songs originally performed by women (and vice versa) are usually embraced, and my experience is that songs from 1990s Disney movies, like "I Just Can't Wait to Be King," "A Whole New World," or "Under the Sea" are (almost) always a big hit.

6. Keep it brief. I was once at a karaoke dinner bar and a friend chose "Freebird." Bad choice. The live version is over fourteen minutes long, and you have to really know what you are doing. When the song finally came to a close, the host said, "That was really, um, long. I sure hope your food didn't get cold." A sure sign of a poor song selection. Live and learn.

7. Rehearse the words ahead of time. Yes, they'll be on a screen if you need help or forget, but if you're relying on the prompter completely, people will be able to tell. Plus, you'll need to bank on the fact that your vision won't be blurry.

8. Timing is everything. Even though you've prepped and chosen your songs ahead of time, do NOT go first. Hold out until at least a few others have warmed up the crowd a bit.

Once you've got a short list of at least five songs (and have practiced them at home to make sure you know the words and that the melodies are in your range), you're good to go. Just give it your all, and if it doesn't work out, don't worry too much; most people will either have had too many cocktails or will be so preoccupied by what song *they* are going to choose that they probably won't remember your performance anyway.

Quick tip: Here's a short list of some crowd-pleasers to get you started:

For everyone:
"Sweet Caroline" (Neil Diamond); "I Want it That Way" (Backstreet Boys); "We Didn't Start the Fire" (or almost anything else by Billy Joel); "I've Got Friends in Low Places" (Garth Brooks); "Wannabe" (Spice Girls); "Total Eclipse of the Heart" (Bonnie Tyler); "Y.MCA" (Village People)

For duets:
"Summer Nights" (from Grease)

For guys with no shame:
"F*ck Her Gently" (Tenacious D)

If you actually have a *good* voice and some stamina:
"Bohemian Rhapsody" (Queen); "Livin' on a Prayer" (Bon Jovi); "Don't Stop Believing" (Journey)

And a personal favorite:
"American Pie" (Don McLean)

How to Improve Your Party with Dry Ice

Dry ice is pretty much the coolest thing ever. It's inexpensive, and there's almost no type of event that it can't make more festive (except maybe a wake, where it'd just be creepy).

I'd feel guilty if I didn't give you a few basic dry ice facts and safety tips before getting you started. First off, dry ice isn't really ice at all, but solid carbon dioxide. Because of this, when it steams (making that cool-looking smoke), it can potentially displace oxygen in the air if the room isn't well ventilated. Don't let this scare you—it just means you need to use it in a larger room or open up a window. Dry ice is also *really* cold (hence the name *ice*), so don't handle it without gloves.

Dry ice is surprisingly easy to find. Liquor, grocery, and hardware stores all potentially carry it; it's just a matter of calling around to find a place near you that sells it. Depending on how much you need, you could even have it delivered. Make sure, though, that you purchase only food-grade dry ice. Non-food-grade dry ice is what's used in science labs and has other added chemicals you don't want anywhere near your punch bowl. Also, make sure you purchase the dry ice the day before, or day of, your party—any earlier might leave you short, because dry ice evaporates over time.

Dry ice is pretty much a must for Halloween parties. One fun way to use it is to break it up into chunks about the size of your fist and put the chunks in bowls of hot water. This will create dry ice "smoke" (remember that a big chunk of super-cold ice will cool the water, so if you want to keep it going, you might want to use a trivet under the bowl). Place fans on the floor to circulate the smoke, creating a thick layer of delightfully eerie smoke around your guests' feet. Just hope no one loses a contact.

Remember when I mentioned punch bowls? Well, that's another good place to put dry ice. It'll make the liquid in the bowl bubble and appear to smoke, turning your ordinary rum punch into a veritable witch's brew. It's safe to ingest it, but most people prefer to have it floating in a punch bowl and then use a ladle to scoop the punch (sans dry ice) into the cups, because if it ends up in your glass you could seriously burn yourself.

Besides looking spooky, dry ice is practical as well. Putting food and drinks on dry ice at parties will keep them chilled and also save you the trouble of having to mop up pools of melted ice (aka water). When you're done with it, just throw it out—no cleanup required.

Don't limit yourself to Halloween when planning parties with dry ice. The smoke effect can work really well with strobe lights to create a nightclub vibe. Just add a disco ball and it'll be like Studio 54, right in your living room.

How to Throw an Impromptu Dinner Party

The great thing about impromptu parties is that, well, they're impromptu, which means absolutely no planning is involved. No one expects anything, so everything you come up with is gravy. In fact the definition of impromptu is "something that is made or done without previous preparation." So if you want to look good in front of all your friends and keep your own stress levels to a minimum, impromptu parties are the way to go.

The key is to keep a few essential items on hand at all times. This way, when you decide that it is the perfect day to ring in the start of summer with a BBQ, or your spouse gets a promotion at work and you want to celebrate with ten of your closest friends, you're ready to go. Although I believe there are no "shoulds" in life, this is one place where I make an exception. We should all look for reasons to celebrate—often. Because we can. And because people love it.

So keep key items in your freezer; at the very least, hamburger meat and buns, and some frozen party foods like pigs in blankets or mini quiches. And ice. Lots of it. These staples don't have to be fancy; remember it's about the company, not the perfect meal. There is always a way to have a dinner party without having it be all about the food.

Drinks, however, are crucial (hence all the ice); after all, nothing boosts the mood of a get-together better than a well-stocked bar (see

"How to Stock the Perfect Bar," page 294). Keep on hand for ("emergencies") a few kinds of liquor and mixers and at least four bottles of red wine and four bottles of white wine. Even if it's not for a dinner party, you never know when guests will stop by or you'll need to drown your woes with a bottle of pinot (for more tips on wine selection, see "How to Choose and Serve a Bottle of Wine Like a Pro," page 302). Having a few of both red and white ensures that whatever you end up cooking, you'll have enough of a paired wine to go around. For decor, all you really need is to keep a stockpile of candles on hand. Just vary the types and sizes—candlesticks, tea candles, pillar candles, and so on, and an everyday room becomes party ready in an instant.

Keep other fun things around as well, like a plaid tablecloth that you can either break out for an impromptu picnic in the park, or use to turn your kitchen into an Italian bistro for the evening. Consider buying a Polaroid camera; if you take pictures throughout the evening and hand them to your guests on the way out the door, they'll remember your spontaneity for years.

> Don't discount the old potluck. If you assign people things to bring, your party planning just became even more of a cinch.

How to Throw a Successful TV Show Viewing Party

TV viewing parties are becoming increasingly popular. They're great mixers, especially if some people in the group are shy or you aren't familiar with everyone in the room, because they provide at least one guaranteed topic of conversation. They're also easy to plan; plus, it's fun to make TV a social event, instead of something you do in your sweatpants on the couch.

Although you could have a viewing party for just about anything, they're usually reserved for special occasions like season premieres or finales. There are four key components to any great viewing party—food, drink, decor, and rules.

Let's start with that last one, which doesn't exactly scream "fun party." Rules are important for a TV viewing party because some people at the party might not be as into the show as others and therefore may not realize it's not okay to talk while all the mysteries of five seasons worth of *Lost* are being revealed. It's important to let everyone know the rules *before* you start the show. And they are: no talking until the commercials *or* only talk in whispers (whichever suits you). Other rules might include betting: place wagers on the show for things like how many times a character will say a certain phrase, when certain long-lost characters will reappear, or whether or not two characters will *finally* get together.

As far as food goes, the obvious choice is theme food for whatever show you're watching. For example, oysters and cocktail sausages if you're watching *Mad Men.* Or red foods, like red velvet cake, and brie with strawberry jam, for bloody shows like *True Blood* and *Dexter.* You can also always go with cuisine native to a show's setting. Shows like *Breaking Bad, Burn Notice, Weeds,* and *True Blood* have distinct settings that are known for certain types of food (the Southwest, Florida, Southern California, and Louisiana, respectively).

If you just can't come up with *anything,* check out websites like www.slashfood.com, which has a lot of creative theme recipes, for inspiration. If you can't find one that makes sense for your show, just stick with a crowd-pleaser that's conducive to viewing—stuff that's quiet (no potato chips, please) and doesn't require a lot of work on your guests' part. Cheese and bread, cookies, and finger sandwiches are all good examples. Or get creative and make "TV dinners" and serve them on little plates lined with aluminum foil or TV trays.

Naturally, you'll also want theme drinks for your viewing party. If you're watching a show without an obvious drink theme idea, you can just name drinks after characters or things in the show. Browse your local liquor store to see if there are any wines or liquors that share names of characters on your show for a fun (and easy) theme drink, like Grey Goose *(Grey's Anatomy),* Jack Daniel's *(24),* or a nice merlot (which is the inspiration for Sam Merlotte of *True Blood*'s name).

When it comes to a viewing party, you can't go too far with the themes. And that means costumes. Medical shows like *Scrubs* or *House* are good opportunities to break out your hospital garb, *Mad Men* is the perfect opportunity to bust out (no pun intended) that little Joan Holloway number, and *Lost* is a great excuse to whip out the inflatable palm trees and tiki lights you've been dying to use.

One last thing: If you have a DVR, you might want to record the show, then wait sixteen minutes (for hour-long shows) before starting it. This will allow you to fast-forward through the commercials and end the show on time. On the other hand, commercials are the perfect time to gab during the show without breaking the rules.

How to Impress People with a Magic Trick—and Then Get Them Off Your Back Before You Have to Do a Second

I'm no magician, but knowing one solid magic trick can make you the talk of a party or gathering, if it's done right.

A sleight of hand (the kinds of tricks real magicians do) can take years to perfect, so I recommend choosing a trick at a local magic shop. But some of these can look cheap and unimpressive, so don't just buy the first thing you pull off the shelf. Ask the shop owner to perform a few tricks for you, though know you'll never be let in on the secret until you actually purchase the trick. I highly recommend choosing a trick that can be done with everyday objects (or fake replicas of everyday objects) so your audience won't be able to tell it's store-bought. Select the one that's the most stunning. (You probably don't need anything too fancy, especially if you've got a group of novices on your hands. They'll fall for anything.)

If you can't find a magic shop, look online (www.magictricks.com is a good place to start). Some favorite starter tricks include putting a pen through a $20 dollar bill (and then pulling it out with the bill intact) and a coin trick called "Scotch and Soda" that involves making a coin vanish from an audience member's hand.

Don't ever purchase a magic "kit" unless it's a gift for a child. Sure the kits are cheap, but so are the tricks. Plus, you can bet that everyone's seen them before—like when they were five. Invest in one solid grown-up trick—it might cost a bit more, but it's worth the investment.

Once you buy the trick, the key is practice, practice, practice. You should be able to seamlessly perform it with your eyes closed, otherwise you'll get nervous in front of a crowd and potentially mess up.

Once you've performed, the crowd will likely ask you to either do it again or do another trick. *Never* do the same trick twice for the same group of people. They'll be looking more closely, and if anyone figures it out, the entire effect is lost.

If you don't have a second real trick prepared, you need an easy out. Consider going with a "joke trick," which starts out looking like a magic trick but turns out to be a joke. Try this one. First, ask a volunteer to take out a ten-dollar bill. Ask her to fold it in half lengthwise, covering up the wings of the eagle on the bill. Then ask her to fold it in half, lengthwise again, and hold it up to a light source to make sure the wings of the eagle are covered up (this is all really to confuse the audience). The person should now be holding a long, skinny, folded bill. Next, ask her to fold it in thirds, like a letter, and put the bill in your palm. Make a fist, wave your other hand over it, and say some fun magic words. Finally, open your fist (the bill will still be there, of course), pocket the cash, and give your volunteer a hearty thanks.

Your audience will be confused at first, but when done right, this joke trick usually gets a laugh (it's cheesy, but since they're expecting a trick, that's part of the appeal), and it usually gets the group off your back. They'll forget about wanting to see another real magic trick, and they'll think you're as funny as you are magical (though you may want to eventually return the pocketed cash).

How to Write a Toast

Even if your oratory skills are less than spectacular, you may someday, somehow find yourself in a situation where you'll have to make a toast. And even though toasts are often personal, you can learn, with just a few basic skills, to write a toast for just about anyone and come off looking like a pro. Yes, believe it or not, I have been hired to write a toast for a client to give to a bride at her wedding (thankfully, I wasn't asked this by the groom!).

Start by jotting down a few key things about the person you are planning to toast. These should be *personal*, but not *too* personal (no embarrassing childhood anecdotes), and *specific*. The more you celebrate the person's unique personality traits, the better. Of course, this only applies if you have time to prepare. Often, you may be called upon to give an impromptu toast and believe me, when put on the spot like that, it's impossible to graciously refuse. For that, well, I can give you a few tips that will come in handy, but you'll have to wing it to some degree.

The number one key to a successful toast is to *make it about the person you are toasting*. Let me say it another way in case you didn't understand: don't talk about yourself. It's fine to let people in on some little secret, but if you're going to include yourself in the story, you'd better make it something *really* funny or interesting. Honestly, no one cares about how much beer the two of you used to drink in college. Think of something great to say about the person, or keep your mouth quiet.

The next rule of toast writing is to *know your audience*. For example, is the room full of family and aged relatives, or close childhood friends? The latter gives you a little more permission to tell all. Still, unless it's a bachelor or bachelorette party, keep it PG, or at least PG-13. And though some teasing is fine, don't go overboard. Nothing will make a bride madder than too many jokes at her or her beloved's expense. Make sure you steer clear of humor involving sex, physical features, or any other areas that might offend. Jokes should be short and sweet, like the rest of your toast.

Which brings me to the next rule of toast writing, and perhaps the most important one—*keep it brief*. Whatever the occasion, you're making people put their meals and conversations on hold while they listen to you, so once you cross the five-minute line, you're in dangerous territory.

Rehearse your toast beforehand and time yourself, keeping in mind that there will (hopefully) be pauses for laughter.

A good formula for success is this: introduction (briefly state who you are and your relationship to the person), joke, joke, a few heartfelt words (not too many—or you may come off as too heavy or corny, and you'll lose the crowd), then raise a glass. And before you sit back down, don't forget to acknowledge and thank the audience.

Remember, you can always do something out of the ordinary. Try this for an added twist of fun to a wedding toast. Have the couple sit back-to-back. Have them remove their shoes and instruct them to keep one of their own shoes and hand their other shoe to the other person. You will then read a series of questions and have them vote by holding up a shoe. The shoe they hold up is who they are voting for. Questions can be anything you choose, for example: Who is a better dresser? Who calls their mother more? Whose mother calls more? Who is better in bed? Keep it to five minutes. Then, end with the heartfelt words. This is a crowd-pleaser and a great way to get both people involved.

One last tip: It's fine to have notes, but don't write the whole toast out, or you'll sound inauthentic and rehearsed. The key to writing a toast in advance is making it seem like you didn't. Here's to you and your future as a toastmaster!

A good quote (as long as it's relevant) can give your toast a punch. And it lets you get away with having less original material, while still making you look like you put some real time and effort into the whole thing!

⌇ How to Hire a Rock Band

Ever dreamed of having Bon Jovi do a private show for you and your friends? Want to surprise someone at his birthday party with his favorite band? This sort of thing doesn't just happen on TV and in the movies. If you make the right connections and have a big enough budget, a big-name band might just be willing to take the gig.

If we're talking really big band, though, it will come at a price. I have found that you usually won't be able to get anyone huge for under $50K (unless someone is doing you a major favor), and most really famous bands will likely charge much more. If money is no object, the key is to get in touch with the agent or manager for the band—and all big-name bands will have one. If you have any friends in the music industry, in any role and at any level, start by calling them. They may not know the specific manager or agent you're looking for, but they can likely get you one step closer, and you'll work your way up from there. If all else fails, search on the Internet. All bands have websites that should list the name and agency representing them. Put in a call and see if the band is available for private functions. If not (or if the price is too high), here's a tip: suddenly reconceive your event into a charity function, ideally for a charity or cause the band has supported in the past. Call again (best to use a different name), and tell them it's an event to support whatever organization you've chosen, and this time, the band may just give it a second look, and perhaps even lower their price.

If that doesn't work, you can always get a lesser-known (or totally unknown) band (maybe one that specializes in covers of your favorite rock band) for a much lower fee. They may not have name recognition, but the music quality can be surprisingly phenomenal. Small local bands are easy to find and simple to book, and they'll probably jump at the chance to perform at your event. The trick is finding the right one.

You can find an incredible, local band in two ways. The easiest and fastest way: the Internet. MySpace has also become a destination for aspiring musicians, and many pages will feature not only information about the band but also samples of their music. And don't worry—a "local" band isn't necessarily a "lame" band. Breaking through in the music industry can be incredibly difficult, so you could find a rare gem just by surfing MySpace or similar websites. Who knows, maybe you'll even discover the next big thing. Everyone starts somewhere, and these days, it's usually online.

If you can't get a full sense of the band from their website or social network page, a second way to find a local band is to go see them live. Or better yet, find out if there's a "battle of the bands" or similar event at any local venue in the near future. That way you'll be able to hear a handful of up-and-coming bands at once. Choose your favorite, then see if you can talk to a band member right then and there. Surfing the Internet may be the simpler solution, but seeing a band live will give a true sense of what they'll do at your event. Remember, live music adds an element of fun to any event, so let the good times roll.

How to Create a Carnival for a Party

Creating an outdoor carnival is one of the most impressive and extravagant ways to celebrate a special occasion. It may seem daunting to create, but in reality, if you have enough people pitching in, it's one of the easiest types of parties to throw. Besides, who doesn't love a carnival? If you can think of anyone who doesn't, be sure to leave them off the guest list, and make sure your party is the talk of the town.

Here's how to throw together a carnival faster then you can learn to juggle. First, you need a staff, preferably energetic young people who are patient with kids (even when you're throwing a carnival for adults, this rule of thumb still applies). You can find willing teenagers in a couple of ways: try asking friends of your kids (or kids of your friends) or contacting youth groups or school clubs. You probably won't even have to pay them much; some teenagers will work a party just for free food. If you can't find anyone (or anyone who doesn't have twelve piercings and a rap sheet), party-planning companies can usually find you a staff, but it'll cost you a little more.

Once you line up your team, have a planning meeting. A carnival is all about *games,* but don't go crazy trying to come up with them all yourself. Put your staff members each in charge of his or her own game, from conception to completion. Letting everyone design and run his or her own booth not only saves you time and hassle, it will make your staff feel like they've accomplished something.

The types of games are completely up to you and your staff (be creative!), but remember that no carnival is complete without face painting. This will be an instant hit, and now everyone will be in "costume." Another must-have is balloons, and these can take any form. You can rent a helium tank and blow up balloons on the spot, or buy them already blown up. Another idea is to have someone make balloon animals. Kids love this, even if your balloon twister is a total novice. I once had a friend volunteer to do balloon animals at a party I was planning and when I got there, I found a line of kids clamoring for "worms and snakes." Turns out, those were the only animals he could make. At first, I was devastated, but then I realized that the kids didn't mind, so don't make yourself nuts trying to find the next Picasso of balloon art.

No carnival is complete without prizes, so pick up a few rolls of tear-off tickets from a party supply store, and make sure all booths have a bunch to give out to the winners of their games. Then, set up a prize booth, where you can give away cheap, disposable party favors of your choosing. They don't have to be the most amazing prizes in the world. In fact, quantity usually trumps quality at carnivals. Simply letting guests walk away with something they "earned" captures the true spirit of a carnival.

Quick tip: Don't forget to think about food, and coordinate it with your theme. Anything on a stick screams carnival, especially corn dogs. Popcorn and cotton candy do, too, so consider renting an authentic popcorn machine or a cotton candy spinner. Most party rental companies will be able to track one down for you and if you can't find one, call a caterer, they'll know. The best part is that most "carnival food" is very easy to "cook."

Last, no carnival is complete without a main attraction. Personally, I favor the dunk tank. You can search online to rent one of these, but you might be able to do better. The last time I was involved in planning a carnival, we rented a makeshift dunk tank from the local fire department. They had actually built it themselves for their own party. Fire departments are often involved in planning local fairs and carnivals, so it's worth checking to see if they have anything that could be of use. If not, they might even be willing to build you something; it's relatively easy for them to do, and it earns the department some extra cash.

Always have a rain plan, whether it's a giant tent, a rain date, or a way to move the carnival indoors.

How to Customize Anything

Few of us are likely to have a building named after us or to ever see a golf course, concert venue, or even a park bench emblazoned with our moniker. But that doesn't mean we need to tuck our dreams of building our own personalized empire of stuff on the back shelf.

With today's advances in digital printing, creating custom items has never been easier. I customize all kinds of items for clients' parties all the time. Going skiing with friends? Create a logo for your group and put it on fleece jackets. A simple birthday celebration? How about custom napkins with funny sayings about the guest of honor? Whether it's a tote bag, a CD case, or a jelly jar, the variety of canvases on which you can express yourself has never been as limitless, nor the means of doing so as easy. I use any chance I get to have a little fun with customized stuff.

One popular request is for customized bottles of all kinds—water bottles, wine bottles, beer bottles, and so on. To create unique beer bottles, for example, just buy a brand that you like, soak off the labels, and then stick on some that you've designed yourself, either with a program like Photoshop or from a simple website such as www.myownlabels.com or www.bottleyourbrand.com. You can order customized labels from the preceding sites that you can stick on any kind of bottle and for a variety of occasions too.

For a less slick, more homemade gift or party favor, scan a picture of your kindergartner's latest artwork (or a picture of your little artist for that matter) onto a customized label that you can apply to just about anything. At www.stickergiant.com you can print custom stickers, create magnets, or design other paraphernalia with your own personalized artwork or messages.

Whether you're promoting your company, throwing an event, or simply want to send a present with a little personalized touch, putting your unique signature on an everyday item is easy, inexpensive, and fun.

How to Hire a Mariachi Band

Anyone can put out a bowl of chips and salsa, crack open a few Coronas, and call it a theme party. But if you want to host a truly memorable Mexican-themed event, I highly recommend hiring a mariachi band. I've done this many times for clients and it's always a hit. So where does one find this particular type of musical artist? Glad you asked.

The easiest place to start, of course, is online, but it may not be the best. There are countless sites where you can hire bands for gigs (including www.rentmyband.com, www.gigmasters.com, www.bookaband.com, and many more), but since anyone can register on these, there's no guarantee the band you choose will be any good. So before you book, listen to samples, and talk to a member of the band on the phone, or better yet, listen to them in person. On sites like these, it's easy for any band, like a punk rock band or a country western band, to check off the "mariachi" box when they sign up, hoping to come up in all search results and thereby book the most gigs. Without seeing the band in person, you run the risk of a hipster singer-songwriter showing up with a trumpet and a sombrero and pretending like he's done it for years.

The best strategy is simply to just visit the one spot you're most likely to find a mariachi band: your local Mexican restaurant. Search online for nearby restaurants, and check their websites (or call) to see if they employ a mariachi band, and if so, which night(s) they play. You may have to travel one or two towns over, but you should be able to find one. Take the family, enjoy your tacos, and pay extra special attention to the music. If you like the band, and they feel authentic, they'll be better than anything you can find online, and since they're local, it will be convenient for everyone.

Speak to the owner of the restaurant, or to a member of the band himself after they're done with a set. For the right price, they'll be at your next event, as long as the restaurant is willing to do without them for a night. Just make sure they know how to play more than one song. "La Cucaracha" gets old.

How to Hire a Lion Tamer for a Party

The weirdest party I ever went to was in Los Angeles (shocker). It had dancers performing on tables (that people were sitting at), a bona fide tattoo artist (none of that henna stuff for this crowd), and for the truly adventurous (or truly drunk), people swinging from the rafters, and bathrooms with no doors. But as strange as all this was, at least I never feared for my life.

If you want to throw a truly wild—and memorable—party, and the standard tricks of the trade just won't suffice, the one surefire way to get a reaction out of your guests is to instill the fear of death. You could do this with fire breathers, snake dancers, or blowfish appetizers, but I say go straight for the king of outrageous party entertainment: a lion tamer.

But finding one—and keeping your guests from being maimed—is easier said than done. Lion tamers likely won't appear in the Yellow Pages, and an Internet search may take you to some weird and disturbing places. So to find a real-life lion tamer you'll have to go to the source: the circus. If you're able to plan ahead, search the Internet to find out if any traveling circuses will be in your city around the time of your party. If you live in a large city, be sure to check for circuses visiting nearby suburbs as well. If you find one, you could try a phone call, but the kinds of people who work for traveling circuses aren't always easy to reach by phone. So the best thing to do is to wait until the circus comes to town and stop by in person. You may have to face your fear of clowns or women with beards, but the lion tamer shouldn't be too hard to spot, assuming the circus has one. From there, just be honest about your intentions, and ask if he (or she) is free for your party. You may have to offer a pretty penny to steal him from the circus for a night, but he'll probably be excited for a change of scenery—and the extra publicity.

If there's no circus in town, take a trip to the only other place where lions can be found in this part of the world: the zoo. You likely won't be able to talk to a lion tamer directly at first, so visit the zoo's administrative offices and talk to someone in charge. That person will let you know if the zoo has a lion tamer and would be willing to let him do some moonlighting. Be sure to mention that you'd be willing to make a nice-sized donation to the zoo, and personnel may be more inclined to help. (I figure if you have the means to hire a lion tamer for your party, you can afford to make a generous donation to such a worthwhile and probably under-funded institution.) And a word to the wise: Don't show up looking like a crazy person. Wear your Sunday best and be your most polite self. Who in his right mind would put his lion in the hands of a nut job?

Once you book your lion tamer, make sure you keep your guests out of harm's way—or at least make sure your insurance covers you if they do get mauled. But really, make sure your motto is, safety first. Bring the lion tamer to the party venue ahead of time and decide where the lion will be and how to keep guests out of reach (preferably behind a barrier). Plan everything out with him in advance, and you'll be good to go. If your lion tamer decides to stick a guest's head inside the lion's mouth, don't worry. It's probably safe. Well, maybe consider using a guest you don't really like too much, just in case.

Remember, hiring the lion is not quite as simple as hiring the tamer. You will most likely need to transport, feed, and clean up after your rented three-hundred-pound entertainment.

How to Be the Most Interesting Person at a Party

I'm not saying that I'm the most interesting person at a party, nor has anyone hired me to teach them how to be (I try not to read too much into this). But because I plan so many parties, I've not only seen interesting, I've been studying interesting people for years, and I think I've got it down. Someday, maybe I'll actually give it a try.

First thing I noticed pretty consistently is that the most interesting people wear clothing that is designed to draw people's attention (an anthropologist might call this "peacocking"). This doesn't necessarily mean they look *good*, mind you; it means they look *odd*, or unusual. This kind of outfit compels people to talk to them, if only to ask what they're wearing and why. If you decide to try this, don't feel that you need an entire crazy ensemble; just one item that's out of the ordinary, like a cowboy hat or a feather boa, should do the trick. When people ask why you're wearing it, have an equally odd line prepared, something like "Oh, my dentist gave it to me." The response should be completely confusing, and it shouldn't answer the question at all. If you have an answer for everything but your answers make no sense, people will want to keep talking to you for as long as it takes to figure you out.

Which leads to the next thing about interesting people—they don't do the typical. For whatever reason, interesting people scope out the wall-flowers or people whom others don't seem to be paying attention to, then wander over and start asking questions. This interesting technique enables them to become more interesting as they are spending time listening to the people others don't know anything about. Yes, interesting people are interested. Remember that and you're almost guaranteed a spot on the interesting list.

Another thing interesting people do is always come prepared with conversational topics. Most books and websites would probably advise you to bone up on current events before a party, and to not only be up-to-date on the major things happening in the world, but also to have an opinion on them. I disagree. Think about what people *really* talk about most at parties. Sex, relationships, and pop culture, certainly not politics and other such sticky matters (unless perhaps you're at a political fund-raiser or live in Washington, D.C.). So instead of scouring the op-ed pages and trying to parrot back what you read (which won't impress any-one, anyway, since all the other guests probably did the exact same thing), watch late-night TV. Pick your favorite host, and watch his or her mono-logue (the first seven or eight minutes is all you really need) from the past week. If you run in worldly circles and think some topics from the head-lines might come up, just add *The Daily Show* or *The Colbert Report* to your viewing lineup. These shows offer some of the wittiest opinions and sharpest satire on television, and they're almost guaranteed to clue you in to another side of the week's top stories. Armed with Jon's and Stephen's opinions, you can talk insightfully about any current event that comes up at the party, while still keeping the tone lighthearted.

Finally, always come prepared with two or three great anecdotes about yourself—preferably ones involving sex or relationships. These are your standbys, and they don't need to change (unless you go to parties with the same people over and over again, in which case you should mix it up). The stories should be general enough that you can find an easy way to work them into almost any topic of conversation, and funny enough that people will remember them—and perhaps ask you to tell another. If your stories are good enough, and you milk them for all they're worth, you'll have a large crowd eating out of your hand for hours.

Some interesting people tell jokes, usually dirty ones, but not everyone can pull this off (and some crowds will be more receptive than others), so proceed with caution.

But look, being interesting is not for everyone; a lot of prep time and patience goes into being *really* interesting. The easiest way to be the most interesting person at the party is simply to go to uninteresting parties with uninteresting people. But then again, that's not very interesting.

How to Sponsor a Parade

Do you love a parade? Well, if for whatever reason you want to set one up, hopefully so do all your neighbors. They should, seeing as parades build community and encourage civic engagement. But before you go all Macy's Thanksgiving on them, you're going to need to get a permit.

Permits for parades take a little time to get, so the further out you can plan, the better. Two months, possibly more, would be best, depending on your local ordinances. Generally, the larger or more elaborate (floats? fireworks? acrobats?) the parade, the longer you'll need to wait for approval. And while you're at it, get a permit for an alternate date as well—in case the weather is not cooperative.

Here's where things can get tricky. Although most places will let you fill out (or at least print) the permit application online, depending on where you live, there could be several different possible authorities in charge of approving them, and this has to happen in person. Start with the local police department (the *non*emergency number)—chances are someone there will be able to tell you with certainty exactly who you need to contact to get a permit. Other possible contacts include your local Department of Parks and Recreation and the local chamber of commerce.

I once looked into this for someone in Aspen, Colorado. Now, Aspen is a town that celebrates everything. It hosts amazing fireworks more than once a year, and the whole town comes out for the annual Fourth of July parade. Since it's a tourist town, some locals thought it would be a great idea to have a "local's day parade." (*Note:* Being a "local" is a subjective thing in Aspen; anyone who visits a lot usually thinks they are a local, but ask a local, they'll beg to differ. If you want to fool them, see "How to Make People Think You're a Local Even If You're a Tourist," page 46.) So I looked into the details for the parade. First, you need to rank the size of your event—major, minor, or moderate. Then, you need to submit an application to the special events coordinator at least thirty days prior for a minor event (*minor* meaning fewer than five hundred people for a day or less) and sixty days in advance for a moderate event (up to thirty-five hundred people, including street closure). For a large event, (anything over thirty-five hundred people and/or spanning multiple days), ninety days' notice is needed.

Once you've filled out the application (get some coffee for this, they're pretty lengthy), you'll have to pay the fees, which will depend on the type of application you're submitting and your plans for the parade.

Next, your permit is reviewed. It might be approved immediately, or you might have to get further permits from other departments, depending on what's involved with your event. Simpler (small crowd, no streets sealed off, no alcohol) always costs less (but will also be less fun), so before applying, figure out if you really need the twelve-foot-tall Abominable Snowman float that shoots fire. The permits only get you permission; then it's up to you to *make* your parade come to life!

Remember: You don't just need people to be *in* the parade for it to be successful—you'll need spectators as well! So once you've got your approvals, go with a theme and then pull together a work group to start rallying the troops. You'll want to get the schools involved (if you get the kids in on the fun, you get the parents, too, and all of a sudden the crowd starts to grow). Then, break out the costumes and start promoting!

Sadly, the locals in Aspen let the red tape rain on their parade and they never pulled it off, but who knows, one of these days they may just make it happen. It can be a lot of work to organize a parade, but it's well worth it, so march on!

How to Install a Bowling Alley in Your Basement

Most people underestimate the popularity of bowling. Did you know that there are over 100 million bowlers worldwide? Or that it is one of the oldest sports around and that bowling pins date as far back as the ancient Egyptians, over fifty-two hundred years ago! Then again, it shouldn't really come as much of a surprise. Who doesn't enjoy the thrill of watching a bowling ball sail down the center of the lane and hearing that satisfying crash as it knocks all ten pins down. The only thing that could make bowling more fun is having it happen from the privacy of your own home. What would be better than having your own bowling alley? Instant entertainment and exercise, right there in your basement.

There are a few options for at-home bowling. Before we get to the more involved of these choices, you might ask yourself, what about Wii bowling? It's relatively inexpensive, fun, and you won't have to tear apart the house to play. But still, it's not the same and you know it. So, if you can get over the visions of the last scene in *There Will be Blood*, you just may be ready for an in-home bowling alley.

Now you'll need two things: (1) a large home you don't mind ripping up, and (2) a bunch of spare cash. No problem, right? When I say "large," I'm not kidding: you'll need a minimum of a hundred feet in length and fourteen feet in width for two lanes, and installers suggest a ceiling height of fourteen feet. Of course, that doesn't even count the underground trench that will be required if you want a ball-return system installed. And when I say "spare cash," I'm talking $45,000 to $50,000.

If you've got the space and the dough, you'll need to find a professional company to install it, because unless you're Bob Vila, this is not a DIY project. Bowling Equipment (www.murreybowling.com) and United Bowling (www.unitedbowling.com) are known to be the best, and their websites have a variety of photos so you can see what the final installation will look like. United Bowling even has a preinstallation guide, which will tell you what to check on ahead of time. Most companies can also send someone to assess your situation and figure out what's possible to build. If you're going to make the investment, you may as well get it right, so let someone who knows what he's doing in on the game.

But here's the fun part—you can re-create everything you like about actual bowling alleys (like electronic scoreboards) and leave out the things you don't fancy (like those hideous shoes). You won't just be paying for a lane in which to bowl, you'll be creating an entire *experience* in your basement, right down to the beer and black lights. Plus, it's great for parties, and you may just bump your social status to the kingpin of your block.

How to Make a Grand Gesture —In Skywriting

How do you say happy birthday to the man who has everything?

Vintage wine and classic old cars and singers in costumes had all been done before. Yes, my client's beau was *that* kind of birthday boy. This year, he would be celebrating with his closest (a hundred or so) friends on the beach and they were stumped for a gift, so it was up to us to come up with something "original." Then, we got it. Just as the Superman cake was served, someone yelled "It's a bird, it's a plane . . ." and pointed to the sky, where his own personal happy birthday message had magically appeared. It was well received by all, especially, the guest of honor.

When you want to send a powerful message, nothing beats the ease of e-mail, or the pleasure of a handwritten letter. But if drama and flair is what you're after, it's hard to compete with skywriting. Remember how the Wicked Witch of the West in *The Wizard of Oz* famously scrawled her own smoke message, "Surrender Dorothy," as she swooped across the Emerald City on her broomstick? It worked for her, but the less self-propelled among us will need to do a little more planning.

Believe it or not, there's more than one way to send a message via skywriting. The cheaper and easier option is to have your words emblazoned on a banner and hire a pilot to tow it from the back of a plane like a streamer. The more dramatic (but more costly) alternative is to go the Wicked Witch route to express yourself. Traditional skywriting involves a single plane, looping through the sky emitting smoke in a controlled way to form words (usually it can only write words of six letters or less because the smoke fades so quickly, which is bad news for those would-be grooms proposing to girlfriends with exceptionally long names). For those with bigger budgets, there's digital skywriting, which involves five to seven planes flying parallel and at equal distances from each other, like a typewriter ribbon moving across a page. The word may not look quite as pretty—think block letters rather than cursive—but can often be longer (around twenty characters) and stretch farther (around five to eight miles) than the traditional form.

This really isn't a do-it-yourself kind of thing, so unless you happen to be an incredibly skilled pilot (think Tom Cruise, as in *Top Gun* skilled pilot), you're going to have to hire a professional. Finding companies that offer skywriting services, especially of the smoky variety, can be harder than you think, but the site www.manta.com offers a list of fifty-one aerial advertising companies across the United States, who would be just as willing to broadcast your marriage proposal as they would your advertising copy.

Warning: Although you can expect to pay less for banners than for cloud writing, the bill for either can be as much as several thousand dollars, depending on the length of the message, how often you'd like it repeated, and how far the plane will be required to fly to get to you. If you do decide to go ahead with it, be mindful of where and when you want your aerial art performed. If you live in an area that tends to be overcast, this may not be your medium. Skywriting generally needs clear skies and light winds of no more than three to five miles per hour. September and October are ideal months, although colder months can work too.

It's not easy to pull off, but the payoff may be priceless. After all, who could ignore a message that's written fifty-two hundred feet in the air and is visible for a seven- to eight-mile radius?

7. seemingly impossible

How to Get Your Guy to Ask for Directions

For a guy, the process of asking for directions is pretty close to the five stages of grieving. First, denial; he's not lost, he knows *exactly* where he's going. Then, anger: "Stop asking if we're lost, you're distracting me!" Then comes bargaining: "If we don't see the exit in twenty miles, I'll stop and ask." That's followed by depression, as indicated by his icy silence. Finally, acceptance, as he pulls over, asks for directions, and finds out you're somewhere in Canada.

But if you don't have the time (or patience) to let your man go through these phases, here are a few tactics to get him to ask for those directions *before* you unintentionally cross an international border.

Remember the first rule of thumb for convincing a guy to do something: make him think it's *his* idea. So instead of "Why don't you pull over and ask for directions," try "Do you think this map is right?" That should be just enough of a nudge to plant the seed of the idea in his head. Plus, if it's a problem with the map, not him, he's more likely to seek out confirmation.

If he doesn't take that bait, you can use plenty of other tricks to get him to ask for assistance. Keep giving him liquids like water, coffee, or Gatorade so he has to pull over at a gas station to use a bathroom. If he's already stopped the car, he's more likely to ask someone for help (or you can dash into the station while he's in the john and ask for directions yourself). Also, if you can control your travel schedule, make sure you're on the road on a day when something *he* wants, like a Yankees game or poker night, is waiting at the destination. If he's really in a hurry to get home, he'll do whatever he can to find his way. And if it's not game night, there's always the promise of a hot night at home to motivate him, so casually mention how much you were looking forward to the ride of a different kind you're planning to give him if you make it back at a reasonable hour.

Don't *ever* try to navigate. He either won't listen, or he'll do the opposite. You might try a little reverse psychology here, like urging him to go left when the correct turn is right, but be warned, this can backfire. Plus, no one likes a backseat driver.

Another tactic is to make someone else the messenger. Fake a phone call from someone who'd know how to get there and casually mention where you are on the road. Then turn to your husband and say something like "Patrick says we're not where we should be," and give him the directions from your "friend" (aka the GPS on your phone). The same thing can work at a rest stop—just pretend like you had a conversation with someone in the ladies' room and she said you're totally lost.

If all else fails, just drug him and take the wheel. When he wakes up at your destination rested and on time, he'll (probably) thank you.

How to Solve a Rubik's Cube (in Under a Minute)

For most people, the word *cubism* brings to mind the work of Picasso. For some, though, it conjures up images of that maddeningly addictive childhood toy, the Rubik's Cube. You may not have seen one of these since your third-grade science fair, but believe it or not, I know plenty of otherwise sane adults who still lose sleep over that deceptively simple thirty-year-old puzzle.

If you're tempted to cut corners, good luck. There are, of course, hundreds of websites, including www.puzzlesolver.com and www.rubiks solver.com, which take you through various steps toward the solution. YouTube even has several videos demonstrating solutions. But with literally billions of possible configurations, taking the easy way out still involves a significant investment of your time and energy. Plus, it's not nearly as satisfying, right?

So assuming you can resist the urge to cheat, now what? First, study your enemy. Know its form, its structure, and its anatomy. The cube is made up of twenty-six smaller cubes, including a dozen two-colored edge pieces, eight tricolored corner pieces, and six center pieces. The center pieces don't move, so they establish the color of that side . . . it can be hard to get your head around, but knowing this is critical. Taking apart the cube will help you understand this concept better and prevent you from trying to make impossible moves like attempting to put an edge piece in the corner. On top of that, you must contend with different parts of the cube, including faces (sides) and layers (top, middle, and bottom rows).

Get to know your cube intimately. Once you're more comfortable and familiar with what you're dealing with, you'll need to understand algorithms (also called "move sequences"). Don't let the large word bring back memories of high school trig class and scare you away; algorithms are just combinations of moves used to get a piece where you want it to go.

Memorizing a few common algorithms will make it easier for you to solve the cube quickly. You can learn these algorithms from websites (maybe it's okay to cheat—um, I mean educate yourself—just a little) . . . so to get started, first learn the lingo.

Cube junkies have coined their own "cube terminology" to communicate a sequence of moves, using letters to identify the faces of the cube (F for front [the side you're looking at], B for Back, L/R for Left/Right, and U/D for Up/Down) and using symbols to indicate the type of turn (no mark means a clockwise turn, ' [the apostrophe] indicates a counterclockwise turn and " [the quotation mark] or 2 [the number two] is used for two turns). These terms are put together into a notation that represents the move sequences. For example, a single sequence might look something like F D F' D' R' D' R. If you spend long enough with these letters, I'm sure you can come up with alternative words that these letters represent. And, who knows, a new mantra may help you speed through the cube to a solution.

After you've mastered some basic sequences, start building up speed. Solving a Rubik's Cube is essentially a matter of trial and error, and the faster you go, the more sequences you can try. Practicing like a fiend helps, as does a lot of patience and concentration. As you begin to master the sequences, it will be easier to learn patterns that signal the next move sequence.

If you're confused by all of this, you can learn several simpler methods, including: the block method, the corners-first method, or the most common method, a layer-by-layer approach, which starts by forming a cross. Learn these and you can work your way into the more detailed variations. A few techniques you can study to help you get faster are the Fridrich, Petrus, and Roux methods (all easy to find on Google).

If you get really into it, there's still more fun to be had even once you've solved the puzzle: "speed cubing" as it's called, is a world unto itself, with its own websites, competitions, rankings, and records. The current record holder, according to the World Cube Association that governs competitions for all puzzles labeled as Rubik puzzles, can solve that sucker in just over seven seconds. So go on, get twisting!

If all else fails, and you think you'll be able to live with yourself after, consider buying an extra set of stickers and placing them strategically over the existing stickers (or taking the cube apart and rearranging the pieces correctly). Hey, maybe you won't prove to yourself that you have a beautiful mind, but at least you'll be able to convince some of the people, some of the time.

How to Say No

"Would you like another piece of fruitcake?"

"Can you help me move this Saturday?"

"Can you train the new intern?"

"Can you organize the bake sale again?" "Drive me to the station?" "Cat-sit?" "Come out for drinks after work (for the third night in a row)?"

Maybe you're the type who feels good about doing things for other people. Or maybe you worry that saying no will hurt the other person's feelings. Or maybe it's just a matter of pride. If someone asks you to do something—say, volunteer at your kids' school, or take on an extra project at work—the reason has to be because you are valued, because they think no one can do it as well as you. Right?

Well, no.

Whatever your reason, saying yes when every fiber in your being is screaming "No!" doesn't do anyone any good in the long run. Think about it. If you really don't have time to train that intern on top of your regular duties at work, and deep down you resent being asked, the intern won't get a good training. Or if you don't really feel like going out for drinks after work (again), you won't be good company, and both you and your friend will have a terrible time. Remember, try as you might, you'll never please all of the people all of the time, and it's frighteningly easy to forget about pleasing yourself at all. The more you say yes when you want to say no, the harder the habit can be to break—and the closer you'll be to a breakdown. You might think you're being nice, but don't discount the fact that people may be taking advantage of your "good nature" (otherwise known as "lack of backbone"). Some people are very good at recognizing a sucker in their midst. Don't let that sucker be you.

So if you're a yes man (or more likely a yes woman, since for whatever reason, women seem to have a harder time with this), it's time to start training yourself to say no. This could take a little time. The first thing you need to do is get into the habit of never responding to any request right away. It doesn't matter what the request is, your immediate answer should be "let me get back to you." Why? Think about all the times you've agreed to do something because you felt pressured to give an answer on the spot, only to kick yourself for it fifteen minutes later. It's time to eliminate this pressure. Depending on the time frame and urgency of the request, give yourself anywhere from an hour (unless someone is on fire, no request is so urgent that it can't wait an hour) to a week (for the really big decisions) to get back to them. This will not only stop you from blurting out those knee-jerk yeses, it will give you a little time to stop and think what was asked of you and decide if this request is worthwhile, or a complete waste of your time and energy.

If you aren't sure, one way of gauging whether something is too much of a sacrifice is to imagine someone just made this same request of your best friend. What would you suggest *she* do? Most of us would never let our best friends overcommit or get pushed around. If you wouldn't let her say yes, why let yourself?

The next step in deciding what your answer should be is to take stock of your priorities. You might think you know what these are—for example: family first, then your own health, your friends, your home, then your job, your hobbies, and finally the community at large. But it's useful to stop and rank those priorities if you haven't for a while. Write them down. Have you been devoting more time to raising money for the new library but making it to yoga class less and less frequently? If your activities are at cross-purposes with your priorities, it's time to start saying no to the things that are tripping you up.

Still, even once you've made up your mind to say no to something, it can be hard to actually get the words out. I understand, really. But get over it. You don't have to say no the way a two-year-old would. There are a variety of polite methods to employ. "I'd love to, but I have another commitment already" is a good one. Or, "I'm sorry, I just can't right now." Remember, you don't have to describe why not. This may take some practice, but you should restrain from saying why you are saying no, or making up any type of excuse. No means no, remember that. You have your reasons, and they should be respected. Plus, it's a much more powerful no if you leave your reasons vague; if your excuse is too specific, it will be easier for the person to poke holes in or argue with it. Let people believe whatever it is they want to believe; it's better to keep 'em guessing.

Of course, you don't have to say no to everything. But the truth is, it's healthy to say no now and then. Try it out and see how good it feels. "No, I will not babysit your two-year-old twins tonight." See, felt good, right? Now light some candles, draw a bath, and turn off your phone instead. Should you feel guilty? No.

How to Get Tickets to a Sold-Out Baseball Game

You've been waiting for your team to make it to the playoffs for decades, and *finally*, their time has come. Problem is, fifty thousand other equally devoted fans also want to witness the historic moment live and in person, and tickets are scarce. So what do you do if you can't get a ticket? This dilemma has a number of solutions, but you want to be sure that you stay, you know, "legal."

Let's start with the basics: scalpers. Obviously, you can always find people who want to sell unwanted tickets on www.stubhub.com, Craigslist, or at the actual game. There are two types of scalpers—the first is the "amateur." This is the guy who bought a ticket for his girlfriend and then got dumped, so he's just trying to unload the ticket for what he paid, maybe a few bucks extra. This is who you want to do business with. Generally, the closer it is to the game, the easier it will be to find someone looking to unload the extra ticket for anything he or she can get (even if it's less than what the person paid for it), so if you can live with the uncertainty, try to wait until a few days or even a few hours before the game before purchasing your scalped ticket.

The second type of scalper, who is to be avoided unless you are absolutely *desperate,* is the "pro." This is the guy who buys up tickets he has no intention of using so he can sell them at excessive prices to suckers like you. These guys usually have whole operations online (sometimes they operate their own sites) and they'll also show up at the stadium, where they'll probably approach you and shiftily ask you if you're looking for a ticket. If money is no object, congrats, you've got yourself a ticket. If, however, you're trying to save cash, first figure out what is the most you're willing to pay, then tell the pro that's all the cash you have. If he's desperate enough (and again, the closer to the game, the better the odds—after all, once the game has started, it's worth zero), he'll settle for that.

Word to the wise: If you go the scalper route, be careful. Although there are no federal laws saying scalping is illegal, it is in some states. In addition, other regulations say you can't scalp certain things like NFL tickets or tickets to raceways. Although scalping laws are not always enforced and you probably won't get busted, be sure you know what the laws are in your state so you know what you are getting yourself into if you take the risk.

Another, more law-abiding—and certainly classier—way to get into the game is to see if you or anyone you know works for a company that has a private box or club access. A lot of major companies do, and with this route, it's just a matter of knowing someone who knows someone with enough pull to get you in. Sometimes you'll need to call in your favors, but hey, these kinds of situations are the reason you do favors for other people in the first place.

I'm not necessarily advocating these next two, nor have I done them myself, but I have heard from reliable sources that these methods work.

Say you already have two tickets but want to get a third friend in. Start by selling one of your tickets to your buddy on www.stubhub.com. He'll get an e-mail that can be used as a ticket, leaving the two of you with your other ticket, and the e-mail about the ticket you sold. You and your buddy enter the stadium with these two "real" tickets, and go to the bar, where your hands will be stamped (they always stamp your hands at the bars at sporting events so that you don't have to show your ID every time you order a drink, even if you clearly look over twenty-one). Once you've got the stamp, take one of the valid tickets to a third friend outside, and keep your invalid ticket (the one you sold) crumpled in your pocket, and reenter with him. His ticket will check out, and with your hand stamped, you can probably just wave the crumpled (invalid) ticket and the security guard won't bother to scan it. Complicated, but the best plans always are.

Finally (again, I'm not advocating this), a good old-fashioned bribe can do the trick. If you see a sympathetic-looking (or just apathetic-looking) guard, strike up a conversation and make an offer. Everybody's got a price and if the price is right, there's a good chance he'll let you in.

How to Survive a Weekend Getaway with No Way to Connect

Though it seems like a distant memory now, there was once a time before cell phones. How did we survive? We planned ahead. We followed itineraries. We arranged to meet certain people at certain times in certain places, and then we showed up. Crazy, right? But now that we're used to having a cell phone with us at all times (and used to everyone else we know carrying one, too), we rely on it, and our lives seem to revolve around our mobile device.

So what to do if you suddenly find yourself out of range? Though cell-phone reception is pretty good these days in most places, if you're traveling to a remote area—like camping in the woods, for example—prepare yourself for the reality that you may not have cell service. In such a case, the best thing to do is probably ditch the phone altogether and just make the necessary preparations ahead of time.

If you are going to be off the grid for a while, though, don't forget to turn on your "out of the office message" (you can do this for your personal e-mail account as well). If you use a social networking site like Facebook, you might want to also update your feed to let people know you're gone. It takes a bit more work, but you might also want to change your cell-phone's voice-mail answering machine to let people who call know you're not available for a few days. Just don't forget to change it back when you return to civilization!

Consider investing in a set of walkie-talkies for your group, especially if you'll all be in a contained area like a small town, convention center, or ski slope. They'll work even without cell service, and you can feel cool, like a true undercover agent.

Once you find yourself successfully disconnected from the folks back home, you still may need a way to coordinate meeting times and places with everyone else on your trip. The key to this is to be *specific*. Saying

"We'll meet up at the hotel at 10:00 A.M." isn't enough. Will you be in the lobby? In your room? The most important thing to do is to set very clear meeting times and places just in case you get split up. Sounds like common sense, but you'd be surprised; when we're without our devices, just meeting people can feel like the modern-day version of a scavenger hunt, especially if you have anyone from the "younger set" with you. Yes, there is now a whole generation of people who have *never* had to make a plan to meet someone at an exact time and at a specific place.

If you are the type who has trouble disconnecting, think about finding somewhere remote to go . . . consider it assisted R&R.

How to Get Rid of Morning Sickness

Does the smell of freshly ground coffee—which used to be your reason for living—suddenly make your eyes water and your stomach churn? Does your coworker's once pleasant perfume now seem like an affront to humanity? Do a few bites of your usual morning egg bagel all of a sudden produce fits of nausea that send you running to the ladies' room? In case you can't figure out what's going on, it's highly unlikely that you have a flu bug and you may want to run out and buy a pregnancy test.

If the pregnancy wasn't planned, you have bigger problems than a touch of morning sickness. But if it was, the euphoria about your impending arrival can fade fast once the morning sickness sets in. Some women never get this unfortunate side effect to pregnancy, but most do, and if you've ever been one of them, you know that "morning" has little to do with it. It can strike at any time of the day or night, though it generally favors an important breakfast meeting, or during lunch at a five-star restaurant, or when you're stuck in traffic on the commute home (i.e., the worst possible times). Though most women feel fine by about the thirteenth week of pregnancy, for some unlucky souls, the condition lasts until they go into labor (and then the fun really begins!).

Although there's no real cure for morning sickness, some techniques can help alleviate it. Common strategies include eating small meals throughout the day, taking B_6 supplements and ginger in any form (ginger root, ginger tea, ginger gum, you name it), sniffing peppermint essential oil when you feel the queasies coming on, and trying to eat Saltines or dry toast before even getting out of bed (yes, permission granted to eat carbs, just don't fool yourself into thinking you'll just be purging those starchy calories anyway); morning sickness tends to attack when your stomach is empty (hence the breakfast meeting trouble), so if you get something mild in your belly before starting the day, that first meal might actually stay down.

For the überorganized, keeping a morning sickness journal is not a bad idea. Jot down when you feel as if you're about to toss your cookies (and note if you actually do), and keep track of what you eat and when. You might notice some trends that weren't at first obvious. Write down the foods and smells that make you wish you had never put that bun in the oven in the first place, and keep such odors out of your life until you return to your previous self.

Others swear by acupuncture or wearing Sea Bands, and still others try Preggie Pops and Queasy Drops, available at maternity stores and online. Licorice works well—the real stuff, not the sugary red kind. Or pick up some ajwain seeds at any Indian grocery store and see if that does the trick.

If you think you'll be living with morning sickness for a while but refuse to let it cramp your lifestyle, consider treating yourself to Morning Chicness Bags, the "morning sickness vomit bags for the chic expectant mother" (www.morningchicnessbags.com). And don't be shy about telling your coworker who seems to bathe in Rank Flowers No. 5 to lay off the habit until the baby is born. You're pregnant, and for a little while, you're the Queen of Everything—that means you get to make demands and all nonpregnant people have to heed them, no matter what (you can use this cardinal rule to your advantage in a lot of other ways, but I digress). Most important, just keep reminding yourself the morning sickness won't last forever—and enjoy the fact that at least you're still getting a full night's sleep.

How to Get Rescued from a Desert Island

Read this one carefully, and try to commit it to memory, because chances are that unless you're very, *very* lucky (and if you're stuck on a deserted island in the first place, you're probably not the lucky type), you won't have this book with you when you get stranded. Of course, I hope it never comes to that, but it never hurts to be prepared.

So let's say your plane goes down, or your cruise liner gets shipwrecked (hey, it happened to the *Titanic*) and you manage to swim to the nearest landmass, which obviously will be an island in the middle of nowhere. Now what? These days, airlines and cruise companies track the whereabouts of all their vessels using GPS devices, so unless you're on the island from *Lost*, chances are rescue teams will be able to find you in a timely fashion.

That doesn't mean, however, that you can't try like hell to speed up the rescue process. Start by forgetting every episode of *Gilligan's Island*. They tried it all and nothing ever worked, so quit trying to think like the Professor and focus on the task at hand.

Next, exhaust the obvious solutions: cell phones, radios, or any other kind of communication device. You're on an island and stranded, so I've got to imagine that any electronic devices got wet in the process if they even floated up on shore at all. But still, if any did get washed up with you, lay it out in the sun for a while and see what happens. It's worth a try, and you're likely to have plenty of time on your hands.

Then, find the highest point on the island and go there—the higher you are, the more visible you'll be to any ship or plane that happens by. Next point of order is fire. During the day, smoke (if there is enough of it) can be seen for miles and is sure to attract boats and potentially even aircraft. The drier the material you're burning, like dead branches or pine needles, the blacker the smoke, which means the easier it is to see. But don't just build a fire and stand there. Use a branch or shirt to block and release the smoke, creating smoke signals, which are the universal sign for HELP and your best shot at being discovered quickly (and if that doesn't work, you'll still need a fire to cook fish over and keep you warm while you wait, right?). So practice rubbing two sticks together to get that fire going.

It may take a while, but keep at it. It'll hopefully serve you better than working on your tan.

Another strategy for attracting attention in the daytime is to use a large piece of aluminum or other shiny metal to reflect sunlight. Hopefully, some scraps will have washed up on shore from whatever vessel you were on. Wait until you see a plane or boat, then hold up the metal (the bigger the better) to the sun, Move it back and forth rapidly, so the light bounces around, and hope it is enough to catch someone's eye.

Finally, depending on your supplies, you can also make a sign. The problem with this is that signs must be HUGE to be visible, so try writing in the sand with a large stick. If brightly colored clothes or objects are available, tying them to the tops of tall trees might help draw attention to your message.

Of course, everything is easier when you have a shoulder to cry on, so if you are stranded by yourself, make a friend to talk to. An old volleyball named Wilson saved Tom Hanks from going completely crazy in *Cast Away* (though I hope you'll be rescued sooner than he was), so maybe an old shoe can do the same for you.

How to Recover a Cell Phone

Leaving your cell phone in a cab (or anywhere else) is universally a sure-fire way to put a damper on your day. The *worst* is when you realize it *just* as the cab is pulling away—a second too late for you to catch him. The first reaction for most of us is to panic. It was already a jam-packed day, and now you have to spend the next few hours tracking down your phone . . . but you have no way to make a call or check messages or send a text. You are completely disconnected. Oy.

You can try calling the police, but most likely they'll laugh at you and tell you to get a new phone.

One way to make reclaiming your phone easier (though it will still be annoying) is to get into the habit of always getting a receipt from the cab driver. That's the only way you'll know which cab you were in, so when you call 311 or the cab company, they'll be able to track the driver down. Just remember that most drivers are too busy eating a sandwich and talking on their own cell phone to notice your orphaned phone languishing in the backseat. So more often than not, the next passenger will grab your phone, and (hopefully) contact you, which is better for you, and actually the way you're most likely to locate your missing phone. This is why it's a good idea to program your e-mail address or an alternate phone number into your phone. Some phones will let you do this right on the home screen; if not, enter the info in your address book under "if lost" (or you could enter it under "mom," as that's the number most people who find a lost phone call when they can't locate the owner. Of course, that might get confusing for you when you try to call your mother and instead reach yourself.).

If no one contacts you, the first thing you should do is call your own number and hope someone hears it and picks up. I've had to recover a lot of lost phones for clients and when I do get a phone back it's usually because it was on and someone else answered when I called. Otherwise, I spend the day purchasing and hooking up a new cell phone for the client.

Better safe than sorry. As annoying as it is to have to enter a password every time you want to use your phone, think about setting one. After all, if you ever lose your phone, do you really want some stranger to have access to all the information you keep in there?

How to Lay Off Chocolate

I *can* get just about everything done; that doesn't necessarily mean that I *choose to.* Some things—like laying off chocolate—are just better left undone.

I mean, I can easily find enough studies that will confirm the fact that chocolate is good for you. It's good for your brain, it's good for your moods, it's been linked to reduced risk for all kinds of diseases. And there are even people who say it will keep you slimmer; yes, just eat it before a meal and you'll consume fewer calories during the meal (works for me). Plus, did I mention it's delicious?

So sure, I could tell you how to lay off chocolate (if this is one of your New Year's resolutions, see "How to Keep Your New Year's Resolutions," page 206), but I choose not to. Trust me, it's for your own good.

How to Refuse a Dare

Dares bring back memories of being thirteen and going to coed sleepover parties. What do you play at a coed slumber party (besides Spin the Bottle, of course)? Truth or Dare. At thirteen, it's usually a relatively tame rendition, but Truth or Dare, nonetheless. I can remember I was once dared to let two other people in the room lick my ears at the same time. Eww.

I also remember sitting there, trying to think of a way out. Do I politely refuse? Try to make a joke out of it? Tell them I have a contagious ear rash (though, come to think of it, that might have worked)? Let's be serious, when you're thirteen and given a dare, there *is* no way out. And sadly, the truth is, it's not all that different once you're a grown-up.

So I went through with the dare. And it was kinda gross. But after about five seconds tops, it was over! I got off easy. But some dares can be a lot more painful, embarrassing, or even dangerous, which is why you need a foolproof strategy for how to get out of them without looking like a chicken.

If the dare is quick and relatively painless, like having your ears licked (who even thought of that one?), I suggest you do the same thing I did: just go through with it. A grown-up version of this might be: "I dare you to go ask that guy for his phone number." That same feeling of revulsion might creep up, but really, what's the worst that can happen? If he says yes, you take down the number and never call; if he says no, who cares? The whole thing will be over in sixty seconds. (And if you don't protest, you're likely not going to be the person who is dared the next time. You're no fun, you'll do anything.)

Of course, if this person is the secret love of your life, the dare just got a little scarier. In this case, your best weapon is sarcasm. Something like "Yeah, right, *great* idea, why don't I propose to him while I'm at it." Then change the subject. If you treat the whole thing like a big joke, it might go away quickly.

Or use the distraction method. Bring up some controversial conversation topic—current events or politics work well—and try to get everyone so riled up they forget all about the silly dare. When someone finally remembers, you'll have the perfect opportunity to say, "I'm done with this game, aren't you guys?"

Another option is to turn the dare around on the person who proposed it. If she won't do the thing she's dared you to do, you've cornered her. Just beware: If you use this strategy and someone else actually *does* do it, and then expects you to do it, too, you're in even worse shape than when you started, and you have very few options other than going through with it—or moving out of town.

But really, you're not thirteen anymore, so if the dare is really something you're uncomfortable with, I double dare ya to just man up and say so. You may feel a little lame, and your friends might make fun of you, but honestly if they do, they aren't really your friends in the first place.

How to Get a Dinner Reservation at an Impossibly Overbooked Hot Spot with a Three-Month Waiting List

Most restaurants inhabit a run-of-the-mill culinary abyss filled with lackluster menus, indistinguishable food, and interchangeable dining experiences. But there are always a few eateries, whether by dint of their mouthwatering creations, unique settings, or storied reputations, that stand out from all the chaff and not only survive the cutthroat restaurant business, but thrive.

The problem is, unless you're a celebrity, social A-lister, or friends with the owner, securing a seat in such a luminous hot spot can be a serious undertaking—one that requires considerable, if not eternal, time and patience.

But it can be done. If you're not a "somebody," the best way to assure yourself a table at the newest and trendiest hot spot is to book it three months in advance (by which time it will, of course, no longer be the newest and trendiest hot spot). But what if you want to get in *this Saturday* at 8:00 P.M.? Trickier, but it still can be done. The key is strategy. That, and a little sucking up.

First, try the obvious routes, like adding yourself to the interminable wait list. When you do this, be sure to get the name of the staff member whom you've spoken with. This will enable you to strike a more familiar, intimate first-name chord on the many follow-up calls you'll be making, or at least allow you to name-drop if another person picks up the phone later. Call at least once a day up until the morning of the day you want to visit, and ask if any tables have become available. If not, ask if you can get bumped up to the top of the waiting list. Although the answer will likely be "No, who do you think you are?," it never hurts to ask. Here is where a little groveling goes a long way. Also important is timing. Don't call at a busy hour when no one will have the time or patience to speak with you.

Your best bet for getting off the wait list is going to be snatching up a last-minute cancellation. These usually happen when the host begins confirming reservations for the evening, so start checking in at 4:00 P.M. on the day of, and keep at it.

If you still can't get a table, a bar can be an overlooked backdoor pass to the main show, so ask the staff if they have one and, if so, whether you can reserve a spot there—even if it's not their usual policy. But even if they don't serve dinner at the bar, once you've secured a seat *somewhere,* you're more likely to get reassigned to a table in the main dining area if and when it becomes available.

Also consider stopping by the restaurant to put a face to your name—it's much harder to blow someone off in person than it is over the phone. If they're not freaked out by your obsessive persistence, they may just be impressed enough by your dedication to at least put you ahead of other walk-ins. Plus, peeking inside the door gives you a chance to point out any open tables.

The greater your flexibility, the more likely you are to land a reservation. That might mean taking the 10:00 P.M. slot, even if it isn't your ideal hour to be settling down to Moroccan cigars and chicken tangine. And show up at least thirty minutes early. Fancy places tend to pad the schedule and can run ahead, so you'll have a good chance of grabbing an earlier slot if you're already there.

Don't dismiss the idea of slipping the hostess some cash. Everyone has his or her price, even if the person doesn't want to admit it. With a little practice you can learn how to make a handshake look natural, even elegant, while slipping a bill in almost undetected.

One thing I would *not* recommend is sneaking a look at the reservations list and using someone else's name. This *never* works, particularly at a nice place, and you run the risk of being called out in front of your dinner companions.

If you insist upon being underhanded (and are prepared to suffer the consequences), consider using a little white lie method. Call up the restaurant, and if you want a reservation for 8:00 P.M., say "I'm calling to change my reservation from 7:30 to 8:00." Of course, they won't be able to find your 7:30 reservation, since you never had one, and this is when the outrage should begin (this one is better over the phone than when you are standing there with all your friends in tow).

What do they mean they can't find your name on the list? You made this reservation weeks ago (or months ago). Don't let up. Tell them this is your anniversary, or birthday dinner, or other special event. How can you possibly reschedule it now? Or that your companion, who is a food critic, local journalist, or high-profile blogger (dining under a fake name, of course), has been looking forward to this dinner for a long time. They probably won't buy it, but if you're lucky, they'll decide it's not worth the argument and will squeeze you in.

And don't worry: You're not screwing someone else out of a table. I've made enough reservations for VIPs to know that every restaurant keeps a few tables unreserved for "emergencies" like this. Plus, they can easily add an extra table to the dining area if they know about it before the dinner rush. Trust me. If they really want to, they'll find you a seat.

Best method of all: If you know any famous people (or someone who *looks* like a famous person), invite him or her to dinner. You'll get a table instantly, and the chef might even send over some goodies.

How to Get Rid of the Last Five Pounds

Why does shedding the last few pounds always seem to take the longest? And why, even if you do manage to get rid of them, are they always so quick to return? Being so close to your goal can be as detrimental as it is inspiring. It's easy to start slipping up—snacking unnecessarily, skipping the gym, and so on—because you're *so close* that it seems OK and you can easily rationalize that "you deserve it."

Obviously, you should still stick to your diet or exercise regimen, because regardless of how close you are to your goal, you're not there yet. You wouldn't quit running a marathon when you were five miles away from the finish line, would you? Plus, you were the one who set the goal in the first place. I'm guessing you chose that goal for a reason so don't move the goalpost.

If getting rid of those last five pounds is an issue for you, you've probably heard all the typical things, like make healthy eating a lifestyle change, not a diet, or get a great trainer or a workout buddy to get you to the gym. But since sticking with a diet and exercise regimen is mostly mental, I have an additional strategy: trick yourself. If you want to lose fifteen pounds, set your goal at twenty pounds. It's kind of like setting your clock five minutes ahead to fool yourself into leaving the house on time in the morning. Sure, you might know deep down you're not kidding anyone, but it can still be a powerful motivator, especially at first. If you think about it, it's really a win/win—if you lose the fifteen, you'll still be pushing to get to twenty, but if those five won't budge, you still reached your "real" goal.

And hey, what if it's all in your mind? If you keep telling yourself that you need to "lose" five pounds, the second they're gone, your brain will look to find them. So instead of looking to lose the pounds, look to reach your optimal weight.

Another trick you may have heard is to buy an article of clothing that you really love but in a size that you won't be able to fit into until you reach your goal. To be even more motivated, make the item expensive, tear the tags off right away so you can't exchange it for a bigger size, and hang it somewhere that you see it every day staring at you . . . just waiting to be worn.

Or, try this: Hide your car keys from yourself for a week to force yourself to walk everywhere. Then take the money you save on gas, and put it toward a new pair of sneakers. You might find you enjoy walking so much, you'll continue to do it after the week is over.

Still can't get yourself moving? How about buying a Nintendo Wii? These have plenty of fun games that also provide a great workout, including WiiFit, a straightforward fitness game or a game like Dance Dance Revolution. Of course, this shouldn't *replace* your normal exercise routine; it should supplement it. As an added bonus, if you have kids, it's a fun thing you can do with them. Not into working out indoors? If you are serious about making a real, lasting lifestyle change, take more drastic measures and move somewhere it's easy to take up a sport, like California or Colorado. Take a look around at how fit everyone is before you choose your destination.

Finally, if those last stubborn pounds just refuse to come off, consider that maybe it's because you didn't need to lose them in the first place—you're already at your ideal weight! Refreshing, isn't it?

How to Get on a Reality Show

Think it's time for your fifteen minutes of fame? Or just looking to make a little extra cash? You're in luck. There have never been so many reality shows—requiring so little talent—on the air. So if it's your moment to shine, there's sure to be a show that's just waiting for you. Still, for the more popular shows, the competition to get on them can be fierce, so here are some tips to help you secure yourself a spot.

For talent-based shows, like *American Idol* or *Top Chef,* networks hold open auditions, or casting calls, in many major cities. All you need to do is find out where and when (if they don't announce the audition details on the show, check the show's official website or www.realitywanted.com to find out casting info) and bring your "A" game when you show up. For other shows that don't involve some sort of on-air talent (which is most of them, unless you call getting drunk and hooking up talent), you'll need to fill out a paper application and make an audition video. Info for these applications can be found on the network's website.

The tough part is not so much finding where and how to audition, but figuring out how to ensure that you get picked once you do. Think back to every reality show you've seen—who stands out? Was it the guy who was polite and relatable? No, it was probably the crazy lunatic who threw a vase of flowers at someone. This is because reality shows are looking for one thing: drama. The people who stand out to producers are those who seem likely to cause trouble on the show. This is not to say that *all* reality contestants are crazy, or that you should chuck heavy objects at someone during the audition, but they definitely skew that way, so if you appear to be a loose-enough cannon that the producers think you *might* go a little nuts, it can only help your chances for being chosen.

This is not to say you shouldn't be yourself when you audition (unless you are boring, in which case, don't even bother auditioning), but that when answering questions on the application or in your video, you should try to be as provocative as possible. Often, how you phrase your answer can say a lot more about you than your answer itself. For example, if one of the questions is "Are there foods you won't eat?," don't just give the polite answer and say "I'm fine with anything other than broccoli." Say something like "I will vomit if someone even shows me a *picture* of broccoli." The more laid-back and even-tempered you seem, the less chance you have of standing out.

On the other hand, it's dangerous to go *too* crazy, because producers don't want the legal hassle of putting someone violent or dangerous on their show. So you might want to refrain from saying something like, "I will punch someone in the face if they even show me a picture of broccoli." Just think quirky and opinionated, and steer clear of creepy or violent.

Your personal story is also important. Imagine your life is a movie—how would you sell it to make it more interesting? You don't have to lie, just choose your anecdotes carefully. Stories about deep personal conflicts or unusual relationships or upbringings will make you pop out at producers, who want people from clashing backgrounds.

Last, looks are important too. You don't have to be a supermodel, but don't roll out of bed and film your video—get a little gussied up. Again, producers are looking for people who will attract attention (and that audiences will want to watch), and the better looking (or at least more interesting looking) you are, the better your odds are of being chosen.

Before you audition, put some serious thought into whether you really want to be on the show. Being in the spotlight can be fun and all, but do you really want all your flaws and insecurities exposed in front of a national audience? Plus, reality TV fame is fleeting, and if it's a serious acting career you're after, a spot on a reality show could actually work against you. Just because you show you can cry on camera doesn't mean you'll get cast in the next Merchant Ivory flick.

How to Get an Autograph from a Reclusive Celebrity (Without Ending Up with a Restraining Order)

Celebrities are just like the rest of us, in that they have a right to their privacy. At the same time, fame comes with glamour, glitz, and admirers. And admirers want autographs. Yet many celebrities bristle at any interaction with fans, when really, they got what they wanted: to be rich and famous. So now why shouldn't you get what you want: an autograph?

In case you ever find yourself within stalking distance of George Clooney, here are some tips on how to get your much coveted autograph. First, be subtle and inconspicuous. Whatever you do, don't draw attention to the celeb. You'd be surprised how good many famous people are at keeping a low profile. I know, I've traveled with some well-known personalities and as long as they keep their security a fair distance away, put on the big glasses, and throw their hair up or put a cap on, they can pretty easily go incognito. So even if you do recognize someone, you may be the only person in the vicinity who does so, and if that's the case, the superstar would probably prefer to keep it that way. If he or she wanted to be spotted, the person would lose the big glasses, wig, and trench coat, don'tcha think?

So screaming "OHMYGODIT'SBRADPITT" is exactly what *not* to do. An "of the moment" personality is much more likely to sign something for you if you casually and quietly approach him and politely say, "I hate to interrupt, but I'm just a really big fan and I'd really love an autograph."

The key is to act natural and treat Brad like a normal person. Pretend you're asking a random stranger on the corner for the time, rather than an international megastar for his John Hancock. Just don't get *too* comfortable. One mistake many autograph hounds make is trying to become the celebrity's best friend. Don't try and make idle chitchat or ask too many questions about their current or past projects. Just get in there, say a nice word or two, get the autograph, and leave him or her alone. Think low-key and low profile. It takes a celebrity about a second to decide whether you're a rabid and annoying psycho, or a respectful and quiet admirer. And make sure you have a pen and paper ready—nothing will make things more awkward than having to ask a passerby for either.

If you have a child, now would be a good time to put him or her to use. It's much harder to say no to someone who tells you her six-year-old is a big fan, especially when said six-year-old is staring up at the celebrity with those big saucerlike eyes.

If the celebrity is truly reclusive and you don't foresee a face-to-face meeting, the mail is always another option. Like an in-person meeting, simplicity is the name of the game. If you enclose a respectful (and short!) letter requesting an autograph for you or a loved one (who, depending on how comfortable you feel "bending" the truth, may or may not be terminally ill and may or may not have requested the autograph as her dying wish) and include a self-addressed stamped envelope, you've made the whole process as painless as possible for the celebrity. I've worked as an assistant for several celebrities, and they will usually set aside time to sign photos for fans; they know it's just part of the job. Your best bet is to send the request to the person's assistant or manager; you might have to wait a little longer, but eventually your request will get in front of the star.

Whether in person or by mail, a good tactic to use when making a request is to tell celebrities how much you loved one of their lesser-known works. So instead of telling Brad Pitt how much you loved him in *Mr. and Mrs. Smith,* tell him how much you admired his work in *Kalifornia* or *Twelve Monkeys.* It may sound odd, but it's more flattering to hear compliments about something most people have forgotten. Plus, it will show how knowledgeable you are of his work.

Another, effective, if slightly more involved approach is to get involved with a charity that you know your hero supports. Then once you've contributed some time and money, ask someone how you would go about getting an autograph.

Whatever you do, don't stalk. Waiting outside a celebrity's house is in fact stalking. Following the person to the gym is stalking. Hanging out at the Starbucks you know a star frequents is borderline stalking. Just be cool, low-key, and uncreepy and you're likely to get that autograph.

Photos of yourself with the star are the new autograph; just assure them you're not going to post the pic on your Facebook page. And if they still refuse, Photoshop can work wonders.

How to Get 1,000,000 Hits on YouTube

Millions of videos exist in that vast sea that is the Internet, and the ones that go viral seem to be completely random and have very little in common (other than being outrageous and entertaining). So how can you make yours one of them? First off, know that the videos that go viral on YouTube and other sites are those that are *original* and unexpected—something most people have never seen before, which, unfortunately, means there's no model to follow. So you'll have to come up with something unique on your own.

Even if your video is original and utterly hilarious, that doesn't necessarily guarantee it will become an overnight sensation. If you think viral videos become viral magically, just by virtue of their content, think again. But this is where you can help yourself. Almost anything that's ever received 1,000,000 hits has been shamelessly promoted—that's the only way to get it noticed in the first place. If the content is not *worthy* of 1,000,000 views, promotion can only go so far, and you'll eventually hit a dead end. Still, I'd have to imagine that countless entertaining, shocking, and sidesplitting videos have gone unnoticed because the person who posted it didn't know how (or wasn't willing) to get the word out and kick-start the viral campaign.

Though there are no guidelines for content, you'd be wise to follow one important stylistic rule: Keep it *short*. No one wants to watch anything more than sixty seconds or so, and some of the most successful online videos are one minute or less.

The easiest way to start your viral campaign is to use social networking websites like Facebook, MySpace, Twitter (if you're not on them, now is the time to join). Post the video to your profile or feed, but don't stop there. Add your video link to other people's walls or feeds and include personal messages encouraging them to go watch. If it's only on your profile, only your friends will be able to see it, but if you post it on other people's profiles, your friends and *their* friends will see it, and even if a small percentage forwards it on to others, the chain will continue to grow.

Next, try posting your video to sites like Digg (www.digg.com) and Buzz (www.buzz.yahoo.com), which are like news feeds for everything on the Internet, sorted by popularity. The more votes your video gets, the higher it will rise on these sites, and you'll see the snowball effect start to occur. The more views you get, the more votes you'll get. To get that cycle started, encourage your friends to "digg" or "buzz" your video; and after that, if your video is indeed worthy, it will continue rising.

If you really want to make this happen (and don't mind spamming your friends), you should also e-mail it to everyone in your address book, and maybe even promote it on any listservs and online groups you are a part of.

Then there are of course the old-fashioned, off-line ways to promote. College campuses are great places to do this. Consider making flyers and passing them around campus, just to get the buzz going. Of course, the flyer must also be clever and compelling enough that people will actually remember to look up the video once they're back at their computers.

Obviously, getting celebrity endorsements also works wonders, so you may need to get to know some influencers or their agents. Hey, if you can get Paris Hilton to guest star in your clip, you'll be on the fast track to 1,000,000 in no time.

Quick tip: To get to 1,000,000 hits, a *lot* of people you know are going to need to see the video, so use your grandma as a gauge. If you wouldn't want your grandma to see what you're posting, don't share it with the world, or it may come back to haunt you later.

Only with a combination of entertaining, original content, and a fair amount of hard work to publicize your video can it become viral and get to 1,000,000 hits. If it *does* become that popular, you might also think about transferring it to a site like www.Revver.com, which pays you a few cents per view (this can add up to thousands of dollars with enough hits). If you did all that work, you might as well get some cash out of it, right?

Here's a general rule of thumb: Think about the things you would do if you were running for office, and then shamelessly use the same techniques to get the word out about your video—networking, endorsements, people campaigning; you get the gist. If you do these well, your following will continue to grow and grow, and someday people may even vaguely remember you as an Internet phenomenon.

How to Get Back a Lost Wallet

Recovering a lost wallet at—of all places—Disneyland seemed like a Sisyphean task if ever there was one. But that's exactly what I found myself doing a few years ago when a client I was strolling down Main Street with realized he was traveling a little bit lighter than he had been in Critter Country. For at least an hour, the Magic Kingdom lost its sparkle as we frantically looked everywhere for the missing wallet—under benches, in public bathrooms, even in the flower beds lining the amazingly litter-free sidewalk.

In this case, we got lucky. We eventually—and somewhat miraculously—located it untouched, at the lost and found, where it had been safely recovered and returned by a security guard. But in instances where luck isn't on your side, the first key to the retrieval of a lost item is simple: creativity. And by that I mean brainstorm every possible path that your rogue item may have traveled, and go down them all. Cast your mind back. Where have you been? What route have you taken? Write it down. It sounds obvious, but it's vital to think clearly in the face of impending panic if you want to construct a clear time line and avoid needless backtracking. The second key is persistence. Lose your cell phone in a cab? Call every dispatch station in the area. Lose your car keys at the mall? Call mall security, as well as every store you so much as stepped foot into. Ask to speak to the people who were working/on duty at the time you were there, and if they are already gone for the day, get their cell phone numbers. Be shameless. Ask the manager to use the loud speaker, and if that doesn't help, insist on coming in and doing your own search. No matter where you lost the item, you'll always do a more thorough search than the people who work there and have nothing to gain from its recovery. That said, if you can't go back and look for it yourself, do the next best thing and offer a reward for the finder.

Prevention is, of course, always better than a cure. So if you are prone to misplacing your wallet, or just paranoid about doing so, keep a tracking device in your wallet. You can purchase a small GPS tracking device at www.globaltrackinggroup.com. Also, arrange for your credit-card company to notify you if your card is used after you've reported it missing (you'd think they would do this automatically but you'd be surprised). Tuck your cell-phone number into your wallet in a visible spot, with a note to "Please Call If Lost!" That kind of plea won't work if you've been hit by a pickpocket, but it could be all that's needed if you've absentmindedly left it somewhere. For an all-out war against wallet-walking, there are actually movement sensors. Check www.loc8tor.com/Store/ for a device that will bust an Artful Dodger in midheist.

And of course, you can always contact the police. They aren't likely to call all cars, but you never know, a Good Samaritan may have turned your wallet in. Just make sure to repay the favor if you ever happen upon someone else's lost item. What goes around comes around.

Move recently? If your driver's license still reflects your old address, call the people living at your old residence in the off chance someone was nice enough to take the time to look at the address on the license, go to the post office, and mail the thing back to you. If it was your old address, now is the time to update your records.

How to Send Flowers to Someone Without Knowing the Address

Let's say you want to show your appreciation of (or interest in) a certain someone by sending her a fresh bouquet. Problem is, you have no idea where that certain someone lives. Well, I'm often faced with this dilemma and seem to get the job done, so don't worry, I've got you covered.

Not knowing someone's address should not stop you from sending the flowers. Yet you'd be surprised how quickly people give up! You can ensure those flowers make their final destination in a variety of ways, whether or not you know where that destination might be. If you have that person's work e-mail address, invent a reason to send an e-mail; many people list their office addresses in the signature part of their e-mail reply. If the person doesn't have that address listed, keep your Sherlock hat on and figure out the name of the company based on the e-mail extension (hint: if the e-mail address is jsmith@widgetsinc.com, the person probably works for a very exciting company called Widgets Incorporated), and then look up the office address.

Next, either send the flowers to the office and hope that you've got the right place, or contact the main office number and ask an assistant if he can get you the person's home address. You may think that getting someone's personal information from a receptionist at the person's company is a sticky wicket but honestly, you'd be surprised how many people are suckers for romance. Explain what you are doing and you probably won't need to dig any deeper.

If no one will talk, there's one way to get this information, but it may involve bribing the flower delivery guy. Give him a few extra bucks to go to the recipient's workplace (at a time you know the person won't be there) and tell someone there that he absolutely has to hand-deliver the flowers to the recipient's address *today* or he'll be fired. If he's wearing a uniform and carrying the flowers around, *someone* is bound to give him the home address. If you can't get the delivery guy to do it, get your buddy. All he has to do is wear a pink shirt and people will assume he's got on the uniform from the flower shop. Piece of cake.

What if you want to get a bouquet for someone who doesn't work in an office, like that cute waitress you talk to all the time but haven't exactly gotten to that "address/phone number exchange" part of the relationship? Assuming you're not the type to follow her home (which is good news) and that she has a distinctive enough name, try www.switchboard.com. And these days, lots of people (wisely or not) also post their home addresses on social networking sites like LinkedIn or Facebook, so don't forget to check there.

Finding someone's address is as easy as finding your own way home after one too many cocktails. It can be a little confusing, and may involve unplanned detours, but you'll get there eventually.

How to Get a Package Delivered on Christmas Morning

It's Christmas Eve and, of course, it never fails. Someone forgot to get something very important delivered to someone very important. Guess who gets the call. Hint: not Santa. Let's just say Consider It Christmas. Few things in life are more difficult than getting anything done on Christmas Day. In most parts of the United States, 90 percent of all businesses are closed, including the post office and most parcel services. But whether you were just late finishing your shopping, accidentally overlooked someone on your list, or just want to give someone that special moment of a surprise delivery on Christmas morning, there are a few ways to get your gifts delivered on the big day.

Here is how it goes, just so you know.

U.S. Postal Service: The only way to get your package delivered via U.S. mail on Christmas Day is by accident. If a package is guaranteed to be delivered by Christmas and something interferes with the delivery, the USPS will step up and deliver it on the twenty-fifth. At least this is what they will tell you if you call, and although I'm sure this line sounds good for customer relations, I've never actually seen a U.S. Postal truck driving down the street on Christmas Day, so I think it's safe to write it off as a pretty unreliable option.

UPS: If you send your package regular UPS delivery—or even overnight delivery—you're out of luck. These services won't deliver on Christmas. For a high fee (how high depends on the weight/location of the package), however, you can use "UPS Critical Express," which will deliver no matter what the day—even on *Christmas*.

FedEx: This carrier doesn't offer any delivery service on Christmas, so as far as the big three options for packages, UPS is probably your best bet.

That said, a lot of companies (especially smaller, local ones) will, for the right price, deliver gifts on Christmas. Local gift basket companies, for instance, are known for being pretty accommodating with delivery times and dates, and you can probably even schedule delivery for an exact time if you plan ahead and pay them enough. The smaller the business, the better your shot, because while larger chains have standard rules, mom-and-pop operations play it pretty loose and will accommodate on a case-by-case basis. This means that when purchasing your very last-minute gift, you may have to choose based on the shop, rather than the gift itself.

Quick tip: If you are spending the holidays in a tourist town (like a ski resort), you are in luck. This is their busy season, and many shops are open Christmas Day. So, if you are a chronically last-minute shopper, you'd be smart to spend the holidays vacationing somewhere you know you can always pick up a last-minute gift.

As I mentioned, I have, on more than one occasion, arranged delivery on Christmas morning. But usually, since no one else will *guarantee* that it will get there, I send someone to hand-deliver the Christmas cheer, just to be sure. So my advice, if you really want to ensure that your packages get delivered on Christmas morning: deliver them yourself. Or avoid the issue by doing your holiday shopping the day after Thanksgiving, like everyone else.

Remember: Whoever shows up at your doorstep on Christmas morning with your package, it's important to share some Christmas joy; so even though you are the recipient, be sure to give the delivery person a nice tip.

How to Get a Ticket to Anything Sold Out

Whether it's for a game, a concert, or a Broadway show, when most people see the words *sold out*, they change their plans. But what they really need to do is change their way of thinking. "Sold out" doesn't really mean sold out; it just means you'll have to get a bit more creative. Because what most people don't know is that since many venues that require tickets—from movies to art galleries to buses and trains—have transferable tickets (either officially or unofficially), there's always some way to get into something that's supposedly "sold out."

I figured this out when I was once traveling by train from New York to D.C., with some clients, four men in suits who were very eager to get to their next meeting. The schedule was tight (as always) and when we arrived at the station to get the train, we discovered there were only three tickets left—we were two short. I had to think fast. We *had* to be on that train for my clients to make their meeting, and it was all on my shoulders to get us on it. Good thing I work well under pressure. So here's what I did. I bought the three tickets and then purchased two additional tickets for a later train. Then we simply got on the train and grabbed five seats, problem solved!

See, on most regional rail lines, your ticket isn't checked until you've boarded the train and it starts moving; even if you've got the wrong ticket, you won't get kicked off. Plus, most train tickets are transferable anyway (in case you miss the train or plans change), often for many months or up to one year, so if you just tell the ticket checker you missed your earlier train, they'll almost always let you on (the same applies for bus tickets). You shouldn't feel guilty about taking a legitimate ticketholder's seat, either; plenty of people are no-shows, so fear not, no one will be left-standing.

This basic strategy works for most kinds of tickets. Buy a ticket for a time that's not sold out, and then go at the time that is. It sounds simple, and it really is; it's one of the few things in life that might even be easier done than said. And if a ticket taker stops you, just play dumb; pretend you just can't *believe* you mixed up the times, but you're here now so can he *please* just let you in? The person almost always will.

Quick tip: If you get to the train or bus station and notice that the ticket agent is checking tickets *before* people board the 2:00 P.M. voyage, you can simply ask people waiting in line if they'd be willing to swap with you for your 3:00 P.M. ticket. Give them a little incentive. Cash usually does the trick; if you have no takers at first, up the ante until you do. I've said it before, but the fact remains true that everyone has his or her price. Look for people in casual clothing who seem relaxed, like they don't need to get anywhere fast, as they may be willing to make the switch. It's a little risky, but there is usually someone who can be bought.

Getting into a sold-out movie is even easier. If the movie you want to see at 7:00 P.M. is sold out, buy a ticket to a less-popular movie at 7:00 P.M., and then just sneak into the movie you want to see. This only works at large multiplex cinemas where they take your ticket at the front entrance and give you access to all the theaters at once, but these days, most of us end up at multiplex theaters anyway. Again, don't feel bad that you're taking someone else's seat: theaters plan for this sort of behavior. A multiplex employee I once spoke to told me that they call a showing "sold out" after selling about 90 percent of the seats to allow themselves a little wiggle room.

Quick tip: At some of the *most* popular movies, they'll check your ticket again at the door to the specific theater. If this is the case, wait until the previews begin and come running to the door with some popcorn. Tell the ticket taker that the rest of your party is already inside, that you just ran out to get popcorn, and left your ticket stub in the pocket of your jacket back at your seat. No theater employee is going to care enough to follow you in just to check out your story, trust me.

If you want to get into something that's sold out and does *not* have transferable tickets, like a concert, or a sporting event, you sometimes have to be a little more creative. Sure, you can find the scalpers outside, or scalp a ticket online at sites like www.stubhub.com, but you may have to pay big bucks. There is a better way. Go to the venue, get in line, and befriend someone who actually has a ticket. Have your new friend go inside with the ticket, then "come back to the gate to say hi" to you near where they are taking tickets. Your friend should not come outside but should sneakily hand you the torn-in-half ticket stub. Wait a few minutes, then go to a different turnstile and tell the ticket taker that you were already inside and you must have kept the wrong part of the ticket (this is more believable if the show or event has already started). Oops, silly me!

How to Make a Citizen's Arrest— or Not

Imagine you are walking down the street and you see an old lady get robbed by a pickpocket. Have you ever considered accosting the perpetrator and making a citizen's arrest? If you answered yes, you have probably been watching too much *Law & Order*.

Still, the idea of making a citizen's arrest—and being a hero—sounds irresistibly cool. Unfortunately, there are no rules as to how you can actually do it. The laws as to whether or not you can intervene and what you legally have the right to do vary widely from state to state and depend on the nature of the crime (misdemeanor or felony).

Plus, it isn't always the safest course of action. Imagine this scenario:

You see a robbery taking place. You walk up to the crook and say, "Stop right there, Buster, I'm making a citizen's arrest." What do you suppose the hooligan would do? Would the thief: (a) immediately surrender his weapon and then wait calmly while you call the police or (b) put your health or continued existence in question?

If you announce a citizen's arrest and the criminal does not choose (a), which seems likely, you might have to resort to physical violence to subdue the outlaw, which puts you at risk of being charged for assault or possibly other crimes. And I have to believe that (no offense) if it came to blows, the thief could probably take you.

So instead of attempting a citizen's arrest, I strongly recommend calling 911 or the local authorities and reporting the offense. If you want to do a good deed, watch carefully so that you can help identify the suspects. And if you think you may be interviewed as a witness, immediately make notes of anything that you remember seeing because memory is quirky and your testimony may become hazy as time passes.

One thing is for sure—certain things in life are always best left to professionals. Crime fighting is one of them.

8. life and death

How to Conduct a Séance

The closest most people have ever come to experiencing a true séance is five people gathered together around a Ouija board at a seventh-grade sleepover. Of course, the most fun part was moving the thing around and pretending to wonder who was doing it. Good times.

Although I've yet to be hired to plan a séance, I'm not a complete disbeliever in the ability to talk to dead people. After all, I'm always living in the anything's possible realm, and I've seen enough reality shows about paranormal activity to know that sometimes things happen that can't be easily explained. Some believe that people who claim to be able to channel the dead—mediums—are the best con artists in the world, but hey, what if they aren't? Stranger things are true.

If you believe in the stuff wholeheartedly or just want to try it out for fun with a few friends, conducting a séance can be an interesting and spiritual experience—regardless of whether or not you actually make contact with the other side. First, gather your group together, and openly discuss your goals. If you're just doing it for fun, say so, but if you actually want to try to connect with a ghost, spirit, or person who has passed away, make sure the group understands that this is serious, and make sure everyone's on board. The easiest way to ruin a séance is to have a vocal dissenter, so ask him to step out for a few minutes. You know who the cynic is in your group of friends; don't invite him.

Next, choose a medium, or decide if you'll all fulfill this role together. If anyone has done this before, or believes he or she has special spiritual abilities, that person is the obvious choice. The medium does *not* necessarily need to have a personal connection with the spirits you're trying to reach.

Quick tip: Never conduct a séance with children, or with someone who has a particularly hard time dealing with death. It will likely ruin your séance—and possibly their mental health.

Once you're ready, prepare the room. As with any party, atmosphere and decor are extremely important. Dim the lights, or turn them off altogether (if you can handle it), and place a spiritual centerpiece in the middle of a round table. If you can't find a crystal ball or deck of tarot cards, use an item of aromatic food, like soup, which many believe will help attract ghosts and ghouls. Others believe that the table should have a deep connection to the earth (i.e., where the people you're communicating with are buried), and suggest using an actual piece of earth (i.e., a bowl of dirt from your backyard) as the centerpiece. One last thing to have on hand, is a favorite or often-used item that belonged to the person you're trying to reach. Rings, watches, even car keys work well as these items are said to carry some energy from the person who was most often in contact with them. Finally, light some candles—because everyone knows you can't have a séance without candles—and then join hands in a circle around the table. Joining hands is key because it signifies the séance is in progress and when the connection is broken, the séance will be over.

You're finally ready to summon the spirits, so follow the medium's lead. If you happen to be the medium, and have absolutely no experience, do your best to feel the presence of the person on the other side, and if you don't feel anything at first, fake it till you make it. Start with a chant to summon the spirit, and have everyone join in. Begin by asking yes or no questions. Decide what the spirit should do to answer yes (perhaps one rap on a door or window) or no (perhaps two raps). It might be for real—you never know—and even if it's not, all it takes is a couple of conveniently timed house noises to convince your group you know what you're doing. You will want to come up with a list of questions in advance and have it handy, so that you don't get caught up in the moment and forget what you wanted to ask or say.

If it's going well, move on to more complicated questions that require more than a yes or no answer. If you're the medium here, do not censor anything. Share whatever you feel or think you hear with the group—they can decide if they buy it.

Remember: If it gets too intense, or anyone starts freaking out, break the circle and stop immediately. Nothing is worth that kind of psychological damage.

Don't know a chant to summon the dead? The most common is some version of this: "Our beloved [name of spirit], we ask that you commune with us and move among us." Be creative, and make up your own chant—as long as you use the word *commune*. That seems to be important.

And if it doesn't work as planned, speak to an expert. Believe it or not, there are people out there who know *a lot* about this stuff. Remember, if the whole thing gets to be too much trouble, there's always a backup option: the Ouija board.

How to Create a Bucket List

If you've seen the Jack Nicholson movie *The Bucket List*, you know what I'm talking about here. If you haven't, a "bucket list" is a list of everything you want to do before you, well, kick the bucket. Sounds morbid, but let's face it, we're all going to be at the end of the road sometime, and we all have things we want to do before we get there, so why not make a list? There's really not much to it, but there are ways that you can make the experience more satisfying, and meaningful.

First off, remember that your bucket list is a very personal thing. It's your list and not anyone else's. I recommend that it be handwritten, on a stationery-sized sheet of paper. A typed list just doesn't have the same feel; plus, you want something you can carry around with you and add to at all times. You can keep an updated copy of the list on your computer if you want, but your real list should be something that you can tuck into a wallet or purse and scrawl on whenever something occurs to you. It will mean more if it's something that's always with you, plus, on those days when you are caught up in annoying meetings, or stuck waiting for the subway in the sweltering the heat of the summer, you can pull out your list to put things in perspective and remind yourself what's really important.

Your bucket list should include all those major, life-changing experiences that you've sworn to have, like travel. Obviously, trying to visit everywhere you've ever wanted to go may be unrealistic (not to mention expensive), so stick to those places you would never forgive yourself for not visiting. If someone gave you a plane ticket to anywhere tomorrow, where would you go? That's the sort of place to put on your list. But don't just make it "Go to Egypt" or "Go to London." Make it more specific, something concrete that you will *do* there, like: "See the inside of a pyramid." or "Have tea at Buckingham Palace." This will make it far more fulfilling when you cross it off the list. Don't worry about *how* it is ever going to happen. Just write it. Trust me on this.

But your list shouldn't just include once-in-a-lifetime trips to far-flung corners of the globe. Little things close to home can be just as meaningful, like telling your high school crush how you felt, finally finishing *War and Peace,* or planting an apple tree in your backyard.

One final note about bucket lists—unless you know exactly when you're going to die (and if you figure out how to predict this, please let me know), it's impossible to tell when you'll run out of time to complete the things on your list. What I'm trying to say is, it's never too early to start. Don't *wait* to start crossing things off your list; do them as soon as humanly possible! You can always add *new* things to the list, but waiting years to start in on your list is the same thing as not having a list at all.

How to Avoid a Hangover

A few years ago, I discovered something called "Hangover Tea" in a specialty store. "Perfect for the morning after!" the box exclaimed (perhaps unnecessarily). So, a few months later, when a client called to ask for a housekeeper to clean up from his party the night before and happened to mention he'd had one too many . . . I remembered the tea and decided to run out and grab some for him. I figured it would be a nice gesture, plus, it would be a good way to figure out if the stuff was a scam, or if it really worked (without having to actually endure a hangover).

He called the next day to say that it had seemed to kick in about an hour after he drank it, but that he didn't really start feeling completely better until that afternoon, after he'd had two or three cups. Curious as to whether this was the effects of the tea, or if it was just the hangover wearing off, I decided to do a little more research. I took a look at the ingredients and compared them with those in other herbal teas I had lying around. Oddly, I noticed very little difference. There was certainly no "secret ingredient" that magically made his headache go away or the room stop spinning.

It's tempting to think some sort of miracle cure exists that will immediately make your hangover disappear, but in reality it seems that hangover tea—not to mention hangover pills, hangover powders, and any other sort of hangover treatment—is just a trick to get you to drink water. After all, a hangover is basically a symptom of dehydration. When you drink at night, the ethanol in the alcohol dehydrates you, only you're too tipsy to notice you're thirsty (or you just think you're thirsty for beer, which doesn't help matters). So you don't drink water, you get more and more dehydrated, and the next morning, by which time your brain is sober enough to communicate with your body, you experience the headache, dry mouth, and nausea otherwise known as a hangover.

Bottom line: The best "miracle cure" for eliminating or, better yet, avoiding a hangover is plain old H_2O. It's that simple.

But you knew that already, right? Then why are you still getting hangovers? The problem is that on any night that could result in a hangover, you'll be too blasted to remember to drink enough water. That's why, like with hangover tea, you have to trick yourself, or at least leave reminders for yourself ahead of time. If you're planning a night of depravity, leave glasses of water—or better yet, resealable bottles of water—around your kitchen, bedroom, and bathroom. When you get home, you might be too far gone to remember to pour yourself a glass, but if it's already sitting there, all you have to do is drink.

And if you're not thirsty? Some may have the willpower to just down it. And if you know what's good for you, that's the way to go. But if you really can't stomach water unless your brain demands it, then you'll have to trick your brain. So eat a salty snack (incidentally this is why people crave salt when they've been drinking), but not too much—you don't want to swap your hangover for a stomachache. Plus, you have your figure to consider. Popcorn is best, since you get the most surface area for salt while limiting caloric intake—and late at night, after a few cocktails, limiting caloric intake is often a bigger challenge than avoiding a hangover. Instead of adding butter, add more salt. In no time, you'll be reaching for multiple glasses of your new favorite cocktail: ice-cold water.

The smarter strategy, though, is to start drinking water *before* you start boozing, and continue drinking it. Alternate every drink with a glass of water—and if you feel uncool ordering water in a bar, get a seltzer with a twist of lime. It will be just as hydrating, and your friends will assume it's a gin and tonic. Of course, the *best* way to avoid a hangover is to limit the amount of alcohol you consume. But that's no fun for anyone.

Moneymaking tip: Make your own "hangover cure," then stand outside a club at 3:00 A.M. and sell it for an overpriced amount. Think of it as a lemonade stand for grown-ups. As long as it has a lot of water, it's guaranteed to work. Just don't quit your day job . . . yet.

How to Go Skydiving

Jumping out of a plane from ten thousand feet in the air is the ultimate rush. Anyone I've ever arranged such an adventure for comes back grinning like the cat that ate the canary. Of course, death-defying feats aren't for everyone, but if you're daring enough to consider doing it in the first place, you're pretty much guaranteed to have fun (even if you don't recognize it as such until your feet are safely planted back on the ground). Here are some tips to make it happen.

First, find a group of people willing to go with you. Friends (or family) can provide the moral support you need to get through the day, especially a day that involves death-defying activities. Trust me, no matter how brave you are, there will likely be multiple points at which you'll want to back out (like when you watch the "safety" video that lists the various injuries you might incur, and when you sign the waiver that limits the pilot's responsibility if you *die*). The people who go with you will also be the only ones who will truly understand the experience you've had, so it will be a bonding experience you can share with them for the rest of your lives. Plus, the more witnesses to this historic event, the better.

Next, find the skydiving company, which can be done with a quick Internet search. Though some people will tell you that scenery makes a difference (in which case you might consider skydiving in the mountains or near the ocean), in reality, the first time you skydive, it will go by so quickly that you'll barely have time to register the beauty of it all. Instead of location, choose a company based on its safety record— which you can obtain by calling the company directly and simply asking for it—and its certification. Yes, you'll want to be *sure* the company is certified by an independent oversight agency (like the U.S. Parachute Association, at www.uspa.org). In all likelihood, though, a skydiving company that's open for business will have a perfect safety record and will be fully certified.

You'll then have to decide what type of jump to do. First-timers will want to consider a tandem jump, which means that you are strapped together with an instructor. With a tandem jump, you don't have to do anything at all—the pro initiates the jump, guides the free fall, opens the chute, and navigates the way back to the landing strip—while you just kick back and enjoy the ride. The alternative (which isn't even offered everywhere) is to jump solo. If it's your first time, you have to use a static line, which means that your chute will open automatically as soon as you exit the plane, eliminating any of the free fall portion (which, to most people, is the essence of skydiving). The only way to jump by yourself *and* free-fall (safely and legally) is to take a certification course, which lasts several weeks, can cost thousands of dollars, and most likely begins with a tandem jump anyway.

Last but not least, calm your nerves. The company is required by law to tell you that you might die, but you won't. Skydiving, especially today, is incredibly safe—much safer than, for example, getting in your car. Companies have multiple safeguards, including a backup parachute that's programmed by computer to open automatically at one thousand feet above the ground, to make sure you land safely and in one piece even if something goes wrong.

If you're still nervous, or they don't explain these features thoroughly, ask questions before you go. Make sure they explain every safety feature before you board the plane so that you feel confident jumping—it would be a shame to spend the entire free fall needlessly worrying about the parachute.

Once you're calm (ish), just go! Don't think about it too much. Trust your instructor, trust the parachute, and enjoy the ride.

Quick tip: Before you leave, buy a T-shirt (or any article of clothing with a logo) as a souvenir. Why? Skydiving comes with bragging rights, which you are free to exercise whenever you wear the shirt. Plus it's a handy morale booster on a day that you're feeling less than daring.

Another cool extra is to get a video of your jump. If you want to purchase a video, most companies will send another instructor with a camera attached to his or her helmet to jump with you. The price tag will be a little bit higher, but skydiving is costly anyway, and may be a once-in-a-lifetime experience, definitely landing it in the priceless category.

How to Go Shark Diving

If you're looking for thrills, shark diving is pretty much as intense as you can get (except for maybe jumping out of a plane; for that, see the previous entry). But don't let the name intimidate you, it's not exactly as dangerous as it sounds. You aren't going to just be jumping into the ocean and swimming with these flesh eaters; rather, you'll climb into a large metal cage and be lowered from a boat into the ocean. Sharks will swim around, and at times even approach the cage, giving you a close-up and (relatively) safe view of these living Cuisinarts. I once organized a trip for a bunch of guys who had done just about everything, and shark diving was a way for them to feel like they were living on the edge and pushing the limits. But don't worry, they all made it back in one piece.

Still, don't try this on your own. Newsflash: Sharks ain't dolphins. And let me remind you, you are not a professional, so I'd recommend that you hire one. A number of companies offer shark-diving trips, and best of all, you won't necessarily have to travel too far to see sharks. Check out www.sharkdiver.com, which organizes shark-diving trips all over the world, including some just off the coast of San Diego.

And if I could offer a suggestion here: when choosing an outfit to take you on a shark dive, you will want to place safety high on your list of priorities. Whatever type of guide you go with, remember: You are going to be *locked in a cage beneath the ocean with a pack of sharks.* There are no do-overs, so inquire about safety issues now, because it may be your only opportunity.

Mostly shark diving is done from a liveaboard boat, and your trip will usually be two to four days long and fall somewhere in the $2,000 to $3,000 range. The price should cover the royal treatment—transportation to and from the outfit's headquarters to the designated dock, the boat ride, equipment, accommodations and, meals on board the boat. Many companies base their pricing not only on the length of the trip, but on the type of shark you're going to see. Great whites, being more rare, tend to be the most prized to dive with, so those packages will cost a little more than a tiger shark package. Some companies also operate day dives, but these are often hit-or-miss. No, not as in coming back alive, but as in seeing sharks. Just remember, a shark-diving trip is *not* something you want to do on the cheap—make sure the outfit is reputable and licensed.

You don't need any qualifications or skills (besides being healthy enough to not have a heart attack when Jaws lunges at your cage), but most of the better outfits will give you a short course (at least an hour) explaining what you can expect as well as updating you on safety precautions.

Finally, know that shark diving will not harm the animals. As a general rule, shark-dive operators respect and care for marine life.

Best perk of all: Most dives also feature a video camera in the cage, so you can go home with footage of your shark dive to show your kids . . . right before you forbid them from ever going shark diving.

How to Find Out If Your House Is Haunted

Before you go any further in investigating whether or not your house is haunted, ask yourself the following question: Do I believe in ghosts, spirits, or the supernatural? If you answered no, then your house is not haunted.

Perhaps this is not enough. Sometimes, in severe circumstances, reasoning is overlooked, and despite your stated disbelief in the paranormal you may not recognize the cause of that creaking noise in the floorboards simply as planks of old, deteriorating wood rubbing against each other. Or perhaps you will have a hard time attributing that chill you feel each time you pass the credenza in your living room to the draft that seeps through your poorly insulated picture window. Then again, who am I to say that ghosts *definitely* aren't real? Just because I haven't seen them personally doesn't necessarily mean they don't exist. I did have a client who swore her house was haunted. She and her husband even called me over late one night after they had seen the apparition (a friendly one, they described it, not exactly like Casper, but a friendly-looking person) to see if I could see it too. We waited and waited, night after night for weeks (I told you I get a lot weird requests from clients), but the ghost never appeared again. So either it didn't exist, or it didn't want to meet me.

Regardless, once you've got it in your head that your house is haunted, logic probably won't be enough to convince you otherwise, so you'll need to do whatever it takes to get to the bottom of it. You'll have to creep around the house for "proof" that everything is all right, and confront your fears head-on . . . and if it turns out to be real, you can go ahead and say I didn't warn you.

The first thing to do is make a list of unexplained phenomena. Keep a journal, and record everything out of the ordinary. And then—this may be scary—personally investigate any problem areas. If a closet door opens and closes on its own unexpectedly, go inside the closet and snoop around (if you're going to be a baby about it, do it when there's some daylight). Is there a loose hinge on the door, perhaps? Or evidence that a mouse or other four-legged creature has recently taken up residence (which may or may not be scarier than a ghost)? If strange noises are coming from the attic, go up and spend some time looking for rotting floorboards, drafts, and (sorry!) rodents (again, for peace of mind, take another person up there with you). If you see a strange shadow, don't run away: go toward it. With a baseball bat.

If, after all this, you still can't find a rational explanation for what's happening, call upon a friend; one who doesn't believe in this sort of thing is a good choice here. Ask your friend—and new paranormal investigator—to stick around and observe some of the phenomena that take place at night. If even *he* sees doors open or close unexpectedly, hears cries or whispers, sees lights turn on or off when no one else is around, feels hot or cold spots, sees objects levitate or move, or actually catches a glimpse of apparitions or ghosts, then your house might actually be haunted.

If this is the case, it's time to call in the experts. Believe it or not, ghost whisperers aren't just on TV—they actually exist, and there's likely to be one in your general area. Just search on the Internet for paranormal investigators in your state, and invite them to come take a look. If they find evidence, they may be able to conduct a ghost exorcism, which might be a creepy experience but should rid your home of spirits for good. It might cost a pretty penny, too, but if you're convinced your house really is haunted, it'll be a lot cheaper than moving.

People may laugh at you for believing in ghosts in the first place, but try not to take it personally. Lighten up and try to laugh at yourself a bit. Look at it this way: neither you nor they will *really* be able to prove or disprove the existence of ghosts, so you might as well seek some common ground here.

How to Keep Your New Year's Resolutions

New year, same resolution. How can this be? You make a resolution on January 1 and then work at it, for one, maybe two weeks . . . and then something (or more like nothing) happens. Maybe it's a universal understanding that says we should just make resolutions that either aren't very meaningful (like lose five pounds) or are next to impossible (like lay off the chocolate). Or maybe we just tell ourselves it's OK to break them, because that's just what happens to New Year's resolutions.

But what if you actually stick with your resolution for thirty days, then sixty days, and then before you know it, it's December 31 and it's been a habit for so long, you can't even remember when it wasn't? Then, the following year, you'd have the opportunity to make an actual *new* resolution instead of the same one you've been making for . . . ever. Just think. If you stuck to just one resolution each year, what an evolved person you would be ten, twenty, thirty, and forty well-kept resolutions from now!

So here, as I see it, is a quick way to stick to the plan. Self-discipline is all about the reward in the short term, right? You *say* you want to go to the gym, because in the long term, you want to be healthy, but in the *short term* you don't get the reward. Sitting on the couch with a pint of Ben and Jerry's on the other hand, now that's rewarding.

Since most resolutions have to do with long-term goals (getting in shape, writing a novel, etc.), they often don't have a short-term benefit. You can almost always put these things off until tomorrow with no negative result . . . but the problem is that tomorrow turns into the next day, and the next day turns into the next week, and suddenly you forget that it's on your list of things to do at all.

That's why, to stick to your resolutions, you would greatly benefit from setting up a short-term reward for each step you make toward achieving that long-term goal. One of the most rewarding things I can think of is cash, so set up a system where you gain money every day you stick to your plan—and lose money each day you don't. First, get out two jars. Label one with something that you would *love* to have at the end of the year (like a vacation), and label the other with the name of a charity of your choice. Select a daily amount—let's say a dollar. Every day that you stick to your resolution, put a dollar in the reward jar, and every day that you break it, put a dollar in the charity jar. Sure, giving money to charity feels good, but let's face it, a trip to Hawaii feels better.

If the jar system doesn't work for you (I know it can be tempting to dip into those jars when you're short on cash), check out www.stickk.com (don't forget the two k's). It's a new website that runs a program with a similar strategy that takes care of all the monetary arrangements. The difference is, though, that you aren't rewarded for sticking with your resolutions. You only get money if you *don't* do the thing you say you're going to do. That's why I'd recommend *not* going with this plan. It puts a whole negative twist on things right from the get-go. Go with the fun and empowering version!

If you've tried the same resolution year after year with the same (lack of) results, do yourself a favor and give something new a try this year, *pretty please!* Even if it's only to give us all a break from that same damn resolution already! Besides, sometimes taking the focus *off* something and concentrating on something new is just what you need to have them both come to fruition.

And if you're disciplined enough to stick to your resolutions, consider celebrating by matching the money in your jar and making a donation to the charity of your choice—a true win-win all around!

How to Write a Will

How to write a will? Hire a lawyer.

Look, it's one of those little things that you can convince yourself you don't *really* need, until you do. If you don't already have one, at the very least include it on the "things to do before the baby arrives" list. And if you're up to child number four and you still don't have one, finish this page and stop whatever you are doing and get started—you know it's the right thing to do. And take care to do it right. To *ensure* that it's completely legally binding and in accordance with your state's laws (every state has different laws regarding wills and inheritances), you really need to hire a lawyer to make sure your exact wishes are carried out when the time comes.

Still, doing it yourself is a lot better than not writing a will at all. Start by stating your full name, address, and other identifying items, like date of birth and/or social security number. It might sound obvious, but you need to make your will completely idiot-proof, or someone who gets the short end of the stick could challenge it in court fairly easily. After you've written everything as plain as day so that the reader won't confuse you with anyone else by the same name, state that you are of sound mental health, and you know exactly the contract into which you are entering. Again, this will all help it hold up in court.

Next, divide up your estate, and make sure you use simple, direct language that can't be construed in any other way. Use short, declarative sentences, and be extremely specific. Divide up your monetary assets in percentages, not actual dollars or shares, because you have no idea how much or how little money you'll have when you pass away. For example, "I leave 10 percent (10%) of my assets to my sister Susie-Q," or whatever the case may be. (Obviously, make sure the total of all percentages does not exceed 100%.) Be crystal clear. Also, it's good to add a "residuary clause," which indicates where any unspecified assets will go. These include new assets you acquire after you write the will, or anything that was supposed to go to someone (like Susie-Q) who has died before you do. Write something like, "If there are any other assets remaining in my estate, I give such residuals to my sons (Jim and Joe)." You may want to include more than one or two people in the residuary clause, because if you outlive them all, your residuals will go to waste or get stuck in legal limbo.

Next, you must name an executor who will carry out your will; it's a good idea to ask the person you name before you do it. If you wish, you can authorize the executor to pay any debts, funeral expenses, and taxes and to sell any stock or real estate you own as he or she sees fit (again, this is not something I would do before talking it over with that person). You may wish to name a backup executor, in case you outlive your first choice, or in case he or she cannot perform the role for whatever reason. Finally, take a copy of your will to a notary public and sign it with three witnesses.

Once it's signed, give one copy to your executor (and perhaps another fourth copy to your alternate executor), and keep at least two for yourself.

Store one in a safe place in your home, like a home safe (see "How to Keep Your Valuables Safe in Your Home," page 336). Store the second copy outside of your home, in case something happens to your house. A safe-deposit box in a bank is pretty standard, but it's up to you. Whatever you do, don't simply type up a will and leave it on your computer; it could be shot down in court easily if it's not signed and notarized. After all, anyone could make the claim that your computer had been tampered with, plus, without a signature, there's no way to prove that you really wrote it and approved of it in its current form. Even worse, someone *could* tamper with it on your computer.

If this all sounds time-consuming, think of it this way: it took you a lifetime to acquire your assets, so the least you can do is spend a couple of hours arranging for their final resting place.

Note: This bare-bones method covers only a fraction of the legal language you'll want to use, and the extra precautions you'll want to take depend on the specifics of your estate. If you choose not to go with a lawyer (and did I mention that it's a really, really smart idea to use one?), do some more research online (many sites have templates available) before you sign and notarize the document.

How to Ship a (Dead) Body

Most people don't normally think about how dead bodies are transported. I, for one, assumed that they would either be driven or flown on special cargo planes. Turns out, dead bodies fly in the cargo hold of passenger airplanes routinely, often multiple times a day, into and out of every major airport. So, odds are, if you're a frequent flier, you've been on multiple flying mortuaries—though, for everyone's sake, next time you fly, better to just not think about the casket lying a few feet below your seat.

If you ever have the unfortunate task of transporting a body, know that because it is so common, airlines are fairly accustomed to the request. Tarmac crews are used to lifting and loading coffins, so you won't be creeping anyone out. Just call up the airline of your choice and speak with customer service. But be prepared to pay a heftier fee than you'd pay for normal baggage—the price of flying a body and casket (with or without a body in it) ranges from about $300 to close to $2,000, depending on the airline, origin and destination, and sometimes the weight of the cargo.

Alternatively, you can ask the hospital or funeral home from which the dead body is being transported to make the arrangements. Both of these establishments have more experience dealing with these situations (hopefully) than you have and should be able to pull it off without a hitch.

And although it's no longer mandatory, it's good to get yourself (or another person close to you) on the same flight as the casket, in case anything goes wrong at the last minute. If the flight is delayed, canceled, or the casket gets placed on the wrong flight (after all, if they can misplace your suitcase, they can just as easily misplace your great-uncle Lenny), it'll be easier to figure out a quicker way to get the body home if you're present at the airport. Don't forget to arrange for someone to pick you and the casket up—you can't just stuff it in the back of a taxi. Your local funeral home will be able to help with those arrangements.

Quick tip: Consider embalming the body—a process that sanitizes and preserves the body with various chemicals to stall decomposition—*before* you ship it. If you don't, a few hours in the hot cargo hold of a passenger plane could get very messy. Plus, airlines generally require the body be embalmed or packed in dry ice (if embalming is not desired for religious reasons).

Sending a body to another country can be a bit trickier, and the consulate of that country will need to get involved. But again, any local funeral home and whichever airline you choose should be able to assist with the arrangements, since they do this sort of thing all the time. If you're shipping a body to Italy, beware: Italy is notorious for its strict laws in this area, and no other country's regulations come close. The body must be embalmed and sealed in an airtight container, the death certificate must be translated into Italian, the Italian consulate must approve of the transport, the funeral director must describe how the outer container was built, *and* the medical examiner must certify in a letter (which much be translated into Italian) that the person did not die of any communicable disease. I'm not kidding. In other countries, you'll get some of these rules, but not all of them. So no matter where you're shipping a body, be prepared for these types of questions, but if you're shipping to Italy, well, after what you just read you may want to reconsider.

Quick tip: Bodies do not need to be sent inside a casket. Most airlines will provide an "airtray," which can transport the body safely—and many airlines require that airtrays be used in addition to a casket. So be sure to confirm it with the airline when you book your ticket, and consider purchasing the casket in the city where the burial will take place to avoid damage to the casket in transit.

How to Bury Someone Who Served in the Military

The prospect of having to bury someone who served in the military isn't fun to think about, but unfortunately, it's something that many Americans are forced to do. Since January 1, 2000, the United States Department of Defense (DOD) has been responsible for providing military funeral honors to veterans. The Department of Veterans Affairs can also assist, if the deceased is being buried at a VA national cemetery. But while they can provide some much-needed assistance at what is sure to be a troubling time, the government is the government, and you'll still need to monitor everything they do to make sure the funeral and burial are up to standards. To do that, you need to know what those standards are.

First, you should know that the new law, called "Honoring Those Who Served," requires the DOD to assist with military funeral honors only for those families who request it. So step number one: Request it. Most local funeral homes should be able to assist in contacting the appropriate branch of the DOD, but for more information, and a direct contact, you can visit www.militaryfuneralhonors.osd.mil.

Next, you should understand what a military funeral entails. First, a United States Burial Flag must be used to drape the casket (or accompany the urn); at some point during the ceremony it will be folded, according to military procedure, and then given to the next of kin, if they are present. Use VA Form 21-2008 (available at www.vba.va.gov/pubs/forms/vba21-2008.pdf) to request a flag. The second traditional part of a military funeral is the playing of "Taps"; the funeral home you use should be able to help arrange that. In addition, military funeral honors require two or more uniformed military personnel to be in attendance, and at least one of them must be from the veteran's parent service of the armed forces.

You must also consider the headstone, and, unfortunately, you may have to arrange for this in advance (before the veteran's death). If you choose to bury the body in a national cemetery, a military gravestone comes standard, but if you go with a private cemetery, you'll have to apply for a military headstone, which the DOD requests that you do in advance. The papers won't be filed unless necessary, of course, but if you send them in as a precautionary measure, as soon as your loved one is deployed, you'll be able to avoid the messy bureaucratic finagling in the event that the worst happens. *Note:* It's a good idea to just make the request when signing up to serve. That way it's not something you have to remember to do when you actually are deployed. The good news is that the VA furnishes these headstones at no charge; you can request a headstone using VA Form 40-1330, or ask your funeral home for assistance.

Quick tip: To honor the deceased beyond just a standard military funeral, you may also want to apply for a Presidential Memorial Certificate, which is engraved and signed by the current president. To find out about this service, e-mail PMC@mail.va.gov.

There's no question that it will be difficult, but if you have a loved one in the military, it's wise to make all these arrangements ahead of time, no matter how remote the possibility is that he or she may be killed in action. Most likely, and with all good luck, the plans you make will never have to be carried out, but if they do, you will have saved yourself a huge headache—and possibly some heartache—by having the arrangements out of the way so that you can focus on what's really important during the funeral and burial: saying good-bye.

How to Plan Your Own Funeral

Even if it's your ninety-five-year-old grandparent and it's clearly time to say good-bye, planning a funeral is not something anyone wants to do. Unfortunately, most of us will eventually be confronted with this reality at some point. At a time of loss and grief, it may seem callous or even sacrilegious to deal with the "business" of a funeral and all of the practical details, but try to keep in mind that it's the means to an important end: giving the deceased a proper, respectful send-off that will allow family and friends to celebrate the life that was led. So when it comes to your own funeral, why leave it all up to someone else? Instead, why not make all the arrangements you would make for a loved one's funeral, for yourself?

Since you obviously won't be around when your own funeral takes place, the most important thing is that you communicate your plans and wishes to your loved ones. It may seem morbid, but it's the only way to be sure that your wishes will be honored. Make sure to also include anything relevant to your funeral arrangements and expenses in your will (see "How to Write a Will," page 207). Be sure to address all the little details: what type of funeral and burial you would like (religious, secular, or a more informal memorial service), who should lead the service (a clergy member, a funeral home professional, a friend or family member), where it will be held, how long it should last, who should deliver the eulogy, how much money you'd like to spend, what should be on the program, and so on. In addition to all these arrangements, another step you can take is to purchase a burial plot, particularly if you wish to be buried near certain family members or in a certain spot in the cemetery. Again, as with writing a will, it's never too soon to think about these things. Even if death is nowhere in sight, a burial plot will be used *someday*, so you might as well buy it now to ensure it will still be yours when the time comes. Just talk to the cemetery owner and make arrangements now. But choose carefully, because once the spot is reserved, it'll be yours forever.

Quick tip: If you can't stomach discussing these things with anyone (or your friends and relatives simply refuse to discuss it with you), at least put your wishes in writing. No one will read it until you're gone, but at least you'll have the final word.

If you have reason to believe this sad day is imminent, visit a funeral home and make the necessary arrangements (if not, it's okay to leave this to family members, assuming you've properly communicated your instructions). To choose the right funeral home, first think about location. Is this home convenient for people who will be attending the service, or if the service will be elsewhere, is it convenient for your guests, and is it near the cemetery? Also, ask friends to recommend a funeral home they've used in the past. Feel free to shop around, but don't go crazy—if you have one or two good recommendations, you can trust the operation. Ask about pricing to make sure it's affordable and double-check that they offer the services you are looking for and that the space can accommodate the number of people you expect will attend.

One of the major costs of the funeral will be the casket and tombstone, which the funeral home can help you choose. Though some funeral homes may have displays, make sure you ask to see a full price list, since some of the less expensive caskets may not be on display. Don't fall victim to scams, like paying extra for a casket that's sealed to prevent decomposition (which is impossible). Do some research online to verify you're not paying extra for false promises. As for the model of casket and tombstone, consider a design that suits your style (choose between something simple, or something ornate), and lean on your support team of family and friends if you're having trouble making a decision (or affording the perfect item).

Quick tip: By law, funeral homes are required to accept and use caskets or tombstones that were not purchased from their establishment, so if you don't see anything you like or can afford at the home you choose, shop around.

One final step to ensure that you're remembered exactly as you wish to be: write your own obituary, and send it to the local paper. After all, they keep celebrity obituaries on file for years and years in case the celebrity dies suddenly, so why not yours?

How to Have an Eco-Friendly Burial (i.e., Cremation)

Cremation is much more common than it used to be. It's generally less expensive than a traditional burial, and the ashes can be handled in a number of ways, ranging from keeping them, to spreading them in your own backyard, to dropping them from an airplane over the Ganges River.

But amid the chaos following the death of a loved one, it's easy to get talked into an expensive burial. And while grieving, it's often difficult to remember that cremation is a respectful, viable, and yes, even eco-friendly option. So, if it's what *you* want for your own body (I know, it's not fun to think about but it's going to happen eventually), you should make it clear in your will (you have one of those, right? You should! See "How to Write a Will," page 207). In fact, you should really make it clear to your family as early as possible; often wills don't even get read until after the burial has taken place and then it just may be too late for your last wishes to be carried out.

If you are the next of kin to someone who has died without expressing his wishes for how his remains should be handled, you are now the official decision maker. So consider the options and remember that cremation makes the funeral process simpler (no protracted caravan to the ceremony, no digging), less expensive (no pricey coffin necessary), and environmentally friendly (no embalming, no taking up space in a cemetery).

Some people think that cremation means forgoing a proper funeral. That's not necessarily the case. If you've decided on cremation but also want to have a service, just get in touch with a funeral home and make it clear to the funeral home director that you have chosen cremation. You can still have a wake or viewing, but bear in mind that for these you'll then need to pay for a casket, so be sure to ask for a list of special cremation caskets (often these can get quite pricey, but sometimes they can be rented so be sure to inquire).

In most states, a body can't legally be cremated until at least forty-eight hours after the time of death. This gives family members the time they may need to make sure they all agree (or resurface, as in the case where there is a sizable inheritance—see "How to Squeeze Your Way into a Will," page 115) with this decision. Cremation is, after all, irreversible. Plus, if there is any suspicion of foul play, it gives the authorities time to check out (and hopefully rule out) this possibility. After cremation, the body cannot be exhumed, remains cannot be reexamined, and there can't ever be an autopsy, so the exact cause of death may never be determined. Many states also require that cremation be authorized by a medical examiner. If this is the case where you live, you'll be informed of this by the funeral director. And be sure to let the funeral director know if the deceased has any inorganic material he or she should be aware of—pacemakers, prostheses, implants, gold fillings, and so on—before they prepare the body, as these will need to be removed to ensure a safe cremation.

This next bit isn't pretty, so if you are squeamish, you may want to stop reading here. After the cremation process, the only things that will remain of your loved one are the bones. These are then pulverized and turned into what we call ashes. They are technically not ashes; they are crushed up bone fragments, but they look like ashes and it sounds much nicer than saying, "That lovely urn on my mantle contains Great-Aunt Betty's pulverized bone fragments." Plus, sometimes people scatter the remains in public places and you really wouldn't want to tell people you're scattering bone fragments around; it tends to make them uncomfortable.

By default, the ashes will be given to you in a temporary container, but the funeral director can provide you with options for a permanent vessel (usually some type of urn). A special container is not required (you could even put them in a cereal box if you really want to, although I sincerely hope you won't—that's the kind of thing that makes for a really bad sitcom plot), but a tasteful and elegant container is a nice touch. So better to go with some type of ceramic, glass, stone, or even titanium urn, with a nice airtight seal to prevent spillage.

From here, how you want to remember your loved one is up to you, be it displaying the urn in your living room or scattering the ashes across the sea. Some parks require permits to deseminate cremated remains, but as you can imagine, these rules are difficult to enforce, so I wouldn't worry too much about it. And remember: There is no rule that says you need a body to set up a tombstone, so you can still have a headstone or memorial placed somewhere so that relatives and friends of the departed have a place to pay their respects for generations to come.

Interested in a space burial? Check out www.celestis.com.

How to Write a Eulogy

Eulogies are often not easy to write. Someone close to you has passed away, and it's up to you to pull it together in front of a crowd of relatives and friends; choosing a few words that will best honor the memory of the departed. I mean, writing a normal speech is hard enough, and the pressure is now drastically increased by the idea that this will be your last chance to say something about the deceased in front of family and loved ones.

The thing to remember when writing a eulogy is that, just as with a toast (see "How to Write a Toast," page 147), it's not about you. Let me say it again—it's not about you. A eulogy is about the person who just passed. When people are grieving, they tend to want to talk about all the times *they* had with that person. If you are the person designated to speak at this important event, remember that it is a celebration of your *loved one*'s life—the person's entire life, not just the parts that involve you.

I was recently at a funeral where the speaker asked us to turn to the person next to us and describe three great things about the friend who had passed away. Then we were asked to turn to the person on the other side and say another three great things about her. This allowed us all to connect to who she was to others and to share what we would miss about her. After sharing what was great about her, we were then asked to share what we would do in our lives as a result of having known her. It was powerful. Not only did we have the opportunity to express our sorrow, but we were left with a reminder of the real and tangible difference she had made to the world she left behind.

If you prefer to give a traditional eulogy, it should *absolutely* be no longer than five minutes, unless you're the departed's spouse or child, and/or there aren't many other speakers. Again, the funeral or wake is about the deceased, and an overly long eulogy usually tends to shift the focus to you. I know you have a lot you want to say, and it can be tough to keep it brief, but really, keep your eulogy to a few minutes. Talk about who this person was, discuss his or her accomplishments, and offer a couple of meaningful anecdotes.

The best eulogies are the ones that keep it real. At a funeral, people are craving intimacy. In other words, avoid generic phrases like "He was a great father who loved his kids and always showed us how much he cared." Make it personal, and specific, like "He was a great father, I remember how Dad would always come home from work early to coach our soccer team and at the end of each season we'd celebrate with a party, win or lose." From that simple sentence, everyone in the room can truly connect with just who he was as a father.

When you sit down to actually write the eulogy, write it in the form of bullet points instead of a word-for-word transcription of what you intend to say. If you write in complete sentences, you're more likely to simply recite what you've written, which will make you come off as robotic and insincere (even if you aren't). Bullet points will remind you of what you want to say while giving you the freedom to improvise a little and let your emotions shine through.

As with all public speaking, practice. Although it may feel weird, and it may be difficult to do while you're so upset, it'll help you be better prepared. Bottom line: Giving the eulogy won't be fun, but if you think about it as an opportunity to honor the departed, give comfort to the people in mourning, and empower them to live their own lives to their full potential, it will often be much easier than you think.

How to Find a Good Taxidermist

It sounds bizarre, but people need taxidermists for a variety of reasons. Maybe you or someone in your family hunts; maybe your favorite pet has passed on and you want to preserve him forever (see "How to Find a Pet Psychic to Channel Your Dead Pet," page 220, if you need a pet psychic); maybe you just want to mount a moose head on the wall. Whatever the reason, taxidermy isn't just for backwoods inbreeds or serial killers anymore, so you'll want to know how to get the best taxidermist your money can buy.

A great place to start is the National Taxidermists Association (www.nationaltaxidermists.com). You might be tempted to write this off as just a group of rifle-toting hunting freaks, but it's a reputable organization, one that also serves as a kind of Better Business Bureau for taxidermists. Membership requires approval and all members must follow bylaws that ensure they are operating in a safe, humane, and legal manner.

Even though anyone on this list is most likely legit, you'll probably want to do a little more research before deciding who to go with. Taxidermy, like tattooing, is an art that must be done right the first (and only) time, so a good taxidermist will understand if you have a lot of questions about the business. And be sure to ask for references or photos of their work before committing.

Of course, if you happen to see a particular piece of taxidermy that strikes you, perhaps in your friend's basement, or at your favorite ski lodge, just ask the owner where it was done. Believe it or not, people who use taxidermists are usually proud of their game, so to speak.

But the tricky bit isn't so much finding the artist as it is transporting what you need mounted to the shop. If you're going hunting, it's a good idea to make arrangements with the taxidermist *before* you bag the deer, so you're not driving around for days with a three-hundred-pound corpse in your car. Some taxidermists might come and pick it up from you, or alternatively, you might have to ship it (and hey, good luck explaining that to the guy at the FedEx counter). If you do have to hang onto the carcass for a while, be sure to keep it below forty degrees Fahrenheit. Although there are no strict guidelines as to how long it will keep, obviously the carcass should get to the taxidermist ASAP.

If you're having a pet stuffed, know that a taxidermist will not be able to create something cuddly that your two-year-old can play with. If you must see Fluffy every day, your best bet (other than a nice portrait, that is) is to put the body on ice as soon as your pet dies and immediately start making calls to find out the next step. If you already think this is what you'll want for your pet when the time comes, it doesn't hurt to start researching now. The sooner an animal is brought to a taxidermist, the better the chances it will be preserved correctly. One note about mounting pets: It can cost a lot more than wildlife. There are stock parts for bears, deer, fish, and other common hunting game, but the artist will need to design custom fittings for your pooch or feline. So while preserving your pet's memory forever may be priceless, having it mounted on your wall isn't.

Finally (again, much like a tattoo), it's a good idea to provide the artist with a photo. If it's your pet, provide some snapshots. If it's something you hunted, a picture that shows that type of animal in the desired pose will help ensure you get what you want.

Let me reiterate, it's best to find the taxidermist *before* the hunting trip and not the other way around.

How to Find a Pet Psychic to Channel Your Dead Pet

To others, he was just another pooch. Or a typical house cat. Or your average hamster. To you, he was a beloved and irreplaceable friend whose death has left an empty void that cannot be filled. As painful as losing a pet is, it can be even worse when mysterious circumstances surround his or her death. So if you want to find out how exactly how your little friend Fido died—or simply get some closure—it's time to get in touch with your dearly departed.

Pet psychics, like their human-convening counterparts, may not be for hardened cynics. But if you're open to the Other World, they could be a viable option. So when one of my clients wanted to find out how his cat had died without subjecting the body to an autopsy, I offered him the pet psychic option.

When choosing a pet psychic, be aware that not all mediums use the same methods. Some channel, some read palms (yours, not the corpse's), some use tarot cards, some use crystal balls. Some psychics do the talking with your animal's spirit, while others let you have a direct conversation. Some may also use a picture or object that belonged to the animal (such as a collar or a leash) to facilitate communication and to better channel your beloved pet. There is no right or wrong when making your choice, just go with whichever method suits you and choose someone with whom you feel a connection.

As with most oddities, Google and Craigslist are great for drumming up leads (be sure to ask for references to find out how past customers rate the readings), but a safer bet is a referral from a friend or someone whose opinion you trust. That's how I found Jane, a Massachusetts-based animal communicator, who revealed to my client that his feline, Moshe, had suffered a brain aneurysm after jumping from a high perch and hitting his head. Suddenly the unusual thump my client had heard in the middle of the night that Moshe died, a week earlier, made sense.

The reading was done over the phone. Jane had my client send in a photo prior to the call and as the conversation began, she summoned up Moshe. (All psychics have different styles of getting connected to the deceased; some take their shoes off, some repeat a chant. There are many different ways, and it is just a matter of what works or how your medium was trained.) Then, channeling the cat, she spoke directly to my client. He went into it with an open mind, and via Jane, Moshe was able to pass his final words of good-bye on to my client. "I didn't know this was going to happen," Moshe told his owner. "I wish I hadn't left you so suddenly. I wasn't in pain . . . I am at peace and I will miss you."

My client was still devastated, but at least he now had closure.

If you don't know anyone you can ask for a referral (or even if you do), visit the would-be clairvoyant yourself and see if your own sixth sense picks up on anything about the person—good, bad, or otherwise. This is one instance where you will really want to trust your gut. Because honestly, when it comes to the supernatural, what other choice do you have?

Be aware, of course, that going the psychic route is likely to raise a few eyebrows. You may not be perceived as being of sound mind, but if it brings you peace of mind, who cares?

Trust the process. What have you got to lose?

9. home sweet home

How to Make Your Move Smooth and Easy

Moving is all about boxes.

If you are moving, boxes will consume your life. Everywhere you look, there will be boxes. Boxes, boxes, boxes. So to make your move smooth and easy, the key is to focus on the boxes.

We recently had a client who just didn't want to think about the boxes—packing them, labeling them, or moving them. He simply packed his suitcase, said good-bye to his apartment, and handed us the keys to both pads. After a short weekend away, he got off the plane and opened the door to his new apartment, which had everything unpacked and in its place. He never saw a single box.

How do you make this magic happen? Three words: call a professional. Professionals guarantee that your boxes are safely packed, clearly labeled, and that they get unpacked, and disappear as quickly as possible from your new home. Definitely outsource your move if you don't want to deal with boxes. If you think you *might* not want to deal with boxes, I'll bet you that you don't. I get people packed up and moved into their new homes *all* the time, and what usually happens is, people *think* they *should* pack their own boxes, so they get some cartons and spend a few weekends thinking about how they really need to start packing up the stuff they are going to move. But then they don't actually do it, and when moving day rolls around, they have to have someone to pack them up anyway. Believe me, you don't need this kind of stress.

If you don't want to pay for movers and have to pack your own boxes, my first piece of advice is to purchase more boxes than you think you'll need and get them in various sizes. Trust me, you'll always end up using more boxes than you anticipate, and even if you do end up with extras, it's worth the price to have all different sizes on hand at your disposal. When you choose which carton to use for what, consider the weight of what is going inside. For example, don't use huge boxes for books. The book boxes may look small, but books are heavy. Plus, having extra boxes will encourage you to *not* pack every single box to the brim, and to pack like items together (for easier organizing when you unpack). Last thing: Don't forget to order packing tape and paper to wrap and protect delicate items.

Now for the labeling. The absolute most important thing you can do to make your move smooth and easy is to *label every single box as specifically as possible*. Too many people make the mistake of just writing "Living Room" or "Books." General words like this will not be very helpful when you're unpacking; it's a lot more difficult than you'd think to find your favorite cookbook amid thirty random boxes marked "Books." I always hire professional movers to pack and even if the moving men say that they are labeling the boxes, then, I always follow them around with a marker so I can note more specifically what is inside each carton.

In addition to the box's contents, be sure to write the *destination room* on the outside of the box. If it's not clear, your bathroom boxes may get mixed in with your kitchen boxes and having to lug heavy boxes to the other end of the house is a pain. Don't forget to write on two sides of each box (not just the top in case it ends up at the bottom of a stack).

If you use movers, make signs and hang them outside each room in your new place to help the movers easily identify what goes where.

After everything is packed up and ready to go, do a walk through the entire place. Check closets, drawers, even the oven. Be sure there is not a thing left. Then, if you're game, take a moment and say good-bye to your place. This may sound silly, but you lived there. You have memories (good, bad, or otherwise) there and it's nice to close one door before you transition into something new. Take a minute to reflect on your place and say good-bye before opening a new door, for new experiences, in a new home.

After all the boxes are moved into your new home, before you breathe a sigh of relief, walk down to the street and take one final glance in the truck to make sure that everything has been unloaded, *before* the movers pull away. Once that's done, it's time to unpack.

Now you're really in the homestretch. All your boxes should be in the correct rooms and the outside of the boxes are clearly labeled so that you know exactly what you are going to find when you open the boxes. Do yourself a favor here and unpack as quickly as possible. The goal is to get rid of the boxes. Call in favors and enlist the help of anyone who asks if you need anything. Yes, you do. You need to get rid of the boxes. If none of your friends are game, consider hiring an organizer to assist you in getting the job done quickly. It's money well spent (and I'm not just saying that because it's what we do all the time).

Don't obsess over putting everything in the perfect place (it's easy to move your wine glasses to a lower shelf later on), just get things put away neatly—somewhere.

Finally, once all the boxes are gone, throw away the bubble wrap and break out the bubbly! Welcome to your new home.

Be sure to have a box or two designated for the things
you will need immediately: bedding, towels and bathroom items
(including toilet paper and soap), box cutters, and your iPod dock!

How to Organize Your Closet in Twenty Minutes

Okay, it's time. Your closet has looked like a clothes jungle long enough. Sorry, but I have to say it: you need to organize that sucker.

But don't fret. No matter how much clothing you have jammed in there, organizing your closet doesn't have to be an all-day affair. In fact, you can do it in just twenty minutes. To get started, go to The Container Store, Pottery Barn, IKEA, or some other organizational store (*Note:* This does not count as part of the twenty minutes.) and buy a bunch of matching hangers. You can even do this online (check out www. henryhanger.com). Remember: The "matching" part is important; your closet will look *far* more organized if everything hangs on identical hangers. Don't believe me? How many clothing stores have you seen hang their wares on a variety of hangers?

That's what I thought.

It's not just because of the matching colors, it's also because different types of hangers hang clothes in different ways, taking up extra space and making your wardrobe look jumbled. Go for some version of flat wooden or nonslip hangers, *not* wire ones. Trust me here, it's worth the splurge. Don't get all ambitious and try to color-code the hangers for different types of clothing (black for formal, blue for everyday, red for ninja wear, etc.), because this never stays organized for long. Plus, every time you purchase a new item, you'll also need to make sure you have the correct color hanger. Just keep it simple and make sure the hangers *all* match.

Once you've procured your hangers, get some paper shopping bags— the nice-looking ones, in good condition. Now, you're ready to start the clock. Take everything out of the closet. *Everything.* Toss it on the bed and get sorting.

Everything should go into one of three piles: donate, keep or can't decide (yes, you get to keep those for now), and store.

The "donate" pile should contain everything in less-than-perfect condition or that you can never imagine yourself wearing again. It's easy; anything with stains, tears, or from the 1980s should go into a bag (a trash bag is fine for this), and be promptly donated to charity (see "How to Easily Donate Clothes," page 376).

The "keep" pile is what you wear most often (black V-neck sweater, I'm looking at you) or your go-to special occasion getup. This actually shouldn't even really be a pile—anything you're keeping should go right back into the closet on one of your shiny new matching hangers.

See how easy? You're almost home.

Remember those nice empty shopping bags? Well, one of them is for whatever you can't decide whether to keep. These are the items you haven't worn since Bush (hopefully W.) was in office but aren't quite ready to part with because you may wear them *sometime*. Maybe it's the (expensive) cashmere sweater you bought and only wore once but the guilt would be too much to take if you just gave it away. Maybe it's those jeans you're saving for your extra-skinny days that are right around the corner . . . yeah, right.

Whatever the case may be, place these items in one of those nice shopping bags and give it a home in the bottom of your closet. If you find that another entire season (or year) goes by and you haven't even peeked into the bag (write a date on the bag so you can keep track), kiss it goodbye and send it off to the Salvation Army (or any other charity). You can use the tax deduction to purchase something you'll actually wear. If, over the course of the next few months, you do take items out of the "store" bag and wear them, hang them with your "keep" clothes. The beauty of the shopping bag is that the items are there if you need them and if not, simply pick up the bag and take it right out the door, guilt free.

Last step: storage. This is for clothes you really like but don't wear all that much—maybe it's a climate thing, or you just don't have the occasion to wear them often. Whatever the case, it's time to give these babies a new home. Either find another closet to use, or rent a storage unit. There are also services (like www.garderobeonline.com) that not only store your clothes for you, they take photos of your clothing and let you access your own wardrobe online (kind of like in that scene from *Clueless*). When you decide what you want to wear, they'll send it right over in clean and ready-to-wear condition. And if you need anything for an upcoming vacation, just let them know and your clothes can even meet you there.

Congratulations! Your closet should now look neat as a pin. Beautiful, isn't it? Go ahead, take it all in: you're organized, and in record time. Go, you.

How to Get Your Scummy Landlord to Replace Your Broken Refrigerator

Getting a scummy landlord to fix just about anything can be challenging, to say the least. A nice landlord, maybe, but a "scummy" one—well, you're talking about the ultimate test. Getting him to change a lightbulb here and there, replace a part on a leaking sink, or investigate that weird creaking noise that's keeping you up till 3:00 A.M. . . . that's doable. Getting him to replace a major appliance like a refrigerator, on the other hand, is a bigger challenge. Many landlords won't want to go near this fragile but crucial piece of equipment, because the cost of fixing a broken refrigerator, even if the symptoms are mild, can approach the hefty price of a brand-new machine. But know that if you're renting, and the refrigerator came with the apartment, it's your landlord's responsibility to replace it when the time comes—whether he likes it or not.

For this reason, even if you think that the time has come, your landlord may believe that food stored slightly north of room temperature is perfectly fine to eat. For cases like this, there's strength in numbers. If you complain, no matter how many times, it will likely fall on (willfully) deaf ears. But if everyone in the building complains, your landlord will be left with no choice.

But how do you round up a building full of people with whom your most meaningful interactions are "Hi" and "Cold out, isn't it?" First, draft a letter explaining your situation, why you think your refrigerator (or whatever else is broken) should be replaced, and that you think you'll all fare better against your landlord if you work together. Make sure to include your e-mail address, and ask people to contact you if they agree and would like to help. Then just slip the note under your neighbors' doors, or leave a stack in the front hall. If you're having this kind of trouble with the landlord, chances are many of your neighbors will have had similar tangles with him in the past and may be happy to help you teach him a lesson. A growing trend for large apartment buildings is to have some sort of electronic communication service that links everyone in the building. If your building has a system like this, you should be able to e-mail everyone in your building directly.

Once you have the neighbors on your side, arrange a short, informal meeting. All co-ops and most condos also have a residents' association of some sort, usually with a board made up of a handful of elected residents who tend to wield influence with the building's owner. If you don't already know them, now is the time to make friends. Explain your situation in person. They can help organize a meeting or fold the refrigerator issue into the agenda of an already scheduled one. If everyone's on board, you or your elected representative should present a united front against the landlord; and with enough support, you'll have a new refrigerator in no time.

If your neighbors refuse to rally (selfish!) and you're all on your own, tell your landlord that a working refrigerator was part of your lease agreement (make sure that's true, of course) and threaten legal action. If he calls your bluff, it's not worth actually hiring a lawyer; instead, let the food in your broken fridge spoil, throw it in your trash, then "accidentally" leave the trash where he'll be sure to smell it. That'll send a message—but beware, you'll either get a new refrigerator, or you'll get evicted.

Another plan (when you are talking scumbag, it usually helps to have more than one plan): Purchase the new fridge yourself and subtract the cost from your next rent payment. Might as well splurge on the chrome subzero model with a fancy freezer while you're at it. It will cost him a lot more than the new icebox to take you to court.

Last ditch option: Have someone else, like a friend or family member who doesn't live in the building, ask him. This often works, I know, because I do it for my clients. Since I'm not living there, I can yell and scream all I want (and get what my client is entitled to) without fear of repercussion. I have nothing to lose, so it's much easier to for me to negotiate.

Then, there is the opposite plan; you know, kill him with kindness. Just when you're the most pissed off, leave a fresh-baked batch of cookies on his doorstep. And keep being nice, until he feels guilty. Yes, even scumbags have feelings.

How to Locate a Matching Spoon for Your Grandmother's Silver Set

My first project when I opened the Consider It Done office in New York was to arrange a move. I hadn't been in town more than a week when I bumped into someone on the street who recognized me from Aspen. She had a friend who could use my help with his move. Of course I was game. It turned out it needed to be done right away. (I have theories on moving, one of them being that because people don't like it, they put it off, and subsequently become even more frantic as the big day approaches.) In this case, the client was moving, while his ex-wife was staying in the apartment. I got his items out of the apartment and moved into his new place smoothly and easily (see "How to Make Your Move Smooth and Easy," page 222), but then he called Saturday morning and said, "You have to help me get the artwork." Of course I would help, I said, and I offered to schedule the art movers for first thing Monday morning. That wasn't going to work. He wanted the art out immediately and wanted my help doing it. I mentioned the fact that it was *pouring* rain outside, but he didn't care. So I arrived with a box of extrastrength trash bags, some tape, and the biggest umbrella I could find. And we moved the art. Although I really don't recommend this method for moving expensive (and um, yes, in this case museum-quality) artwork, I got the job done and managed not to ruin any priceless Picassos in the process. This was my first client in New York City.

Since this day over a decade ago I have arranged more moves than I can count. Moving often unearths many family treasures and I'm usually the person clients ask, "What should I do with this?" or "How can I find the missing pieces for my grandmother's silver set?" This one can be particularly challenging, especially if the set is really old. But as you've probably realized by now, there's nothing I like more than a good challenge.

To locate a matching item—say, a spoon—from an old silver set your first stop should be to check out www.replacements.com, where you can search by name for the particular set you have. That is, of course, if you know the name of the set you have, or the designer or manufacturer. Any of these pieces of information will get you one step closer, but nothing is guaranteed to be an exact match. Caution: If a vendor says that he has a knife from the same set and can custom make you a spoon, I would advise against it. I tried this once and the piece ended up looking like a spoon with a knife handle and quite honestly a bit weird. (The place did take it back at no charge.) Also, a custom-made utensil could be at a different stage of wear and tear and might not blend in with your set exactly.

In all likelihood, however, you may not have any information about the spoon other than what it looks like, or what other utensils in the set look like. In this case, try www.silversmithing.com. You can't buy straight from this site, but you can browse through patterns, and if you see one that looks like yours, you'll at least know what it's called. Also, check auction websites, like eBay, which generally post photos of the items. Anyone selling antique silverware online may have even more in stock, so even if you don't see your particular pattern, feel free to contact the seller directly—you might find that she has a large antique warehouse and can help you find exactly what you're looking for from her supply. Many sellers rotate the inventory that they post online, so this will cut out the waiting time.

But if you really want to be sure you have an exact match, photos won't do. You need to see and feel the real thing. Instead of an online auction house, visit a *real* auction house. They may be old-fashioned, but they can actually be quite fun. Speak to the manager of the auction house, and find out the next time antique silverware will be up for sale. Be prepared to spend some money—but remember that it's a family heirloom you're replacing, and family heirlooms are priceless.

If you can't find the matching pieces that you need, consider selling what's left of your set. Obviously it's rare enough to be worth something.

How to Make Sure Your Renovations Are Completed on Time

Most people who have lived through a renovation project will tell you that this one is impossible—that there's no way to make sure renovations are completed on time. They're not entirely correct. Of course, I can see why they think this. I remember how once, in the early days of Consider It Done, I packed my weekend bag to go to Palm Beach to oversee a small renovation project. Three months later I returned home. I have since perfected the art of getting renovations done on time and can tell you that, while not easy, it's not a futile effort.

Yes, one common characteristic among contractors, even the best ones, is that they are *usually* behind schedule, so the only foolproof strategy I can let you in on to ensure that your renovations are completed on time is this: Give your contractor a fake deadline, two weeks earlier than you actually need the renovations completed. But don't even consider letting the contractor or anyone working on the job in on this. You will want the contractor and any of his crew to think that all your furniture and personal items will be arriving on the date that you agreed upon, and that everything *must* be completed by then. Even if it's not complete by that date (and it probably won't be), this strategy *will* get it all finished up within two weeks of that date—which, for all intents and purposes, is the real end date anyway.

There are other ways to at least attempt to speed up the process. First, get both cost *and* time estimates from a few different contractors before you begin, and cross-check the estimates with their references. A shorter (or less expensive) estimate doesn't necessarily mean anything if they can't pull it off. Specifically ask the reference you call if the job took much longer than promised (and/or was way over budget). Again, contractors almost always run over their estimate, so if you find someone who worked with a contractor who at least *came close* to sticking to time and budget, you're in good shape. But be sure you are comparing apples to apples; if an estimate looks low, it may be because it doesn't include *everything*. Make sure you ask a ton of questions to avoid any such surprises.

Another trick is to work a clause into your agreement that gives your contractor a bonus for on-time completion. Don't worry, you probably won't have to fork it over, and if you do, it'll be money well spent. In fact, it's probably money saved—if the renovation takes longer, it's going to cost more money anyway. But that added bonus can give your contractor the extra incentive he needs to finish quickly, since he'll get to keep the entire amount of the bonus instead of having to spend it on additional parts and labor.

Once the job begins, know that how close he comes to the proposed finish date has a direct correlation to the time and energy you put in as a spectator and inspector, so be vigilant. Stop by the job site, daily if necessary. If the renovations are being made on your own home, it's easy to become complacent and not "visit" the site, since you figure you live there. Notice if you may be subconsciously avoiding that area of the house, even though you're just a room away, because there's a chaotic renovation going on, and be sure to regularly venture into the rooms being renovated. Spend some time there—more than just a five-minute walk-through. Review the to-do list with your contractor weekly, if not more often. If you are too laid-back and relaxed, your contractor will be too, and these are not qualities that bode well for on-time completion. Your presence at the site—and the fact that you're staying on top of the progress—will keep everyone working as quickly as possible.

If you need the renovations done in time for a specific event, do yourself a favor: plan the event so that it doesn't depend on the renovations (in other words, don't get married in your childhood home if it means adding a new wing to your house to do it). Contractors are good with hammers, but not so much with schedules, or deadlines.

How to Furnish a Home Quickly

Some people get such a thrill from designing and decorating their home that they stretch it out for months (even years!). Sure, we all want to find the dining room table that perfectly complements our antique china, and the sofa pillows in the same shade of blue as the stripes in the rug, but let's face it; to decorate your entire home so that everything is perfectly pulled together, you need to have impeccable taste *and* endless amounts of time and patience. Which brings us to the others, the people who just don't have time or interest in all this hassle and who don't like living in limbo. They want the moving truck to pull up and their new home to be ready, set, go.

Many of my clients want it all (and they deserve to have it all, as do you!). They want a perfectly pulled together pad, and they want it now. I remember a client who called from Utah to let me know that he would be in New York in two weeks and, by the way, could we have his apartment ready? He didn't care what the place looked like as long as he could just walk through the door and feel "at home." With just two short weeks to pick out everything from paint colors to bathmats, it was like being on an episode of *Extreme Makeover*.

But amazingly, it turned out great, so if you find yourself in a situation where you need to furnish your home quickly, here's the skinny.

The easiest and most obvious way to furnish a home is to hire an interior designer who can do the entire job for you. Keep in mind that this does not necessarily come cheaply, nor is it guaranteed to be quick. If you go this route, make sure it's someone whose style aligns with yours. If you want to save money, one way is to seek out a designer who is just starting out. Plenty of beginning designers are looking to build a portfolio and will jump at the chance. You can find them at design schools or sometimes working in furniture showrooms. Choose a showroom with a style you like and then find out if someone who works there can help you pull it all together. Another option is to ask your realtor to recommend a "stager" (aka someone whose job is to make homes pretty so they will sell faster). These people are pros at pulling a room together quickly.

Whether you're working with a designer or giving it a go on your own, if your intention is to be quick, you'll need to be flexible. For one, you'll want to choose items that are in stock, so you can have them delivered immediately. Floor samples and closeout merchandise are great, because they are sometimes sold for less money and are ready to roll out of the store. Just look for things that don't have much wear and tear (i.e., have not been on the floor long!). The best part about going to a store (as opposed to ordering online) is that you can enlist an in-store designer. Don't be shy about taking up such designers' time. That's what they're hired to do, and you'll be laying down plenty of cash at the end, so there's nothing to feel bad about. At Crate & Barrel, you can schedule a free forty-five-minute makeover with one of their consultants. To use this time efficiently, be sure you show up with measurements and floor plans.

It can be helpful to check out catalogs to get inspiration and to see completed rooms. Pick out the main pieces first—what's absolutely essential as far as giving a room a pulled-together look—and then fill in the final touches at the end. Also, consider getting a couple of impressive, more expensive pieces, and then mixing in some IKEA. At first glance, your house will still give the impression of high end (this is a trick the wealthy pull off all the time. It's how they stay rich!). And don't ignore knockoffs. There are some really good ones out there, and the best part is, if you ever suddenly find yourself with the time and desire to *re*decorate, you can toss them, guilt-free.

How to Be Sure You Have the Necessities in Your Kitchen

Some people think that in order to cook up a gourmet meal, your kitchen needs to look like the showroom at Williams-Sonoma. It doesn't. When I get clients moved into their new homes, one of the things they often need help with is making sure that they have the necessities to get them started. So I know for a fact that it *is* possible to be fully functional in the kitchen with nothing more than a few pots and pans, a couple of knives, and a few other basic kitchen devices. Here's a quick rundown of all the equipment you'll need to create a feast at a moment's notice out of whatever ingredients you happen to have on hand.

Let's start with the basics. Anything you cook is going to require at least one of the following: a large pot for boiling water, a strainer, a heavy-bottomed frying pan or wok, or a thin-bottomed pan (usually for sautéing). Cast iron is an excellent choice for the heavy frying pan, while stainless steel or aluminum is a better material for the lighter cookware. You also want to make sure to have at least two smaller saucepans for cooking and reheating sauces, gravies, and compounds.

For preparation, all you really need is a sturdy cutting board and a set of good knives. For the cutting board, wood is the standard and all around best. Avoid plastic ones, because they can be damaged easily and can even melt on contact with hot surfaces. You can buy knives in sets from many home furnishing or kitchen stores, like Sur la Table, or Williams-Sonoma, or even IKEA, but if you don't want to invest in a whole set, the main three go-tos are a French knife (large, sharp blade for chopping vegetables), a paring knife (smaller knife for delicate work like peeling vegetables or deveining shrimp), and a cleaver (for meat and bone cutting). You might also invest in a peeler and a pair of kitchen scissors. A food processor or blender is also useful for many recipes, but a clever cook can figure out other ways to achieve similar effects with a little elbow grease (remember you've got a cleaver and a cast-iron skillet).

As for the food itself, it's impossible to keep every ingredient you might ever need on hand, but a few items are so commonly used and are great staples to keep in your pantry at all times. Have at least one red and one white vinegar on hand for salads, sauces, and flavoring. Also, be sure never to run out of olive oil (extra virgin is what most recipes call for) and kosher salt.

Every cook should also have a few basics in the seasoning department. Cilantro, chives, basil, thyme (lemon thyme is terrific), parsley, rosemary, cinnamon, and nutmeg are good starters. Penzey's Spices (www.penzeys. com) offers customized spice racks containing all the spices you will need for a multitude of recipes—everything from Italian to Indian to baking. They are well worth the minimal investment in time and flavor.

Now that you're prepared with all the basics, you're ready for anything. So just stop in at your local farmers' market or grocery store and decide what's for dinner. Bon appétit!

How to Disassemble and Reinstall an Antique Chandelier

You're moving your grandmother's belongings out of her house and you suddenly realize it never occurred to anyone what to do about the chandelier. Sounds like a pretty unlikely scenario, but I have actually run into this on more than one occasion. Antique chandeliers are fragile, tough to reassemble, and expensive (if not impossible) to fix or replace, so you will definitely want to put a little thought and planning into this if you ever want to use (or sell) the chandelier again.

First off (and this is actually good news), know that your movers generally won't touch it. They will have you call an electrician (unless it is so old that it uses candles, not electricity). A skilled electrician should be familiar with the process of dismantling chandeliers, but call around until you find someone who knows what he or she is doing. If you can't find an electrician, call an auction house. They also deal with chandeliers and can usually recommend a pro.

If you want to give it a go yourself, first break out the digital camera and take a ton of pictures of your chandelier from all possible angles. Get a ladder out if you need to (you probably will need one when you disassemble the chandelier anyway) to take close-ups as well as wide shots. You can't take too many photos, and the more angles you have, the easier it will be to reassemble the chandelier later. I'd recommend taking "before" pictures even if you've hired someone who claims to know what he is doing. Once it's down, it's down, and though you may think you remember *exactly* what it looked like when it was assembled, after it's taken apart, all the pieces will look the same and putting it together will feel like a giant 3D jigsaw puzzle.

Quick tip: Before you begin disassembling, put a towel and some cushions on the floor below to catch any pieces you might drop. Just one broken gem can ruin the entire chandelier.

In addition to taking pictures, you may want to create a blueprint of where each piece goes and how it fits together with the other pieces. If spatial relations isn't your strong suit, invite a friend over to help draw the map—just make sure the friend sticks around for the reassembly or you might not be able to decipher his scribbling. Not reassembling it right away? You should. If that's not an option for whatever reason, at least practice putting it together once so that you know your guide works. It may seem like a lot of extra effort while you're in the midst of moving boxes, but if you put the box in storage and wait months (or even years) before reinstalling, it'll be that much more difficult to remember how to put humpty together again.

Quick tip: Now is also a good time to clean your chandelier. If you have a crystal chandelier, call a lighting retail shop to recommend cleaning products. I've read there is a mixture you can create at home consisting of one part isopropyl alcohol or ammonia to three parts distilled water. But I can't vouch for having tried this so I recommend calling in an expert.

Finally, once all the prep work is done, to reinstall your chandelier, start from the inside and work your way out, following your guide as carefully as possible. After each small section you assemble, cross-reference the photos you took to make sure they match. If your map or guide has enough detail, and if you took enough photos of each part of the chandelier from various angles, it should be fairly straightforward. The mistake most people make is thinking that reassembly will be easy and intuitive, but the process is actually as delicate and intricate as the chandelier itself.

How to Get Your Movers to Rearrange Your Furniture One Last Time

Moving into a new home is exciting. That is, once all your furniture is moved in and your boxes are unpacked (see "How to Make Your Move Smooth and Easy," page 222). But until you get to that point, moving equals stress—especially when large pieces of furniture don't fit through doorways or the cat goes missing amid all of the chaos, and of course these crises inevitably happen at just about the time that the cable company shows up and wants to know where the TV is . . .

Most of us only go through this moving hell a few times in our lives, but imagine if you did it day in and day out. I suppose you would save money on a gym membership, but still, being a mover doesn't top the Dream Job list for anyone. So treat your movers nicely—they're doing a job that, quite frankly, blows.

If you want to get your movers to go the extra mile for you, politeness is of utmost importance. "Do you mind being extra careful with that?" and "I changed my mind again, can we move everything in this room to the room upstairs?" are requests you'll want to deliver as sweetly as possible. After all, they're handling all of your precious possessions and will likely be more careful with things belonging to someone who is nice to them. So call them by name, smile, and remember your pleases and thank-yous.

Consider politeness a prerequisite. But here are a few additional little tricks to get your relationship with your movers off on the right foot. The best thing is to do something extra nice for them *before* they even get started. Why not have donuts and coffee for the movers when they arrive. Make this a continental acquaintance breakfast—learn your movers' names and a few details about their lives. Just five minutes of small talk can create a real bond, one that will come in handy when they're handling your antique china. Movers will often bend over backward for you if you make them feel appreciated.

Even more than keeping them feeling appreciated is keeping them well fed. After the heavy lifting is done, these guys probably have worked up a huge appetite. So order a pizza (or two). Believe me, this $20 investment will pay off in the end when you're asking them to move your couch to a different spot just one more time as you practice your feng shui skills.

If you don't have time to plan these niceties for your movers, tipping generously works well too. Consider tipping them before the day begins so they'll want to go the extra mile for you before the last box has been unloaded, and then again at the end if they've done a good job. A general tipping gauge is $5–$10 per man per hour, depending on how happy you are with the service.

Last piece of advice: Develop a relationship with someone in the main office. If there's a problem, it's better to call the company than to confront your movers face-to-face. You should remain on good terms with the muscle and let their office set them straight.

Keep plenty of water readily available—you'll need it too!

How to Fix a Hole in the Wall

No, I'm not going to tell you how to fix the hole that some guy punched in the wall of the fraternity house after his girlfriend broke up with him. I'm talking normal, smallish holes, mostly from screws and nails. Walls get holes, and holes need fixing. Luckily, this can be done pretty easily and quickly.

Smaller holes, like from a nail, screw, or small crack, can be filled with caulk and painted over. Mighty Putty also works like a charm on smaller flaws—it can fill up a crack perfectly and be smoothed out so cleanly that it's almost impossible to detect once it's painted over.

This works if all you care about is not seeing the hole, but if you need to put another screw or nail into exactly the same spot, here's a great tip. Go get some sawdust, which you can find at lumberyards, hardware stores, or pet stores (they use it in the bottom of the gerbil cages) and mix it with some Elmer's glue. Just patch up the hole with your concoction and let it dry, then paint over it. It's practically free, it works like a charm, and you'll feel really handy. Because let's face it, everyone likes to feel handy.

If the hole's a little larger, like the size of a fist (though hopefully not from an actual fist), find a tin can lid that is slightly larger than the hole you're repairing and drill two holes in the lid so you can string a wire through like a hook. Slip the lid through the hole, then pull the wire so the lid's face is pressed against the hole. Apply caulk, plaster, or Mighty Putty to the can lid to hold it in place, remove the wire, and finish patching it up and painting it over. Again, good as new! (This trick also works for slightly larger holes—it's just a matter of finding a piece of metal big enough to bridge the edges of the crack.)

Any repairs bigger than that are out of my league and may require a professional, or a trip to Home Depot. They sell repair kits (as do most other hardware stores) that are easy to use and come in a number of varieties depending on the size of the hole and the type of surface you're dealing with (though they usually just consist of pieces of drywall of various sizes and thicknesses). Snap a picture of the hole and the surrounding area and show it to someone at the hardware store. Photos always seem to help.

With a little time and effort, you can make any wall look as good as new. But the next time you get angry, do yourself and your wall a favor and just take it outside.

In the event of a major hole, the kind that looks like a cartoon character came crashing through your house leaving a perfect outline of its shape, you'll probably want to hire a contractor.

How to Move a Twenty-Gallon Fish Tank

Fish are great pets. You don't have to play with them, you don't have to clean up after them, and sometimes you don't even really need to feed them. Even if you have dozens swimming around in a giant aquarium, they are no more trouble than your average houseplant. But as easy as they are to care for (and stare at), if you ever need to move the tank—maybe you got a sudden job offer in Peoria, or you're just oh so ready for a change of pace—you may no longer think fish are so easy.

The reason? Water is heavy. Really, really heavy. And even a relatively small tank holds at least twenty gallons of the stuff. Excluding the glass, lid, filters, and attached paraphernalia, twenty gallons of water weighs 167 pounds. Even if you could lift it, moving a giant glass tank can be hazardous.

As part of my business, I get people packed up and moved all the time, with or without fish. So I know that moving is often a traumatizing experience, even when it's an exciting change. It's stressful to be removed from the environment you are comfortable in, and it's a huge hassle to pack up and transport all your worldly belongings. So when I have clients with large aquariums, I usually recommend leaving the tank (one less thing to deal with) and just starting over with a fresh one in their new location.

But if you don't want to invest in a new tank, or worry that it will prove too disorienting to your fish (or your kids), the first thing you should know is that although a mover will move an empty tank, they will almost never move the actual fish. They really don't want to be liable for this sort of thing. So you'll have to do it yourself. For a price, your local fish store may be willing to come in and handle the process, but if not, here are some key things to remember.

When moving into a new home, make the aquarium move the last step in the packing process and the first step when unpacking (I usually recommend the wine be the last packed up and the first unloaded, but we all have our different priorities), so the fish are out of their environment for the shortest amount of time possible. This is important, because when fish are put in small, unfiltered containers, the ammonia and nitrite levels in the water can get dangerously high (a condition called "new tank syndrome"). You may even consider holding off on feeding your fish for a few days before you move them so there will be less waste in their temporary home during the move. Less waste means cleaner water; plus waste can suck the oxygen right out of the water, and if left too long without oxygen, the fish will suffocate. Don't worry, they won't starve, and once they're in their new home, feeding can resume as usual.

You will need plastic bags or jars to transport the fish (just like how you would bring home a goldfish from a carnival) and a cooler big enough to fit the bags side by side without overlapping. You'll also want to transport your filter media in a sealed plastic bag filled with tank water to minimize the damage to bacteria colonies. Do the same with any plants and decorations, but leave the gravel at the bottom of the tank. When it's almost time to move the fish from their tank to their travel containers, you should even prepare your net by soaking it in water for at least ten minutes. This will soften it, so it's less likely to hurt the fish. Fill the bags or jars with enough tank water that fish will be fully covered even when the bags are set on the floor of the cooler, and gently drop little Nemo and his friends in. Finally, empty the aquarium itself, saving as much tank water as you can, and pack it carefully.

When you get your aquarium to its new location, pour the tank water back in and add as much new water as necessary. Get the filters up and running, and set up the decor as it was before. Don't worry about redecorating; just get the fish back in the tank that they know and love. If all goes well, they'll be untraumatized and back to their old tricks—subtle though they may be—in no time.

Consider a new plant or figurine for a tank-warming gift.

How to Get Rid of a Mildew Smell

Ugh, mildew. How is it possible that, with all of the great-smelling soaps, shampoos, and fresh towels in your bathroom, you've got mildew? And if you've got it, that dank, musty odor will be the only thing you can smell.

The worst part about mildew is its ability to permeate *everything*—tile, fabric, and even wallpaper. Not to worry, help is on the way!

Let's clear one thing up. The best way to get rid of a mildew smell is to get rid of . . . you guessed it, the mildew. If you don't eliminate the root of the problem, the best you can hope to do is mask the stench, but that's going to be a quick fix and will only work for so long.

Mildew is caused by prolonged moisture and humidity, hence the bathroom being its favored location. That means every time you take a shower and leave excess water, mildew will start to form. Air circulation helps, so turning on a dehumidifier or exhaust fan or opening up a window after a shower is a good way to prevent it. Make sure that you also hang up towels and bathrobes separately so they can dry thoroughly. Even your kid's sneakers from the last rainy day can grow mildew if not dried property, so stick them in the drier before the stench starts to set in.

Not unlike the flu, once you have mildew, you have it until you figure out how to kick it. Luckily, there are a few quick elimination options. The first is a store-bought cleaner, of which there are many. Anything that's specially formulated for tile or is advertised as mildew fighting will do.

But if you don't have time to run to the store for a cleaner, you can try a handy (and cheap) household remedy. Baking soda, whether by itself or mixed with water to form a paste, will quickly both dissolve the mildew and eliminate the smell. Use an old toothbrush to spread it on tile and glass, concentrating especially on the grout between the tile and the areas on glass where water beads collect.

Vinegar also works well as a mildew fighter, but this replaces the mildew smell with a vinegar smell. Same with bleach—it'll get your tiles shiny at the cost of nauseating vapors. Remember that it can be dangerous to breathe in bleach fumes, so if the room doesn't have windows or ventilation, be sure to give yourself plenty of time to air out the area after cleaning.

To get mildew out of shoes or clothing, just buy some Borax at a supermarket or drugstore and mix it, in equal parts, with *powdered* laundry soap (not liquid). Pour the mixture in the washing machine, start the water, and then pause the cycle to let the items soak for about twenty minutes or so before you run your machine on the regular cycle.

If all this sounds overwhelming, think about it this way—just like almost anything else, it's all in the prevention. If you eat healthy, you'll be less likely to get sick. If you brush your teeth, you'll be less likely to get cavities. If you do just a few minutes of scrubbing each week (especially if you live by the water), you'll be that much closer to never smelling mildew in your home again!

How to Turn a Closet into a Baby's Room

Anyone who has ever watched *Dirty Dancing* (and that's most of us, admit it) knows that "Nobody puts Baby in a corner." But what about putting baby in a closet (or similarly small space)? Your first sonogram probably had you dreaming of a roomy nursery filled with fluffy toys, a comfy rocking chair, and a nice big state-of-the-art crib, but the harsh reality of your limited real estate means that Junior's first digs may be snugger than you'd initially hoped. Whether you're an urban dweller renting a studio apartment in a city where a square foot costs into the quadruple digits, or a suburban homeowner without a room to spare, a former closet or storage space may be the best (or only) option for your pint-sized new addition. Fancy wallpaper, plush rugs, and rocking chairs may be tantalizing, but let's face it, that stuff is really more for your benefit than the baby's.

Clearly not all closets are equal when it comes to baby conversions, so picking your location is key. Forget anything in an attic or basement; the last thing you're going to want to do when it comes time for the 3:00 A.M. feeding is to walk up and down lots of stairs. Obviously, the more space the better, so walk-in closets with double doors and the most room to maneuver are best. Clean out the junk (now is the perfect time to get rid of the wedding gifts you'll never use), put in a rug, and give the walls a fresh coat of paint. You'll ideally want some shelves, so think about units that are light (closet walls aren't always the sturdiest), easy to install, and multipurpose, like wire shelves that you can also hang things from. If there's no room for a changing table, put it in your bathroom. It doesn't even need to be a real changing table. Any bench or table your little one won't roll off will do. Investing a little extra in matching baskets and nice hangers can make all the difference when it comes to transforming a storage space into a welcoming and color-coordinated baby zone; these are items that won't break your bank and that you'll surely get use out of later.

Of course, the closet-turned-nursery is only a temporary makeshift solution. At some point, when your child gets a little bigger, you will have to find more space. But for now, pick up some paint, order a crib (hint: that's what baby shower registries are for), and install hooks and shelves (clear Lucite shelves, which are inexpensive, sturdy, and clean looking, work well) for the supplies that you'll be constantly reaching for, like creams and diapers. After that all you'll need are a few stuffed animals to watch over your bundle of joy.

If you start to feel guilty, don't. Closet living may seem like inhumanely cramped quarters for us adults, but babies seem to love these cozy nooks that are just their size.

How to Set Up a Darkroom in Your House

I had assumed that in the age of digital photography, darkrooms were pretty much out of date, until a client asked us to turn an unused bathroom into one. As it turns out, some things never go out of style and developing your own photographs, from yes, a good old film camera, is still an incredibly fun and rewarding hobby (and contrary to popular belief, not that difficult).

Many people choose to set up darkrooms in their basement, which has the advantage of being dark and secluded so no one else in the house will accidentally turn on a nearby light. But if you don't have running water in your basement (running water is key to developing prints) or you don't have a basement, a bathroom may be your best option.

And it's a good one. Easily accessible running water makes everything go faster, and the smooth surfaces in most bathrooms are ideal to work on. Plus, you can simply throw unused developing chemicals right down the drain instead of trekking them through the house. The downside, however, is that bathrooms tend to be smaller, and if it's a bathroom you use regularly for, you know, normal bathroom things, you may have to make your darkroom a temporary setup. For this reason, a "spare" bathroom that isn't used very often is the ideal spot for a darkroom.

Your first step is to purchase an enlarger. This will be the biggest, most expensive piece of equipment you'll have to buy, but there's no getting around it. An online auction website like eBay may be a great place to look—tons of people who traded in their darkrooms for digital cameras are likely looking to get rid of these big, clunky machines for a low price. You can find a decent enlarger on eBay for $40 (compared with an over $100 price tag at a specialty photo store).

Next, visit a professional photography store in person or online (I recommend B & H Photo Store, at www.bhphotovideo.com, or Freestyle Photo Supplies, at www.freestylephoto.biz), and buy the materials necessary for developing prints. This includes (but is not necessarily limited to) paper developer, fixer, at least four plastic trays, measuring cups, and a ton of glossy photo paper. Speak with someone at the store (or call customer service, if ordering online) to make sure you have everything you need.

Setting up the darkroom all depends on the layout and size of your bathroom. If your counter is big enough, that's a good place to put the enlarger. If you have a bathtub, this is an ideal spot for the four plastic trays used for developing each photo. If you want, you can also put a piece of plywood over two-thirds of the tub and use that as an elevated developing surface—but leave the third of the tub closest to the faucet and drain clear so you have easy access to running water. You'll also want to install a red lightbulb, since photo paper isn't sensitive to red light like it is to white light. This will allow you to see what you're doing without ruining the paper.

Last—but definitely not least—cover up any windows in the bathroom with something opaque, like a plastic trash bag or some cardboard. Make sure the window is covered completely, so that not one bit of light shines through. Honestly, if *any* white light leaks in, your photos will be toast, so go as far as to stuff a towel under the bottom of the bathroom door.

Note: Stick with black-and-white photos. Not just because there's something classy and artsy about black-and-white photos (which there is), but because color prints require more materials, are more sensitive to room temperature, and the whole printing process takes much more time and practice.

Now that you've got everything set up, actually learning to *use* your darkroom is another story—ask a friend, take a course, or search on the

Internet to get going with that. And although developing your own photos is a really cool thing to learn, expect that somewhere in this process, you may develop a new appreciation for that digital camera (or yearn for the days of Polaroids).

How to Keep Your Basement Organized

A basement is an often overlooked luxury. Take it from someone who's lived in an apartment and gotten excited by having access to a five-by-five bin in the dark and dingy bowels of the building. Nevertheless, basements often become a receptacle for unused junk, and it is the rare person who keeps a clean and well-organized basement. It is, after all, the one place in the house no one wants to go. Most cellars are cold, damp, smelly, and dark—and often whatever gets tossed down the stairs to the basement is something that you don't really want anyway. But honestly, this is a huge waste of what is (for some people) highly coveted real estate. So here are some tips on how you can organize your basement to get the best use out of all that turf.

When you find your underground space in need of an overhaul, the first thing to do is clear the area of everything. Organizing a basement is the same idea as organizing a closet (see "How to Organize Your Closet in Twenty Minutes," page 225), but with a basement you will be throwing many more things away and will usually need additional cleaning supplies—so allow yourself more time than twenty minutes. Get rid of anything and everything that you do not like or never think you will ever use again. Don't think too much. Just toss. Then clean. Sweep, scrub, mop, scour, whatever you have to do to get the basement looking as clean as a room you'd actually want to spend time in. Then let the real fun begin.

Since many basements aren't the most pleasant areas of the house, take some steps to make it more appealing. Paint the walls and consider installing nice floors or if your basement is not too damp, carpet. Bring some speakers or a radio down there as it always helps to have music to listen to while you work. You probably have some furniture that you wanted to toss down there anyway (even if it is just folding chairs), so start with that and turn your basement into a real room, not just a storage space. You can even rename it the "rec room." If your kids are old enough, get them some paintbrushes and let them take ownership of the redesign. It's just the basement so it doesn't have to be perfect—just cheerful and inviting. Think about moving a TV, or video-game system, or even a Ping-Pong table down there as well. Suddenly, the basement will be the most desirable room in the house. Plus for kids it will feel like a secret hideaway. Let's face it, parents were once kids and every adult remembers what goes on in basements, so let's just leave it at that.

Once it feels like a real room, it will also be even easier to organize. The key to organization is easy-to-access storage units like shelves and large plastic bins (airtight because basements can be damp). Even if your basement doesn't seem big enough for shelving, you can almost always fit a few shelves *somewhere*. Shelving units are easy to assemble and fairly inexpensive, and plastic bins are even cheaper. The Container Store, Bed Bath & Beyond, or a similar store should have all the organizational supplies you'll need. Be sure to label everything because as you know, things down there don't see the light of day very often. Don't overload bins or shelves; a good rule of thumb is to keep everything visible. In addition, separate your things into categories so that you can find everything relatively quickly. It's really that simple.

Quick tip: Don't get burned out. If you're tired of organizing, stop! Start again the next day, or take a few days off. A messy basement can be a huge job, so don't force yourself to finish right away—take your time, and stay sane.

Over time, as you bring more and more stuff into the basement for storage, make sure you also review your older things to see if you're ready to part with anything. With a little bit of prep work, a small investment in storage supplies, and diligent maintenance, you can keep the basement organized for a decades. And if you are fortunate enough to have space down under, remember to be grateful, and know that you are the envy of every apartment dweller you know.

How to Add a Room to Your Apartment

Open-plan spaces and lofts look great in glossy design magazines, but they aren't always practical for everyday realities. After all, do you really need to subject yourself to the sight of Uncle Max sleeping in his underwear when he drops by unexpectedly for a weekend visit? And let's face it, it's nice to have the crib off to the side in your room for the first few months, but after that novelty wears off, you'll realize there is plenty of opportunity for family time during the day and physical dividers are good for everyone.

If you're not up for a major remodeling job, putting up a temporary wall can be a relatively easy, inexpensive, and speedy solution to partition problems. Running between a few hundred and a few thousand dollars (compare that with the cost of a full renovation), they're quick to put up (it takes less than a day), simple to remove (so landlords are less likely to object), and (this is the best part) are usually undistinguishable from your other walls. Really.

If temporary walls conjure up uneasy memories of the wobbly backdrop on the set of your high school play, think again. Today's room dividers aren't just sturdy; they come in a variety of shapes ("L" or straight) with an impressive range of add-ons and features—including windows and doors (French or sliding)—that provide ventilation, light, and help the wall blend in with the rest of the apartment or house. Some companies even add on features like windowsills, built-in closets, noise-reducing insulation, and fans for better air circulation. With such an array of choices out there, faking it has never been easier.

Companies like those accessed at www.citywallny.com or http://thewallpeople.com/home.html offer a variety of different walls to choose from and get them up quickly (they'll even take the walls down when you move out!). If these companies don't serve your city, call a contractor; he'll either be able to get it done for you or recommend a company that can.

Believe it or not, it's also possible to actually lease rather than buy a temporary wall. So if you're only renting, or planning on moving out relatively soon, you may want to think about that option. You can usually get a quote online if you provide measurements and other relevant information about your apartment and building, although some outfits only give a price once they've seen the space in person. Before work can begin, you may also need to notify your building's doorman or super and pay a deposit (typically a few hundred dollars). Last, you'll want to find out if your building needs a certificate of insurance from the installers, who might require a floor plan and a signed lease if you're a renter.

If a temporary wall is still really out of your budget, but you simply must have a divider for Uncle Max's "guest bedroom" or to keep your kids out of your hair for just a few hours, consider a thick curtain. It will feel like you have your own space, and it beats drawing an imaginary line down the middle of the floor.

Money tight? Put up a wall, and then get a roommate.

How to Get Rid of a Stubborn Smell

A while back, I was hired for the unusual task of helping a client banish an awful smell from her office. Sounds easy, right?

Well, after a very thorough cleaning service failed to get rid of the smell, we tried some plug-in room deodorizers. Unfortunately, they just created another obnoxious smell *on top of* the existing smell.

But then I remembered an old secret a perfume executive I know once let me in on—coffee. An open can of coffee, she told me, can absorb just about any smell, from cat litter and wet dog to cigarette smoke to paint. If you don't believe me, ask the staff who work at a Starbucks and they'll tell you that coffee can overpower just about any other scent (of course, wherever you try this trick it may smell like your local coffee shop for a bit, but that's usually preferable to paint or smoke or wet dog).

**In my line of work, I pick up tidbits of information everywhere.
Some are more useful than others, but one thing is for sure: when
a perfume executive lets you in on a secret about smells, trust it.
Their nose knows.**

How to Baby-Proof a Tiny Apartment

For months you've been enjoying your little bundle of joy. But now that she's finally crawling (or soon to be), it's time to prepare for the major changes that are about to descend upon you. Yes, baby-proofing is just one of the many preparations for your new life as a responsible parent, and it's a great way to get you off to a safe start.

The home is a potential minefield for little ones. So it's worth starting off with a list of all the elements in need of attention. You'll want to do this *before* your little one is on the move because once she's going, she's gone.

First deal with the basics: cover electrical sockets and soften sharp corners. It's easy to find socket plugs and edge and corner guards on www.amazon.com. Install cabinet and drawer locks, and make sure floors are clear of any small objects that can be tempting to curious mouths.

Breakables and valuables may need to find new homes for a while, and don't forget about house plants: some are poisonous if eaten. Shorten or cut cords that hang from blinds and curtains, and put slip-proof mats under rugs and carpeting. Cover doorknobs (doorknob covers are also available at amazon.com); that way, you'll be in charge of whether your little adventurer stays in the room or gets to wander. And make sure you have working smoke detectors. After that, think about specific needs for particular areas, like toilet locks in the bathroom, and oven latches in the kitchen. The list may at first seem endless, but like almost anything else, once you start, you'll see it's not as insurmountable a task as it at first seemed.

A good rule of thumb: You should baby-proof to the point that should you get locked out of your house for three hours, the worst thing that could possibly happen to your baby is a bruise.

Quick tip: There are companies that will come in and make sure you have taken everything into consideration. For recommendations, ask your pediatrician, or check www.totsafe.com/checklist.htm or www.babycenter.com for articles and lists to help baby-proof your own home.

A tiny apartment may cut down on the number of rooms and acreage you need to worry about, but living in a glorified shoebox presents its own special challenges when it comes to eliminating potential baby death traps.

The key, when floor space is sparse, is to think Manhattan. Just twenty-four square miles in size, the island has long looked to the skies in order to grow. So follow the Big Apple's example and make use of the empty room *over* your head by putting up shelves for neatly storing anything you don't want a baby getting his or her hands (or mouth) onto. If space is really tight, consider a storage facility. Any inefficiently used real estate must be relinquished *now;* that dusty cabinet where you've been storing your fondue pot is a prime place for keeping everyday items that are suddenly off-limits—like cleaning supplies and spare change.

Given that you're a gigantic monster (even without the baby weight) compared to a crawling or newly vertical tot, it's easy to quite literally overlook things that may be hazardous to fingers and mouths operating near ground level. So get down on your own hands and knees to see the world as your baby does; it can bring dangerous items into view that you might not notice from your vaulted vantage point.

And remember, when you live in tight quarters, safety isn't just about getting rid of sharp edges and breakables; it's about staying sane too. So baby-proof yourself, and get a sitter once in a while.

How to Keep a Plant Alive

The primary obstacle in keeping a plant alive is remembering to water it. We all know that plants need to be watered. It's just that, like exercising, or calling Great-Aunt Clara on her birthday, we often forget to do it. Every type of plant, indoors and outdoors, will have different needs as far as temperature, sunlight, repotting, and so on. But every plant needs water, and it needs a little bit every day. Too much, and it'll drown; too little, and it'll dry up. There's no way around it.

So if forgetfulness is your problem, try making it a habit to water the plant in conjunction with another activity you do every day. For example, every time you pour your coffee in the morning, or feed the dogs, or turn on *American Idol* (that's on pretty much every day, right?), water the plant as well. The first few days, you'll have to be especially conscious and remind yourself, but after that, it should become automatic.

If that doesn't work, see if you have an old digital watch lying around. You probably have at least one in that drawer full of stuff you'll never use again. Find one that's still working (or buy the least expensive one they have at a sporting goods store), and set the alarm for a time you'll always be home, either in the morning before you leave the house or sometime at night. Put the watch next to the pot (this also works if there is anything else that you need reminding to do every day, like take your vitamins, go to the gym, brush your teeth—just be sure you get watches with different-sounding alarms or it will get really confusing). And after about thirty days, or once it becomes a habit, remember to turn off the alarms so your next houseguest doesn't think you've seriously lost it.

If you still can't handle this task, consider these other ways to make sure your plant doesn't go thirsty. First, and easiest, is to outsource. Whether you have a mini botanical garden in your home, or just a small houseplant or two, get a neighbor—maybe even a kid who wants a little extra cash—to come by and water the plants for you (if you don't know anyone offhand, call a local gardening store or florist and see if they know someone with a particularly green thumb).

If you don't feel comfortable having someone come into your home every day, there is a yet another solution. Almost all gardening stores (and a host of websites) sell some version of an automatic watering device; the most common are called "watering globes" or "watering spikes." These have large reservoirs that store water and channel it though stakes that you drive into the soil. The stakes have small openings at the ends that release water to the plant slowly, so you don't have to worry about it (though you'll still have to refill the globe every time it empties out).

And although the key to keeping a plant alive is water, remember that every plant also needs love. Talk to your plant (though you may want to do it in private). It may seem weird at first, but every living thing needs affection and you'll see, the plants you talk to will thrive. Plus, it's a great way to vent about your problems without annoying your friends (or paying a therapist).

How to "Green" Your Home . . . and Get Your Kids Involved

A client recently wanted to "go green" and teach her kids about the environment in the process. Bigger concepts like electric cars and solar panels are out of most young children's realm of understanding, but we found a ton of cheap, easy, and fun ways to actively teach kids about being environmentally conscious while taking steps to "green" a home.

One fun project to do with your kids that will also cut down on household trash is to make a compost garden. Food waste, even if it's rotted, is completely natural and makes for healthy soil for various plants. If you think it will gross you out or smell bad, think again, compost pails now have stench-proof lids and liners (plus, anything that you may consider disgusting will probably up the cool factor for a kid). If you don't have a yard, you can even install a compost garden on a ledge outside a window in your kitchen. If you're not sure how to compost, check www.composting 101.com or search for "composting garbage" on YouTube, where you can find numerous videos that take you through the steps. Having a visual makes it as easy as it looks.

If you instill in your children a sense that objects can still have a useful life even after their original use is finished, they'll carry this value with them forever. Most kids are into arts and crafts, so simply start turning their regular craft projects into "green"-inspired ones. Go to www.make-stuff.com/recycling/paper to find out how to make recycled paper out of old newspapers. Then, use it for painting and drawing. This is two activities in one, since the process of making the paper is a craft in and of itself. Convert old coffee cans into flowerpots or tiny herb gardens and decorate the outside of the cans. Maybe spruce up an old milk carton with paint and/or stickers and turn it into a bird feeder. Or cover cereal boxes with paper grocery bags and color on them to make magazine organizers. Just think, it's fun for kids, and it'll help you get organized.

Although I shouldn't have to remind you, the other easy changes you can make right away, and in front of your kids, are to always turn off lights when you leave a room and turn off the faucets while you're brushing your teeth. Also, remember that appliances can eat up energy even when they are turned off, so *unplug* things completely like the coffee machine, your cell-phone charger, and even your televisions, when they're not in use. Model this behavior for your kids, and they'll follow along. Or turn it into a contest and have them keep track of how many things they can unplug or turn off each day.

Next, take your kids to the hardware store to replace your lightbulbs. Buy some fluorescent bulbs to replace the incandescent ones you likely use now. Major advancements in fluorescent lighting have been made in just the past few years, so you'll be surprised how soft and bright these bulbs are. Fluorescent bulbs cost about the same amount as the incandescent kinds, but they last much longer (up to ten times longer), and they use about a third of the energy, so they'll also save you money in the long run.

Another thing you can do is subscribe to a "green" blog and check it with your kids each morning. There are plenty of blogs out there, and the ones geared toward families have suggestions for new green activities your kids can do. Try www.TreeHugger.com, www.TheDailyGreen.com, or peruse www.BestGreenBlogs.com, which is a directory of (duh) the best green blogs around.

10. lions and tigers and pets, oh my!

How to Sneak an Elephant into a Public Park (for an Indian Wedding)

So you want to have your dream Indian wedding in Central Park (or another large public space), but Hindu traditions dictate that an elephant must be present. A client once told me that he wished he'd known me a year earlier, when he was trying to get an elephant into Central Park for his wedding. I was so intrigued that I had to do the research and figure out how to pull it off.

First things first. Begin by planning the wedding, sans elephant. Holding your ceremony in a place like Central Park is not exactly a cakewalk, with or without wildlife. Know that the only way to have your wedding in Central Park without a permit is to have fewer than twenty people, and no camera equipment. But, most likely, that won't be the case; if you are going to the trouble to get an elephant, I imagine you'll want to document it and have more than twenty of your friends there to witness it firsthand. Plus, having a permit will give you the right to kick out any bird-watchers or wandering tourists who might try to crash.

To get a permit (sometimes an additional photography permit is required) visit www.centralpark.com, and click on the "weddings" link. You'll have to pay a small fee, but the park workers can help you plan the entire ceremony, and will put you in touch with the Central Park Conservancy to obtain the proper documents. Do this *far* in advance. Especially in the warmer months, the number of permits awarded are limited and the best spots in the park will be reserved well ahead of time.

Warning: Central Park in New York City is one of the most controlled, regulated, and carefully monitored parks in the country and the Conservancy has strict rules for weddings. For example, anything that affects the soil is not allowed in the park, which means no tents, tables, or chairs. So be sure to learn all the rules before you start planning your party in the park.

But what about elephants? You might be able to sneak a couple of folding chairs into the park without anyone noticing, but don't count on an elephant going unnoticed. Elephants tend to draw a crowd. And when they do, and you haven't planned everything ahead of time, you could wind up paying heavy fines, and possibly facing jail time (which would undoubtedly put a damper on your wedding day). So, once you've obtained your wedding permits, now it's time to deal with the elephant in the room. Well, the elephant in the park.

The Parks and Recreation Department rules (at least in New York City) allow the park commissioner to grant special permissions that override preestablished rules (like a ban on elephants). So set up a meeting with the commissioner and plead your case. Guarantee that your wedding will be contained in a private area and that the elephant will be restrained and under control. The list of "Prohibited Uses" of the park include the following: "No person owning, possessing or controlling any animal shall cause or allow such animal to be unleashed or unrestrained in any park unless permitted by the Commissioner in accordance with these rules." So whatever you do, don't plan on bringing a wild elephant to your wedding and letting him roam free.

If the commissioner won't budge, it's time to go to the press—or at least threaten to. An elephant at an Indian wedding is religious tradition, and the commissioner wouldn't want to deny freedom of religion in his park, especially not in an election year. (*Note:* For best results, coordinate your wedding with an election year.) The threat of negative publicity might be enough to change his mind. And if he does, consider returning the favor by inviting him. Who knows, if the local news catches a glimpse of him at your wedding, it could be just the positive press he needs to make the jump from city parks and recreation commissioner . . . to state parks and recreation commissioner. Wow!

There is a sneakier way to pull this off that I think can work. Often, park rules are relaxed for movie filming, so hire a filmmaker (aka videographer) and have him get the proper permits for his low-budget movie about an Indian family with a wedding scene in Central Park . . . wink wink. This might be pricey, and you may need to carry a lot of liability insurance, but if you claim financial hardship, there could be ways around that. Besides, if you're set on having the kind of wedding that involves an elephant, I'm guessing you're prepared to spare no expense.

Now there's just one last detail—locating the elephant. You'll most likely be in the rental market for this wedding prop, and luckily, there are rental options, though not many. One is a small family zoo in Goshen, Connecticut, that rents animals—including Minnie the elephant. Simply call her booking agent (yes, it seems elephants have booking agents; you can find his phone number at http://amazinganimalproductions.com), and for as little as $7,500 (including insurance), she'll be all yours for that special day. If Minnie is booked, her agent may be able to put you in touch with an elephant named Dondi, who has participated as a flower girl in a wedding outside of Boston. Of course you could also try the circus, but it is less likely that the circus owners would let their elephants participate in a show other than their own, so a privately owned elephant is really the way to go.

But before you go through with it, be sure that you also consider the risks. Elephants in heat can go on rampages (it happened recently in India). And of course, animal rights activists don't think riding elephants is the most humane idea (they've protested it before). So, although it's possible to have your dream wedding, and I would never say to give up or settle for less, just know what you are getting yourself into. And remember, elephants have this way of stealing the spotlight; if you really want your wedding day to be about you, consider swapping the elephant for a really big horse.

∞ How to Swim with Sea Lions

Sea lions are basically the golden retriever puppies of the sea, and swimming with them is an absolute blast. Naturally, you won't be able to do this at your local swimming pool, so the next time you're headed on a vacation to a warm coastal area, look into places that will let you go for a dive with these friendly water mammals; it's the memory of a lifetime!

A great vacation for me means a challenge or an adventure, which I guess is why I didn't think twice about boarding a plane to spend a month in Mexico with nothing more in mind than getting a scuba certification and swimming with the sea lions. Call it luck, or call it a knack for getting things done, but Mexico's Sea of Cortez turned out to be an amazing choice. There are tons of sea lions off Isla Espiritu Santo, and on a calm day, the channel crossing is only a slightly treacherous paddle across. How did we do it? Rented kayaks, of course. The sea lions turned out to be extremely friendly, and excellent swimming companions. If you are ever up for a unique experience, give this a try. Really, they are as harmless as goldfish and you'll have nothing to worry about—just have some fun.

There are, however, easier ways to swim with sea lions than renting your own kayaks and journeying to the tip of a remote island. Mountain Travel Sobek (www.mtsobek.com) offers a kayaking package that will take you all over the Sea of Cortez, right to the sea lions' doorstep, as it were. Their trips have a way of making you feel like you are roughing it, even though you'll never have to light your own campfire or catch your own dinner.

Quick tip: If you *do* decide to go the tough-guy route and do it on your own, bring cigarettes. You will need them to trade the fishermen for your dinner. It's not as easy as you think to catch a fish off a kayak, trust me.

Florida is another option if you want to swim with the sea lions. Although perhaps not as daring as braving the open seas in a small plastic vessel, for a close-to-authentic experience, try a sea lion swimming program in an enclosed area of ocean water or saltwater lagoon. For around $120, you can get an instructional session and some one-on-one time with one of these aquatic pups. Some companies will even throw in a video or photograph of you with the sea lion—perfect for your annual Christmas card. Check out www.theaterofthesea.com and www.dolphinsplus.com.

Just remember to do a little research on any company you use. Swimming with sea lions is a great time, but you don't want to patronize a company that's mistreating its sea lions!

How to Get a Rare Tropical Bird as a Pet

So you want a rare tropical bird as a pet. But do you, really? In theory, birds are a cool idea; you don't have to walk them, they look pretty, and some of them can even talk. But too many people make the mistake of adding "they're easy to take care of" to the list. Let me be the one to give it to you straight—they're not. We have clients who frequently travel, and when they are out of town, they hire us to care for their birds. Just like any other pet, birds require *a lot* of care and attention. Not to mention, they're messy; and if you don't particularly have an affinity for birds, they're annoyingly loud.

But if you do come to the conclusion that a bird is the pet for you, you might as well get a rare and tropical one. Here are a few key tips to contemplate. First, birds are expensive, especially exotic ones. They can cost anywhere from $100 to $1,000, and if a bird is really rare, it'll need expensive vet visits as well. So if you're getting a bird because you think it'll be less expensive than a puppy, think again. Second, if you think a tropical bird won't take up a lot of space, well, you're once again mistaken. Most exotic birds need large cages, and the bird's domain will likely extend to the area around the cage as well. That's because with birds, unlike, say, fish, the mess is not contained within their living environment. Food will fall out of the cage, as will bird droppings (not easy or pleasant to clean up). The noise will reach beyond the confines of the cage—and likely the room—as well. This is an important factor that most people overlook. Birds are loud—really, *really* loud. Especially if you get the kind that can talk, and *especially* if you've trained and encouraged it to talk. Plus, according to Murphy's Law, your bird will refuse to speak on command when you want to show it off to your guests, but it won't shut up at 2:00 A.M. when you're trying to sleep.

And if that weren't enough, the amount of time and energy your bird will require is more than you think. Tropical birds have sleeping patterns that resemble those of newborn babies, so be prepared to care for them at all hours of the day and night (note that a parrot's average life expectancy is around fifty years; anticipate spending a lot of time with it for many years to come).

Despite all these negatives, exotic birds have some upsides. They really are beautiful, and if you treat your bird right, you could end up with a friend for life (literally).

So how to go about getting one? Start at your local pet store. They are sure to have birds, but maybe not as exotic as you'd like. If they don't have what you want, just talk to the shop owner and describe what you're looking for. The pet-selling community is relatively tight-knit, so the person should be able to refer you to someone who sells the breed of bird you're after.

Depending on where you live, certain tropical birds just may not be available in your area at all. For the rarest breeds, you'd have to travel to another country, and bringing it back into the United States can be a challenge. Because birds can carry diseases like avian flu, the United States currently has a ban on importing birds from more than forty countries, including China, Japan, Israel, Egypt, Iran, Iraq, Turkey, and many others. Even if you import a bird from an approved country (most European countries and many South American countries), all birds, except those imported from Canada, must undergo a thirty-day quarantine at a USDA Animal Import Center, at the owner's expense. You need to make reservations ahead of time, and it can be quite costly depending on the quality of the center. (For the complete list of countries you can import a bird from, and for more information on the quarantine process, visit the USDA's Animal and Plant Health Inspection Service website at www.aphis.usda.gov.)

If you opt to pick your new friend up yourself, you may be able to make arrangements to have a bird shipped to you, but check your airline's policies before coming home. With the proper documentation, most airlines will allow the bird on board, but some airlines don't allow birds in the main cabin—especially tropical birds, because they're so loud—and you'll have to pay extra (sometimes several hundred dollars) to check it as baggage in the cargo hold.

Probably the best place to get an exotic bird is Florida. This way you avoid the international restrictions, and because of the state's tropical climate, you'll have countless varieties to choose from. And if you can't stomach going all the way to Florida just to buy a bird, make a vacation out of it. Who doesn't like an excuse to visit Disneyworld?

How to Get and Keep a Pet Lion

I once received a call from a client who, after an innocent matinee of *The Lion King*, decided she wanted a Simba of her very own. Was it legal, she wanted to know? Could her family keep one at their home in Texas?

Turns out that there *are* ways to purchase an exotic cat, although in my opinion, when it comes down to a pet feline, it's better to think domesticated—small and fluffy and staying that way. But if you have your heart set on a king of the jungle, first and foremost you need to find out what the law in your state is for owning a lion or similar exotic animal. Some states (like West Virginia) are just fine with keeping a three-hundred-pound carnivore in a private home, while others (like most of the rest of them) aren't. Texas will allow it, although a permit is required. At www.bornfreeusa.org/b4a2_exotic_animals_summary.php you can find a state-by-state breakdown of these laws, though you might notice that even where legal, private ownership of exotic animals is discouraged. That's because most exotic animal owners (and breeders) either don't take proper care of their pets or simply don't have the space that an animal of that size needs to thrive. So if you're an exotic animal lover, taking an annual African safari vacation might be the more humane choice.

But let's assume you live on a giant ranch (or some other location that both allows lions and has large open spaces) and you are a responsible person. Where do you go about finding a pet lion? Generally, from a breeder. It's difficult to locate lion breeders, let alone reputable ones, so you might have to go out of state or even out of the continent. There are websites devoted to exotic animal breeders, but, like anything else online, many are shams, so it's important to make sure there are photos of the animals and that you check the breeder's credentials and references before any money—or any large animals—change hands.

Assuming this all works out, before bringing your lion home, you're going to need to lion-proof it. This is a lot like child-proofing a home—the big difference is that a child can't eat you. You'll need a large pen for the lion (I hope I don't have to tell you to try not to keep it *in* your house) that's connected to an extra large, fenced-in outdoor area. And please make sure these fences are sturdy. Lions like to climb, so the roof of your pen also needs to be sturdy enough that he can't push his way out. True, letting your lion escape is one way to make headlines, but it's also one way to land yourself in jail. Your lion house (or den) should also have at least two separate rooms that can be sealed off, so that you can safely enter to feed and clean the lion while he's locked on the other side.

The lion must have a place to clean himself, so you'll either need a pool (preferably one with flushable plumbing for easier cleaning) or a stream on the premises. Lions also need huge supplies of drinking water (not as much as elephants, but they do get very thirsty).

As far as food goes, if you thought your teenage son was eating you out of house and home, you haven't seen anything yet. Your lion will need 5–7 percent of its body weight (around twenty pounds) in raw red meat every five days. In the wild, lions hunt, gorge, and fast, so to replicate their natural feeding patterns, give your lion a huge pile of meat (you're about to be the local butcher's new favorite customer), wait a few days, and then replenish. Ideally, you'd feed your lion more than just the raw meat because it is better for lions to consume entire animals (the hide, the bone, etc.), but unless you plan on hunting down the dinner yourself, this may be a challenge.

And let's not forget about health care. What if your lion gets sick? It's not easy to find a vet who will make that house call.

Suffice it to say, this is all extremely expensive, time-consuming, and easy to screw up. So although my client thought having a four-hundred-pound cat for a pet sounded great, after learning what was involved, she decided (much to my relief) that her visions of a lazy afternoon lounging around with her lion curled up by the fireplace or riding her pet lion to work, were better left in her head. If you are ever similarly tempted, consider volunteering your time at a lion nature preserve like Lions, Tigers, and Bears (www.lionstigersandbears.org) or Cooper's Rock (www.cougarsanctuary.org) instead. This will give you the chance to feed, clean, and bond with real lions and other exotic cats that have been freed from abusive zoos and circuses. It's fun, free, and unlikely to result in your neighbor's kids mysteriously disappearing.

Hakuna matata!

How to Get Your Dog to Bring You Your Slippers

Your dog won't fetch? You throw a ball or a bone and he just stands there and stares at you wondering what's going on, or at least why you are crazy enough to think he's going to chase after it? That's because you didn't teach your dog to retrieve anything while he was young. You've heard the saying that you can't teach an old dog new tricks. There's a reason for it.

The truth is, trying to teach your dog to bring you your slippers at any age is probably more trouble than just going to get the slippers yourself.

But it'd be *so cool*.

It would impress everyone who comes over, and it'll probably impress you every time he does it, which, if you go through all the effort to teach him, should be every day.

So if you decide to give it a shot, know that training your dog is all about repetition and association. First, teach him to fetch and to give up the object when he brings it to you (many dogs will want to get into a tug-of-war instead) by having him do it over and over and rewarding him with a treat every time he does what you ask.

It also helps to institute a secret code word. It could be "Slippers," or it could be random, like "Macaroni" (more fun when you perform the trick for strangers). Say this code word or phrase when you toss the slippers ("Macaroni!") and then again when the dog brings them to you and lets go, but this time with the word *good* in front ("Good macaroni"). And again, *always* remember to give him a treat.

It might take a while, but your dog will start to associate "Macaroni!" (or whatever word or phrase you choose) with your slippers. Just make sure you don't use this phrase as a command in any other scenario (like trying to get him to come for dinner), or he'll get confused. Then, slowly begin to expand the training. Instead of tossing your slippers, place them on the other side of the room and point to them when you shout "Macaroni!" If that seems to be working well, start placing them in another room (your dog should be able to smell them). As long as you keep saying the code word, and keep giving him treats, you should be able to eventually modify the trick so that you can just plop down on your favorite chair, yell "Macaroni!" and your dog will appear, slippers in mouth, seconds later. The more you practice, the better, and if you do it enough times, you might be able to phase out the command completely. With time and patience, your dog could simply bring you your slippers as soon as you sit down in your favorite chair.

Sick of having to keep treats by the couch? You can phase out the treats, but you have to do it slowly. Begin to combine the treats with praise, petting, tummy rubs, or whatever your dog loves. Slowly transition to more affection and fewer treats until a pat on the back is all your pooch needs to feel satisfied for a job well done. *Note:* This also works for husbands.

The better trained your dog is from puppyhood, the easier it will be to teach him this trick. But there's one small snag—your dog will get used to the look, feel, and smell of your slippers, so when you get a new pair, you'll have to go through the same process all over again. It should be faster, but there will still be a decent learning curve.

Quick tip: Some dogs, like retrievers, will pick up on tricks like this faster, but all dogs should be able to catch on in theory. There's only one hard and fast requirement: the dog must be able to fit the slippers in his mouth.

Don't despair if your dog is a lost cause in this particular matter. After all—and I mean this literally, not metaphorically—sometimes you really can't teach an old dog new tricks.

How to Keep Your Pets from Scratching the Floors

Hardwood floors can be classy, and easier to clean than wall-to-wall carpeting, but it can be tricky to keep hardwood floors looking good with pets in the house. If you insist on having it all—that is, gleaming, finished floors and a giant Great Dane—here are some tips to help minimize the scratching damage.

As far as pets go, cats shouldn't be much of a worry when it comes to wood floors, but watch your carpet and your furniture. They tend to like scratching softer things, such as couches and upholstered chairs. Some of them do have a thing for wood, though, and if yours is one of them, consider strategically placing multiple scratching poles or sisal mats, sprinkled with catnip, around your house or apartment. Cats' instincts to scratch are strong, because it's how they leave their scent behind (cats have sweat glands between their paws) and also how they file down their nails, so it's better to just give them an outlet rather than try and stop them. Of course, declawing is an option, but it can turn friendly cats into biters, plus, cat lovers tend to find the procedure just plain cruel.

Dogs are a bigger issue as far as keeping your floors scratch-free. The best way to minimize the damage is, first and foremost, to keep their nails trimmed (long nails are actually bad for dogs so don't feel guilty about doing this). Standard nail trimmers can leave sharp edges, however, so you may need to file; if your dog will tolerate it, you could even use a Dremel tool, a high-performance rotary tool that can grind your pets' nails into rounded edges that are less likely to gouge into your floors. Taking your dogs on long walks on pavement can file their nails well. Such walks, and good exercise in general, have the added bonus of tuckering dogs out. A sleepy dog is one that will do less frolicking—and less damage—inside your house.

A few more quick tips:

1. Try out doggie booties, if your canine isn't too embarrassed by them. (Maybe take them off if he has a playdate.)
2. Give your dog a little haircut. Some dogs grow long fur between the pads

of their feet, which makes them slip and slide on wooden floors, so they have to clutch with their claws to get around. Trimming this fur helps.

3. Apply wax. No, not to his fur. Depending on the finish of your floors, you might want to apply a few coats of floor wax. It's a pain to get it down, but it will protect your floor's finish and improve your best friend's traction.

4. Take a spa day. If you don't like trimming your dog's nails yourself, take him somewhere to get his nails done. You could make an outing of it and schedule a pedicure for yourself while you're at it.

5. Try Soft Paws. These are glue-on nail caps that last four to six weeks and are made for both dogs and cats (www.softpaws.com).

6. Try the old inexpensive standby, duct tape. It's not stylish, but if you put it on his paws, it will last for weeks.

7. Deal with it. If your dog is going to be a real member of the family, you'll have to live with some wear and tear, and maybe someday get the floors refinished (probably around the same time that you need to repaint the walls to cover the mural your two-year-old has made in your living room). There are worse things in the world. And keeping a hardwood-floor scratch paint pen on hand for touch-ups is a good idea as well.

If you're worrying about this before choosing a type of dog, know that all breeds have the same-length nails. It doesn't matter if the dog is large or small; that will only mean a small difference in the size of the scratches.

You might also consider covering wood floors with a coat of paint. Looks good, and you can retouch quickly and inexpensively.

How to Have a Dog in a 10 x 10 Apartment

Determined to fit Fido into your tiny studio apartment? Okay, then. Before you do anything, make sure your building *allows* dogs. This is something to take seriously: it's pretty easy to conceal cats in a no-pet building (you didn't hear that from me), but it's not as easy to be sneaky with dogs. They not only need to be walked but will probably make enough noise to tip off the neighbors of their presence. So, if your intention is to *ever* have a dog in an apartment of any size, choose a dog-friendly space before you move a single box.

Once you're cleared to have dogs, the next step is to choose your best friend and might I add: choose wisely. If you're moving into your tiny digs *with* a dog, she's hopefully on the smaller and older (read: less energetic) side. A golden retriever may not be an ideal breed to have in a small apartment, unless you're able to exercise her frequently (read: live near the park). Even with access to a nearby dog run, larger dogs can still get depressed in small spaces, so you will want to know that there is somewhere else your pup can spend her days before you decide to cram her into your shoebox.

If you're getting a new dog, think small, for the dog's sake. A great site is www.petfinder.com, which allows you to search locally for dogs that need homes; you can narrow the search by size, gender, breed, age, and so on. The Humane Society or animal foster homes are also good places to adopt a dog. This isn't just a nice thing to do. Very often, foster care dogs are already trained and are generally a little older, meaning they'll be better behaved and less lively (i.e., good for smaller apartments).

Mutts vary from dog to dog, but in terms of actual breeds, you want one that doesn't require a lot of exercise (again, unless you live near a dog run or are training for a marathon). Cocker spaniels, corgis, dachshunds, and pugs are all good small dogs that are generally okay with lounging around the house in your absence. Also, keep in mind that in a tiny space, it's not ideal to have a small dog that's prone to yapping a lot, like a Chihuahua or a Yorkshire terrier.

Once you've found the right pooch, you'll need to make the apartment dog-friendly. No matter how small your space is, devote one section to the dog. Put a small bed there, and keep his toys, food, and water all in that area. Whenever you see things out of that corner, move them back there. After a while, the dog will understand that that is his area and will keep his things in that corner. Yes, in this case you often can teach an old dog new tricks. If you're having issues with this, spend a few bucks and bring in a trainer. A good trainer can teach a dog to do just about anything. (Well, maybe not how to do the dishes.)

To keep your sanity while cohabitating in such a small space, routine is the key. Walk your dog twice a day at the same time each day and he'll begin to expect this and adjust his clock to yours. For some extra exercise (and entertainment) while you're at work, consider buying a Roomba or other automated vacuum cleaner. He'll have something to chase around, and your place will always be clean.

Finally, just remember: At the end of the day, it's not so much about space, but about you. As long as you give your dog the same love, affection, and care you'd give him if he lived on a farm, he'll be happy.

How to Make a Custom Sweater for Your Dog

Although some controversy exists among veterinarians and pet owners about whether dogs really need anything besides their own fur to get them through the winter, pet clothing was a $300 million industry in 2009; clearly, plenty of people believe in dressing up their canines. If you're one of those dog parents who is worried about keeping your pooch warm—and besides, isn't he just the cutest thing you've ever seen when he's bundled up?—you have oodles of options, some pricier than others. Don't know where to start? Read on and I'll throw you a bone.

First, there is beauty in the magic of recycling. An item of old clothing that looks terrible on you could be just right for your dog. So either dig that hideous old Christmas sweater out of the attic, or find something at a thrift shop that fits your dog's personality. Who cares if the pattern or style brings to mind an Austrian toddler at the turn of the last century? Dog fashion has its own rules.

Here's an easy method for converting a human sweater into a cozy dog outfit in no time (this will probably only work for smaller dogs). First, take some measurements of your pooch: along the back, from neck to back legs, and underneath, from the neck to the front legs. Then, measure and cut a single sleeve of the sweater so that it is the same size as the back of your canine. Take a piece of chalk and use the second measurement to mark the spot for the leg holes. Cut a hole for the tail (usually at least two inches back, but it depends on the size of your dog). Snip another hole (for the other leg), hem all the raw edges, and voilà!

For another great do-it-yourself dog jacket or vest, use an old pair of shorts. You'll only need half the pair, so use the other half to make a matching outfit for your dog's best mate (the only thing cuter than a dog in a sweater is two dogs in matching sweaters, right?). Measure your dog: neck, waist, and body (back of the neck to the end of the torso). Mark the dog measurements on your shorts. Cut as needed and hem the ends. Put the shorts on the back of your dog and you'll see right away where you need to add snaps down the center so that it closes.

If this is ambitious, start small and knit Fido some leg warmers. They are simple to make, fit any size dog, and by the time you've done the fourth leg, you'll have gotten such a hang of it, you might feel ready to give a full-sized sweater a go.

Toddler sweaters or doll clothes can also fit small dogs, but if your dog is larger, try www.thedietdiary.com/cgi-bin/chart_dog.pl. Just enter your dog's measurements and the company will send you a custom pattern for the doggie sweater of your dreams.

Alternatively, you can go the easiest route of all and either go to a dog boutique (these are surprisingly easy to find, and if you're the dog-dressing type, I suspect you already know just where to find one) or go online to have a sweater custom-made for your dog. One company that specializes in this can be found at www.Ruffknits.com. In addition to sweaters, it lets you custom-order sweatshirts, rain gear, and even a tuxedo (in case your dog will be the ring bearer at your upcoming wedding). Hey, it might sound like a little much, but dogs deserve dapper duds too.

How to Wash Your Dog

Let's face it, cute as they are, after a while, dogs start to smell bad. But getting your frisky puppy into the bath can sometimes be quite the struggle. If you get to the point that you can't even get close enough to pet him without gagging at the stench surrounding him, you know you can't put off a bath any longer.

Easier said than done—unless you choose the outsourced route: have him professionally groomed, bath included. Sure, that's a quick fix this time, but it may not be so easy on your wallet, especially if it's done on a regular basis (once a month should be your absolute minimum). And really, if you take on the commitment of owning a dog, you should really be able to bathe him yourself. A professional groomer should be the exception rather than the rule.

So how can you do this with the least amount of mess and hassle? First off, it's best to do it outdoors (unless, of course, you have a very small dog and can give it a bath in your kitchen sink), and be prepared to get wet. Trust me, you'll thank me for this tip later. If you have an old kiddie pool lying around, that's a good place to do it, mostly because it will keep your dog contained and prevent him from splashing too much water all over you. If you don't have one on hand, just use a hose—that's more of a shower than a bath, but it works. However you do it, make sure you buy a pet shampoo made specifically for dogs; the kind of soap or shampoo you'd use on yourself won't fight the especially strong dog odors or bacteria particular to dogs.

If your dog smells *really* funky (like mine sometimes did), a bath will help, but it may not *always* get to the root of the odor. To cover all bases, you'll want to make sure you brush his teeth, too, using special dog toothpaste from a pet store. You'd be surprised that your dog's breath can often be ten times worse than the stench emerging from the rest of his body.

Once you've got him all washed off and smelling clean, back up. Way back. Dogs don't like to be wet so get out of his drying zone quickly before you become the one getting the bath.

Quick tip: If you really don't have the time to invest in your dog's personal hygiene but can't afford a groomer, this is a good job to give to your kid or your neighbor's kid. They'll usually want to make a quick buck and might even enjoy the bonding time with your pup (at least until they catch a whiff of him). Plus, it gets him or her outside and away from the Wii for a few hours.

How to Plan a Birthday Party for Your Dog

The best thing about throwing a party for your dog is that you can make it any kind of party you want. You can choose the theme, the guests, the food, and the music, and you will not have any arguments from the guest of honor. If it is a surprise party, even better—you can talk freely about it as often as you'd like and you don't have to worry about anyone letting the cat (or the dog) out of the bag.

It is common knowledge that people throw parties for all kinds of pets: cats, fish, horses—even iguanas and snakes. But the abundance of merchandise available for dog parties in particular shows just how widespread the practice of celebrating a canine pal's birthday has become. For a hefty fee, some doggie day-care centers will throw your dog a party on-site (think a Gymboree party, only for dogs), but if you want to do it yourself, here are a few tips to help you honor your pooch in style.

Invitations: Yes, special doggie birthday invitations are available online (in fact, you can buy a whole birthday package of supplies at some sites), or get creative and make your own. The only real unofficial requirement is that you incorporate a photo of your dog. Also, be sure to make it clear that this is not a drop-off party. There has to be at least one human for every beast, to ensure any tussles are broken up easily.

Speaking of which, think carefully about which of your dog's friends you ought to include. This is your home we're talking about here, not the dog park, so they must all be well socialized (and housebroken) mutts. And maybe avoid inviting that gorgeous new Lab puppy from down the block. He's bound to attract too much attention and make the birthday dog jealous.

The Big Day: If your dog will tolerate it, have her wear a special birthday hat or bandana, or something to show she's the main attraction (plus it will make for cute pictures). Have party hats on hand for all the guests, too, so no one feels left out. If the weather's good, an outside event is best—consider your backyard or a nearby park—just make sure plenty of drinking water available. Don't plan on too many organized party games. Dogs tend to prefer to mingle on their own and won't want to be corralled into playing blind dog's bluff, sniff the tail of the donkey, or whatnot.

Vittles: Food can be a tricky element of a dog's birthday party. Depending on size and breed, different dogs have different tastes and needs—it's not like you can just order a pizza and everyone will be happy. Remember, eating is the best part of the day for many dogs, but it can also bring out the wolf in them. Some dogs have serious food-guarding issues—let's just say they aren't great sharers—so it might be best to keep the treats in their goodie bags and let them dig in when they get home. If you're determined to do a cake and sing "Happy Birthday" (the temptation is understandable), do everyone a favor and make it a cake for people. Dogs don't like frosting, anyway.

If the humans are well socialized, snacks for them are fine. But just in case there are any food snatchers among the canine guests, don't serve anything made of chocolate, grapes, or onions—all of which can make a dog sick. If you insist upon serving food that the birthday girl and her friends can eat (I suppose that's only fair), go to www.tailwagging.com to order a carrot and apple wheat-free dog cake mix and a bone-shaped muffin pan to make a tray of pupcakes.

Entertainment: Not sure if this is for the dogs or the humans, but a dog trainer with a pooch who can do great tricks is always a hoot (or a howl as the case may be). The best entertainer I've seen brought a dog who could smile on cue. Cute.

If you think your guests are evolved enough to handle structured entertainment, obstacle courses or races are a lot of fun (greyhounds will have the distinct advantage). Put all the dogs on leashes, have someone stand at the other end of the field or yard, and when the whistle blows, let the dogs go! Or set up a scavenger hunt—just hide a bunch of bones and see if they can find them all. *Note:* You will probably want to do this in a fenced-in area or your party will quickly get out of hand.

Favors: Send each guest home with a goodie bag. Include snacks such as homemade biscuits or jerky treats, as well as a squeaky toy, perhaps personalized with your dog's name and the date of the party. Consider a custom CD that the owner can enjoy listening to on his early morning walks with his pooch—filled with songs like "Who Let the Dogs Out?" or other canine-themed favorites.

How to Get Your Dog to Stop Barking at the Mail Carrier

If a dog is man's best friend, why is he the mail carrier's archnemesis? It can get pretty frustrating, not to mention a bit embarrassing when day after day your adorable pup shows no love for Mr. or Ms. Postman. You know, the person who works so hard in rain and sleet and snow, just to get . . . barked at? Not cool. For whatever reason, most dogs see the mail carrier as a malevolent intruder, and not the friendly bearer of our Netflix. Most dog owners yearn for the day they'll glance outside to find their bundle of joy sweetly nuzzling the mail carrier as he or she fearlessly hands the mail to an adorable tail-wagging pup who runs it right up to the doorstep and deposits the day's mail at her owner's feet. It could happen. Or not. But there is hope.

The quickest, (though harshest!) solution to the postal carrier conundrum is an antibark collar, available at most pet stores or online. Most no-bark collars work in one of two ways: one is by releasing a citronella spray (yes, the same thing that keeps mosquitoes away) whenever a built-in microphone detects barking. The spray doesn't harm the dog (much), but the strong and sudden smell confuses and distracts Fido long enough to stop his barking. The second type emits a gentle electric shock every time the dog barks. Both types are a bit on the cruel side, if you ask me, but after a while they will condition your dog to permanently stop barking.

Besides being somewhat inhumane, the other problem with these collars is that they will eliminate just about *all* barking, and that means, good-bye watchdog. Many people rely on their dogs to bark when strangers are at their door, so if you want your dog to stop barking at the mail carrier but to continue to bark at potential burglars, you'll need a more precise method. With practice and dedication, it's possible to train your dog to do this. Ironically, the best way to train your dog *not* to bark is to train him *to* bark—but only at specific times.

You'll want to train your dog to respond to a specific command, for example, "speak," means bark. You might need to bark yourself for him to get the idea, and then reward him when he does. Once your dog understands the speak command, use the same method to teach him to "hush." Eventually, he'll associate "speak" with barking, and "hush" with being silent (if only this also worked for humans).

Once he has learned the commands, start telling him to "hush" every time the carrier comes by, then reward him when he's quiet. In the same way that repetition taught him the "hush" command, constantly rewarding him for hushing when the same person comes by each day will make him associate being quiet for the mail carrier with receiving a treat.

The following method only works if you have a smart dog (not to be mean, but seriously, you know whether or not your dog is smart). Also, it will only work if you have one mail delivery person dedicated for your route (some areas rotate carriers, while others have one consistent person for years). Let your dog (on a leash) sniff the carrier every day for about two weeks while you speak to the person in a friendly and calm voice (the smart dogs will sense this, but the slower ones may not). Pretty soon your dog should recognize the carrier as a nonthreat and should stop the infernal noise.

One last option: Leave a few treats in the mailbox, and have the mail carrier give the dog a treat if and only if he sits quietly. Trust me, this one works.

If the barking *still* continues, I don't know what to tell you. Consider going completely paperless, or learn to live with the barking and give your carrier a huge tip at Christmastime.

Keep in mind that at least in this instance: It's better to bark than to bite.

How to Make Your Old Dog Become Best Friends with Your New Dog

A loving family I know has two black poodles—one standard, one miniature—with sibling rivalry issues. The standard is male, and the miniature is female. When the family got the miniature, the standard poodle had been living with them for five years. They didn't think much about how to integrate the new dog into their home and make their old dog comfortable in the process. Sound familiar? If you have more than two dogs in a single home, well, let's just say they're not always going to get along.

Make no mistake, as with siblings, when two or more dogs live together, there's going to be a pecking order. Most people think the best way to deal with this is by letting the dogs figure out the order themselves, the way I almost did when a client had me purchase a new puppy for her daughter. But it was a good thing that I did my homework, because after talking to a professional dog trainer, I realized that when fighting for dominance in the household, dogs can get violent.

Luckily, this can be avoided by stepping in right from the start. Instead of letting your dogs decide which one will be the leader, *you* must intervene to let them know who the top dog is in your house—and that would be you.

Here's how it goes. Pay constant attention to both dogs for the first few weeks. This means being present whenever your dogs are together, inside or outside of the house, and breaking up any dog fights that might erupt. Playing around is fine, but you should be able to sense when playtime turns into a real fight. If you set the right precedent for the first thirty days, they'll get the picture, and you can back off.

But you can't possibly be watching over your dogs twenty-four hours a day. That's why most dog trainers highly recommend using a crate for new dogs (and often for *all* dogs). Whenever you're not around, your new dog should be locked up in the crate. Even if it seems like doggy jail, don't feel guilty; most dogs actually enjoy (or at least require) time in their crate because they can get some rest. You wouldn't deprive your pup of food would you, so why consider depriving him of some quiet R&R?

The main benefit for putting your new dog in the crate early on is that it allows the dogs to sniff each other to their heart's content (to get to know each other, as it were) but still provides an attack barrier (the crate). Stay nearby, at least initially, so that if your old dog begins growling or barking, you can nip it in the bud. Your old dog should know that *you* are the leader in this pack and that you absolutely won't tolerate any aggression toward the new dog.

Quick tip: There are countless dog-training books out there, many of which deal with this subject in depth. But there's no substitute for hiring a professional dog trainer, who can help with all your dog issues. Try www.apdt.com (the Association of Pet Dog Trainers) to find one near you, or ask your friends who have dogs if they can refer someone. Or, simply ask your local vet for a recommendation.

Often people try to make their new dogs feel welcome by giving them extra attention in the early days. Although attention is important, it's a dog-eat-dog world, so watch out that your first dog does not become jealous of your new addition.

Dogs are a lot like children—treat them as you would treat your kids if you were bringing home a new baby. Remember to give them each some one-on-one time with you and then spend time with both of them together. Ideally, before you know it, they'll be best of friends.

How to Get Pet Insurance

You might *think* your whole family is insured, but have you ever wondered what you'd do if something happened to Mittens or Spike? Health care for animals is expensive, and unless you happen to work for the ASPCA, I'm guessing your pet's bills are *not* included on your plan.

Well, wonder no more. The good news is that pet insurance, unlike people insurance, is pretty easy to apply for, and it doesn't take very long to get. Approximately thirty companies nationwide offer comprehensive pet insurance. The differences between these companies have to do with coverage and exclusions (some don't cover routine care, while others don't cover congenital diseases) and length of policy plans (some last twelve months, others are for a lifetime and automatically renew year after year). State-to-state differences appear to be minor (some accept annual payments, while some only accept monthly payments, etc.).

Once your pet is approved and a policy is in place, you'll generally pay out-of-pocket for vet visits, then apply for reimbursement from the carrier. If you're forgetful about mailing things, it might be a good idea to fill out and stamp a few envelopes to the insurance company and have them on hand whenever you get back from a visit to the vet.

Finding the policy that's right for your pet is as simple as checking www.petinsurancereview.com. You'll be able to easily compare insurers' rates and coverage, and read comments and reviews from people who have actually purchased policies. But just in case you're too lazy to do the research, here are some of the top providers I found on Pet Insurance Review.

- *PetPlan:* This is the official insurance of the Humane Society. It has a high deductible but does offer lifetime coverage. It doesn't offer routine care (regular checkups, medicines, etc.), but unlike most other companies, it does cover congenital and hereditary diseases. In addition to veterinary fees, it covers kennel and cattery fees, coverage if your pet is lost or stolen, and it will even reimburse you for the reward money you have to pay out to get back a pet who has strayed.
- *Veterinary Pet Insurance:* VPI plans have a low monthly rate and deductible, and the term is one year. VPI reimburses most veterinary expenses relating to accidents, illnesses, and injuries for dogs, cats, birds, and exotic pets. VPI is the nation's largest licensed and the number one veterinarian-recommended pet health insurance provider.
- *Pets Best:* This plan has lower monthly rates but higher deductibles. The term is one year and covers accidents, medical, illness, injuries, and optional coverage for routine care. Pets Best also offers holistic care (dog acupuncture, anyone?).
- *Embrace:* This plan's deductibles are high, but it offers cancer treatment, diagnostic testing, surgery, hospitalization, alternative therapies, accidents, drug and dental coverage, wellness, and genetic/ breed-specific conditions. However, Embrace doesn't cover deliberate injury, breeding, pregnancy, behavioral conditions, or costs of burial.

Whew! Still wondering if you need pet insurance? Ask yourself this question: If you just took the time to read through those boring descriptions of the various plans, the answer is probably yes. Go to the companies' websites for more information and decide which is the best plan for you and your pet.

How to Care for a Dog That Suffers from Separation Anxiety

I spend a lot of time in people's homes, taking care of *everything*, and often my clients decide to share odd things with me, on the off chance that I can help. So when one client started telling me about how she might have to get rid of her dog, because of his severe separation anxiety every time she left the house, I took it upon myself to look into a solution. A little research, and some patience and persistence by the owner, was all it took. I also learned that pet separation is quite common and that many pets suffer from it. See if this sounds familiar.

Before you leave for work in the morning, you turn to your dog and say: "Good-bye, Rufus. You be a good boy now. No messes, OK, Rufus boy?"

You give him a good loving pat, scratch his ears, kneel so you can look at him right in his golden eyes, and bid him farewell.

Before you've even shut the door, Rufus starts to emit a low whine that soon turns to a howl. You run inside, pat him one last time, remind him again to be good, and slip out the door. The howl, which has now turned into a mournful bark, continues. But you're already late, so off you go, leaving Rufus alone till dinnertime.

At the end of the day, you come home hungry and exhausted, and here's what welcomes you: a pee puddle in the middle of the living room rug; your favorite pillow on the couch chewed to shreds, feathers everywhere; the remote control gnawed into black bits; a hole scratched in the screen door; and so on. Stuffed in your mailbox is a note from your cranky neighbor saying Rufus has been barking all day, and she just can't take it anymore. Your dog has done a dozen things he shouldn't have, as if he were furious with you, but the minute you walk through the front door, he is overcome with ecstasy. You are his greatest love.

If this goes on for much longer, you're not sure you'll be able to keep Rufus.

Turns out, this kind of separation anxiety is an extremely common reason that families decide to give up their dogs. Luckily there are things you can do to ease your pet's distress—and cure his misbehavior—before giving up on your four-legged friend.

First, make sure he actually *has* separation anxiety. Mild destruction—

chewing on a few things—is not separation anxiety; it's boredom. Dogs with real separation anxiety chew on things that have your smell on them (hence the remote and the pillow). They work on escape routes. They whine and bark nearly nonstop while you're gone. When you get home, they greet you wildly and stay anxious and clingy for a time, following you around the house for hours.

It makes sense; dogs are pack animals, and separation from the pack goes against their instincts. Sometimes a dramatic change—a move to a new house, a new baby—can trigger this behavior in a dog that had no trouble being left alone in the past. Whatever the cause, quitting your job to stay home with him full-time is not an option, so here's what you can do to calm Rufus down when he has to be separated from the pack (i.e., you).

Make sure he's getting enough exercise. I know, you're exhausted already and can't imagine getting up a half hour earlier to take a longer walk with him, but it might be worth it if it'll save your furniture—and your neighbor's eardrums. A well-exercised dog is a tired, happy dog. Besides, if this whole situation is stressful for you (which it must be at this point), a little exercise will probably help reduce your stress as well. So get your butt out of bed. It will be good for you both.

Don't make a big deal out of your departures and arrivals. In fact, if the radio and the living room lights are on as you're getting ready to go, leave them on (it's not the greenest solution, but desperate times . . .), so the change isn't so dramatic. (Just be sure the radio isn't playing loudly, giving your neighbor reason to be annoyed not only at your dog, but at the music coming from your apartment.) Simply put on your coat and walk out the front door. Don't give Rufus a talking-to before you go. When you do that, all he'll hear is: "I'm leaving now, I'm leaving now, I'm leaving now." And when you come home, don't gush all over him, even if he's been good. Make it seem as if the whole thing is *no big deal*.

Give your dog "jobs" to do while you're gone. The best activities for most dogs involve food. Stuff a rubber Kong (a popular toy you can get at any pet store) with peanut butter, maybe mixed in with some of his kibble, and leave it for him—he'll be entertained for hours trying to get the treat out of the little rubber toy. There are other toys like this on the market—a cube you fill with kibble that Rufus can push around the floor, knocking out the occasional piece of food. Another trick is to hide treats around the house before you go (if you can do it without him noticing). Make some of them easy to find, so he'll catch on to the game quickly.

It's also important to try to desensitize your dog to your leaving. He may get anxious when you start with your regular getting-ready-to-go rituals, like organizing and snapping shut your briefcase, getting your coat on, taking the keys from a hook by the door. So on a Saturday morning, try doing these same things in the same order you usually do, but then don't go anywhere. Do this several times over the course of a few hours, or however long it takes for the cues not to upset him anymore. It might require a lot of repetition, but it will help him dissociate those cues with your leaving, which will make it less upsetting when you do leave for work.

You also might want to consider crate-training your dog, and then leaving him in his crate when you go out. For people not used to the idea, it can seem cruel to shut a pet up in a cage. But if you do it the right way (and you should follow the guidelines in a dog-training book or ask a trainer to help you), a crate can seem like a den to a dog, a safe place to be while he's alone. If not a crate, you might try keeping your dog in a contained part of the house—just one room, or just downstairs. You might think he needs the space to run around, but if he's had enough exercise, he'll mostly be sleeping anyway, and too much space can overwhelm an anxious dog.

Finally, as a last resort, consider enrolling him in doggie day care. He'll be excited to play all day while you're at work and pretty soon won't seem to miss you at all. Our client took the preceding advice, and in a matter of weeks, Rufus had calmed down—as did the upset neighbor.

Since 2007 vets have been prescribing antidepressants, including Prozac, to dogs. But with dogs, as with people, the conclusion seems to be that good training, exercise, and patience work better than drugs.

How to Move Your Pet Overseas

Moving overseas? The first thing you should worry about transporting is your four-legged furry friend. Moving pets requires time, patience, and a *lot* of preparation. Once, when I had to assist a client with getting a dog to the United Kingdom on short notice, we actually had to first route the pup to another European country with more lenient laws. At that time the United Kingdom had a law stating that all dogs from the United States had to be quarantined for six months before entering the country, but lucky for Fido, the way we got around that was by sending him on a vacation to a farm in France for a few weeks. Quite honestly, I'm not sure the little guy actually wanted to leave the farm when the time came, but off to London he went.

The United Kingdom has finally (but only recently) changed that long-standing law that forced owners from other countries to keep their pets in a government-run quarantine for *six months* before being able to rejoin their families. But the process, although now a little easier, still requires many steps, and you will ideally need seven to eight months of lead time to guarantee everything goes smoothly (the process varies for other European countries, but it can still be quite lengthy).

The easiest way to move your mutt is to hire a pet relocation service. Yes, these exist and they will handle everything for you, including pick-ups, deliveries, flight bookings, airport check-in, customs clearance and import handling, assistance with health documentation, and everything else you and your pet might need. For more information, contact www.petrelocation.com or 877-Pet-Move. The one hiccup is that door-to-door service will run you from $3,000 to $20,000. That's a lot of dog food. If you decide to undertake this task on your own, the best thing to do is to follow a process called PETS, which you can read about at the website just listed.

Whichever way you go, it's crucial that you jump-start this process as soon as possible. There will be paperwork, shots, and health exams, and, depending on where you are moving, perhaps a period of quarantine. (FYI: Quarantine is like a kennel. It's not a problem to visit your pet, but the cost is still fairly steep—about $15–$35/day—and your pet definitely won't have the comforts of home.)

If there is a quarantine period and you are short on time, consider leaving your pet with someone in the States until the waiting period is up.

Fortunately, most countries aren't as strict as the United Kingdom, but be sure to check out www.aphis.usda.gov/regulations/vs/iregs/animals/ for a country-by-country breakdown of the laws. You'll also be able to find a local pet inspection vet, which is important since a health certificate will likely be required wherever you go. Once your pet's shots are taken care of, your vet will give you the certificate, which you'll then need to take to an official USDA Inspection veterinarian to endorse.

But wait, there's more. Not only must you meet all the requirements for the country you're going to, don't forget that unless your pet is a *really* good swimmer, you're going to have to fly him there. Which means you must meet all requirements of the airline that will be transporting him—and all airlines have slightly different rules. In general, to avoid being quarantined at the destination, pets have to fly as cargo and travel on specifically approved airlines and routes. The good news is that airlines will get your pet through customs so you'll just have to meet him in the reception area. Airlines don't need much advance notice that your furry friend will be traveling with them (at least two weeks is best, just like regular airline tickets), and ticket prices depend on the size of the animal plus handling fees in both the United States and the destination country. You will also want to be sure to get an airline-approved kennel with ventilation on all four sides. Flying is understandably an incredibly stressful experience for animals, as they're away from their familiar environment and owners, cooped up in a tiny box, and surrounded by loud noises and intense air pressure. Most animal experts recommend putting some of your old clothing in your pet's travel crate with the pet, so the animal has something familiar to sniff and hang on to. Dogs will calm down considerably if their owner's smell is present.

Finally, once your pet has safely arrived in his new home, you'll have to devote some time to making him comfortable in his new surroundings. Moving is an adjustment for *everyone*. Remember that you and your family will be the only familiar things to your pet; his home, neighborhood friends, and probably even his brand of food will be different. So make sure to surround your pet with all his old toys, blankets, and anything with a familiar scent, and for the first few days after your pet arrives, try to keep to the same schedule you had at home, so he understands that things are more or less the same.

How to Clone Your Pet

Most dog and cat lovers go through multiple pets in their lifetimes. And although each provides a different type of companionship at a different point in our lives, let's face it: there's always that one pet we become more attached to than any of the others. So much so that no future pets will truly live up to. If you feel that way, you're not alone. This is why, in the past decade, huge advancements have occurred in the science of animal cloning. It may sound like something that could only happen in a bad science-fiction movie, but today it is actually possible to get an exact replica of one's former pet, genetically speaking, at least.

Yes, people call Consider It Done to find out about *everything*. So the day a client called and asked if I knew anything about how to clone a pet, I didn't flinch. I didn't have a clue, but of course I would find out. Here is what I learned.

Animal cloning is scientifically possible, but if you have your heart set on doing it, you may have to wait awhile. Although a company called Genetic Savings and Clone (seriously!), working in conjunction with another called BioArts (which holds the sole worldwide rights to clone dogs, cats, and endangered species), did successfully clone its first cat in 2001, and multiple dogs between 2006 and 2008 (and opened its business to commercial clients in 2004, charging around $50,000 to clone a cat and $150,000 for a dog), in September 2009 the company issued a press release saying it would be indefinitely ending its commercial cloning services. Though there were legal reasons for this decision (most of them patent related), the company also reported some physical abnormalities in the cloning process. Despite early success, it seemed that cloning couldn't be done safely in all cases—at least not yet. As the company's press release stated, "This technology is not ready for prime time."

In the meantime, though, various services offer gene *banking*, which allows you to preserve your pet's DNA when it passes away, so that when commercial pet cloning does become available—and it likely will—you can just pull your old pet's DNA from storage and give it a shot. To find a gene bank near you, it's best to speak to a local vet, but you can also visit www.viagen.com, which offers gene banking as well as cloning services for cattle, horses, and pigs (just not for pets).

A word of caution: If you do decide to put your pet's genes in a freezer so you can clone them at a later date, it's important to remember that a cloned pet is a genetic copy, but it's not necessarily going to be the exact same pet. Though some of your dog or cat's behavior is determined by genetics, a lot is determined by its environment. The circumstances in your home when you raise your pet, the amount and type of attention you give her, the manner in which you train her, and so on, will all affect the personality and temperament of your cloned pet. And while your new dog or cat may look a lot like your old one, it's not guaranteed to be identical. Quick science lesson: Unlike identical twins, whose DNA matches entirely, a clone will match its host in nuclear DNA but not mitochondrial DNA, which just means that small differences can, and usually do, occur. So before you go to the trouble of cloning your pet, think about mating (if that's an option) or simply getting a new pet of the same breed.

My client agreed that it wasn't quite the right time to be cloning her pet. Instead, she got a new puppy and let her older dog spend time with the pup. You know how when you are around someone a lot, oftentimes many of their habits and behavioral patterns start to wear off on you? Believe it or not, the same is true for dogs. The new puppy developed a personality that was so similar to the client's favorite pet, it eased the pain of saying good-bye to her longtime pooch when the time finally came.

Better yet, if you've lost a beloved pet, consider adopting your next pet from a shelter. Sure, he or she may not have the same rugged good looks or charming disposition as the departed, but if you save a dog or cat from suffering, I guarantee it will bring you just as much joy. Plus, it's way less bizarre—and it will save you $150,000.

How to Kill a Cockroach

The only thing worse than an uninvited houseguest is when that uninvited guest is (horror of horrors) a cockroach skittering across your floor. Like burglars, roaches make us feel like our homes have been completely violated; plus, they are just gross. They say that cockroaches live forever, but the good news is, a roach is actually pretty easy to kill. The bad news is that if you see one roach, more than likely you're *not* seeing a bunch more.

So if you're determined to kill that (hopefully) little sucker—and his little friends, too!—it's usually best to resist the urge to jump up on a chair and start screaming. It won't be easy, but instead of running away from the roach, follow him (at a safe distance, of course). Try and track the roach you see. Where is he off to? If you see one or more roaches in the same area of your home over a period of time, I'm sorry to say, chances are they have a nest somewhere nearby. It may make you feel better to spray an entire can of Raid in that direction or swat at the individual offenders with a rolled-up newspaper, but don't kid yourself. That's a short-term fix and you're gonna need a long-term solution to make your home roach-free.

Store-bought roach traps aren't pretty, but they work, and are completely safe if you have kids or pets in the house. Alternatively, there are two homemade ways to combat roaches. The first is a simple solution of soap and water—roaches breathe through their skin, so if they're exposed to soapy water, even a few drops, the solution will stick to their gruesome roach bodies and basically suffocate them. So instead of those unsightly traps, leave trays of soapy water around, or fill a spray bottle and spray it in the direction of their nest.

The other more complicated method is a mixture of boric acid, sugar, and flour. Boric acid is easy to find at the hardware store, cheap, and not externally harmful to pets or humans (meaning it won't hurt you unless you ingest it, so if you have small kids at home you should obviously keep it out of reach). The sugar in this powdery mix is the bait, while the flour makes it stick to surfaces. The boric acid is the killer, and just a tiny bit will dispense with your roaches in a matter of hours. I know what you're thinking—you want them dead, and you want them dead *right now*—but the lag is actually what makes this method so lethal. Because the death isn't instantaneous, the roaches will track the stuff back to the nest and spread it to their comrades. Sprinkle a new layer every couple of weeks for about a month and a half to destroy the entire nest.

For a fee, there is obviously the exterminator route. The downside is that it is less personal, and you want to send a *message* to those pests.

Once you get rid of them, remember to seal your food and keep your home clean to avoid attracting more. Duh.

11. food and drink

How to Choose the Ripest Watermelon

Sure, you can find mealy, pale chunks of watermelon in a supermarket fruit salad in the middle of January, but to most people, watermelon means summer. To me, watermelon means summer on a Greek island, where they serve the sweetest, juiciest watermelon as an afternoon snack and after meals at night. But whether you are at an open market in Mykonos or landlocked in the Midwest, follow these tips to ensure that you'll bring home the ripest of these sweet giants.

First, look at the shape and size. Unless the melon is one of the new tiny varieties that are bred to be about the size of a cantaloupe, the name of the game here is the bigger the better. If the melon is large, that means it was left on the vine long enough to ripen. Another sign of a ripe watermelon is that it should be fairly symmetrical in shape.

As for color, start by looking at the "belly spot," the area of discoloration on the bottom where the fruit was resting on the soil. If it's light green, the fruit is not ripe. But if it's a creamy yellow, you've probably got a good one. Next, check the stripes. If a watermelon's stripes really stand out, chances are it's not yet ripe. The color should be a relatively uniform green, and only a subtle contrast with the stripes. Also, be sure your choice has no bruises, cracks, or soft spots. Those types of flaws aren't just ugly, they actually affect the taste, as they're signs either of rough handling, which may have spoiled the fruit, or of overripeness.

Now pick up your new darling. A watermelon is 90 percent water, which means it should feel even heavier than you expect it to. A heavy melon means a juicy melon, but rock it a little and listen for any sloshing—that's a definite indicator of a fruit past its prime. And finally, the thumping test. Some say to use your index and middle fingers pressed together, some the palm of the hand. Everyone agrees the watermelon should give off a hollow sound when its side is tapped. If you hear a solid thud or a high-pitched tone, put it back.

Some people swear by the following method too: Take a long, straight piece of dry grass and set it crosswise on the melon. If the fruit is ripe, they say, the grass will spin and align itself lengthwise with the fruit. Maybe it's an old wives' tale, but if you're bothering to thump, check the belly spot, and cradle the thing, why not try this, too? You might get some odd stares from fellow shoppers, but that's a small price to pay for a refreshing, healthful summer dessert of perfect ripeness.

A watermelon is no banana. Once it's picked, it doesn't ripen any further. So make sure you're taking home the best one you can find.

How to Find a Fishmonger in Your Area

When I first started cooking fish regularly, I would buy it at—where else?—the supermarket. In the beginning I assumed the bland flavor and rubbery texture were a direct by-product of my undeveloped cooking skills, but as my skills got better and my fish didn't, I knew I had to look beyond my comfort zone. So I went farther down the street, past the chain supermarket next door, to a specialty market, the kind that you can just call "super" because customers feel hip shopping there. At the chain store, the fillets of fish were gray, mealy, and prepackaged in blue Styrofoam. Here, they were firm, glistening white, and nicely displayed on ice. And when I took them home and cooked them, they were indeed more tender and flavorful. Problem was, my wallet was also much emptier. That's when I sought out a true fishmonger.

At first I didn't even really know what the term meant. Turns out it's just a guy who sells fish, but without the middleman. Fishmongers get fish directly from the fishermen who catch it—and in some cases, they *are* the fishermen.

The "net" (get it?) result: Fishmongers sell fish closer to the time they are caught and for a lot less money. You get the freshest fish at the best price.

Now, finding a good fishmonger is obviously easier if you live by the water but still possible if you don't. Start by searching for specialty local food markets, not the kind in shopping centers with fancy neon signs out front, but the kind in parks and on sidewalks, with makeshift tents and no signs at all. If you're in a city, try traveling through ethnic neighborhoods; in New York City, for example, markets in Chinatown, Koreatown, and Little Italy have some of the best fish in town (not to mention all kinds of other fresh vegetables and meats). Sometimes, farmers' markets will pop up one day a week in certain towns and cities (go to www.localharvest.org to find the ones that set up shop nearest you), and they are likely to sell fresh fish, as well.

If you don't have a local outdoor market, and you live anywhere near the ocean, your best bet is to travel toward it. The closer you get, the fresher the fish—a few miles for you could mean a few days in terms of freshness. Find the nearest port and walk around the boardwalk until you see the fishing vessels. Most of the day's catch will go off to other markets, seafood restaurants, and wholesale distributors, but a local fishmonger usually sells a small portion right then and there.

If you don't live near a specialty shop, a farmers' market, or along a coast, you should be able to find a local fishmonger in the Yellow Pages or on the Internet (though they may be a day or two behind in freshness). But don't go with the first one you find. Every fishmonger will tell you all his fish are fresh, so don't take this at face value. Even the best fishmonger gets a bad batch of tuna every once in a while. For example, at a local fish store in Massachusetts I visited, a giant sign above the cash register read, "Everything's fresh. If you ask what's fresh, go to the back of the line." He was like the soup Nazi of fish, but he had no right to be: I'd tasted fresher seafood at Long John Silver's.

The point is, everyone will tell you their stuff is good, so instead of asking what's fresh, ask what came in when; if the salmon came in that very morning, it's obviously going to be fresher than the sea bass that came in the day before. Still, the fishmonger might tell you that everything in the store was still swimming that morning, and there's no way for you to double-check freshness other than by tasting it. So try a few different fishmongers—and a few different types of fish at each one—and then choose a favorite to be "your guy." (It's always good to have a guy.) Once you become a regular and develop a relationship with your guy, you'll actually be able to get an honest answer when you ask what's freshest. Bottom line: Even if you live in the middle of the desert, you should still be able to get fresh fish if you know who to ask—and how to ask for it.

How to Entice Your Kids to Eat Their Vegetables

The local and organic movements have taken off, and farmers' markets are popping up all over. But as you happily dig into your braised butternut squash and baked kale chips, are your kids still stuck on hot dogs and macaroni? If so, you're not alone. It's the age-old dilemma: how to get your kids to eat their veggies. As any parent knows, just getting a vegetable to cross their lips (let alone talking them into chewing and swallowing it) can become a nightly struggle at the dinner table. And if you're a real foodie, or take pride in your culinary abilities, it can be all the more frustrating to see Junior wrinkle his nose at the fruits (or more accurately the veggies) of your creations.

Luckily, I know a few tricks that might help get veggies into their little pieholes.

1. *Make your kids chefs for the night.* Start the process by sitting down and letting them plan the menu—with the caveat that at least one green item must be included. Subtly make suggestions, disguised as questions, like "Would you like to serve spinach or brussels sprouts with your meal tonight?" Then take your kids to the grocery store to pick out their food. After they have planned, shopped, and helped you prep the food, they will be proud of what they have made . . . so proud that they might actually eat it. You could even have them create physical menus—hand colored, of course—while you finish up the cooking. If you want to get creative, have them come up with the names, things like "Ricky's Radishes" or "Susie's Steamed Green Beans." How can they refuse something that's named after them?

2. *Use reverse psychology.* Fill *your own* plate with vegetables and tell your kids they can't have any. There's nothing more appealing to a child than the forbidden, and pretty soon they'll be begging for that sautéed Swiss chard on your plate (*Note:* This technique generally works with husbands too).

3. *Give the food nonfood names.* I discovered this creative tactic while babysitting. The little devil wouldn't eat the broccoli, but when they were "trees" he couldn't get enough. More trees please!

4. *Sneak them in.* Of course the most well-known trick these days is the one Jessica Seinfeld promoted in her cookbook, *Deceptively Delicious* (and she may or may not have cribbed from Missy Chase Lapine's *The Sneaky Chef*). The idea, to sneak vegetable purees into child-friendly foods like cakes, brownies, and chicken nuggets, is not a new one, but it became a lot better known after Lapine sued Seinfeld for "vegetable plagiarism," as the latter's celebrity husband termed it. Media circus notwithstanding, it's a method worth considering. If your kids really won't down a single green bean, why not avoid the dinnertime battle and sneak some healthy stuff into the foods they already know and like. It's a victimless crime.

5. *Embrace your inner artist.* Wouldn't it be nice if your kids *knew* they were enjoying the cauliflower you were hiding in their macaroni and cheese? If you want to take the straight and narrow, turn on the visual artist inside you and make the food look fun. Turn a salad into a smiley face: use baby spinach for hair, grape tomatoes for eyes, a carrot nose, and a green bean for a mouth. Stick a bowl of salad dressing alongside it for dipping. Dipping all kinds of veggies into hummus, guacamole,

or yogurt not only makes everything taste better, but it feels more like an activity than eating and can work wonders. One other suggestion: stuff cream cheese or peanut butter into some celery and dot it with raisins to make ants on a log. If the name sounds gross to you, chances are it'll have some appeal to your kids.

6. *Make them suffer.* If all else fails, try starving them! OK, not quite, but twenty minutes or so before you're ready to serve dinner, when your kids are clutching their stomachs and claim to be dying of hunger, put a bowl of baby carrots on the table. Or even some stir-fried broccoli. Get the vegetables out there first. You'll be surprised by what hunger pangs can do to their antiveggie stance.

How to Find a Weird Culinary Concoction That No One Has Ever Heard Of

Chicken soup is widely hailed in the culinary world for its miraculous restorative powers—for the body as well as for the soul. Less familiar, perhaps, are the healing properties of jellied monjaline—an obscure and virtually undocumented colder cousin of the ubiquitous poultry-based broth.

As I found out firsthand, as with any obscure food item, getting hold of this admittedly unappetizing-sounding substance is no walk in the park. Finding monjaline, jellied or otherwise, can be a challenge for even the most intrepid foodie. I hadn't ever heard of it before (or heard of it since) the summer a client asked me to deliver it to a friend who was ill, but I said I would locate it and so I did. Although, admittedly, I didn't ever discover exactly what it was.

A first step to tracking down elusive edibles is, of course, to use the electronic highway. But if, as in this case, all Google comes up with is a bunch of random websites in a language that looks like gibberish, try specialty grocery stores (ones that cater to the item's specific cuisine, if possible, although in general, Japanese markets are good places to find exotic ingredients). If they don't carry what you need, ask one of the clerks if he or she knows other places that might.

If you still come up empty, you could try your hand at making it yourself—assuming that your sought-after vittle doesn't need to be stalked, slaughtered, or skinned. Of course, you'll need a recipe for the do-it-yourself approach, which in our case, was something that we could not locate. So if Martha and Moosewood can't help you, you may have to find someone who's familiar enough with your dish to fill you in on the ingredients and preparation.

If it's one of those old country, like-your-grandmother-used-to-make types of concoctions, try someone from an older generation who may either know what's involved or else have firsthand memories of what it tasted like. Don't pal around with too many old-timers? Try a friend's relative or, if you're really desperate, visit a nursing home.

In my case, by asking around at each grocery and specialty shop, I was able to find a foodie whose grandmother used to make the soup. Just because your dish isn't common here also doesn't mean that it's not popular elsewhere in the world. So find out where it's from, and get in touch with a native to get the scoop.

If all else fails, wing it. If jellied monjaline's your goal, for example, and you know it's vaguely like chicken soup, only, well, jellied, mix chicken broth with gefilte fish jelly. Maybe even add a couple of matzo balls for that homemade feel. It may not be monjaline to the tee, but if it's that hard to find, chances are no one will really know the difference anyway. This was my solution to the jellied monjaline delivery. I called a chef (because chefs can make anything taste good) and had her create a cold chicken soup with some jellylike stuff. Then I wrapped up a container with a giant bowl and put it in a beautiful box with a big ribbon to seal the deal. I'm guessing the client's friend was so grateful for the thoughtful gift, the authenticity of the soup was probably the last thing that mattered.

So when you need to locate a rare culinary concoction (or anything else rare for that matter), keep in mind that if it's rare, most people don't know what it is either. There is always a way to wing it and in my case, it was easy, because after all, it was a gift, and gifts make everyone feel better.

How to Truss a Chicken

Ever wonder why your roasted chicken just doesn't quite look like the one you pick up at the grocery store? To prepare a roasted chicken and have it sitting pretty on your dinner table, you'll want to truss it. Trussing is just a fancy word for tying—so don't get nervous. Although trussing a chicken may seem like an advanced chef technique, it's actually really easy, and it'll help your chicken to cook evenly.

All you need is a long piece of butcher's twine (don't worry about it being too long, because you can cut it when you're finished), maybe two to three feet long, depending on the size of your bird. Do any fancy work, like stuffing or applying a rub, first, and tie last.

Lay the chicken breast side down on your counter. Tuck the wing tips in so they resemble your arms when you pretend to do a (hence the name) chicken dance (arms toward your chest, elbows out), and grab the twine. Run the twine under the drumsticks, and bring it up to make an X above the chicken. Then bring the twine down between the legs and pull it tight, so the back portion of the chicken gets squeezed together. Then wrap the ends of the string around to the front of the chicken, flip it over, and tie the ends together under the nub where the chicken's neck would be. Tie it in a bow, snip off the extra string, and you're done!

Bon appétit!

How to Stock the Perfect Bar

Take a look at your liquor cabinet. Is it a little bare? A little lopsided (i.e., three kinds of fruit-flavored rum with nary a whiskey in sight)? Are you missing ingredients that you need for most basic cocktails? Well, if so, it's time to revamp your bar.

Unless you actually own your own cocktail lounge, it's extremely costly, and nearly impossible, to furnish your liquor cabinet with *everything* someone could ever want, but it's easy to collect enough of the basics to be able to accommodate most standard drink orders. First, you'll need to make sure you have at least one of each of the five major liquors—vodka, gin, rum, whiskey, and tequila. Most rum cocktails call for silver (or "light") rum, so start with that. As for whiskey, rye or bourbon mix the best, so if you're only getting one bottle, go for one of those over scotch or Irish whiskey.

Depending on your budget, you can get a wide range of quality for each of these liquors. Unless you're stocking up for something fancy, it's best to get bottles in the $20 range. Tequila tends to be a little pricier, but you can still get a decent brand (e.g., Jose Cuervo) for around $25.

Once you have your base liquors, it's time for the tricky task of finding liqueurs, the sweet-flavored liquors with lower alcohol contents that many mixed drinks require. Liqueurs are where many people can get overwhelmed, but they're actually not that daunting, as many are similar and you will be able to get away with a few key essentials here.

You *must* have an orange-flavored liqueur, so get some Triple Sec, Cointreau, Grand Marnier, or Curaçao (clear *or* blue, they're both the same). Vermouth is also a must—Martini & Rossi is the standard, but if you have a preferred brand, go with that. Crème de cassis and peach schnapps are used in many Champagne cocktails, so if you and your friends tend toward festive occasions, a bottle of each is a good idea. Depending on your tastes and those of your guests, you might also want to have a coffee (Kahlúa or Tia Maria) or chocolate liqueur (like crème de cacao) for good measure. Also invest in a bottle of bitters—there are a number on the market, but Angostura is still the most popular and the most common for cocktails.

Next, mixers—tonic water and seltzer are essential. As far as juices go, orange, lime, and lemon are pretty common, so be sure to have some of each. Finally, garnishes—cherries, olives, onions, limes, and lemons are pretty much all you need. Mint is helpful for mojitos, but there aren't many other drinks that require it.

So to recap, you want at least one each of the five liquors, an orange liqueur, a peach/blackberry liqueur, a coffee/chocolate liqueur, a bottle of bitters, some tonic and seltzer, some citrus juices, and a selection of garnishes. If you have all that, you'll be much better prepared than the average home-bartender. Just be sure you keep everything up-to-date and replenished—a party is the wrong time to discover your orange juice has gone bad or that you've run out of rum! And don't worry if you don't know how to mix the drink someone asks for; with this kind of bar, you'll be able to create a good substitute, and you'll certainly look good trying!

How to Make the Perfect Martini

Making your own martini can seem daunting—not necessarily because of the cocktail itself, but because of the glass you're required to drink it out of. Those first few sips can be treacherous, and the distance from the table to your lips can seem like miles when liquid is threatening to overflow on all sides.

But whether you're like me, too intimidated by the threat of spillage to go anywhere near a martini, or whether you drink them daily, the martini is one of the classiest drinks around—just ask James Bond. When prepared correctly, it's simultaneously the most refreshing and impressive drink to serve to guests . . . or yourself.

The great irony about making your own martini is that you don't even need a martini shaker (sorry, Williams-Sonoma). Instead, just start by filling a pint glass with ice. The key to a perfect martini is that it is *cold*, so don't be stingy on the ice. There will still be plenty of room for the liquor. Next, add two and a half ounces of gin, or slightly more or less, depending on your preference (you heavy-handed pourers know who you are). Last step: add one-half ounce of dry vermouth.

Back up: Yes, I said *gin*, not vodka. Some are often surprised by this, but a classic martini is made with gin. If you prefer vodka, go for a vodka martini, but let's call a spade a spade. That's not a real martini.

Next, you'll be faced with the age-old debate: shaken versus stirred. Although Mr. Bond might look good drinking it, he's actually ordering a watered-down martini—oddly out of character, but that's another story—so resist the urge to sound cool (by the way, it doesn't) by repeating his catchphrase. It may not be as much fun as playing Bond, but stirring your homemade martini will keep your drink ice cold and dilute it just enough, whereas shaking will add so much water and make the drink so weak, you might as well be drinking a mai tai at a dive bar on ladies' night.

Now come the martini glasses, and yes, you've got to use them. Don't buy the really cheap ones, either; the small stems will be so fragile they won't last until the end of the dinner party. I once ordered a pack of six glasses for $20; two arrived with the stems already snapped in half, two fell apart in the dishwasher, and the last two are sitting on the top shelf gathering dust.

Once you've got decent glasses, you're ready for the most important step: chill them. Either stick the glasses in the freezer or fill them with ice cubes a few minutes before you're ready to serve. It's the easiest step to forget, but if you can remember to do it, it doubles the impressiveness factor.

Remember: The key to the perfect martini is serving it *cold*, and a chilled glass will keep it colder, longer. Plus, it looks all frosty and fancy.

Quick tip: Traditionally, one would drop an olive or two in the glass, but for a refreshing change, try peeling the skin of a lemon with a vegetable peeler, squeezing a little lemon juice over the drink, and then placing the lemon strip inside the glass. Looks elegant; tastes great.

If you find the classic martini a bit boring, there are countless ways to spice it up with syrups, fruit juices, and other types of liquor. Of course, most apple, cranberry, or chocolate martinis aren't martinis at all, technically. But if it's served in a martini glass, who will question you, especially if it tastes delicious? Bottom line is, if it's got a lot of alcohol, and you don't spill it, then whatever concoction you pour into that martini glass will be the perfect martini . . . as long as it's cold.

If you're entertaining guests, fancy stirrers can be a nice touch. If they want it shaken, instead, that's their loss.

How to Make Irish Cream at Home

Smooth. Creamy. Delicious. An Irish cream is the ultimate in decadence, like a glass of spiked liquid cheesecake. But while it's available at pretty much any bar, there's no law saying you can't also whip up a batch at home. Not only is it a scrumptious drink, it can also serve as a unique dessert topping or coffee creamer (though not necessarily recommended for your morning coffee), so try serving it at your next get-together. It's the kind of thing not everyone wants to *admit* to drinking, but if it's being served in the privacy of your home . . . well, even the manly men will belly up to your bar. Really, it's a crowd-pleaser. Trust me.

The ingredients you'll need are:

1. 1 ²/₃ cups Irish whiskey
2. 1 cup light cream (heavy cream also works and will make it richer)
3. 14 ounces sweetened condensed milk
4. 1 teaspoon instant coffee
5. 2 tablespoons Hershey's chocolate syrup
6. 1 teaspoon vanilla
7. 1 teaspoon almond extract or other flavor extract

For the Irish whiskey, Jameson is a good choice. It's the standard brand, and it's high-enough quality without being too expensive to justify using in a mixed drink. Feel free to experiment with extract; caramel, rum, orange, mint extracts can also work and will give your Irish cream a unique flavor. When it comes to the coffee, be sure you use instant, because you need it to break down and blend with the other ingredients, and fresh ground coffee will leave residue. Finally, for the syrup, Hershey's works, but if you have a preferred chocolate syrup or want to swap it for caramel or strawberry, feel free to substitute to your taste.

Throw everything into a blender and blend for about thirty seconds. You can also whisk it all together in a mixing bowl. Once all the ingredients are blended, pour the mix into a sealable container—airtight Tupperware or a bottle with a screw-on top will work just fine—then chill, shake, and serve. You *can* serve immediately, but for better results, leave the mixture in the fridge for at least a couple of hours. Be sure to shake right before serving, since some of the ingredients will separate in the fridge.

And there you have it—a delectable, decadent, and alcoholic treat of your own creation.

How to Make an Old-Fashioned

Why would you ever need to know how to do this? Well, old-fashioneds are making a comeback, but few people know how to make them, and you'll want to be prepared in case a guest in your home asks for one. I once got a frantic text message from a client asking if I could please advise how to quickly make an old-fashioned in a pinch. You may not always have all the ingredients for this classic cocktail on hand (though to ensure that you do, see "How to Stock the Perfect Bar," page 294), but fortunately, there are a few work-around solutions that will help you serve an acceptable old-fashioned and show off your outstanding bartending skills using what you do have in your liquor cabinet.

First, here's how you make a *real* old-fashioned: Smash (if you want to get bartender-fancy, you would say "muddle") a maraschino cherry and orange slice at the bottom of a short glass. Add a teaspoon of simple syrup, a jigger (1.5 oz.) of bourbon, a dash of Angostura bitters, and top it off with ice and a splash of club soda. Just knowing this recipe will give you instant cool bartender status.

Simple syrup is just water and sugar mixed in equal parts, so you can make that yourself. Boil a cup of water with a cup of sugar, then let it simmer for five minutes until all the sugar is dissolved. Bottle or store it in an airtight container and it will keep for up to a month in your fridge. If you don't want to make simple syrup, just add a spoonful of sugar to the drink and stir vigorously to dissolve the sugar as much as you can.

Simple enough, right? But what if you're out of oranges? Or you open up that jar and find you used your last cherry on that hot fudge sundae you shouldn't have eaten? Or what if you don't even know what Angostura bitters *are*? Worse yet, what if you don't have a muddler?

Well, here's what you do. Remember, drinks are primarily about *flavors,* not textures, so as long as you can replicate the flavors, you'll be fine (plus, if you make the drinks strong enough no one will complain). For the orange, a splash of OJ works just fine. If you're out of maraschino cherries, a splash of the syrup they soak in will do the trick (not quite sure why anyone would keep the jar of maraschino juice, but this may be the reason . . . so before you toss it, consider saving that slightly disgusting syrupy stuff in case you ever need to make an old-fashioned). And the curved end of a spoon works well as a muddler substitute.

Chances are, you have a bottle of *some* kind of bitters somewhere, and they can stand in for the Angostura. If you don't have bitters, a tiny drop of vermouth will work; in fact, the drink works even if you leave the bitters out entirely (I won't tell anyone).

And while the typical old-fashioned uses bourbon, rye or Canadian whiskey can also work, so see what you have in your bar. Just avoid scotch, as it has a darker, smokier flavor than other whiskeys and won't blend very well. And if you're out of seltzer, a splash of lemon-lime or orange soda will give the drink a hint of carbonation with a little extra flavor. Spring water also works if you're desperate, but flat old-fashioneds aren't always popular.

It's fine to improvise, but don't stray *too* far from the recipe. If you find yourself having to make more than two of these substitutions, it might just be better to throw in the towel on your old-fashioned and offer up an old-fashioned screwdriver instead!

How to Brew Your Own Beer

Back in the dark days of Prohibition, it was done out of necessity, but today, brewing your own beer is twice as much fun, half as hard, and one hundred percent legal (if the math doesn't add up, it's thanks to all the beer) as it used to be. This explains why home brewing has become such a popular pastime, with tens of thousands of zealous devotees around the globe churning out all kinds of sophisticated and delicious microbrews, right from their own homes.

So how can you become one of them? Well, let's not get ahead of ourselves. You need to crawl before you can walk (and then you may not be able to walk, once your first brew has been consumed), so let's start with the basics. You'll need a four- to five-gallon steel pot (most home-brewed beer is prepared in five-gallon batches, but single gallon "minibatches" are also popular) and a copy of *The Brewmaster's Bible* by Stephen Snyder, which is, uh, as the name suggests, the bible for all home brewers. Most experienced home brewers recommend getting a starter kit, which you can find on websites like www.morebeer.com and www.beerwine.com. These kits should have all the ingredients and materials you need, and though you could probably find all these on your own, if it's your first foray into do-it-yourself brewing, simplicity is the name of the game. Kit or no kit, you'll need grains, barley, hops, yeast, sugar, a sealable fermenter (which can just be a regular container like a big five-gallon water jug with a stopper, though an actual fermenter, available online or in brewing stores, is preferred), forty to fifty 12-ounce bottles, and a thermometer (a nice handy one that has adhesive on the back so that you can just stick it right onto your pot can be picked up at a brewing supply store, a pet store, or an aquarium supply place). Then, look online for recipes that will tell you the exact proportions of ingredients, because they vary depending on what type of brew you're trying to make.

If you're using a kit (and really, you should, why make life difficult for yourself?), start by boiling two gallons of water in that steel pot. Once the water is 170 degrees, put the grains from the kit in the water, like you would a tea bag. The kit should supply you with a nice mesh bag for the grains; if not, get some cheesecloth, pour the grains in, and tie it with a piece of string to make your own pouch. Let it steep for about half an hour, then throw out the grains. Next, let the water boil again before turning off the heat and adding the malt extract and the first portion of hops. Then bring the water back to a boil and add the remaining hops gradually, every five to ten minutes for the next hour.

Now what you've got is "wort," or prefermented beer. Set the pot of wort in a sink filled with cold water or ice and let it cool down to 130 degrees before pouring it into the fermenter, which should already contain two gallons of cold water. If the fermenter isn't filled all the way (air can interfere with the fermenting process), add enough cold water to make an even five gallons. Then add a packet of yeast, and seal the fermenter with a stopper.

Two weeks later, pour the concoction from the fermenter into the smaller bottles, adding a spoonful of sugar to each bottle to help with carbonation. Seal the bottles, and in another two weeks you've got yourself home-brewed beer.

Now if you want to get fancy, you can also add flavorings to customize your beer. Flavors like coriander seeds, honey, fruit juices, and even chocolate or coffee beans can all be delicious. You'll need about a pound of your flavoring for every five gallons of beer—just add it to the mixture when you add the malt extract.

Two other important tips from experienced home brewers: (1) Before you begin, make sure you *wash and sanitize everything*—the bottles, the fermenter, the pot, *everything*. Nothing's worse than rancid beer or beer with a soapy flavor. And (2) if you're serious about home brewing, get real feedback on your brews from other brewers or beer snobs. It'll help you figure out what works and what doesn't and make you a better brewer. Most of your friends will tell you "it's great, really!" as they choke it down, so ask the one picky drinker who'll give you constructive criticism.

If you get your stuff together and start today, in a month you could be chugging your very own ale. And if you want to get *really* fancy, create your own labels (see "How to Customize Anything," page 152). Whatever you do, just try and save some beer for your friends, okay?

If you're not quite up for the brew-at-home experience, look online for a "Brew on Premises" establishment. They provide the tools, the ingredients, and the instructions. You show up once to create your brew and two weeks later to bottle it. You still brewed it yourself—without making a mess in your own kitchen!

How to Choose and Serve a Bottle of Wine like a Pro

Nothing's more impressive to a group of guests than a host who knows his or her wine, but not everyone has the time or inclination to become an amateur sommelier (that's a wine expert, for those of you who don't have the time or inclination to *look up* sommelier). Fortunately, it's easy to class up your next party with the right vino served in the right way.

When choosing a wine, always consider what food you're serving. Sure, you've probably heard these rules before, but you also probably just simplified them to "reds for red meat, tomato sauces, or chocolate; whites for chicken, seafood, or light pasta sauces." Well, there's a little more to it than that and (unless you routinely dine with wine snobs or foodies) learning just a couple more tidbits is what will get you to pro status at any (novice) wine table.

For heavy dishes with strong, spicy, or meaty flavors, you want a bold red wine, like a cabernet sauvignon or a malbec. Pinot noirs or merlots are good medium-bodied wines that pair well with a lighter red meat dish or a stew. Lighter dishes like chicken, fish, or vegetables go well with a pinot grigio, dry Riesling, or a sauvignon blanc. Be careful, though—for extremely rich savory foods, like cheese or foie gras, most wine experts will recommend a sweet wine, like a Madeira, instead of a robust red. The opposite is true of very sweet desserts, which actually pair better with a more acidic wine than a dessert wine.

So now you know which type of wine, but how do you choose from the millions of labels out there? One trick is to just check the label to see if the wine has been certified. If a wine is certified by its country's wine authority, you know you've got a fine wine. So look for AOC labels on French wine bottles, or DOC labels on Italian bottles, and so on. Wines that are made with grapes that originate from only one vineyard also tend to be better than wines cobbled together from a range of grapes, so stay away from merlot/shiraz/cabernet blends.

When you're selecting wine, also consider the region the wine comes from. Many wines require specific climates, so if you're choosing, say, a pinot noir, you want to be sure you get one from a wet region, like Burgundy or the Pacific Northwest. For more information on regions, take a look at www.winespectator.com, where you can also check out the website's blogs and videos, learn about collecting, and much more.

But what most people don't realize is that choosing the wine is only half the battle. Yes, it's always about how it looks, so you also have to be sure your wine presentation and service is up to par. Provide your guests with the proper glasses (red and white glasses for the corresponding wines, obviously), and be sure to show people the label before opening the bottle. Wine keys, sommelier knifes, and Rabbit devices are all considered proper tools for opening wine, while "wing openers" are viewed as tacky by most fine dining establishments.

When pouring, always pour with the label facing your guest. Start with the ladies in the room, then serve the men, and then finally serve yourself. Give guests a small amount at first so they can taste it before you serve them the full glass. Holding the bottle by its end (don't put your thumb in the indentation at the bottom!), tip the wine into the glass about three inches above the glass's rim, aiming for the center of the glass's bottom. A good pour is about a third of the glass.

Once the wine is poured, wait a few minutes and smell the contents. This is not just something to do because you saw someone doing it in a fancy restaurant or in a movie. A bottle of wine is "corked" (ruined) if it smells of damp newspaper or cardboard, and if this is the case, your guests may be too polite to say anything, so it's up to you as the host to sniff it out.

As you finish the pour, twist your wrist as you bring the bottle up to ensure it doesn't drip. Congrats, you just served a fine wine like a pro!

How to Create Your Own Wine Cellar

True, having a wine cellar in your home will make you seem sophisticated and cool. But that's not the only reason people have them. Wine is best stored between 45 and 65 degrees Fahrenheit, with little exposure to light or humidity. That's why the earliest wine cellars were caves—dark, dry, cool, and likely to stay that way, regardless of the weather outside its walls. For that reason, caves and basements (known as "passive" wine cellars) are naturally good environments for wine. So if you have an underground room where the temperature doesn't fluctuate and you can easily keep the light out, all you need to do is put up some wine racks (ideally, bottles should be on their sides) and voilà. Instant wine cellar.

No basement? There is still hope. You can buy or create an "active" wine cellar, a storage area that is temperature and humidity-controlled to ensure wine is properly preserved. Active wine cellars range in size from a cabinet the size of a dishwasher to a whole room, but unless you're a major wine collector and/or a restaurant owner, you're probably looking for something in the range of the former. Amazon and sites like http://www.winecoolers.com sell such mini wine cellars, called wine coolers (not to be confused with those fruity things you drank in college), and the good ones start around $200.

Quick tip: Consider pairing a wine cooler with some wine glasses, a few bottles, or even a wine-tasting class for a nice wedding, engagement, or housewarming gift for anyone who likes wine (or wants to pretend that they do).

Although it's pricey, you can also have a room in your house turned into an active cellar. Companies like Wine Enthusiast and Wine Cellar Innovations can custom build a cellar to fit your needs. Besides constructing the actual room, they'll also seal it off from humidity and install temperature controls. This can cost upwards of $10,000, but for the true (read: wealthy) wine enthusiast, that could be the value of a single bottle, so well worth the investment.

Finally, you're going to need to stock your cellar. If you're new to this, consider enlisting the help of someone who knows what he's doing (ya think?). Good wine shops will often make recommendations (especially if you are purchasing bottles from them), so ask them to help you make sure your cellar is stocked with the perfect wine for every occasion. There are an abundance of classes you can take to learn about wine if you are interested, but it can be a bit overwhelming in the beginning, so until you know what you are doing, ask the pros.

If you've got a brand-new cellar to stock, you may want to check out a festival like the Aspen Food & Wine classic where you can learn and taste to your heart's content. Just be sure to write down the names of the bottles you like—trust me, after tasting all that wine, you're not going to remember them on your own.

How to Make Your Favorite Cocktails on a Plane

By the time you get through security, wait at the gate for a couple of hours, and finally board the plane, you're ready for a drink. But not just a boring vodka soda or a glass of crappy wine. You've been through a lot and you deserve to relax with your favorite cocktail. Unfortunately, most airlines offer a pretty basic drink selection and may not have the ingredients for your beverage of choice on hand. Not to worry, here are some creative ways to make it happen even if the in-flight selection reminds you of your ninety-year-old grandmother's liquor cabinet.

First off, if you must have your guava mojito while you travel, go by train. Bringing liquids on trains is perfectly legal, so you can just take all the weird nonalcoholic ingredients (and the more obscure alcoholic ones) with you (hint: bring extra, and you'll be the most popular guy or gal on board). When it comes to BYO cocktails, airplanes are another story. Since liquids aren't allowed through security, you'll only have whatever's available either past the security gate or on the airplane to work with. That's okay—that's what improvising is for.

Let's start with the easiest. If creamy drinks are your poison, coffee with cream, sugar, and vodka will make a suitable substitute for a White Russian (even better are those bottled Frappucino drinks many flights now serve), while the same with a dash of chocolate milk will get you pretty close to a Mudslide.

Fruity drinks like margaritas or mojitos are a little trickier, since the key to those drinks is lime, which is not always available on a flight. Here's where you can get clever. And all it really takes is a little thought after you pass through the security checkpoint. Snag some slices of lime at just about any airport bar (simply ask the bartender—a healthy tip should cover it) and stash them in a baggie. Or pick up lemonade, an easy enough substitute. Now, margaritas are pretty easy—some tequila (you can always get tequila on a plane), lemonade, and a squeeze of lime (and if it's your lucky day, some airlines actually have Cointreau or other orange liqueur, but if not, a splash of OJ will do the trick). How to get that nice frothy texture? Grab another handy Ziploc bag from your carry-on, combine all ingredients, give it a little shake, and watch your seatmate enviously eye your glass as you pour.

It's good practice to always carry extra Ziplocs when flying, even if you aren't planning to mix up a traveling cocktail. You never know when you will get the stickler security guard who insists you put your toothpaste or contact lens solution immediately into a small plastic bag.

Next up, if you're dying for a mojito, you'll need light rum, limes, club soda, and mint. So far so good. We covered the limes, so the only new twist is the mint. You could pack some ahead of time, but on international flights it might be illegal (though you could always sneak it inside a sandwich; no one will sniff your turkey on whole wheat). A better plan might be to get some mint tea from a shop and throw a splash in your cocktail for flavor. Or, simply drop an Altoids in and give it a little stir. Works like a charm. Really!

Bonus drink: piña coladas. If you're really lucky, the airport will have a smoothie shop in the security area. Because you choose the fruits and flavors that go into your smoothie, these are perfect for mixing with the booze you'll buy on the plane. Order a coconut and pineapple smoothie and just add rum once you're wheels up. No smoothie shop? Most airport stores now carry coconut juice (it's good for hydration), which is great in a pinch (and consider grabbing some extra to rehydrate before landing).

Being able to sit back with your favorite cocktail can make air travel much more bearable. Just make sure there's a car service waiting to pick you up on the other side.

How to Figure Out What to Order in a Restaurant Where No One Speaks English

Believe it or not, there are still places in the world where not everyone speaks English. Try visiting very remote places and you will come across them. Just a couple of years ago, I was in China, and sure, the people who worked at the big hotels in the large cities spoke English, but many people in many other places still did not. Taxis were challenging, as were restaurants. Yes, the farther off the beaten path your travels take you, the more likely you are to come across people who don't speak a word of English. And while it can be frustrating at first, it's surprisingly fun to attempt to make your way around. So how can you be certain that you don't accidentally order the pig intestines with a side of fried crickets?

Of course it will help to learn a little of their language before you go. We're not talking *fluent*, just a few key phrases. When it comes to eating out, "What's good?" "What is he eating?" and "I'm a vegetarian" are all very useful phrases, and even if you don't understand the answer, it'll give the waiter an idea of what you're looking for. But as I quickly learned the hard way, Chinese is a particularly challenging language, and if you even slightly mispronounce something (and the odds are good that you will), your waiter won't have a clue as to what you are talking about.

Luckily, I've learned some handy shortcuts. Pointing to something appetizing looking that someone else is eating is a good idea, as well as pointing to menu items and giving a questioning look or a shoulder shrug. Your waiter will probably catch on that you're asking if the item is good—you *are* in a restaurant, after all, and that tends to be a universal signal. You might even end up playing a rousing game of food charades, with your server attempting to use signs to tell you what something is. Bonus points if you get him to cluck like a chicken.

If the meat on the menu is unidentifiable, I usually decide to stick with vegetables. But be careful, because I did at one point end up with deep-fried broccoli with sprinkles (yes, the kind used on ice cream) on top. Healthy? Um, not really. Tasty? Not so much. But safe, sure. As far as food preparation goes, I recommend sticking to boiled. Why? If you see a large bowl of steaming noodles, you can pretty much know that whatever is in there has been boiled for at least three minutes, which means it's safe to eat (an old camping trick I like to apply).

But for the truly fearless traveler, there's no more authentic—and exciting—dining experience than just pointing to a random item and praying it's something edible. Hey, part of the fun is trying to figure out what it is, right? If the locals eat it, it can't be poison, so you may as well give it a go.

12. show me the money

How to Get Your Late Fees Waived

I'm a pretty easygoing person, but late fees really irk me.

Late fees no longer equal a couple of cents for forgetting to return your library books. These days, everyone from credit-card companies to cell-phone service providers to cable companies to landlords have jumped on the "charge-you-late-fees-because-I-can" bandwagon. The thing is, when most people see a bill with a late fee tacked on, they figure the easiest thing to do is simply pay it, especially if the fee isn't *that* high—at least compared with what you already owe. So most people choose the path of least resistance. But it's money out of your pocket, and it adds up, so why not put a little time and effort into getting your late fees erased?

You'd be surprised how easy it is to get out of paying the fee. Often, all you have to do is call and ask. Really, you'd be shocked by how many customer service agents have the authority to simply remove your fees, and if you're one of the few people who takes the time to call and explain your situation (very nicely), they'll often do you the favor. Make friends with the person on the other end of the phone, and if it doesn't seem to be going anywhere, ask politely for a supervisor. Again, be as nice as possible, but if you're really coming up against a dead end, you may have to switch strategies (but first try just switching people and keeping with the same strategy).

Plan B? Get mad. Tell them how long you've been a customer, how much you really do love the service but how disappointed and upset you are right now. Threaten to leave the bank or whatever organization it is, entirely. If you're comfortable doing it, yell (and, if you're not, try doing it anyway and consider it a form of therapy). Some people will remove the fees just to avoid dealing with you any further (or at the very least compromise and cut the fee in half).

Your other option? Have an excuse ready for why your payment was late, and make it a really good one. A few surefire get-out-of-anything excuses include: you were away getting married, you were on your honeymoon, or you just had a baby. You could also try saying that you never got the statement in the mail, or that you did pay, so somehow it must not have gone through.

If all else fails, tell them you previously called to let them know that your payment would be late, and the person you spoke with said it would be fine and that the late fee would be waived. Isn't it noted in the system? People are human, so it could be true—and even if you're telling a little white lie, they can't prove it. What's that about the customer always being right?

Still no luck? Go straight for the top. Ask for a manager, and if the person you're talking to says the supervisor is busy (often employees just say this in the hopes you'll give up), nicely tell him or her that you will wait. Keep asking to speak to someone higher up, to the president or CEO of the company if you have to. Try writing a strongly worded letter, and send it to someone at the top. The intended recipient may never read it, but someone will, and it's usually easier for this person to just waive the extra fee than to go through the hassle of dealing with you for an additional extended period of time. A little persistence from the squeaky wheel here could be the key to your fee removal.

Remember: The letter must be strongly worded. They must know that you mean business, and that you're not afraid to pursue this until they waive the fee (just be sure you recognize that you may get so hooked into being right that you forget that your time is also valuable, so weigh that with the amount of the fee). To help plead your case, refer to the following sample letter, which should give you a good start. Just choose the phrases that are most appropriate to your situation. (Kind of like a Mad Lib.)

Dear Mr./Mrs. President/CEO/Important Person:

I recently received a bill from your *venerable/time-honored/pathetic* institution, which I have been a member of for *5/10/82* years, and was *surprised/outraged/sent into cardiac arrest* when I discovered the addition of a late fee. There must be some mistake, and therefore I refuse to pay the additional fee. I *returned my books/paid my bill/ slipped my rent check through the crack in the wall between our apartments* on time, and it is completely due to *a computer glitch/incompetence of your staff/buffoonery of your clerk/misplaced hunger of my Chihuahua* that it was not received on time. This entire situation is *simply unacceptable/completely illogical/possibly illegal, but I'll have to get back to you on that.* I am *a newspaper reporter/a high-profile blogger/a good friend of Brian Williams, the most trusted man in America,* and I will make sure the world knows about this injustice in the form of *an investigative exposé/a three-week web series/a two-hour prime-time special starring John Stossel* if something isn't done to rectify it.

Yours Truly,
Honest Abby

Feel free to add anything else you think necessary, but that should give you a decent start. In a letter, you can never go too far. I know someone who sent a very similar letter to the CEO of her bank, and within a week, the late fees had vanished.

Sometimes just being a big enough pain in the ass is enough to get you out of anything.

How to Cut Your Monthly Dry-Cleaning Bill in Half

Impressed with yourself because you found a $19 dress that looks just like the $200 one hanging in the window of that boutique around the corner? Excellent job, as long as the washing instructions don't say "dry-clean only" or after five or six wearings you'll have spent so much in cleaning bills that you might as well have splurged on the more expensive model. Let's face it; dry cleaning is expensive, so if you want to save money, start at the root of the issue. When you go shopping, look for the items that say "hand or machine wash." This may sound obvious, but how often do you stop to look at the label when you're busy stroking the soft, plush cashmere of that must-have sweater. Looking at the cleaning instructions before you buy an item of clothing should be just like reading the nutritional information before you buy food at the grocery store. Of course, there are going to be some little numbers you simply have to have, dry-clean or no dry-clean. So, here are a few more tips to save loads so that you won't get taken to the cleaners (literally) ever again.

- Know that care labeling laws for clothing require only that the manufacturer include at least one method for cleaning, not all acceptable methods. So chances are even if it says "dry-clean," it's perfectly okay—and a whole lot cheaper—to clean the item by hand. Use a gentle cleanser (Dove dishwashing liquid actually works well, as does baby shampoo or baby laundry detergent, like *Dreft*) and cold water. Don't twist or wring the wet clothes, and of course, never dry them in the dryer. The safest way to dry is to lay the clothing flat on a drying screen or use a layer of towels, and replace the towels when they get soaked through. Note: *Do not use this method if it says "dry-clean ONLY." Otherwise, you're fine.*
- It can't be denied that nothing looks quite as crisp and clean as a shirt or skirt just back from the dry cleaner. To achieve this look, but still save money, hand wash your clothes and then take them to the cleaners for a pressing. This is a particularly good idea for silks, which are tough to get the wrinkles out of on your own.
- Take your items to the dry cleaner as infrequently as possible. You'd be

surprised how many people waste hundreds of dollars a year or more by overcleaning. Plus it's not even good for your clothing. So ironically, the more often you dry-clean, the more you'll be spending on new items. There is no set rule as to how often one needs to dry-clean, but in general, you can spot clean and hang items to air-dry before putting them back in your closet for at least half a dozen wearings and still be fine. Most items that aren't directly in contact with your skin, like suits and coats, really only need a cleaning once a year; and the same goes for leather or suede (just be sure to find cleaners that specialize in cleaning leather). Seriously, it's not good for items to be dry-cleaned often, so rewear your items and save your money for something more important—like shoes.

- Determine if the items are dirty or just wrinkled. This is another common cause of unnecessary extra trips to the dry cleaner, and one *very* common among people of the anti-ironing stripe. Here's how to break this nasty habit. Always hang up your clothes. No matter how late it is and how many cocktails you've had, if you stick that blouse on a hanger, there'll be one less thing for you to regret in the morning.

- Try a home dry-cleaning kit, like Dryel, for example. Toss your items in a bag (which the kit includes) in your dryer. When the bag heats up, it releases chemicals and moisture so that your items come out clean and wrinkle free. This isn't a true cleaning, but it's good for dresses and tops that need a "freshening up."

- If you are of the aforementioned anti-ironing stripe, consider investing in an at-home steamer. After all, it's much easier to steam than to iron. A fabric shaver is worthwhile, too. It will shave lint, fuzz, and loose threads off wool, cotton, and knit clothing, as well as dollars off your dry-cleaning bills.

Mix a concoction of two parts water and one part vodka (the cheaper the better!). No, it's not a cocktail to celebrate your newfound savings. Spray it lightly on clothing to take out smells—even cigarette smoke!

How to Avoid Baggage Charges on a Flight

Many airlines have recently started to charge for checked baggage. This policy is not popular, and for good reason. A piece or two of luggage has always been included in the cost of an airline ticket, so it seems unfair to have to start paying additional fees now. I mean, if you are flying somewhere, you will usually need to bring a suitcase with you so when you think about it, this is really just a sneaky way of raising the price of the ticket. C'mon, who do they think they're fooling?

Well, if they are going to be sneaky, two can play at this game. First off, when deciding which airline to fly, check out the website www.air farewatchdog.com, which keeps an up-to-date chart of how much airlines charge for bags. Currently, JetBlue doesn't charge for one checked bag, and Southwest doesn't charge for up to two.

If it looks like you're stuck with an airline that does charge for bags, though, there are still a few (somewhat devious) ways around it. Whether you have two bags and only want to pay for one, or don't want to shell out any money at all, this plan usually works.

Have you ever tried taking a largish carry-on bag onto the plane, only to be told at the gate that it won't fit in the overhead compartment? If you have, you know about "gate-checking," which is where carry-ons that don't fit are given a special tag and thrown in with the checked baggage. Well, if you're trying to get away without paying to check your bag, this is exactly what you want to happen. It's a bit of a hassle, but the flight attendants at the gate are generally too busy trying to get everyone on the plane in time for takeoff to bother to charge you for your checked bag.

To make this work for you, though, your bag will need to be *close* to carry-on size, or it won't make it through security and check-in. If no one stops you before you reach the gate, when you get to there, head on through with your bag and *just* as you're boarding the plane, tell a flight attendant that you bought some stuff at the duty-free store and now you're worried your bag won't fit into the overhead compartment. Most likely, they'll gate-check your bag for you—free of charge. After landing, you'll usually pick up your gate-checked bags near where the plane disembarks, rather than going to the baggage claim area, but every so often they will route your suitcase to baggage claim with everyone else, so be sure to ask; either way, it's free! Just remember to act like you didn't plan this, as you don't want the airline officials catching on to your scheme. And if anyone asks, you didn't hear it from me.

How to Return Something Past the Warranty Date

Returning something past its warranty sometimes requires a bit of both creativity and persistence. Often clients hand us items and just want them returned. Of course, they don't know *where* the warranty is but they are *sure they had one*. Okay, so we'll just figure that one out. Even if you do have the warranty, it's often not such a cakewalk. It's as if companies include the warranties anticipating that people will lose them and just pay for repairs or replacements. Which is often what happens.

The best way to ensure that this won't happen to you is to keep a file or a household binder for product warranties and file the paperwork there as soon as the item is purchased. Not to worry, even if you forget to do this, there is still hope. The first place to start is the receipt. This will tell the company when you actually purchased the product and sometimes that's all you need. If you don't keep your receipts, you can usually get a copy of your credit-card statement fairly quickly online, giving you sufficient proof of purchase.

If the item was a gift (like that fab washer/dryer your parents bought you as a housewarming present—yay!), you may not have the receipt. But as with everything, you'll probably be able to find a loophole in the policy—if you speak to the right person. Often situations like whether to grant a missing warranty or whether to let you exchange products without a receipt are left to the discretion of the manager or salesperson you're dealing with. So your first move should simply be to try to sweet-talk the salesperson or customer service representative you end up speaking to. You've heard the saying about attracting more flies with honey . . . well, it's true. Be as nice as possible, and be sure to mention how much you love the product—and how you'd never switch to another brand or buy from another store, so is there anything that they could do? It may not fly with everyone, but if on the off chance that it doesn't, you're no worse off than when you started (and besides, it works more often than you'd expect).

I once had a client whose watch broke more than a year after the warranty date. So I called customer service and told the rep how much my client absolutely *loved* the watch and how he had recommended the brand to *all* of his friends (which happens to have been true, but doesn't necessarily have to be to pull off this technique). Even though it was no longer under warranty, they sent him a new watch, free of charge (all they asked was that the broken one be returned). Total time: fifteen minutes, and it saved him hundreds of dollars.

Quick tip: If they believe that you're a trendsetter and that you'll recommend the product to your friends, they might be even more inclined to make exceptions to the warranty policy.

If killing them with kindness doesn't work, don't give up. You just might need to switch gears. Take the opposite approach and suggest that you're in a position to make statements about the shoddy quality of their product that will be widely distributed. Most companies realize it's easier to make an exception (just this *one* time) than to deal with the fallout of a nasty story about them that goes viral. If you don't have the outreach to follow through on this threat yourself (though you probably won't even need to), you may want to call up a blogger or writer for a popular website. If you threaten to have this person write negative reviews of the store or product, it just may scare the company into replacing your item—even after the warranty date has come and gone. *Note:* This is not my favorite tactic, but sometimes, it just happens in the moment.

If you are still not getting anywhere, try the old-fashioned handwritten letter route. Now more than ever, a handwritten note is a great way to get noticed (because it's so rare), so take out your pen and paper and get started. You'll easily find the name and address of the person you need to reach on the company website.

Finally, if you have an American Express card, use it to make all purchases that have a limited warranty, because AmEx will extend the warranty by one additional year, free of charge. They'll even do it retroactively if you forget to extend it when you make the purchase.

And if it is *way* past the warranty date, consider just buying a new one. Honesty is always the best policy, especially if you got years' worth of good use out of the product, don't you agree?

How to Actually Cash in on Your Coupons

You know how it goes. You're constantly getting bonus coupons, rebates, or e-mail promotions, but you never end up actually using them. How many times have you found yourself at the store purchasing an item and you *know* you had a coupon for it stuffed in some drawer at home? Thought so. What a colossal waste! Luckily, I have a very simple system to help ensure that no coupon will go unredeemed again.

First off, whenever you come across a coupon, discount, or promotion, clip it or print it. Then, put it in the *one* place you've designated to store all coupons (like an envelope, a folder, or even a Ziploc bag so that you don't have scraps of paper flying around everywhere). Now, and this is key, until you are in the habit of taking them with you, be sure to keep this baggie or folder near the door, so you'll see it each time you head to the store.

The second huge obstacle to coupon usage (after not having them on you when you need them) is expiration. Most coupons need to be used within a month or two or they become completely worthless. So get in the habit of sifting through your coupons on a monthly (if weekly is too much) basis and sorting them by expiration date. Get rid of anything that's no good, and keep those about to expire at the top of the pile where you can see them. If there are one or two in particular that are such great savings it would be a crime not to use them, put those right at the top, and consider highlighting their expiration dates in neon highlighter. You might even want to plug the dates into your calendar as an added reminder.

Just keep reminding yourself that coupons are essentially free money, and remembering to use them will be a breeze.

While you're at it, don't forget to sign up for rewards programs. Everyone from banks to Staples has such programs these days, and it's money back in your pocket.

How to Create a Budget

Creating a budget for yourself is a sensible way to stay ahead of your expenses, put money aside for savings, and even have some guilt-free frivolous fun once in a while. OK, so you already knew that. Then why aren't you keeping one? Maybe you have put this task off because you've always insisted you're just not good with money (you know that's really just an excuse, right? I mean you don't have a problem with money when it comes to buying shoes, do you?), or because it sounds too complicated or intimidating, or maybe because you just don't want to face the reality of your money issues (aha! sounding more like it?).

But budgeting doesn't have to be that scary. The first step is creating a budget that's realistic, taking into account your finances and lifestyle (the same budget may not work for everybody). First, start by simply being conscious of the ebbs and flows of your bank account. Just like logging food intake helps dieters face the reality of what they're eating all day, keeping track of expenses (and deposits!) forces you to confront your spending (and savings!) habits. Handing over a few dollars at a time may be easy to do at the coffee counter, but it's a different story when you see those daily lattes totaled up at the end of the month.

Luckily, keeping track of spending couldn't be simpler. If you're the old-school type, keep a notebook on you, filled with the headings "Date," "Description" and "Amount," and use it to record every penny you spend. If credit cards are your weakness, leave them at home and use a debit card instead. Be disciplined about monitoring your checking account on a weekly basis, if not more often, and consider an online tool such as Mint. com (or its iPhone app), which pulls together bank and credit-card information, categorizes your purchases, and delivers an instant picture of your financial comings and goings.

Once you've kept an eye on your spending patterns for a month or so, and know what you are working with, establishing a simple budget is pretty easy. Consider a basic 50-30-20 plan: this means 50 percent of your net income should go toward "must-haves"—basic expenses like mortgage or rent payments, child care, utilities, transportation, and groceries; 30 percent should go toward "wants"—like eating out, clothes, and gym membership; and the remaining 20 percent should go toward savings and paying off debt.

For many people, antipathy and anxiety about computing their costs is deep-rooted. Many people are simply too scared to face the truth about their money issues. But planning for the financial future is an important, if oft-ignored, part of life, and the irony is that tackling your finances head-on is not only fairly simple, it's a path to *less anxiety* and greater peace because you'll know that you've taken control of the situation and are up-to-date on where you stand.

There are, of course, more complicated budgets you could try. But start simple—confronting the issue is half the battle, and it's better than not starting at all. And who knows, you may just find out that your finances are in better shape than you think.

How to Get Your Taxes Done (More or Less) on Time

What is it about tax season that can turn high-functioning, responsible individuals into bumbling, hopeless procrastinators?

Does this sound at all familiar? April 15 is approaching. The drawer you shove receipts and statements in is too packed to even shut. Your palms are getting sweaty, and you'd really rather be doing *anything*—like pouring curdled milk into your fresh cup of coffee or opening wide for a root canal—other than organizing yourself to get your taxes done.

If the deadline is drawing near, it's probably too late to implement a brand-new organizational system, but you should get one going as soon as possible so that next year won't be such a nightmare. Seriously, do it this time. I'll keep it simple, so it's not too scary and besides, starting small is always the best way to go. This standard method works for a lot of people. Go out and buy an accordion file. Label each compartment alphabetically with the name of a deduction category. Start in pencil and when you're confident about your categories use an electronic label maker. It will make you feel either like a pro or a complete nerd but will give your system a cleaner look. You'll definitely survive without this touch, so if the thought of going to the trouble to make fancy labels gets in your way of actually doing the task, skip it. Use a crayon if you need to, just label those tabs. Here are some common categories to get you started: cell phone, credit card, donations, household, insurance, office expenses, books/magazines, personal, professional services, professional dues, training/seminars, and travel. From now on, when you have a new receipt in your hand, turn it over and jot down exactly what it was for, then just slide it into the relevant compartment, and forget about it. Keep a section of your accordion file and do the same for all your end-of-year earning statements—W2s, 1099s, and so on. These will likely start appearing in your mailbox in January or February, so have your system in place by then. That way, when the dreaded day does come around, you won't have to ransack your house trying to remember where you put those damn slips of paper from Bank of America.

I know, none of this sounds like fun. But trust me, a little bit of organization will go a long way in making your life easier at tax time. If you have a particular aversion to accordion files (some people do), use file folders or create a folder-less system. The tools are really up to you. Plenty of people stay organized with just Ziploc bags or color-coded envelopes, each one labeled with a Sharpie pen and then stuffed in an old shoebox. If you're the more artistic type, picking out some attractive folders that match your personal style might help spice up the process. You could even go to a flea market or look on eBay and get yourself some sort of fun vintage furniture to serve as your filing cabinet—like a section of an old library card catalog. Refinish it, and use the small drawers for receipts. If you make it seem like a fun home decorating project, you may be able to forget it's related to taxes at all. Organizing doesn't have to turn your house into a some personality-less Staples megastore.

If you're the techy type, or favor a paperless lifestyle, take a look at www.shoeboxed.com. The company offers an iPhone application that lets you take photos of your receipts and statements with your phone and then e-mail them so the company can digitally archive and categorize your receipts. It can even export the digital records to Quicken and other software (if you don't have a camera-phone, you can send Shoeboxed your physical receipts, and they'll scan them for you). The service has a free option, but for the more advanced features you'll need to purchase a paid plan. Even the IRS is looking to save some trees these days, and will accept digital receipts, so dust off your shredder and say good-bye to all that paper!

Yes, organizing your receipts and tax documents really is as simple as filing them in a timely way. Actually *doing* the taxes still won't be a picnic, but it will be easier, faster, and less stressful if you go into it with all your paperwork in order.

Looking to avoid taxes altogether? Pack your things and move to Kuwait, Andorra, Monaco, or Norfolk Island, where there's no personal income tax at all.

How to Keep Your Credit-Card Information Safe

Credit and debit cards have their advantages. They are convenient and, at least in the case of debit cards, can be a helpful way to keep track of expenses and stick to your budget. Plus, you can rack up points that get you airline miles and other good stuff. They have their disadvantages, too, and these are well known. They make it a lot easier to buy things you could live without—like that fruit dehydrator you saw on QVC. The most serious problem with credit cards, however, has to do with security. Currently, the majority of purchases are being made online, which means that credit-card fraud and identity theft are more prevalent than ever. And if this happens to you, not only will you have a lot of annoying but necessary paperwork to complete, it could ruin your credit score completely. So here are a few tips to keep your credit-card information as safe as possible.

First, when you're out shopping, or at an ATM, try to keep the physical card in sight—but only *your* sight—at all times so that no one can copy down the account information from your card. Try not to get distracted while paying for something at a store, and don't let the shop clerk walk off with your card for even a minute. If you're out to dinner, it's best to keep an eye on the waiter or waitress who takes your card, as well. If you're too embarrassed, or think it would seem rude, take cash to restaurants and avoid the issue. And this should go without saying, but when at an ATM, cover the keypad with your other hand as you enter your pin. And if the person behind you is hovering a bit and in your personal space, don't be shy and ask him or her to please move back. Seasoned thieves sometimes use small handheld devices or cameras to take snapshots of people's card numbers and pins as they withdraw cash, so sometimes it pays to be paranoid.

The Internet makes all this even trickier, of course. If you must shop online (and who are we kidding, of course you must), be careful about making an online purchase in a Wi-Fi hotspot. A hacker can use open networks to lift names and passwords, even when it looks as though the password is blocked out. It would also be wise not to do your online banking or taxes at such spots. And check to make sure your home network is password protected, or you might just find yourself unwittingly financing your neighbor's kitchen renovation.

When deciding if a site is safe to buy from, please use common sense. Only shop at reputable sites—that is, places you've heard of before. An "s" after the "http" in the address bar (for instance, "https://amazon.com") indicates a secure page and a safe place to shop. Turn on the antiphishing filter in your browser, and make sure you have up-to-date antispyware and antivirus software on your hard drive.

Another important tip: Be smart about passwords. It's best to have a different password for each online account, and don't use obvious combinations of numbers and letters, such as birthdays or kids' names. If the thought of so many passwords makes your overtaxed brain ache, consider the following method. Think of a phrase rather than five or six letters. An example: "I can't remember my password." Use the first letter of each word: ICRMP. Then for each account, personalize the password. So if it's for Banana Republic's website, maybe make it BRICRMP. To be extra safe (and some sites require it), throw a number in there (BR23ICRMP), and be sure it's one that you'll remember but won't be obvious to someone else—like the number on your son's Little League jersey. And if you insist on writing your passwords down someplace, keep that piece of paper well hidden or in a safe. By that I mean NOT, on your smartphone, on your computer desktop, or in your top desk drawer. Better yet, write them backward. Seems silly, but if someone is trying to hack into your account, they probably won't work hard enough to figure this out. If you have a laptop, I'd also recommend disabling the cookies that allow online retailers to store your credit-card information (you can usually just do this by going to your account preferences and deleting the stored payment information). It's a pain to have to reenter your Visa number every time you want to buy a new dress, but this inconvenience pales in comparison to the hassle of having to cancel all your cards and close all your accounts in the event your laptop is stolen.

> When asked if you want to store your credit-card information with an online retailer, just say no! The risks outweigh the convenience.

How to Eat for Free for an Entire Week

When you own a business called Consider It Done, some people interpret that as a challenge to see if you can do things they think could absolutely never be done. Sure, we've all had free pizza at a club meeting, wine and cheese at an art show, or free sandwiches from a vendor doing a promotion. But how about eating for free for an entire week? A client of mine wondered if it could really be done.

Turns out it could. We tested the theory in the office, just for kicks. Someone in our office managed to eat without buying a single meal for that whole week—although she did have to go to more than her fair share of club meetings, lectures, and other time-consuming events. I'm not so sure it's worth it, but in case you're looking to save a little cash, and this seems like a fair trade-off, here are ways she discovered to get some free eats.

1. *Find God.* I'm not suggesting you pray for manna from heaven here. Many churches and other religious establishments leave out platters of food for meetings, or following services. The larger the group, the less likely they are to notice you (and the better selection of food they are likely to have). Similarly, group therapy meetings, like AA meetings or anger management sessions, may also offer free food. Just sit quietly, and no one is likely to question your presence. These are, after all, anonymous meetings. Plus, who knows what you might learn about yourself.

2. *Go back to school.* Nowhere are meetings at which nobody knows your name and there's a ton of free food quite so frequent and varied as on a college campus. So if you really want to eat free for an entire week, plan on spending a lot of time at a nearby college or university. (If you don't live near a college or university, there may still be lectures or book readings or panel discussions at venues like the YMCA, a library or bookstore, or a bar or coffee shop.) Check out the student center for posters or fliers, and look for any groups that are holding open events: book clubs, foreign-language associations, newspaper and magazine meetings, poetry readings, political rallies, guest lectures, speeches, and more. Most of the time, these clubs will advertise if they're serving food to attract more attendees (a wise tactic). And again, who knows, you might even learn something, or meet a new person (who could potentially offer to take you to dinner—bonus meal!), all while munching on free pizza and cookies.

Follow your nose. There are plenty of places to sniff out free food.

3. *Become a party crasher.* If you're feeling really adventurous, visit local hotel ballrooms and event spaces in search of parties. You'd be surprised how easy it is to crash birthday or anniversary parties, bar or bat mitzvahs, and so on. If it's a wedding, you're really in luck. Vince

Vaughn and Owen Wilson may have been crashing weddings for the ladies, but they got their fair share of free eats, as well.

4. *Become a breakfast person.* Often a tip for dieters, this is a good trick for people looking to eat for free, as well. Most cheap chain hotels serve a free unmonitored continental breakfast, so if you live near one, quickly duck in, load up on pancakes (this probably isn't what the dieticians had in mind), and duck out. It's technically stealing, so you didn't hear it from me, but half the stuff they put out ends up in the trash, anyway, so don't feel too guilty about it.

5. *Samples, samples, and more samples.* Just need a snack between (free) meals? Some grocery stores and many specialty markets serve free samples of delicious food, and if you don't mind the shame of asking for seconds (or thirds), you can get a decent snack. Or stop by a warehouse like Costco, which has a plethora of samples all over the store. Try one of everything, and you've basically got a full, free meal. And samples can be found in places other than grocery stores. Countless organizations give out free food every day to lure you into one promotion or another, and if you don't mind nodding and smiling for a bit, you can eat free for days on end. My local gym, for example, frequently hosts events where nearby health food stores offer free samples to entice the health-conscious consumer.

If none of this works, you can always consider temporary employment in the kitchen of a restaurant. You'll almost always get a free meal at the end of the night . . . not to mention endless snacks while you work.

6. *Give, and you shall receive.* Consider calling catering companies or event spaces and asking what they do with the food that is left over after an event. If they say they usually just toss it, volunteer to take it to a charity, just snag a quick bite along the way (if anyone catches you, tell them you were making sure it still tasted good). Sounds a little shady, but you're actually doing a nice thing, and they were going to throw it out anyway.

7. *Finally, volunteer at a soup kitchen.* They welcome volunteers and generally, if there are any leftovers—they're yours!

How to Split the Check with
Ten Stingy Friends

There's no way around it. When you split the dinner check evenly among a big group of friends, someone usually gets screwed. Whether it's the high-rolling friend who ordered the lobster, or the recently dumped co-worker who decided to drown her sorrows in three martinis, if you're splitting the bill evenly, sooner or later, you're going to get stuck picking up part of someone else's tab.

In most big-group situations, people end up splitting the bill evenly simply because it's easier than doing the math required to figure out what people actually owe. So if you're determined to pay your share and nothing more, you're going to have to step in and take charge, *before* someone says "let's just split it." This means you'll have to pay attention when things seem to be wrapping up—if you want to be the person in charge, now is not the time to make your way to the restroom.

Most people don't really know what they're doing when dividing a check based on meal orders, so chaos ensues. They then overcompensate by asking for extra cash. And nine times out of ten, even after money has been collected, you'll somehow still be short, and everyone will be asked to throw in a few more dollars.

So assuming you *do* know what you're doing, you'll be doing everyone a favor if you grab the check and chart the course yourself. A standard formula that works every time (if calculated correctly) is to add up what each person owes individually, and then add 25 percent for tax and tip. That may sound like too much, but really, it's accurate. Figure about 7–8 percent for tax, leaving around 18 percent for tip. Besides, 25 percent is a good number because it's extremely easy to calculate (if one-fourth is too complicated, just split it in half twice). When in doubt, always round up, and once you've got the number, stick to it. Don't let anyone claim they owe less—insist that you know what you're doing, and you'll give them money back at the end if you overshot it. In all likelihood, most people don't care about the extra dollar or two, they just want it to be *fair*. By adding 25 percent to everyone's individual tab, you're ensuring that everyone pays for exactly what they ordered. What could be more fair than that?

If all of this math is too much trouble, and your group is feeling coura-geous (and not totally broke), why not try a game of credit-card roulette? To play, have everyone put his or her credit card into the little folder con-taining the bill, and ask the waiter or waitress to just choose one at ran-dom and charge the entire bill. It's risky, but it can be fun . . . at least for the people who don't get chosen. And if you get in a routine of using this method with the same group of friends you eat with frequently, it should all even out in the long run.

Quick tip: There are various smartphone apps that can help you split a check (although it can be done just as easily with a calculator). If you're an iPhone user, try downloading SplitCheck or Separate Checks. Both apps are easy to use, and they can assist in splitting the bill based on what each person ordered.

Remember: What goes around comes around. You may not feel like having an appetizer this time, but another time you may decide on two. Think about that the next time you choose between the even split and calculating dollars and cents when your dinner bill arrives at the table.

How to Go to Live Concerts for Free (or Even Make Money)

Every week a client calls asking us to get tickets to some concert or an-other. Of course, they always call at the last minute and always want great seats, so they end up paying a pretty penny, much more than if they had just done a little preplanning. Although my clients may not change their ways, lucky for you, I was recently clued in on a way to get into concerts without paying those ridiculous ticket prices . . . and sometimes even *make* money in the process.

If you want to see your favorite band perform live (for free!), join the street team associated with the concert venue or artist. The "street team" is the group that spreads the word about the concert, usually by putting up posters or handing out fliers near the venue, and they are given free tickets to the show. If seeing the show is your goal, just be sure to confirm that you'll be receiving tickets before you do any work. The easiest way to join the street team is to find a member of the team in action, approach him or her, and ask who you can talk to in order to get a job. If a concert you would like to see is coming up, hang around the venue a few days before the event (or even the day of) and look for people promoting it. If you live in a big city, check the busiest spot in town (think Times Square), because even if the venue isn't near there, street teams will probably be there trying to lure tourists.

Don't have extra time? Get free concert tickets the old-fashioned way—by winning a contest on the radio! Instead of listening all day and waiting for the correct time to call (which can take hours out of your daily routine) like we did in the good old days, now you can also visit the radio station's website. For best results, check the websites of multiple stations, especially smaller, local stations. The fewer people visiting the website, the better your chances of winning.

What if you want to make *extra* money? Simple. While you are getting your early-bird tickets, purchase a few more. As we already established, people don't plan ahead when it comes to concerts, so all you need to do is wait until close to the show, then shoot out an e-mail to a few people saying you have tickets, and let them know your price. Usually, they'll be gone within the hour.

If you really want to make a few bucks, hold on to the extra tickets until right before the show, and then visit www.stubhub.com (there are other ticket resale sites, but StubHub is by far the most popular), and sell your extra tickets. You're almost guaranteed to sell them for much more than you paid for them (sometimes double or triple, if it's a really popular band). In fact, this is a way to go to concerts for free even if you did buy your own ticket; if you do it right, by buying enough tickets early on when prices were low, you'll make back the cost of the tickets you're actually using for yourself. And if you're really lucky, you'll come out ahead, which means you're essentially getting paid to see a concert!

This strategy is real, totally legal, and almost always guaranteed to work (as long as the concert sells out). Even if it doesn't happen *every* time (you may overestimate the popularity of a band once in a while), if you do it often enough, you'll come out ahead overall. The best part: There's very little risk. Shelling out money far in advance may seem a bit scary but rest assured that, if you put the tickets up for auction online, you'll *usually* sell them for at least the same price you paid if not more (unless the band is really bad). The last person I spoke to who did this purchased four $40 tickets to a concert and sold them the day before the concert for over $100 each. Rock on.

How to Tell How Much an Antique Is Worth

Are you guilty of keeping that outdated bedroom set from your grandmother even though it clashes terribly with your sleek modern decor? If so, I'm guessing it's because someone told you it was worth a lot and it would be a crime to let it out of the family, right?

Case in point. I once spent a month in Florida helping a client clear out her home. It was an undertaking; the basement and attic and even the elevator were completely filled with *stuff*. We had a team of people in there (yes, this was a *really* big house) and as we unwrapped and staged every item for the owner to look through, we unearthed all kinds of unique—and antique—items. The funny thing was that with each item we unwrapped, some people would oooh and ahhh, while others thought the item belonged in the donation pile. It was then and there that I realized the true meaning of the phrase "one man's trash is another man's treasure."

So how do you tell what's a valuable antique and what's a piece of junk? Here are some things to keep in mind when digging through your attic. First off, items that are still in their original boxes are always worth more to collectors, especially if they still have their original instruction booklets. In addition, items related to historical events, like paraphernalia from world's fairs, political campaigns, or pieces related to some historical movement, are big sellers. Complete sets of anything are better than a few parts, and even two of a set is better than a lone item, so if you find the Minnie Mouse Pez dispenser to go with that Mickey Mouse one, they both become more valuable.

Finally, erotica never seems to go out of fashion, nor does anything related to gambling, alcohol, drugs, or tobacco, so hang on to that ancient deck of cards, or that old pipe, for example (just what does that say about our culture I wonder?).

These are good rules for collector's items, but what about, for example, your grandmother's gold tasseled lamp? Finding out the value of an antique can be done a few ways. You can call an auction house and see if an employee will come appraise it for you, but if you really have no idea and don't want to risk wasting the person's time in case it's worth nothing, you could check out Kovels.com. Ralph and Terry Kovel have written more than a hundred books about collecting, and their advice is easy for the novice antiquer to understand. If you want to learn more about collecting in general, you can sign up to receive their monthly newsletter. The website and related blog (http://kovels.blogspot.com/) will also give you updates on trends, like what's getting hot and what's losing ground in the antique market. Don't forget to look at the price search section to find out if it's the best time to unload your item.

If you decide that you want to sell, consider hiring a private appraiser. And an Internet appraiser is likely not a good idea. Instead, get recommendations from a trusted source, like a bank manager or an estate attorney. An appraiser will charge you a few hundred dollars an hour, so you'll want to check references before making a decision about this person.

Whatever you do, don't "fix" anything you're hoping to sell. If you've ever watched *Antiques Roadshow,* you've seen the crestfallen looks on people's faces when they learn their Queen Anne dresser is now worth thousands less because they just stripped the original chipped paint and resurfaced it with a modern coat. Let an appraiser look at your item *before* altering it in any way. If you do decide to keep your antique item solely for the sentimental value, then you can feel comfortable painting, refinishing, and altering it as you see fit, guilt-free!

How to Win at Texas Hold 'Em

There are two ways to win at cards: cheat, or be smarter than everyone at the table. Since cheaters never prosper, here are some tips to make sure that you walk away from your next poker night with a bigger bankroll—using the second method.

First, in case you aren't familiar with Texas Hold 'Em, here's a quick (and very basic) overview of the rules. You're competing for the "pot," which is money (or chips) you and your friends have all contributed. You put an amount in the pot based on what you think your odds are of winning, given the hand you're holding and the cards in the middle that are available to all players. Anyone can choose to fold or risk more until the remaining players have a showdown (hence the name "Texas Hold 'Em"). This is where you'll have to show your hand—two cards you're holding and/or a combination of the community cards. The player with the best hand takes the pot.

But as any seasoned Texas Hold 'Em player will tell you, it doesn't end there. The game is *really* won or lost in how you place your bets and when you fold, raise, or call. The experts know Texas Hold 'Em is a *long-term* game, and this is where the real strategy comes in. It's all about odds, and being able to maximize them over time. Suppose you have a total of $500 you can afford to spend in a poker game. You buy into a $500 game, and get all in with double aces against a pair of 2s, which gives you about a 90 percent chance to win. But then somehow, you lose. Don't give up! You may have to *repeat* the process more than a single time to make the odds work for you.

Knowing the odds of various hands is the key to the game, and the easiest way to get a leg up on your friends. For example, the best hand you can have is double aces (sometimes known as "pocket rockets"), because two aces against any other pair has about an 85 percent chance to win. So if you're really committed to going home the winner, you'll want to learn from a pro.

For more detailed tips, read a book like *Theory of Poker* by David Skalnsky, *Harrington on Hold'em* by Dan Harrington, or *Doyle Brunson's Super System* (Volumes 1 and 2) by Doyle Brunson, rather than trying to learn by watching a poker competition on TV (although those can be surprisingly fun to watch). TV poker is usually edited, sometimes only showing half of a hand or skipping some hands altogether. This means that you don't really see the development of a long-term odds beating strategy. And don't rely on trying to read other players' facial expressions. Most real poker players will tell you that "tells" (someone's physical tic that indicates his hand) don't really work. As one seasoned Texas Hold 'Em player puts it, "Don't risk money because someone scratched his face."

How to Earn Quick Money by Being on Television

To make lots of money quickly, some people turn to the lottery, but with terrible odds and no skill involved, it's really not a sound investment. I'll give you a better idea. If you've got even a sliver of book smarts, you're already a step ahead of many people, and if you're ready to put in some time and effort, you can (usually) make just as much money in as short a time by going on a television game show. And technically, you're not just *making* the money, you're earning it. That's something you can feel good about.

Though it may seem impossible to get on a game show, it's actually quite simple, and the odds of actually getting on TV are higher than you'd think. In addition to the staples like *Jeopardy!* and *Wheel of Fortune*, there are *tons* of game shows on TV these days, both on the major networks and on cable channels like GSN (Game Show Network), with more and more cropping up every year. Sure, some of these get canceled quickly—or never make it on the air at all—but the contestants who appear in the taped episodes still get their prize money. So if you stay on top of the television game show circuit, you could wind up a big winner pretty easily.

First, check out the big shows that are on every weekday, like *Jeopardy!*, *Wheel of Fortune*, *Who Wants to Be a Millionaire*, *Family Feud*, *Deal or No Deal*, and *The Price Is Right*. After all, five days a week equals lots of contestants. To find out how to audition, these shows all have their own websites with information for potential contestants. For some, like *Jeopardy!*, you'll have to take an online quiz before you can even go in for an interview, but if you're the type who's always the smarty-pants at your friends' game night, go for it.

It's great if you get on one of those established shows, but because they are so popular, the competition is fierce, so you may have more luck on a new, up-and-coming show. These tend to offer just as much prize money; plus you never know which new show will be the hot ticket tomorrow. Be prepared for anything; some newer shows are getting wilder and crazier, so if you're easily embarrassed, or don't want to do anything like, say, bathe in a tub full of scorpions while stranded on an island with Donald Trump, you might want to go the more traditional route.

Still, there are a lot of choices out there, so to find the show that's right for you, first, do your homework. You can start by checking www.About.com, which has multiple pages related to game show casting. Also check out a blog dedicated to "Viewer Participating Television," at www.VPTV.blogspot.com. These sites can keep you informed of new shows (both game shows and reality competition shows) and whether or not they have open casting calls.

Quick tip: Game show casting calls, and especially reality competition show casting calls (see "How to Get on a Reality Show," page 181), are almost *all* about personality, not brains, so play up any wacky personality quirks and don't be afraid to say or do some crazy or weird stuff. Hey, go big, or go home, right?

Another little-known secret is that most networks, even the big guys like CBS, ABC, and NBC, put their game show casting calls on Craigslist (www.craigslist.org). Most of them tend to be in New York City or Los Angeles, so start by checking the N.Y.C. and L.A. sections of the site, but some do travel (e.g., *American Idol*). If you don't live in either city, poke around your hometown's page and see if anything pops up. You might get lucky if a show is passing through.

Don't limit yourself. Just showing up to a casting call is 90 percent of the battle—most people never even take the time to do that. Once you're there, you've got a decent shot at making it on TV and winning the jackpot. Or not—when I once managed to snag a spot on *Scrabble*, I went home with nothing more than a curio cabinet and a freezer full of Otter Pops.

You may not want to quit your day job. There are rules about how many shows you are allowed to be on over a period of time. I had to sign something saying that I wouldn't be on more than three shows in ten years. Who knew?

How to Figure Out Who and How Much to Tip at Christmas

Christmas comes but once a year (thank goodness!) and *every* year, we ask the same questions: Who do I need to tip? and How much did I give them last year? For some reason, tipping at the holidays is very stressful for people. I get the same calls every year asking about tipping etiquette. Even when people keep a list from the previous year, they *still* want help making their list and checking it twice (or sometimes, even three times!).

The holidays are the perfect time to show the people who help you out how much you appreciate them, but it can be kind of a headache deciding who to tip and how much. And with all the other chaos in the month of December, the last thing you want to be thinking about as you're racing to make the plane for your holiday vacation is, "Oh no! I forgot the piano teacher!"

Well, the good news is: There is no "set-in-stone" rule for who to pay and how much, so you can't get it wrong. It's a gift, remember? Still, you don't want to jilt anyone, and you don't want the process to be stressful, so if you haven't done this already, next time the holidays roll around, make a list of who you tipped and how much, and keep it in a safe place. From now on every year, just after Thanksgiving, pull out your list from last year and take the next two weeks to add or subtract from the list of people. Think about your average week: who you interact with, who performs services for you, and so on.

If you live in an apartment building, for example, you might have a doorman, a super, and an elevator operator, to name a few. If you live in a house, it might be the person who mows your lawn, postal workers, pool cleaners, and so on. If you employ a nanny, housekeeper, or dog walker, they'd definitely go on this list. Be sure to also include people who regularly do things for you away from home, like hairdressers, trainers, teachers—you get the gist.

That takes care of who—now what about how much? For people who provide services you directly pay for, the general rule of thumb is a tip equal to one unit of service. So if you have a weekly housecleaner, tip her one week's pay; for your favorite stylist, tip the equivalent of one session.

It gets a little trickier for people you don't directly pay, like doormen, supers, or trash collectors, since you have no idea what they are making. Plus, their salaries vary widely depending on where you live; it's usually higher in big cities. If you're not sure what to give them, the best strategy is to ask your neighbors what they are giving. And for those who go above and beyond, like the superintendent who comes running when you lock yourself out at one o'clock in the morning or the handyman who fixed your broken water heater, take your best guess as to what you think you should give and double it (especially if you may need them to assist you again in a pinch).

There's also the matter of your level of interaction—if you chat with your doorman every day but go for months at a time without seeing your super, there's no law that says you can't tip the doorman more.

You can use these guidelines, or you can simply tip everyone equally. Make your list, decide on a set amount of money that you are going to use for tipping (consider it your Holiday Tip Budget—Suze Orman would be proud!), then count up the number of people and divide. Once you have it evenly split it up, you can decide who deserves a little more and who deserves a little less and tinker with it until you feel that you have a fair division of your budgeted amount.

One final note: Postal workers, who are often given Christmas tips, are not technically supposed to accept cash gifts. They might still pocket your green, but it's a good idea to just give a gift card instead to ensure they're on the straight and narrow.

If a tip is not in your budget, consider a small homemade gift, and always include a handwritten note!

How to Keep Your Valuables Safe in Your Home

You might think of your home as a more tastefully decorated version of Fort Knox, but trust me, even the most impenetrable of fortresses can suffer a breach in security every once in a while. And all it takes is one break-in and you've lost your favorite piece of jewelry, an irreplaceable heirloom, or your most personal documents. This is why, even if you own two Dobermans and the most expensive burglar alarm system on the market, it's important to have a backup plan.

The best and easiest backup plan? Buy a safe.

A safe might seem like a big step (a safe in your *house?*), but think of it as not just a secure place for your valuables, but also as an organizational tool of sorts. No more tearing the house apart looking for your great-grandma's emerald earrings, or your recently renewed passport; if they're in the safe, you know where they are at all times. Safes are not just protection against burglars, they're a one-stop storage area for your most important goods.

Safes come in many shapes, sizes, and types, and choosing one depends largely on what you want to store in it and what your safety concerns are. For instance, many safes are specifically designed to be resistant to the elements (choose this kind if you live in an area prone to flood or fire); others are geared primarily toward keeping intruders out (choose this one if you don't have the greatest alarm system, or if there are typically a lot of guests or contractors traipsing through your house).

I think installing a home safe is a great idea and often recommend it for my clients. I really don't like finding Rolex watches and diamond jewelry lying around, especially when there seems to be a constant flow of people in and out of someone's apartment. Usually, people agree and we get the safe installed. The issue is that if people aren't used to having a safe, they forget that it's there. Like the client who had us install a safe and immediately filled it with jewelry and even a stash of cash that he had in the back of a drawer. Two years later, I got a call to please get someone to break into his safe. He had completely forgotten the password to get in. When we called the locksmith and had him break into the safe, what did we find inside? His password. Written right there on the instructions for "how to use this home safe." That's why, now, I recommend my clients start with a safe that uses a key. They just have to remember where they store the thing (hopefully not in the safe).

Whatever type of safe you get, you'll want to be sure of two things: (1) that once it's installed, it will be (almost) impossible to move, and (2) that you (and maybe only one other trustworthy soul) will *always* be able to access it.

When choosing your safe, remember that the smaller types can be bolted to the wall or floor of a closet, while larger ones are usually too unwieldy to be moved quickly (unless you are being robbed by Mike Tyson). For this reason I'd recommend having it delivered and/or getting someone from the store to install it for you—these things get pretty heavy!

For the second thing you need to be sure of (being able to access your safe), the trick is that not only will no one else be able to get into the safe, but that *you* will. This means choosing a combination you'll never be able to forget, or at the very least having a surefire way of remembering it. That said, do NOT pick something obvious, like your address, and please do not write it down and label it "combination to safe." One good way to ensure you'll always be able to access the password when you need it is to save it to your phone—not as "safe combination," but as the phone number or e-mail address for a fictional person.

Another, more modern way to make sure you and only you can access your valuables is to buy a biometric safe, which can only be opened by a preprogrammed fingerprint (it's a good idea to make sure at least one other person close to you programs his or her fingerprint as well, though, just in case something happens to you).

If the contents are mostly small things like jewelry or loose cash, a less secure (and also less expensive) method is to buy a small disguised safe, commonly called a "stash box." Stash boxes (which you can usually buy on sites like Amazon.com) appear to be everyday items like books, cans of food, or clocks but have secret compartments within that can be opened with a key. Just make sure you put the stash box in a place where it won't stand out. If a burglar finds a can of Pringles in your sock drawer, the jig is up.

Safes aren't just for protecting your valuables from burglars; they can also store anything you don't want members of your family to have access to . . . from a firearm to a surprise birthday gift to a journal. Your items will be protected from prying eyes, plus it's nice to know that you have a little place you can truly call your own.

If you're really ready to make the investment in a beautiful safe, try www.traumsafe.com, but if all you've got to keep under lock and key is your passport and your diary, consider picking up a much more affordable model anywhere, even at www.staples.com. Better safe than sorry.

13. unusual yet useful

How to Locate a Discontinued Pair of Running Shoes

You finally found the perfect sneakers that transformed your runs in the park from torture sessions into glorious flights. With every stride you felt more and more like Forrest Gump, able to just keep on runnin'.

But just when you begin to feel unstoppable, your shoes fall apart, and annoyance turns to panic as you discover the line has been (gasp!) discontinued. And while your head tells you it's time to move on and try another model, your heart cannot forget the spring of that sole, the firmness of that arch.

There's no way around it, you've got to find that shoe. But how? When I once got a call from a client asking me to order him a specific model of size 10 running shoes, I thought it would be a cinch, that the client must not have looked for his ruby running slippers any farther than his own backyard. Little did I know that the line had been discontinued years before and that dozens of calls to local and out-of-town running stores would turn up nothing. A desperate Internet rummage was also a wash. So I went straight to the source. I called the running shoe manufacturer and explained how much my client missed those sneakers. Everyone likes a fan, and I figured my heartfelt plea might just encourage someone at headquarters to help me locate a pair.

But still no luck. So I inquired about the last retailer to place a large order of the shoe and called him up. None left in stock. Still, no reason to panic. Overstock that is either left unsold at the end of the season or replaced with newer models usually ends up at outlets, so I got a list of numbers and started dialing.

The low point in this great shoe hunt was when I was told I was on a fool's errand . . . there was not a single pair left in all of the United States. But I wasn't deterred; there was always our friendly neighbor up north. And indeed, when I finally called an outlet across the border, I hit the jackpot. The victory lap was ordering every last pair. Thank you, Canada!

My next step would have been to post an ad on Craigslist and hope to find someone with a lightly worn pair taking up space in the bottom of his closet.

If you follow the preceding steps, and your "sole mate" was discontinued within the last year or two, there's a good chance that you'll find it somewhere. But just don't wait too long or your luck may finally "run" out.

How to Purchase a Vietnam Combat Photo

Purchasing a Vietnam combat photo might seem like an odd thing to do. That's what I thought too when a client recently asked for my help in finding one. But then he told me he had a friend who lost his father in Vietnam and had become a Vietnam memorabilia collector. He collected movies, photos, souvenirs, books, *everything*. So my client wanted to give his friend a combat photo—a photograph taken by soldiers during actual combat—which is a rare and coveted item for collectors.

After a little digging, we found that the best places for Vietnam memorabilia of all kinds, including patches, uniforms, bullets, documents, and yes, combat photos, are militaria shows. "Militaria shows" (also called "militaria flea markets") are basically big conventions where collectors flock to trade and sell their stuff (they don't just have them for Vietnam—you can find militaria shows for just about every major American war).

If your area doesn't have any upcoming militaria shows, or you find one but it doesn't have what you're looking for, try the "Collectibles" section on Craigslist. This is one of the best places to go to find oddities of all kinds, from antique gold cowboy spurs, to vintage accordions. And, if you can't find what you're after by searching, you can post a request for a particular item.

Army/navy stores, which carry camping supplies, knives, and combat wear, also often have collections of war memorabilia. And if they don't, most stores employ veterans or military enthusiasts who might be able to help you locate what you need.

Also, finding a few books of Vietnam war photos is a good starting point, so try contacting the author to find out if any of the originals are for sale, or if he can put you in touch with some of the photographers.

These tips don't just apply to hunting down Vietnam War photos, or even war memorabilia in general. Flea markets, trade shows, specialty stores, and especially the Web are the best places to find all kinds of collectibles and memorabilia. Trust me, people collect all kinds of crazy stuff. Never assume what you're looking for is too rare or bizarre to find; it's usually out there.

How to Locate a Fabric from a Photo

A client of mine was once at a dinner party when she fell in love with an upholstered chair and decided she *had* to have the same fabric to recover her worn-out sofa.

Throwing a bit of new fabric over an old frame seems easy enough, especially if you've found the material you love. The only problem here was that said fabric was already stretched across her friend's furniture, and neither my client nor her friend knew where the pattern had come from.

So the day after the dinner party, I got the call to please locate the fabric and get my client's sofa reupholstered. Sounded easy enough (like it usually does). She proceeded to tell me that she would send a photo of the fabric that she wanted. Great, even easier (or so I thought). The chances that you'll find an obscure pattern at your local fabric store are slim (though you should obviously still try), but luckily, most major cities have design centers—huge venues with tons of showrooms where interior designers shop—that sell almost every type of fabric imaginable.

Entry is for "trade" folks, though, so find a designer friend to get you in, or head to a design school and see if a student is willing to take you. Plus the doormen at design centers are usually pretty easy to get by, so even without the official credentials, you may want to give it a shot. Whatever method you use to get in the door, just make sure—and this is key—that you go with a photo of the fabric in hand. No matter how smart you think you are and how accurate you believe your memory to be, you're going to be looking at so many similar patterns that I guarantee you'll get confused if you try to rely on memory alone.

Even if your pattern is distinctive, the vast number of sample books filled with endless swatches that you find at design centers can be daunting to tackle. So look for clues, like a line of fabric that has a similar style to the one that you like. My print, for example, included a monkey, which I assumed would make my job pretty easy. But after endless hours pawing through books and asking around, my confidence (but not my determination) was beginning to fade. That's when I spotted some animal pattern pillows in a showroom window. They weren't an exact match to my fabric, but they had a familiar look, and as it turned out, they were by the same designer.

Unfortunately my Sherlock moment was cruelly cut short when I was told my particular pattern had been discontinued. Undeterred, I tracked down the distributor, who in turn called the manufacturer in China, who let me special order the old design. I had it in hand just a few months later, and my client was thrilled.

> Although it would have been a bit of a monkey on my back, if I hadn't been able to find the fabric, my next step would have been to use the photo as a guide and create my own custom monkey pattern.

How to Send a Banana in the Mail (with No Box or Envelope)

Most people think that to send something in the mail, you need to put it inside an envelope or box. Wrong! This may be true for private delivery companies like UPS, but the U.S. Postal Service will deliver anything with a readable address and proper postage, regardless of its packaging. You can literally put a ton of stamps on a surfboard, scribble the address with a Sharpie, and drop it off at the post office. It will be delivered. Really. It's been done before.

Although a surfboard might be a bit unwieldy (and, could get expensive to mail at forty-four cents for every three and a half ounces) I've learned from personal experience that smaller things, like fruit, for example, are a different story. With all the kooky things people call us to handle, some things just don't sound odd anymore, even to me. And mostly, it's not worth asking too many questions. So my policy is that we are on a need-to-know basis. If I don't need to know why a client needs me to mail a banana, I'm not going to ask. And honestly, when it comes to food-related requests, I don't usually ask.

Like the time I was asked to anonymously deliver persimmons to someone's office in a brown paper bag, no note included. The instructions were: "Don't let him know who sent you." If I hadn't purchased the persimmons myself, I may have feared for the recipient's life. It was all in good fun (or so I assume) and I never found out what it was all about, but I did it. Then there was the time I was asked to get a hotel room ready for someone—and to "be sure to put a frying pan in the dresser drawer." Seriously?! I didn't want to know, and again I never found out. Yes, we hear it all, so when someone calls our office and asks us to mail bananas, not a soul flinches. But this time, even I laughed, because it's kinda bananas.

Here's what went down. First, the instructions were to mail individual bananas to the same person over a period of a few weeks, one every few days, with no note or explanation or hint who it was from whatsoever. I was to use phony return addresses and not put the bananas in a shipping box of any kind. So that's what I did. I wrote the address on a small slip of paper and taped it to the banana. I weighed the banana and securely affixed stamps. Then I just walked into the post office and handed them a banana. And they took it, and mailed it. They have to: in rain, sleet, or snow, no less.

Of course, a few precautions needed to be taken. Because it would take two to three days to deliver the bananas, they might turn brown and mushy by the time they arrived, and my instructions were to mail bananas, not rotten bananas. The solution: green bananas—they would ripen in transit.

Next, the client asked if it would be possible to send bananas from different locations. So, I rounded up some traveling friends and family members and provided them with pre-addressed bananas before boarding their planes. They were also given extra labels and a few bucks in case the bananas got confiscated by airport security. Once in a new city, each had instructions to just put the banana straight into a mailbox.

Not sure how much postage you need? My bananas needed six stamps each, though you should double-check before you send yours as the number will vary depending on the size of the fruit.

The U.S. Postal Service does in fact, have a rule about "perishable items," and they could argue that a banana falls into this category. Though the woman at the post office let me send the first two bananas, no questions asked, the man who was there the next week did not. So, to prevent the bananas from perishing, I started wrapping them in clear packing tape. It doesn't ruin the effect at all, and will keep the banana intact, even if it does get a bit mushy underneath. Then I just slipped the bananas into a blue mailbox on a street corner—I didn't feel like dealing with the post office employees again—and sure enough the bananas all made it to their destinations.

Quick tip: A post office employee at a desk can say no, but once the banana is in the mail, it's easier for postal workers to just keep it in transit until it reaches its destination than it is to return it to the sender. As long as you've got a legible address and enough stamps, they're legally bound to send it *somewhere*.

Punch line: A few weeks later, that same client called and asked me to send an orange, only this time with a note . . . *"Orange you glad I didn't send another banana?"*

And this is how I knew he was just monkeying around.

Unlike bananas, oranges aren't likely to rot and change color, so the address can be written directly on the peel.

How to Put a Photo on a Cookie

Gone are the days of birthday cakes with simple messages written in frosting. The future is here, and that future is edible photo cakes and cookies! I often create photo cookies as a way to personalize a party. After all, what better way to celebrate your brother's thirty-fifth birthday than by serving cookies with his high school yearbook photo plastered all over them? And I've found that cookies with favorite photos of the bride and groom can be a huge hit as wedding or shower favors.

The easiest way to create photo cookies is to go to a site like www.rollingpinproductions.com, www.cookiehq.com, or www.candidcookies.com. These are all reliable; just e-mail or upload your photos, choose the kind of cookie you want, and you'll have your edible mementos in less than two weeks.

These sites do most of the work, but on your end, the most important thing to do is to choose the right snapshot. The higher the resolution, the better. Remember that the icing paper and edible ink aren't exactly of the same quality as photographic stock paper, meaning your picture won't be as crisp (no pun intended) once it's on a cookie. The more contrast your photo has, the better. Go for colorful shots that don't rely on a lot of detail. If you want to use a photo of someone's face, make sure it's a close-up, otherwise it will just look like an unrecognizable blur. It's also key that your photo isn't too small, because the printers will need to resize it to fit on the cookie, meaning a smaller picture will become distorted.

If you want to do this at home so that you can use your own, top-secret Snickerdoodle recipe, you'll need the right equipment. Edible printers (er, printers that print edible paper—obviously, no printer is actually edible) are a bit specialized and require special ink and paper, so they don't come cheap. Check out www.kopycake.com where you can purchase edible ink and then use your own Canon or Epson printer to print right onto frosting sheets. It's a good idea to have a separate printer for food items, though, as you don't want any residual ink contaminating your treats.

If there are a lot of photo cookies (or photo cakes) in your future, a printer from www.photofrost.com might be a sound investment. But ask yourself: "Am I going to put this to good use, or am I just going to print up three dozen cookies with my cat's face on them and then eat them all after a bad date?"

If you even have to think about this, you might want to just stick to buying cookies by the batch.

How to Send a Message on the Big Screen at a Sporting Event

Sports fans often know no bounds. Somehow, perfectly respectable people who go to work every day, who make their mortgage payments on time, and who cook sensible low-fat, low-carb meals for their families turn into complete lunatics and display all kinds of irrational behavior when it comes to their sports teams. They insist on wearing the jersey of their favorite player, the way their kid might wear a Hannah Montana shirt. They develop deep superstitions about their team—refusing to wear clean underwear to a playoff game, or insisting their baby wear team logo socks for the World Series (I speak from personal experience on that one). They might paint their faces in team colors on game day, and believe it or not, even the most mild-mannered Bostonians might have a small Red Sox tattoo.

For these kinds of fans, the perfect place to send an important message to a friend or loved one is naturally on the big screen at his favorite stadium. It used to be that you'd have to know someone to get a "Happy Birthday, Bobby" message up there, but these days you don't need any special connections—just a checkbook.

Here's how you do it.

Contact Guest Services at the stadium of your choice, or look at the team website to find out their options and pricing. At Yankee Stadium, for instance, you can have a personalized message appear on the "Zales Fan Marquee" in centerfield for $100 (which goes to a Yankees not-for-profit foundation). The message will be announced on the PA system while it flashes on the screen, but they'll only show ten messages a game, and all of them during the fifth inning, so reserve your spot early. And don't let your pals head to the hotdog stand in the bottom of the fourth. Other stadiums have various options depending on where they are in the season (playoff games being more expensive), at what point during the game it will appear (halftime is pricey), and how long your message will be in lights.

Wedding proposals have become increasingly popular at sporting events, and stadiums have begun offering options to take advantage of the trend. At Citizens Bank Park, where the Phillies play, you can order an engagement package, where, for $450, you'll get to propose on "PhanaVision." Not only will your proposal be covered live on the left-field video board, you'll get a champagne toast and a DVD of the whole event afterward. Hint to sports fans: If you decide to go this route, please make sure that your one and only is as big a fan of the team as you are (but hey, that's why you're perfect for each other, right?).

When sending a message via the Jumbotron, there are some things to watch out for. First, do make sure the person who arranges it has the correct spelling of every word and name involved. If you make the reservation for the message over the phone, follow it up with a fax or e-mail, to ensure that the staff has the correct spelling. Also, be clear on exactly when the message will appear, and have a plan for how to get the person you're addressing to look at the screen. It will flash by pretty quickly, and you don't want her to miss it because she's in line for popcorn. Finally, if you're going for a proposal package, don't do it unless you're really confident you're going to get a yes. Rejections are hard no matter what, but the humiliation will feel far worse in front of tens of thousands of people.

How to Get a Russian Translator to Pick Up Your In-laws from the Airport

I once had a client whose Russian-speaking in-laws were coming to visit and needed to be picked up at the airport. Wanting to make sure they found their way to his home despite the language barrier, he called Consider It Done to send a driver who could not only pick them up when they arrived but also communicate with them in their native tongue.

So how did we do this? Well, we happened to know a car service owned by Russians, so in this instance it was a piece of cake. But if we hadn't, or if his in-laws had spoken a different foreign language, here is how we would have proceeded. First of all, people of the same nationality living in a foreign country tend to hang out with other people who speak their language. In larger cities, like New York, there are even whole communities of Russian speakers. So we would have located a shop or business that catered to a community of Russian speakers, called them up, and asked them to direct us to a car company that employs Russian-speaking drivers.

If you go this route and it doesn't yield results, don't worry. There are a ton of other options. Most colleges and universities, for example, have foreign language departments where someone is *bound* to speak Russian (or any other language). Plus, college students can *always* use some extra coin. Putting up a flyer or even just wandering around the language department hallways is sure to yield at least one student who's eager to practice his or her language skills, not to mention make some spare change. Even if the student does not own a car, hire him to translate, then find a driver to head off to the airport with your student interpreter in tow.

Another place to look for Russian speakers is Russian restaurants—someone in the kitchen or waitstaff is likely looking to make some extra cash and might even enjoy the opportunity to chat with someone from the old country. Plus, showing up at a person's place of work is a good way to weed out the people who might drive off into the night with your money and your in-laws (unless, of course, that's your goal); the person is probably smart enough to realize that since you know where she works, it would be quite easy for you to track her down.

If none of these pan out for you, or if you're looking for something a little fancier or more official than a Russian Studies major or a borscht cook to pick up your in-laws, you can always hire a driver and a *real* translator. This will make your in-laws feel important, and if you need to keep them occupied for a bit before you're ready to face them, the translator can direct the driver to local areas of interest and answer any questions your in-laws might have about your city.

Needless to say, these ideas also work for in-laws of all nationalities, so avoiding a visit from your spouse's parents on the grounds that you're scared they won't make it from the airport to your doorstep—it's not going to happen. Better to have them picked up and cared for, and then promptly break out the bottle of vodka upon their arrival.

How to Charter a Tugboat

Tugboats, by definition, are small but powerful boats used to pull (or tug, duh) larger ships where they need to go. But if you want to charter a tugboat, and you're reading this to find out how, I'm going to assume you're not a large ship owner. If you are, and you don't already have a relationship with a tugboat company, you need a bit more help than this book.

Instead, I'll assume that there's a certain nostalgic appeal about the tugboat that you'd like to reconnect with. Probably it was all the old cartoons, from Mickey Mouse to Little Toot, or the charming children's book about Scuffy the Tugboat that left an impression of the cute, little tugboat with wide eyes and a perennial smile. So maybe you've decided to design a romantic evening or host a small party on a tugboat. Or maybe you want to use it to transport fireworks to a wedding on an island, like I once did for a client.

Whatever the reason may be, as I learned the hard way, you won't find tugboat charters in the Yellow Pages. I suppose it's just not a common enough request that anyone bothered to list it for the general public. So when my client called in a panic to say that he was surprising his bride with fireworks at his wedding that night, but that the tugboat broke and they would need to cancel the fireworks, we got to work.

We started by calling the local dock and asking questions about tugboats. We were able to speak with a manager and explain our predicament. One referral led to another, and we were finally able to locate a tugboat company that was willing to rent us one. The issue was that tugboats move slowly. Very slowly. So we would need to see if we could first transport the fireworks by truck and then get them to a port. But that got complicated as it was the middle of summer and we would need special permits. Eventually, we did get the fireworks on a tugboat so that they could chug their way over to the wedding just in the nick of time. Still, when you're relying on a tugboat, make sure you have a backup plan. In my case, just as I was congratulating myself for getting the complicated task of transporting fireworks in the heat of the summer done . . . it started to rain on my fireworks parade, literally.

A tugboat may seem like a state-of-the-art maritime vessel when your three-year-old is playing with the cute bathtub replica . . . but in real life, it is slow and no-frills. So if romance on the high seas is what you're after, consider renting a sailboat or a schooner instead—and leave anything that needs to be tugged to a professional.

How to Build a Sand Castle That Won't Collapse

I love my job. One highlight was the summer I got hired to organize a beach party. The hit of the afternoon was a sand-castle-building contest, and just for the record, the adults had more fun than the kids.

It's a fact of life that all sand castles will eventually fall over, get washed away, or get stepped on by a big, fat bully. But if you ask me, their temporary nature is part of their appeal. There's something special about a work of art that blends in with and then becomes part of its environment. Still, we all want our sand castle to at least stay standing while we're building it, and preferably for a bit longer, so that other people can admire (and in this case judge!) it.

To build a sand castle that doesn't (immediately) collapse, you could follow all the tricks of the trade. There are countless books and plenty of websites describing everything from how wet the sand should be to how to pack and sculpt sand like a pro. You can mix sand with just the right amount of water before putting it into a mold. Or you can learn to form the perfect bricks to make a foundation that will be structurally sound. You can even buy sand-carving tools to shape a sturdier castle than you could build by simply using your hands.

But let's clear one thing up. The irony is that to build a sand castle that won't collapse, you'll really want to build something other than a castle. Yes, when we think of structures people make out of sand, we think of castles. Sure, an elaborate sand castle is impressive, but it takes years of practice and patience to build a structure that actually looks like a castle—and won't topple over at a moment's notice. Instead, build a structure that's equally impressive as a giant, ornate castle . . . but a lot more durable, and easier to construct.

To get inspired, search the Internet for sand castle contest photos. Though some people actually build castles, most don't, and the winners (and most of the amazing entries) are usually not castles. I've seen "castles" in the shape of alligators, sea monsters, sunbathing sand people, turtles, fish, starfish (lots of sea creatures—you get the idea), plus surfboards, cars, mermaids, and much, much more. Take a look around to get inspired, and then add a creative twist of your own.

The reason these other structures are less likely to collapse than traditional castles is that they are generally lower to the ground (if you choose to build something tall and narrow, it will topple just as easily as a castle, if not more so; stay away from a sand giraffe, for example), and they usually have wide, strong, easy-to-build-on foundations. Plus, low-to-the-ground structures are easier to repair; if you make an alligator, and then accidentally step on it, you should be able to salvage it by simply filling in the one spot that is ruined. If it were a castle, one small misstep might cause the whole thing to collapse. And just because you're building something *shorter* doesn't mean it has to be *smaller*. I've seen sand monsters that were *enormous* and spread out over several yards, but they never collapsed because they weren't very tall.

If you must have an actual castle, do yourself a favor and dig a big "moat" around it. This may be the reason why people started building castles in the first place: because the moat gathers the water before it reaches (and destroys) the castle wall. You can use this moat technique with any sand creation; you just might not want to call it a moat if it's constructed around the sphinx or people may start to wonder if you've been out in the sun too long.

And finally, if it's annihilation by a foot-stamping bully you're worried about, consider surrounding your construction site with police tape to keep away the riffraff, or find the two toughest-looking kids on the beach and offer to buy them ice cream to guard your design.

In the contest I put together, it was the people who spent a little time preplanning who prevailed. Isn't that always the case? So give your design a little thought ahead of time, and if your creation does collapse, remember, at the end of the day it really is all about fun, and let's face it, sand structures aren't designed to last forever, anyway.

It's extra-impressive to build a re-creation of a well-known landmark, like the White House, the Pyramids of Giza, Mount Rushmore, or Stonehenge. Some of these can be very challenging because of the detail involved, but just think short and wide and your monument will be more likely to stand strong.

How to Fit More TV into Your Life

In the past ten years or so, the numbers of mediums and options for TV viewing have grown exponentially. Today, we can watch any one of thousands of shows broadcast on any one of hundreds of channels not just on our TVs, but on our computers, our DVRs, and even our smartphones, whenever we wish.

But even so, for a lot of people, finding the time to watch TV is challenging—work, family, and other daily tasks sometimes make it almost impossible to fit it all in. Let's face it, in today's hectic world, it's hard to find the time to keep up with the Kardashians, let alone your dozen other favorite reality TV families. Fortunately, though, it's easy to fit more TV into your life—it's just a matter of knowing a few key tricks!

The first of these tricks is literally the most beneficial for your health—the gym. These days, you don't have to suffer through endless loops of football replays on your gym's perpetually-tuned-to-ESPN communal TV. Instead, anyone with a video iPod or an iPhone can download almost any TV show from the iTunes store and watch it during your workout. Sure, the screens may be tiny, but most cardio machines have a place where you can dock your device so it's right in your field of vision as you sweat, and some newer machines even let you hook up your device so you can view your shows on the machine's larger screen.

Watching TV while you work out not only lets you fit some viewing time into your day, but also really helps your workout go by faster—one episode of *The Biggest Loser* and you'll fit in a workout that would make Bob Harper proud.

If you don't care what's on, but just want some more time for TV watching, doctors' offices, manicurists, and hair salons have TVs in the waiting rooms and sometimes even in the service areas. Hey, it may be daytime, but it's still TV! If you travel a lot, you can also grab a seat at an airport waiting area near one of their flatscreens, or use your wait time to watch something on your iPod or laptop. In fact, if you own one of these gadgets (and, who doesn't) just about anything that involves waiting—including dentists' visits, road-trip rest stops, car tune-ups, and the dreaded jury-duty waiting room—can all be places to tune out and tune into *American Idol*.

Finally, just about any household task, like folding laundry, for example, can be done while watching TV. Put a TV or computer in the kitchen, so you can also have a show on while you cook or wash dishes.

The bottom line is that any electronic device with a screen—an MP3 player, a smartphone, or a laptop—can be your personal, portable TV so you don't ever have to have a dull moment (and by that I mean a TV-free moment) again!

> If your goal is to watch more TV, remember that you don't need to give most shows your full attention (let's be serious, most require 10 percent of your brainpower, tops), so think multitask and you'll be up-to-date on *The Bachelor* in no time.

How to Record Your Own CD

Recording your own music used to be expensive. Extremely and prohibitively expensive. You needed a studio, special equipment, a recording dock, mixing machines, and multiple technicians to get it done. The cassette tape made things cheaper, and the CD improved audio quality, but nothing has made recording your own music as easy and cost-effective as the laptop computer.

Assuming you already own a laptop (or a desktop, in which case you can still record music, but only in the same room you keep the computer), you're just a few clicks—and possibly a new software package—away from making your own CD. First, choose your recording location. It doesn't need to be a foam-padded studio, but it should be a room with decent acoustics: one with a carpet and some furniture, not the empty, echoing garage you usually practice in. The importance of this depends on what you're recording: if you've got a rock band, acoustics are key, but if you're performing spoken-word poetry, you could probably record in your bathroom.

This brings us to the next step: equipment. You don't need much, and again, it depends on what you're recording. If your band is just one or two people, with minimal instruments, one microphone might do the trick, and if audio quality isn't a major concern, most newer laptops have built-in mics that should be fine. If you have more band members and additional instruments, you might want to invest in a set of decent mics (one for each person). This will allow you to adjust the levels and mix each track after you record.

Then, think about software. There are countless PC programs designed for home recording—a basic Internet search should give you enough results to choose from. Some software will even come with hardware, like microphones and mixing docks. If you have an Apple computer, a program called GarageBand is usually preinstalled, and it works wonders.

Quick tip: It'll take some time to learn the software, so make sure you play with it ahead of time and run some tests before the big day. Luckily, you won't be paying by the hour for the studio, so it's OK if your recording session doesn't go perfectly the first time around. Still, it's good to get well acquainted with the software you choose.

After you've made your recording and done any sound mixing, you can burn your CD, but in this day and age, with CDs becoming more and more obsolete, make sure you consider the alternatives before you make a thousand copies. If you want to sell your music in person, perhaps at a venue where your band is performing, then CDs are a good choice. But if you just want to get your tracks out to friends, a digital MP3 file costs nothing and can be e-mailed or posted to a website; plus, most people just rip CDs onto their computer so they can listen to the music on their MP3 players anyway—why waste your time and money on a bunch of plastic disks if they're just going to end up in the trash?

All that being said, if you want a really professional recording, you should head to a studio. You'll end up with much better sound quality and experts will be able to help you with everything from "tracking" (the process of recording songs) to "mixing" (blending the individual tracks together for the best sound) to "mastering" (turning your collection of individual songs into an album or playlist) to full production. This process requires a *lot* of editing and the pros really know what they are doing. Plus, some studios will even provide you (for a fee) background vocals and instruments, and they will also often recommend artists to design your cover and even help get your CD manufactured. So if you have the extra cash, a studio is really the way to go. Not to mention that you'll feel like a rock star in there with the huge headphones on while someone works a bunch of controls behind a glass panel.

If you are releasing your own record and it's not all your own work, make sure you are doing everything legally. Take a look at www. musicbizacademy.com/articles/legalchecklist.htm.

How to Get Open the Plastic Bags That Come in Rolls

You know the bags I'm talking about—the produce bags at the supermarket, the clothing bags at the gym. Right, the thin, slippery ones on those giant rolls that are damn near *impossible* to get open gracefully. Okay, so I know it's not the hugest ordeal in the world, but it's annoying nonetheless. So, worry no more. Here are three strategies for quickly opening these suckers without throwing a temper tantrum in the middle of the produce aisle.

The reason these bags are so hard to get open is because the two sides of the bag get stuck together from static cling that occurs when they're packaged. So the trick is to separate them. As you start to pull the bag off the roll, rub your thumb and forefinger together around the edge of the bag for about five seconds and the sweat from your fingers will loosen the bag up. Once you get even the smallest gap, you should be fine to just pull it open.

For really stubborn bags, slowly rub the bag between the palms of your hands. It doesn't need to be a frantic motion. The friction (and heat from your hands) should be enough to separate the edges of the bag.

Finally, if you have a long nail, you can run it along the inside lip of the bag to separate the two sides. A key or thin card (like a library, gas station, or discount card) also works. Once you have a small separation, blow into the bag to really get the two sides apart.

That said, even though you now know how to open them, consider skipping the plastic and doing something good for the environment. You know it's the right thing to do.

How to Turn Your Idea into a TV Pilot

Think your life would make a great TV show? Or maybe you just have an amazing idea that you think could be the next *Glee*. Whatever the concept for your hit show, you will first need to create a "pilot"—a first episode that networks will use to test and see if they think it will become a success. And turning an idea into a TV pilot is something anyone can do (no matter how boring your life is).

What you want to do is develop your idea into a "pitch" (if you are just entering into this business, it's important to know the lingo), basically an outline of why your show would be awesome. To write a pitch, you'll need to have a few things: a show concept, the main characters, and an idea of the storyline. You can send your pitches to agents, development companies, or even directly to networks. Many TV writers get their start by simply selling a show on a pitch.

When you explain the concept, you want to spin the show's content in a way that makes it sound interesting and unique. How is it different from *every* other show out there? What is going to grab people and keep them watching? Is it something *totally* new, or is it an interesting spin on a popular genre/idea? If you were pitching *The Sopranos*, for instance, you wouldn't just say that it's about a New Jersey mob family, as mob stories have been done to death (pun only partially intended). What you *would* say is that it's the story of a mob family whose boss is under a lot of stress and seeing a shrink to deal with his personal and criminal issues. Your concept should be no more than a paragraph and should contain the show's premise and a brief mention of the show's protagonist.

And that brings us to the characters. Even if your show is going to be an ensemble that follows a whole bunch of people, limit your characters in the pitch to the four or five most important ones. Include their names, genders, ages, and major personality traits. Give a little bit about their background, and why anyone would care about them. It's good to mention what challenges the characters will face, as that gives an idea of where the show is headed.

Make sure also that there's some conflict between the characters. Explain why they like or dislike other characters, and make their personalities different enough that it's clear how they will clash. Remember—people want drama, so if all your characters get along, not so exciting. Even *Leave It to Beaver* had conflicts to work through.

Finally, your plot. Think about all the good pilots you've seen: they all have two things in common. First, they put the characters in a situation that's different from their normal lives (well, other than *Seinfeld*, which was such a huge hit because it *was* about daily life, but that show has already been done), and second, they give viewers an idea of what they can expect from the series. Devote a few paragraphs to describing the plot of the pilot and how it sets the characters on the journey we'll see in the rest of the series.

Your pitch should be approximately three to five pages and focus on what makes your show exciting, dramatic, and *different*. If you've done your job, people will want to know more—just be sure you *have* more to give them!

How to Get Permission to Film a Movie in an Airport

Your masterpiece is almost complete. All you need to finish the next *Citizen Kane* is the climactic scene where the hero chases down his beloved in a crowded airport and passionately kisses her at the gate before she boards her plane . . . piece of cake . . . or not. Good luck with that.

Ever since 9/11 airports are about as easy to film in as a maximum-security prison on lockdown. In fact, with heightened security concerns, even public locations like bridges and tunnels forbid filming. But, though it may not be as easy as filming on a street corner in New York City, there *are* ways to get the shot you want; you just may have to jump through a lot of hoops to set it up.

First and foremost, this is *not* something you want to try and do "guerilla style," so get that thought out of your head right now. Filming in an airport without the proper approval is going to land you in deep trouble—trouble that might show you firsthand why maximum-security prisons are hard places to film.

If your masterpiece will not be complete without the perfect airport shot, start by contacting your local port authority or the mayor's office. Most port authorities have liaisons who specifically deal with filming rights, and they'll be able to get you in touch with the people who can get you the permit you'll need to shoot. Be sure to specify *where* in the airport you want to film—the area beyond the security checkpoint is *much* more difficult to film in than the rest of the airport, so for the easiest access, try to restrict your shots to the areas before the security checkpoints.

Everyone involved with your project will most likely need to undergo a background check, so if you're working with any felons, this might be a good day for them to take a vacation.

Keep in mind also that large chunks of many airports are owned by individual airlines, so contacting airline representatives is another good strategy. Depending on the type of film you're making, an airline might be excited about the free publicity your movie could bring. But the airlines alone will not be able to grant you access; you'll still need clearance from the airport itself.

One insider tip: Your odds of getting approval are greatly increased if none of the dialogue or action refers to or comments about the airport. And know that a representative of the airport will be with you at all times during filming to make sure you aren't painting the airport in a negative light. There goes the surprise ending.

The bigger the movie (or the bigger the company financing the movie), the likelier it is you'll be able to get in. Major studios have relationships with airports, so if you're with a studio, you're much more likely to be trusted than if you're just some random independent filmmaker. Think about it: There's a reason most airport scenes in movies occur in wide releases and not independent features.

And one final note: Even if you *do* get permission, if you're doing a scene where the hero chases after his beloved through an airport, catching up to her breathlessly, seconds before she reaches the gate, you might want to rewrite your script. That's *so* cliché.

How to Be a Comedian

Just because your friends laugh at your wisecracks over dinner doesn't mean you should quit your day job. Thousands of people are dedicating their lives to making it big on the comedy circuit, and a very few will become the next Jerry Seinfeld. But I guess you just never know if that someone could be you, so if you're serious about it, here are some tips for breaking in to the comedy business.

Start by writing thirty minutes of the funniest comedy routine you can come up with. Then choose the best three to five minutes of it. That's the typical length you'll get as an unknown act, so those few minutes are what will make or break your mission. Memorize your routine so that you can do it in your sleep. Practice it over and over until you're so bored by the jokes that they don't seem funny anymore (but trust your initial instincts that they were funny to begin with). Then test out your routine on friends and family—especially the people who don't laugh easily. If you can make them laugh, you're on to something.

Next, scout out the local comedy clubs. Speak with someone who works there, and ask for the "booker" or the manager. Typically, first gigs happen at an open-mic night, so ask when the next one is and how you can book a spot. Double-check the length of the set you'll be asked to do—though three to five minutes is standard, it might be longer at a smaller club or on a slow night. When the day comes, *invite friends*—as many as possible and be sure they know to laugh no matter what (they better, that's what they are there for), because their laughter will rub off on the rest of the audience. It's been proven that when one person laughs, others will think they should laugh too. Remember the old sitcoms and how they used to turn up the laugh tracks? Laughter is contagious.

Quick tip: If there are no comedy clubs near you, or you can't get a gig, see if local bars or cafés host open-mic nights. If they don't, start one. Bars are always looking for ways to draw people in, so they'll more than likely be game. Since it's not a real comedy club, there will be less pressure to be rip-roaringly hilarious—plus, alcohol will be flowing freely, and that makes everything funnier.

If you're not into stand-up, try improv or sketch. In most big cities, there are schools or theaters that run these kinds of classes, and if you stick with it, local comedy clubs often take notice. A friend of mine, who has been taking improv classes for less than a year, recently formed an improv troupe with six classmates from his most recent class, and they're beginning to book gigs a few times a month all over the city. If you take the classes, you can end up getting connected with a great improv or sketch group, and start performing with them in no time. Plus, improv is a good life skill to have . . . it'll make you even better at wise cracking over dinner with friends.

If you're trying to get a spot performing at a hot venue, you may need to arrive early (like bring-your-sleeping-bag early) because open casting calls always tend to attract large crowds, and the lines form in the wee hours. At least with comedy auditions, you're almost sure to be entertained with some good jokes while you're waiting . . . and if you're not laughing in the moment, you're guaranteed a good laugh years later when you look back on what you did to get your first gig.

How to Change Your Name Just Because You Feel Like It

Maybe you've born the cross of a name that came out of your parents' flower power days (sorry about that, Rainbow Sunshine Smith) long enough; maybe you're just sick of your boring name (no offense, Mike Jones); or maybe your once respectable name has, for some reason, become embarrassing (I feel you, Paris Milton). Or maybe you are like two of my clients, who wanted to combine their names and choose a completely *new* name for their entire family. Well, I'll tell you, I discovered that it is a fairly complex process, so be sure that you are committed to your new identity before taking it on.

Here is how it goes. Every state (and even some cities) have different regulations and procedures for name changing, ranging from a few forms to court appearances. The most common process, though, is the one in place for New York City residents (where my clients lived). To start, you'll need to get the "Petition for Name Change" form, which might be available from your local government's website, or in hard copy at a local civil court. You'll need to choose a name that is clearly not for fraud purposes (i.e., Michael Jackson Jr. is not a good choice) and one that is free of numbers or other unusual characters (except for Roman numerals).

You'll also need to provide a reason for the name change. It's perfectly fine to simply say that you just don't like your given name, but if (let's hope this isn't the case) you're changing your name because you are fleeing from a domestic abuser or because you were a witness in a criminal trial, stating the reason may help you to get a speedy approval. In this case, my clients simply wanted to combine both their last names to make a new one. Pretty cool. Though, if I were to do that, my last name would become something like Papabotky or Sudopoulos. Needless to say, not happening.

Anyway, once your petition is complete, you'll need to get it notarized. Then, bring the notarized petition, along with your original birth certificate, to the courthouse. Every civil courthouse has an office that deals specifically with name changes, so you shouldn't have any trouble finding the right place to submit your petition. After you pay a processing fee, the clerk will give you a court date to come in and get final approval from a judge.

At the hearing, you'll simply state your reasons for wanting a name change, and, assuming everything appears aboveboard, the judge will grant your request. But hold on, because you're not done yet: most places require you to publish a notice of your name change in a newspaper. This is to give anyone who might object to the name change (like people you owe money to, or your parents) a heads-up (if you're changing your name due to domestic violence or because you're a witness, the judge will allow you to bypass this step for obvious reasons). Seems a little silly, because it's not like the people you owe are scouring the newspapers looking for name-change notices, but, hey, at some point way back this was practical and so it became the law.

After your ad has been published, you'll simply need to provide proof of the publication to the court and the change will be finalized. Soon after, you'll receive a certified copy of your name-change order, which you'll need to produce in order to get replacement ID documents, like a driver's license, social security card, and passport (you can also purchase extra copies of the name-change, which I'd recommend doing as backup).

It may sound like a lot of work, but as long as you're not a felon or deep in debt, the process should be relatively quick and painless. The biggest challenge will be getting your friends and family to learn and use your new name. A nametag or some shirts with your name stitched across the front might help.

This does not apply to name changes due to marriage. For this, all you need to do is get copies of your marriage certificate and head over to the Social Security office. Once you get your new SS card, head to the DMV and from there you'll have the necessary two forms of ID needed to change your passport. It's that simple.

14. annoying (but necessary)

How to Remember All Your Passwords

Keeping track of all your passwords can be tricky, especially since if you try to create a database of all your passwords, you'll probably want to protect it with another password, and then you'll have to remember *that* one, too. E-mailing yourself all your passwords isn't a great idea, because if someone hacks into your e-mail account (unlikely, but possible) or you accidentally leave private information up on the screen of a public computer you open yourself up to the serious possibility that someone could end up with *all* your passwords. (I once used a computer in the library and the person before me did that, but luckily I was the next person who showed up, and I just closed the screen.)

Having a lot of different passwords can be a pain, but, there's really no way around it. If you use only one password for everything, and someone decodes it, that person can now hack into every account you have. Most websites are secure enough that your password will never be shared, but if you use the same password for your online banking as you use to buy clothes at a small online boutique with less security, hackers can start with the easier site and then move on to your bank account. Yikes.

Complicating matters further is the fact that many newer websites with stricter privacy protection guidelines require passwords of a certain length, and with a certain mix of letters and numbers. Some sites even require symbols in your password. So how are you expected to remember and keep track of them all? One trick is to create an acronym for something that is meaningful to you (but not obvious to others). For example, let's say your first pet was named Honey, and your freshman year in college you lived in 314 Silton Hall (though please never use your current address, or any piece of it). It still might be tough, but you'll remember a password like HON&314@SilH a lot easier than some completely random string of symbols and numbers.

Quick tip: Logins are just as important to remember as passwords. To give yourself one less thing to remember (or as the case might, be, forget) always use the same login name and e-mail address when you sign up with new websites. (If you use different user names, you might be getting the password right but the user name wrong, which will cause all kinds of frustration and confusion.) Plus, this way if you forget your password and click on the "Forgot password" option, it'll always send a reminder to the same e-mail address.

Another trick is to double up on your passwords. You should still have more than one, but not so many that you can't remember them without writing them down. I use three distinct passwords, and I've built a three-tier system for websites that require them.

Tier One: I use my most complex password (with symbols) for the most important websites, the ones that would cause disaster if they were hacked. It's up to you to decide what makes it into the top tier, but it could include your e-mail account, your online bank, your Paypal account, your university login, your work's database password, and so on.

Tier Two: This includes (but is not limited to) any type of site that might store my credit-card information. I've saved credit-card numbers for future use on all the sites I shop at frequently, and I'm guessing you have too. This could include websites like Amazon, Netflix, newspaper subscription sites, music subscription sites, and other online stores. I also include websites like Facebook and Twitter in this tier, since they could cause some damage (or at least severe embarrassment) if hacked by the wrong person. Your password for this tier doesn't need to include symbols, but it should include letters and numbers, and should be at least eight characters long.

Tier Three: For this tier you can use something simple and memorable, like a pet's name (but preferably still include letters and numbers to comply with some websites' rules), as long as you only apply it to websites that don't include credit-card information or any important personal information whatsoever.

With this tier system, you'll only need to remember three passwords for the rest of your life, and if you *still* can't handle that, write them down on the back of your sock drawer. Not on a piece of paper, not on a Post-it, but right on the actual drawer. No one will find it there, except *maybe* your spouse or significant other (or all the identity thieves reading this book), and it'll always be there when you need it—if you can remember where it is.

Quick tip: Most Internet browsers today have a feature that remembers passwords for specific websites. Use it *only* if you're using a *personal* computer that only you have access to. But beware—if someone else borrows your computer, that person can gain access to your passwords, so be careful whom you loan it out to.

The memo pad of Outlook is a place to keep a list of your passwords. But key them in backward, to be safe, and be sure to password protect your Outlook—or look out.

How to Get Gum Out of Your Clothes

You're on your way to the wedding. You arrive at the church and slide out of the cab. A few minutes later, someone taps you on the shoulder and whispers that dreaded, "I think you have something on the back of your dress." You run off to the restroom and turn to look in the mirror. Sure enough, you somehow sat on a piece of gum and now you have Orbit spearmint all over your bridesmaid gown. Believe it or not, this is a true story; once while coordinating a wedding, I overheard one of the brides-maids freaking out over this very situation. I whisked her into the kitchen and, before she could say *Bubblicious,* used a simple ice cube to freeze the gum off her dress. Some people believe that getting gum on your clothes is the end of the line for that garment. Well, I beg to differ.

Basically, you can get gum out of your clothing in three ways, all of which are based on gum's unique physical properties (yes, it's all very scientific). Gum in its normal state is difficult to deal with, so to remove it you're going to have to alter its consistency in one of these three ways.

1. *Freezing.* Frozen, hardened gum loses that stick-to-everything consistency, allowing it to be scraped off just about any surface, including fabric. Applying an ice cube to the spot should do the trick, but for stubborn pieces, take more drastic measures and stick the garment in a freezer for a few hours, then immediately chip away at the gum with a table knife (just be careful not to stab the fabric—or yourself!). Repeat as necessary until you get rid of as much of the gum as possible, then toss the clothing in the laundry to finish the job.

2. *Melting.* Ironing is the quickest way to melt gum. Put a piece of cardboard on your ironing board and then place the garment with the gum stain *facedown* on the cardboard. With your iron on medium heat, iron over the back of the fabric with the gum stain. The heat from the iron will melt the gum off the fabric and on to the cardboard. Repeat this until you've gotten it all, then wash. This method is a bit messier than the preceding one, but if you haven't got any ice, give it a try.

3. *Dissolving.* A number of normal household items can break down the gum and make it easier to remove. Two main types of liquids work well: acids and oils. Acids will break the gum down, separating it from clothes; oils will loosen up the gum and help "slip" it off your garment.

If you opt to go the acid route, apply a few drops of gasoline, lighter fluid, vodka, or white vinegar. Be sure to thoroughly wash your garment afterward, though, so it doesn't smell like alcohol or vinegar or, worse, burst into flames if someone lights a cigarette near you.

In terms of oils, liquid dishwashing detergent mixed with water, or even some peanut butter should loosen the gum up considerably (just remember that peanut butter might also create a stain, depending on the fabric, so use caution). Again, be sure to wash your garment immediately afterward.

Go ahead, chew to your heart's content, secure in the knowledge that a gum stain *will* come out. Getting the stuff out of your hair, though, is another story. . . .one that may require scissors.

How to Get Rid of the Hiccups

Hiccups. They rank up there with mosquito bites and people who talk during movies on the list of annoying things that must be eliminated ASAP. But since everyone and their mother (*especially* their mother) think they know how to cure hiccups, it can be hard to tell the just-might-work cures from the that's-just-crazy ones.

Let's start with the basics. "Hiccups" are sudden spasms of your diaphragm muscle. Eating too fast and not chewing enough are the most common causes, so taking your time with that burger is a good way to prevent getting the suckers. But if you *do* get them, here's a little guide to which (in my experience) hiccup-eliminating cures actually work.

First and foremost, *forget the old "scaring them out of you" cure*. These are hiccups, not a skittish toddler, and having someone jump out of the shadows will only make you drop your coffee.

Some tricks (aka old wives' tales) that seem equally silly, can actually be quite effective. These include slowly sucking on a tablespoon of sugar, breathing into a paper bag, or reverse-drinking a glass of water (cover the top with a napkin, bend at the waist, and drink from the opposite side). Some think that these cures work because they either relax or stimulate the diaphragm, but I believe that they may just be a distraction from the hiccupping.

Hiccups can sometimes be caused by heartburn, so if you think this is the case, grab some fresh tropical fruit like papaya or pineapple to neutralize the acid in your esophagus and ease the heartburn, and subsequently cure your hiccups.

These are the most common cures, but there *are* a couple of additional options for the more troublesome cases. Be warned, though, they're pretty time-consuming and/or gross, so you might want to just wait the hiccups out a little longer before resorting to these next two.

1. If your hiccups won't quit, try eating a cup of plain yogurt mixed with two tablespoons of salt. It might sound nasty, but many people swear by this concoction (plus, everyone knows that yogurt is good for you anyway).
2. Boil down two cups of water with a half teaspoon of fresh cardamom powder (you know, that stuff you've had in your spice rack for a decade and never use) until about a cup remains. Let It cool for a minute, and if your hiccups aren't gone by the time you've finished putting together this potion, drink a glassful while it's still warm.

These may sound like hocus-pocus, but if you try enough of them, you'll certainly find your cure. Of course, different methods work for different people, so give them a try to see what works for you.

How to Unclog a Drain

After I saw *Ghostbusters* for the first time, I was afraid to go to the bathroom for a week. Sure, it was a comedy, but the thought of pink slime oozing up and out of my tub and toilet—possibly while I was sitting on it—was just too creepy (and disgusting). After a while, my fear of bathroom fixtures subsided, but it never fully went away. Today, what strikes fear in my heart isn't ghosts, but a similar situation that could present itself if the toilet or drain gets clogged . . . only the goo won't be pink.

Though the quickest fix might be to go out and buy liquid or foaming drain cleaner, with repeated use, these products have chemicals that can damage your pipes. Plus, they cost money. Cleaning a drain is already bad enough; why make it hard on your wallet, too?

For every store-bought method to unclog a drain, there's a homemade version that's just as effective, if not more so. So, the next time you reach for liquid drain cleaner, make a pot of tea, instead. I'm serious.

Most drains can be unclogged with a combination of dish soap and hot water. But why the tea? The water should be hotter than what comes out of your faucet, but not so hot that it boils: the same temperature you'd use for a delicious cup of tea. Pour some dish soap on top of the clogged drain, and then wash it down with the tea-temperature water—not just a cup, but the full pot. Pour from a foot or two above the drain, not right on top of it, and pour slowly, not all at once; this way, you use gravity to your advantage. The force of the water will help clear the blockage. Wait about a minute or two and if it hasn't loosened the clog, try the same process one or two more times. Most likely it'll get the job done. You may even have a bit of hot water left over for an actual cup of tea to celebrate.

Stores also sell drain "snakes," which are pliable long wires with bristles on the end to catch a clog and bring it back up. These are unnecessary. Instead, save some money by uncoiling a wire coat hanger. Snakes work well because they conform to the shape of any pipe, so bend your coat hanger into the shape of the specific pipe you're trying to clear before you stick it down there. Use a vigorous back-and-forth motion to break up the clog. The best part? Snakes often bring up part of the clog when you pull them out, but a coat hanger just breaks it up and pushes it down through the pipes, so you won't have to look at anything too gross.

If your toilet's clogged, there's an easy and immediate solution: a plunger. But when a drain is clogged, either in a sink or shower, plunging usually doesn't even register as an option for most of us . . . but it should. It may sound nasty—and it kind of is—but a good plunger (not the cheap kind) can do the same thing for a standard drain that it can do for a toilet. To use the plunger most effectively, don't just push and pull rapidly. Use three or four very slow plunges to get some suction and eliminate some air between the plunger and the clog, then yank it away quickly, dislodging the obstruction.

And I hope you don't need me to tell you this, but *please* make sure to clean the plunger before you stick it in your sink.

Only as a last resort should you call the plumber. His fee will be scarier than an army of ghosts.

How to Remember to Make All Those Annoying Medical Appointments— and Then Actually Show Up

You're busy, every day. There is hardly a gap for lunch and your to-do list is a mile long, so carving out time for a doctor's appointment hardly seems a top priority, especially when you are the picture of health. You know how it goes. Your overdue checkup starts to hang over your head, but something that seems more important inevitably comes up and once again the MD gets bumped. Remember, even though no one really likes going to the doctor, nothing is more important than your health. So how can you make sure that you schedule—and show up—to all of your doctor's appointments?

Start by putting the various appointments on your to-do list—every day—until they actually end up on the calendar. Soon, the desire to cross them off the list will overwhelm your desire to procrastinate. And when you do finally schedule the appointments, why not kill several birds with one stone and make a day of it. Book all the appointments on the same day, take the day off work, and just pop from one appointment to the next. To make the day less painful, treat yourself to a nice lunch in the middle—you know, to toast to your good health. Think how many items you'll get to cross off your list at the end of just twenty-four hours! And if everything goes well, you won't have to repeat this scenario for another year.

If that strategy doesn't work, try scaring yourself into going. Create an ailment so you'll panic and actually want to go to the doctor. Take a typical annoyance and blow it out of proportion, for example, Does the sun seem to be bothering your eyes more often than usual? The accurate and logical answer might be yes (because it's summer, of course), but don't go with that. Concoct a crazy idea, for example, "Oh no, maybe I'm going blind! Hurry, I've got to make an appointment—quick! I can barely see the phone!" If this fails, watch some medical dramas, like *House* or *Grey's Anatomy*, on TV. They'll scare the healthiest people into believing they too can get some freakishly rare disease. Seriously, fear—even of the irrational variety—is a powerful motivator.

Granted, this next idea is drastic, but another effective technique is to have a baby. Nothing will get you to the doc faster than the knowledge that it's not just your health, but the health of that tiny little being growing inside you that's at stake. And once the baby arrives, new moms have so many aches and pains they need a doctor to not only assure them that everything is fine but also provide remedies to relieve their duress. And for new dads, it's all about ego. They don't want to be that guy who gets out of breath running after a toddler at the park, or the guy pushing a walker at his son's high school graduation.

So if the appointment day arrives and you're considering skipping out, just imagine the disapproving look your doctor (or even worse, your mother) will give you when you finally show up after rescheduling for the sixth time. Do yourself a favor and just get it over with already.

How to Keep Your Linen Shirt from Wrinkling

Linen wrinkles. That's the way it always has been, that's the way it always will be. If you really can't stand being seen in public wearing a shirt that looks a little tousled, don't buy linen (or buy a linen-polyester blend). Otherwise you'll just have to live with it.

You can, however, at least delay the inevitable wrinkling process. Start by ironing. Obvious, yes, but it will smooth the wrinkles. At least for the first ten minutes of wearing the shirt. For a slightly longer-term solution, most people turn to starch, but starch makes the shirt feel stiff and sticky, and if you keep using starch, it will continue to build up until the shirt is basically unwearable. Instead, try something called "spray sizing," which can easily be found online and at certain specialty stores (particularly craft stores, not pharmacies). Spray sizing works on all fabrics, won't stiffen the shirt, and is harmless for you and for the environment. Just spray it on when you iron—trust me, it'll make a difference.

Quick tip: Try wearing a white T-shirt under your linen shirt. Wrinkles are sometimes caused by heat and moisture, so an undershirt can keep heat in and soak up perspiration before it touches the linen.

These things will help, but if you really want to prevent against the dreaded wrinkles, follow these easy steps:

- Don't sit down.
- Don't lean against anything.
- Maintain perfect posture at all times.
- Don't touch anyone or let anyone touch you.
- Don't sweat.
- Don't go anywhere that's hotter than 70 degrees or colder than 65 degrees.
- Avoid excessive movement, like walking or dancing.

Sound like fun to you? I didn't think so.

Look, if you really want to wear linen, you're going to have to adjust your expectations. Linen is *supposed* to wrinkle. It's part of the look, and for many, part of the appeal. That's just the way it is. Trying to keep linen wrinkle free is like trying not to wear white after Labor Day; everyone always talks about it, but it's not something you're actually expected to do. Ironing will at least make it look like you didn't just roll out of bed, but beyond that, expect at least a few wrinkles, and wear them with pride.

A good rule of thumb for all wrinkles, linen or otherwise . . . embrace them, don't fight them.

How to Convert Your DVD Collection to Digital Files

This comes up over and over again with my clients. They have huge DVD collections worth hundreds and hundreds of dollars that they've carefully cultivated over the last ten years, yet these movies sit largely unused on the shelf. Why? Believe it or not, some people have gotten so used to just pushing a button on their digital TV and having the film appear magically. Reaching for the disk, taking it out of the case, and popping it into the DVD player now seems like too much trouble.

Sounds ridiculous, but you may be one of these people. And if you are, seems to me the only solution is to convert the DVDs to digital files and get rid of the actual disks. This isn't just a step to increase the likelihood that you'll actually watch them—it's also a step to protect your investment for the future. Just like VHS tapes are now out of date and almost completely useless (no one even sells new VHS players anymore), in just a few years, DVD players (and potentially even Blu-Ray players) will likely follow suit. And just as digital MP3 files replaced cassette tapes and then CDs in the music industry, so will digital files replace MP3 players, DVDs, and Blu-Ray disk movies, leaving your DVD collection to live on a large hard drive, just like your music. C'est la vie.

With that in mind, it's best to start converting your DVDs to digital files sooner rather than later since, with time, the DVDs will deteriorate and get scratched or dusty, and you may not be able to save them. You can always keep the hard copies for nostalgic reasons, but backing up all your movies on a hard drive will ensure you'll be able to watch them in the future.

Converting DVDs is quite simple. First, purchase an external hard drive. You can get these from any electronics store. Lacie is a very respected brand, though cheaper brands are likely just as reliable. Amazon.com is a quick and easy place to purchase them online, although JandR.com, (an electronics superstore), has very low prices, as well.

The cost of these drives is going down, down, down every day, and you can buy relatively large ones for under $100—or unnecessarily gigantic drives for around $200–$300. They're simple to use and easy to store, and whatever form new movie-players take in the future, they'll undoubtedly be USB compatible, which means you'll be able to load all your converted files onto them from any external hard drive.

Next you'll need to purchase or download a program that rips DVDs. For those who don't know the lingo, "ripping" a DVD is taking content *off* a DVD and turning it into a digital file (not to be confused with "burning" a DVD, which means taking a blank DVD and adding your own content to it). These programs are easy to find, and most of them are free. I use (and recommend) a program called Handbrake, which is available for Macs as well as PCs and is completely free to download (go to handbrake.fr, *not* .com).

The controls and settings on Handbrake (or any other program) can take some getting used to, so take your time and experiment a bit. Once you've got it down, converting your DVDs will just take a couple of clicks, although there will be a considerable amount of waiting time. Every two-hour DVD can take up to one hour to rip, depending on the quality of the files you select. If you have the time, I recommend the highest quality. After all, you're only going to do this once, so you might as well do it right.

Remember to transfer your new files to your new external hard drive, so you save space on your computer. And rest assured, ripping DVDs is perfectly legal (despite the Interpol warnings that appear when you pop the disk in), if you're only burning them for *personal* use. As long as you don't post the files online or start selling copies, you're in the clear.

Before you undertake this project, take a good look at your movie collection and decide if it's worth the time it takes to do the transfers. If you've had the DVD for five years and it's still in the original packaging, you may want to save yourself some time and energy. If and when you decide that you must see it, know that locating almost any flick these days is only a quick click (and a few dollars) away.

➳ How to Easily Donate Clothes

Are your closets so jam-packed with stuff you never wear that you can't even see what's in there? Or, is it finally summer and time to break out the warm weather garb and get rid of the winter items that never quite made it out of hibernation this season? Maybe, it's just time for that closet reorg (see "How to Organize Your Closet in Twenty Minutes, page 225). Or, the best reason to get rid of all the old clothes you never wear, you finally have come to the realization that there are people in need who can make much better use of your seldomly worn items than you can. Whatever the reason, don't wait for the next hurricane or natural disaster to hit to make a difference. It's always a good time to donate last season's sweaters to the less fortunate.

Donating your old clothes may seem like a no-brainer, but I see too many people hold on to stuff because they don't know how to go about giving it away. This really is a lame excuse. Plenty of people out there need clothing and they aren't hard to find, so there's only one reason I can think of that you could possibly use to justify throwing something away instead of donating it: you're lazy. If it's an old T-shirt with stains and fourteen holes in it, okay, but for just about everything else, put in that tiny bit of extra effort to get it into the hands of someone who could use it.

The quickest and easiest way to donate clothes is to call up the Salvation Army, Vietnam Veterans of America, or the Military Order of the Purple Heart. They will come right to your door and carry the unwanted items away, simple as that.

If for some reason none of these do pickups in your neighborhood, both Goodwill and the Salvation Army have drop-off locations, and some towns even have donation centers that are open 24/7 so you can pitch your items at any time of the day or night. If you really can't locate a place, leave your bags on the doorstep of your local church; they'll know what it's for (of course, if you're looking for a donation receipt so that you can deduct this act of kindness from your taxes at the end of the year, you will have to wait until they are open).

So jump online and search clothing donations. It'll take you about ten minutes tops. And don't forget about organizations like Dress for Success (go to www.dressforsuccess.org for a list of their locations) that collect work clothing and distribute the items to disadvantaged women in need of professional attire. Just jot down the address of the donation center, and put it at the top of your list of things to do. Also put the bag of clothing into your car right away so if you happen to be in the neighborhood, you'll be able to make the drop right then and there.

Be the one to organize a donation drive at your church or school. You'll not only get rid of a ton of old stuff, you'll be making a big difference in the lives of others and teaching your kids to do the same.

How to Remove a Stain

What can I say, stains suck.

No promises, but here's what works for me.

- *Ink:* Use hairspray.
- *Gum:* Use ice.
- *Wine:* Use seltzer water and sea salt.
- *Oil:* Use dishwashing liquid (saturate the entire spot, let soak, then wash in machine).
- *Spit-up:* Use OxiClean. Helpful hint: Don't wear black if you have a baby under six months.
- *Blood:* Use Hydrogen peroxide. Always test a small corner of the fabric first and act as quickly as possible.
- *Grass:* Soak the item in detergent for a few hours before tossing it in the washing machine.
- *Brightly colored foods* (like tomato sauce): Scrub with dish soap before washing as normal. If fabric is white, try bleach.
- *Makeup:* As long as you haven't spilled an entire bottle of foundation (in which case I probably can't help you), just wash in the machine.
- *Combinations* (like coffee with cream): Always treat the greasy or oily component first (see above) and then deal with the color.

- *Miscellaneous Stains:* Use baby wipes. I'm not sure why but most types work great for removing random stains from clothing (a little scary as to what they do to your baby's bottom!).
- *Almost anything:* Use Tide Stain Stick. Again, don't know why it works, but this stuff is like magic.

The key to stain removal is to act fast and stay away from any heat. And if at first you don't succeed, try, try again.

How to Break In a Baseball Glove

There's nothing better than that leathery scent of your first baseball glove (especially if you're a ten-year-old boy). It's a big step, and not something to be treated lightly, so if you are in the position to bequeath such a glove to its recipient, be sure to make it somewhat ceremonial.

But as any baseball lover knows, you can't just rip the glove out of the package and hit the diamond. First, the glove will need to be broken in. That's half the fun. The best way to do this is to oil it up—everywhere. Buy a container of glove conditioning oil from the sporting goods store, and smear it all over the mitt. You can also use foam shaving cream, mink oil, or saddle soap. After you saturate the glove, wipe it clean and let it dry. Then, put a ball inside the glove and wrap a belt tightly around it. Now your glove is *almost* ready.

The last step is a rite of passage. Put the glove with the ball still wrapped in it under a mattress and send your little baseball slugger off to sleep, where he'll dream about becoming the next Derek Jeter.

You're not likely to get your little guy to go to bed this early again, so enjoy!

How to Write Thank-You Notes in No Time

After a big event, sometimes the unwritten thank-you notes just seem to pile up, even for the most efficient types. After all, you spent so much time planning for the occasion, now you just want to breathe a sigh of relief, not spend your evenings thinking up creative and heartfelt ways to thank Aunt Mildred for the gravy bowl you didn't need. Sure, you're grateful for and appreciative of all the beautiful gifts, and you want to make sure that people know it, but let's face it, writing thank-you notes can be tedious and time-consuming. I am one of those people who always sends a thank-you note immediately after receiving a gift—yes, one of *those* people. But after having a new baby, I found that somehow I got behind in the note-writing department and suddenly it all made sense as to why so many clients hire us to write thank-you notes for baby, wedding, and even birthday gifts.

Now you may be thinking, *That's so impersonal. How could you hire somebody else to thank your friends and family for you?* But think about it, the people you hire aren't really the ones doing the thanking, they're just doing the hefty thank-you legwork—the pen-to-paper stuff you simply don't have time for. Plus, let me let you in on a little secret about thank-you notes: most people don't care what you write, they just want to know that you received their gift. So the next time you find yourself with unwritten thank-yous piling up, consider ordering some cute note cards, finding someone with good penmanship who needs to make a few bucks, and hiring him to get the job done.

If you do insist on writing them yourself, there is one foolproof shortcut. A photo postcard. Think about it. People really love to see photos (especially if it's a baby), but if it's a wedding or a party that works too. Postcards are easy to make (try an online service like www.zazzle.com or iphoto)—it takes about five minutes for the whole process. The best part is there is not a lot of writing space so you *have* to keep it brief. You could even print them up with one ready-made message (don't worry about sending the same one to everybody; they'll never compare notes). Really, that's why photo holiday cards became popular—a quick photo and no need to even write a thing.

Another trick that works especially well for baby showers: hand out envelopes at the event and have everyone pre-address their own. Your only task will be a quick thank-you for the lovely item.

So whip up some quick photo cards, scribble a few words, and your thank-you notes will be finished in no time flat. Emily Post doesn't know what she was missing.

You can thank me later.

How to Stick to a Workout Plan

Real gym rats know the worst time of year to work out is in January, before all those New Year's resolution people lose interest (until they read "How to Keep Your New Year's Resolutions," page 206), and the wait time for the elliptical machine seems endless. Are you one of those January exercisers who finds it hard to stick to your fitness goals, year in and year out? You could lapse into couch potato status after making a healthy start for a variety of reasons, but a common one is setting goals that you feel you *should* have—when the truth is that you would rather chew glass. And reason number two is that, believe it or not, you are being a bit of a perfectionist.

The fitness pros will say you have to reprioritize your life to make your workouts as important to you as sleeping, eating, playing with your kids, and relaxing. You wouldn't start to skip brushing your teeth, would you, they'll ask? Of course, it's true that exercise *is* of extreme importance. It will keep you healthy, strengthen your immune system, improve your mood, increase your self-esteem, improve your sleep and your work habits, and on and on and on. You already know all of this. In fact, it's *because* exercise is so good for you that you resolved to do it in the first place. Then why does it constantly lose its spot on your daily calendar? Why doesn't it feel like nearly as much of a priority as eating or sleeping? And why do you feel the need to keep letting the excuses roll off your tongue . . .

Let's face it: For some of us, what it really takes is tricking ourselves into exercising. The truth is that just knowing all the benefits of exercising—great moods! increased sex drive! long life!—is unconsciously making it hard to proceed. It's too much pressure! The key is to convince yourself that it is something fun that you get to do, not something you *have to do*. If you're lucky enough to have a sport you like, especially one that can be played year-round, get back into it, even if you haven't played since high school. Make it social: Find a league that plays volleyball at night or rally a tennis partner. Or if you've tried jogging but never stuck with it for long, there are loads of running groups you can join. If you can do it with a friend, even better. You might be too busy in your everyday life to schedule a regular lunch or coffee with her, but if you run together at 6:00 A.M. three days a week, you'll have a guaranteed date that you can look forward to, and a healthy one at that.

If you're rolling your eyes at this ("Volleyball? Hah!" or "If I tried running and talking to a friend at the same time, I'd pass out"), you may want to readjust your thinking a bit and set your goals a bit smaller. Yes, you read this right, start *smaller*. If you set your goals too high, they'll seem unreachable and you'll end up doing nothing! For example, let's say you join a gym and tell yourself you'll go every day after work, but after a couple of weeks, it just becomes too much, and figure you might as well give up on the whole thing.

Try this instead: Go to the gym twice a week at first. Just twice. Anyone can handle this, and when you start sticking to the two days, you'll begin to feel really good about yourself not only because you are working out, but because you are sticking to your commitment. When you become comfortable with your new routine, gradually begin making your goals a little larger. Don't jump from two gym trips a week to signing up for a marathon. Instead, look at where else you can burn a few extra calories. Refuse the ride and walk to the station. Take the stairs to the third-floor dentist's office. Skip escalators altogether. And so on.

Once you find a reasonable plan you can stick with, you'll find that you no longer have to trick yourself into thinking it's fun—it will be! The workouts will be more pleasant. You might look better in those gym shorts, and you'll certainly feel better. When you really start having a good time, you could very well find yourself adding to your routine— voluntarily.

How to Prevent Blisters on a Long Hike

Ah, the great outdoors. There's really nothing like it. But if you love to hike, certain inconveniences just come with the territory. Go hiking in Wyoming and you'll have to be on alert for bears. Backpacking in the Pacific Northwest? Bring a poncho. Choose a trail on the East Coast in the summertime and you'll be swatting mosquitoes all day long. But no matter where you go, you'll always have to avoid one nuisance: blisters.

Blisters will ruin your hike faster than a bear attack or a torrential downpour. Fortunately, they're also pretty easy to prevent, so just follow these tips to keep your tootsies blister-free.

Sure there are the usual remedies, like Band-Aids and moleskin, but let me just cut to the chase. The best and easiest trick by far is *duct tape*. I discovered this while in Africa hiking up Kilimanjaro. It takes about a week round-trip to hike this peak, and so the last thing I wanted was an annoying (and painful) blister. So here's what I did: I took my duct tape (the cure-all for myriad issues and a must-have in your camping bag at all times) and wrapped it completely around my feet. Then I just made sure that it was nice and smooth, put on my socks and hiking boots, and I was ready to go. It may sound a bit gross, but you can even keep the same tape on for days. I don't think I even had to retape the entire trip!

One word about socks: If you're going on a major hike, it's a good idea to invest in a pair or two of good, breathable, synthetic socks. Stay away from cotton, which absorbs moisture (sweat). And be sure your socks fit well.

Also, always drink a lot of water. Not just because it's important to stay hydrated; water also actually helps keep blisters at bay. That's because sweat is made of a mixture of water and salt, so if you don't drink enough and the water dries up, teeny tiny salt crystals form, which will stick to your skin and create friction. Friction is what causes blisters. So if you hydrate and sweat a lot, the salt will wash away. You can also keep your feet dry with a foot powder (talcum or Gold Bond are fine, but powder is messy, so be careful).

Another thing to keep in mind is your shoes. Just as with socks, you want to choose shoes that will let your feet breathe. Leather boots are the old standby for long hikes, because they are weather resistant and have great ankle support, but boots that have mesh or fabric near the toes allow more air to circulate. Your shoes should also have space enough to wiggle your toes, but not enough space for your foot to move around inside. It's a fine balance and believe me, you'll want to get this right. If you are going on a long hike, wear your boots around for a while to make sure they work well for you. Get to know your boots; they will become your best friend.

With the right boots, some good socks, and a roll of duct tape, you'll be able to let your feet do the walking on any trail for miles on end.

How to Keep Up with Sports

Knowing about sports is a good practice. It's one of those things that can really help you score big, not just professionally but in your personal life. Not only is sports talk an icebreaker, it can also be a conversation filler when you've got an awkward moment at the start of a meeting with a new client (or a new date).

Plus, if you have any number of guy friends with whom you hang out regularly, the conversation will inevitably turn to sports at least for a little while, and you don't want to be left in the dust. If you *are* a guy, it looks bad if you don't join in—and even worse if you join in and have no idea what you're talking about. And if you're female, even though you're not "expected" to know the stats and power rankings that overcrowd most guys' brains at all hours of the day, you can often impress the group if you're engaged and informed about the latest NFL news.

Although it seems like you'd have to study all day to memorize the gazillions of personalities and scores and stats that die-hard fans spout off, it really only takes a little bit of time to learn the basics that are discussed around the watercooler. After all, have you ever noticed how many seven-year-old boys can cite the stats for every football player, baseball player, and basketball player? They may not even know how to spell "statistics," yet they can figure out a batting average in their sleep. If they can do it, how hard can it really be?

The first step is to put sports scores and updates on your radar. Make it a habit to scan the sports headlines in the way that you check for other news stories or celebrity gossip. Make your homepage www.espn.com, so that it's always front and center, and bookmark your local paper's sports page or Yahoo! sports in your toolbar, so that it's always at the top of your web browser, reminding you to go there. Once you get in the habit of doing this, it will be easy. If you want to keep track of a sport all season long—not just during the playoffs, when *everyone* is tuned in—it's a good idea to bookmark that sport's official site, like MLB.com or NFL.com.

Quick tip: Subscribe to www.sportsbusinessdaily.com for a daily e-mail with important sports tips and news. After a month or so you may be able to get by on this alone.

You may also find that it's easier to keep up on sports when you have something personally invested in the outcome of each game. Now I'm not condoning illegal gambling or suggesting you bet your next mortgage payment on the NFL playoffs. But there are sports betting sites, like www.sportsbook.com and www.sportsbetting.com, that are legal and allow you to keep your bets relatively low. Try betting twenty-five cents on every baseball game during the season. It's not about the money; just having *something* invested, even a quarter, will make you care enough about the outcome of each game that you'll check the scores and stats frequently.

Quick tip: If March is rolling around, make sure you get in an NCAA basketball pool, even if you have no idea who will win. The NCAA is all any sports fan talks about in March, and having your own bracket to follow will keep you engaged and in the know. Plus, it's usually the people who have no clue about any of the teams who end up winning it all.

If you don't feel like spending money, try joining a fantasy sports league. In a fantasy league, you manage a team of players (which you draft at the beginning of the season) cobbled together from various teams across the league, and each of their individual performances contributes to the performance of your team. Having your own team forces you to be invested in a wide range of players across multiple teams, and the fantasy sports website will link you to stats and news quickly and easily. ESPN runs easy-to-use fantasy leagues, as does CBS sports (www.cbssports.com/fantasy) and Yahoo! sports (www.sports.yahoo.com/fantasy). Warning: I've seen people get addicted to making player trades and checking scores, so know what you are getting yourself into. And please, don't look to join the same league as your significant other. Trust me, it's not worth it.

Finally, learn by osmosis. If you spend time around people who are into sports, it's amazing what you can pick up. After one season of being married to a Yankees fan, I found that I had somehow learned not only all of the players' names but also their numbers and batting averages without even trying. So if this seems like more information than you could ever hold in your head at once, consider this: If you can keep up with *American Idol*, you can keep up with sports.

Start with the big three—baseball, football, and basketball will take you far. If you become really ambitious, throw in a little golf for good measure.

How to Make Sure You Actually Print or Make Albums for All Your Digital Photos

Ever since investing in my first digital camera, I take ten times as many photos as I used to. But I look at them significantly less, and I rarely, if ever, make real prints. Sure, digital photos have their advantages—you can share them with friends on Facebook or over e-mail—but there is definitely something lost by not having actual photographs that you can flip through or put into photo albums to easily share with people. Slide shows are nice, but they just can't replace actual photographs that you can look at in a book. Plus, what happens when fifteen years later your kids want to see photos of themselves as babies and you don't remember your online password or even what photo site you were using at the time?

Printing photographs is actually relatively easy if you keep up with it, but if you don't, it becomes a massively overwhelming project. Clients often call because they want prints of their digital photos but complain that it is just so time-consuming, confusing, and inconvenient. Can we help?

Luckily, today a lot of new ways are available to make the process easier, faster, and cost-effective. For most people, the biggest obstacle in getting prints made is the time and hassle of moving the photos from the camera to the computer. If you're one of them, the best thing going is something called an Eye-Fi. This is a memory card you can just pop into your camera, and it will automatically and wirelessly download photos from your camera to your computer. It rocks. If you don't want to invest in one of these (your loss), the best advice I can give you is to move the photos from your camera to your computer immediately after taking them. If you do it while you're still excited about your brand-new pics, it will seem fun, and you'll never be faced with the task of sitting behind your desk for three days organizing and printing your shots. The key is to make it a habit. For organizing your photos and making basic edits (like cropping or removing red eye), I recommend supereasy programs like Google's Picasa or Apple's iPhoto.

The next step, of course, is the actual printing. If you're into the immediate gratification of printing at home, here's the method I recommend. First, buy yourself a printer that specifically prints 3" x 5" or 4" x 6" photos. Do *not* use your all-in-one printer as your photo printer because every time you want to print photos, you'll have to change the settings and swap out the paper. This may not seem *that* bad, but these minor inconveniences add up, and become the reason most of us procrastinate actually printing our photos in the first place.

Next, stock up on photo paper, and I mean *lots*. Yes, it'll be expensive, but trust me, eventually, you'll use it all. Cost is a huge reason most people don't print photos regularly—it can cost $20 for just one pack of photo paper—but if you purchase a large quantity ahead of time, you'll be forcing yourself to use it. Besides, you've presumably already deleted all the photos where you look ugly or your thumb got in the way so you're saving money by only printing the best shots (and, hey, no one will ever know if you Photoshop those little wrinkles right out).

If you'd rather have your prints made for you, there's no shortage of options. With iPhoto, Picasa, and Shutterfly, among others, ordering a hard-copy photo is a snap! Other great photo-book sites include: Viovio (offers various binding options), Bay Photo (for professional quality books), Scrapblog or Mixbook, (which give you more creative control, like options for adding special backgrounds, stickers, and modifying the page layout any way you choose). Printing a longer photo book? You may be able to save some money by using an online self-publishing site like Lulu or Blurb. Lulu makes it easy to add stock photos to your album . . . so if your pictures from the Great Pyramids didn't come out so great, you can buy a few professional ones to spruce up your book (who will know the difference?). Think those photos from your safari in Africa are professional quality? These sites also make it a cinch to sell your photo book online.

If you can't stomach the price of an album (they're not outrageously expensive, but they can seem that way each time you order), buy yourself a large gift certificate to whatever photo album service you use (anywhere from $100 to $500 should tide you over for a while). By prepaying, you're investing in something that's meaningful to you, and forcing yourself to go through with it on a regular basis.

Remember, a picture is worth a thousand words. So if you feel the need to share every detail about your cross-country road trip, keep your mouth shut and make albums instead. Your kids will appreciate it later.

How to Change a Tire

It's the cardinal rule of driving. No matter where you're going, you should *always* keep a spare tire in the trunk. Of course, an important corollary to this rule is that it's not enough to just have a spare tire—you should also make sure it is inflated and know how to change it. It doesn't take much to learn this lesson. A few years back, while transporting a client's car from Colorado to L.A., we blew out one of the back tires while driving through the desert in Utah. If we hadn't had the spare, we would've been stranded on the side of the highway for hours.

Though I had never changed a tire myself, I had all the tools necessary in the trunk (phew!). This is the second corollary to the cardinal rule of driving: in addition to a spare tire, *always* have a jack, a wrench, and a flashlight in the trunk. Because, trust me, when you blow out that tire, you *will* be on a deserted road with no gas station for miles, and it *will* be dark out. These items should've come with your car but take a few minutes *right now* to double-check. I'll wait. Once you have the right tools, changing the tire is actually easier than it may seem (as long as it's not raining). Here's a handy step-by-step guide:

1. Pull off the road as soon as possible, to a flat area, and put the parking brake on.
2. Take off the hubcap or wheel cover if there is one and loosen the lug nuts (those boltlike things) with the wrench (your mantra should be "righty-tighty, lefty-loosey!) *before* you jack up the car. (Think about it: If your car is raised, the tire will spin when you try to loosen the nuts.)
3. Place the jack under the car frame near the flat tire and pump the handle until you have lifted the car just enough so you can get the flat tire off, and the spare tire on (you may need to look at the car's owner's manual to see the proper positioning, but the jack should be supporting the car).
4. Replace and tighten the lug nuts (turning the wrench clockwise), and lower the car back down to the ground. Then retighten each of the lug nuts.

Quick tip: Be careful that you place the jack correctly so that you don't break the plastic molding on the car. Most newer cars have a small notch just behind the front wheel or just in front of the back wheel to indicate where the jack should be placed. If you can't find it, check the car's owner's manual before you use the jack.

If this has all gone well, once you've got the spare tire on, your next stop should be an auto repair shop or a gas station. Most spare tires are only designed to last for up to fifty miles, but it's best not to push it even that far if possible.

Of course, this is sometimes easier said than done, so as with any good plan, you should always have a backup. If you're a AAA member (and if you drive a lot, you should be), be sure to download their smartphone app in addition to carrying the AAA card in your wallet. This app will help you find the nearest repair shop (based on your location), and if you call the emergency services number, someone on their customer service line can walk you through changing the tire.

If you're not a member of AAA, the National Automobile Club offers a free app that does not require a membership, called "NAC Road Service." I downloaded the app to test it out, and although I can't say it's spectacular, if you have no other options, it's good enough. Essentially, it's an 800 number, and though the call for help is free, if the service sends a repair person to your location, it will cost you. Still, the person on the line can help with flat tires, dead batteries, running out of gas, or other similar problems. Just make sure to get a price quote before you ask for on-site service.

Another free app, good *only* for changing a tire, is called "Car Breakdown." (There is also a version for $1.99, but the only difference is that it doesn't have ads, so it's probably not worth it.) This is basically a very detailed fourteen-page PDF document explaining how to change a tire. Though you could probably get the same information by Googling "how to change a tire" on your smartphone, you might someday get stuck with a flat tire in an area with no cell service, so downloading this app ahead of time can be a useful backup.

It's good not to have to rely on flagging down a stranger in the middle of nowhere, so be prepared whenever you're hitting the road, especially if you know you'll be in a remote area.

resources

The following is a list of online resources mentioned throughout the book (and a few extras). For additional web sites, or to suggest your own resources, please visit my website at www.consideritdone.com.

RELATIVELY SPEAKING (Chapter 1)

Jewelry polish: www.hagertyusa.com   2
Sell unwanted items online: www.craigslist.com; www.ebay.com   2
Remote access to a computer: www.GoToMyPc.com; www.logmein.com   6
Family crest design: www.fleurdelis.com/meanings.htm; www.MakeYourCoatOfArms.com   22
Custom T-shirt ordering: www.CustomInk.com   22
Professional organizers and hoarding issues: www.hapo.net; www.pamguide.com.au/anxiety/hoard_test.php   26
Family portrait artists: www.PortraitArtist.com   27
Portraits painted from photos: www.PaintYourLife.com   27

AROUND THE WORLD (Chapter 2)

Packing tips: www.onebag.com   34
Passport forms: www.travel.state.gov   42

acknowledgments

This book, my business, and all my experiences have been achieved because of the amazing people in my life.

I would like to take this opportunity to specifically acknowledge those who have made a huge difference with this project.

First, Shannon Marven and Lacy Lalane Lynch at Dupree Miller, thank you for believing in my project and supporting it and me throughout the process.

Talia Krohn and the team at Crown, thank you for working so closely with me and for all of your input, creativity, and insight. Your encouragement and hard work inspired me throughout the process.

Renee Duff, Chris Bassler, Rob Cohen, Sarah Davis, Danielle Haas, Elizabeth Otereo, Joanna Gryfe, Gina Fabiano, Alison Oliver, and Elissa Goldman—from proposal to completion, I am grateful for your contributions.

Thank you to my EO forum, Zoe and my Tuesday night group, the Manhattan Mamma's, and Beth, Jeremiah, and Rowan for your encouragement and support.

Laurie, your organization, attention to detail, feedback, and unconditional support was invaluable. You are smart and creative, and I truly value your input and dedication. I appreciate you and hope you know how talented you are at so many things.

My parents, who provided the space for me to figure out how to get things done. I appreciate it now.

Evie and Steve, who encouraged my move to New York and continue to offer support.

Cynthia Britto, your flexibility, love, and fun-loving personality brightened my workspace and lit up my son's world.

Nick, your unconditional love, support, and contribution made a huge difference while writing and always. You are an open, loving, and giving man. You are my best friend. Thank you for your persistence, commitment, and love.

Elias, for the joy you bring to me and to the world.

And to my friend Robin, thank you for the difference you were in every area of my life. I miss you and wish you were here to celebrate this win.

And a final thank-you to my outstanding get-it-done team for your energy and creative solutions. And to my fantastic clients: your requests provide us the opportunity to Consider It Done.

I am grateful and appreciative to you all.